John Hull, the Mint and the Economics of

Massachusetts Coinage

Boston and vicinity, ca. 1705

This map is adapted from a detail of the earliest engraved chart of Boston Harbor. North: To the east of Charlestown is Noddle's Island, it is now known as East Boston and is home of Logan Airport. A branch of the Mystic River separated the island from the mainland but in modern times landfill has joined the former island to the North Shore. The Hammersmith Ironworks was about six miles to the north. West: Cambridge Creek is now known as the Charles River. The trees on the north bank of the river are in Cambridge, the town of Watertown is four miles to the west. The Muddy River has been filled in; the area is now Brookline. South: About a half-mile west and a mile south of Dorchester Neck is the town of Dorchester, Braintree is a further four miles to the south. In Boston proper West Hill is depicted. The water line was at the western boundary of the Boston Common; today the entire Back Bay has been reclaimed from the sea. Reproduced from Winsor, volume two, an unnumbered plate between pages x and xi.

John Hull, the Mint and the Economics of Massachusetts Coinage

by

Louis Jordan

C 4 Publications
The Colonial Coin Collectors Club

Distributed by
University Press of New England
Hanover & London

The Colonial Coin Collectors Club
www.colonialcoins.org

Distributed by University Press of New England
One Court Street, Lebanon, NH 03766

The paper used in this publication meets the minimum requirements of American National
Standard for Information Sciences – Permanence of Paper for Printed Library Materials,
ANSI Z 39.48-1984.

Printed in the United States of America on 70 pound acid free paper in 12 point Times by
Sheridan Books, Ann Arbor, Michigan.

Dedicated to

my wife, Lorraine

my daughter, Elizabeth

and

my son, Louis

fugit hora

Table of Contents

Part One - John Hull and the Massachusetts Mint

The family and homestead of Robert Hull
John Hull is promised the homestead
John Hull inherits the homestead
The homestead at John Hull's death
John Hull's Boston properties
Hull's shop and its relationship to the mint
Contemporary references to the mint house
    Citations to the mint house from 1652
    Citations to the minting facilities from the 1660's
Robert Sanderson and his homestead

John Hull of Dorchester
John Hull of Newbury

    The personal ledger of John Hull
    The shop account

Part Two - The Massachusetts Mint and British Politics

The 1652 backdating hypothesis
Presuppositions
Post-Restoration relations with Massachusetts Bay: 1660-1666
Renewed interest in Massachusetts Bay: the complaints of 1675-1677
The pronouncements of 1677
A reversal of fortune: 1678-1684
From the abolition of the charter to Queen Anne's proclamation: 1684-1704
British opposition to the mint in Massachusetts Bay: a summary

Part Three - The Economics of Massachusetts Silver Coinage

Part Four - Production Issues

Part Five - The Eight Reales and its Value in Britain and Massachusetts Bay

Editor's Foreword

In 1930, many communities within the Commonwealth recognized the Massachusetts Bay Tercentenary with locally sponsored celebrations, parades and historical pageants. Other localities and committees in eastern Massachusetts added to the festivities by striking a total of 50 different commemorative souvenir medals. Five of these medals recalled the famous Massachusetts Mint by presenting a generic rendition of a Pine Tree Shilling, not unlike Noe 16, on their reverse sides, while depicting a theme of local interest on their obverses. The first of these souvenir tokens was struck by the Bourne Historical Society and depicted the legend of John Hull weighing his daughter, Hannah, in Pine Tree Shillings as the dowry for her marriage to Judge Samuel Sewall. The Society used the proceeds from the sale of these coins to support their replica of the 1627 Aptucxet Trading Post, in the Plymouth Colony, which had carried on an active commerce with the Dutch from New Netherland (Shepard Pond, "Medals of Massachusetts Bay Tercentenary," *The Numismatist*, vol. XLIV, no. 6, June 1931, pp. 1-25).

This year, 2002, is the 350th anniversary of the establishment of the Massachusetts Mint which cannot be allowed to pass unheralded. Although this event has great numismatic significance, it will not be honored with the same abundance of medals as the Bay State's 300th birthday, just recounted. In preparation for this observance, I had asked Louis Jordan if he would write for *The Colonial Newsletter* a chronology of the Massachusetts Mint similar to the one that already appeared on the Notre Dame website. He readily accepted this assignment and, while researching the material, happened across Hull's original ledgers at the New England Historic Genealogical Society while in Boston attending the annual Colonial Coin Collectors' Club Convention in November 2000. I can well recall his excitement at his discovery of these important documents.

With the addition of this wealth of new information, the originally proposed article immediately graduated into a book length project. It was soon obvious that a manuscript of this size would be better accessed in a single volume rather than serializing it within a journal over a span of many months. Hence, as a tribute to the Massachusetts Mint on its important anniversary, the complete work is published here in book form under the sponsorship of the Colonial Coin Collector's Club.

Another event in the 350th year celebration of the Massachusetts Mint is Stack's landmark auction sale, *The Hain Family Collection of Massachusetts Silver Coins*, whose catalogue was painstakingly researched and written by Michael Hodder. This catalogue, itself, will become a collectors' item and a permanent reference for colonial enthusiasts to this classic series.

In the Hain catalogue, Hodder reached his conclusions by examination of the coins themselves, whereas here, Louis Jordan based his findings on the interpretation of documentary evidence. These two different methods of approach yielded very compatible results which together help us reconstruct how the early mint functioned. We are pleased that Michael Hodder accepted the invitation to write the introduction to this book, and it is with his opening comments that we can begin unfurling the fascinating story of John Hull and the Massachusetts Mint, so much of which is being revealed for the first time!

Philip L. Mossman
Bangor, Maine
February 2002

Figure A - The Bourne Historical Society token. This example is used with permission from the collection of Louis Jordan. Image is 2x.

Introduction

Massachusetts silver coins are the aristocrats in early American numismatics. Sylvester S. Crosby, whose *The Early Coins of America* is still the basic handbook to colonials, devoted more than a quarter of his book to a study of the Bay Colony's mint and coins, a measure of their prestige. The great collectors of the past, such as William Sumner Appleton, whose collection went to the Massachusetts Historical Society, considered their holdings of Massachusetts silver the centerpieces of their entire collections. These coins were accorded the same pride of place by more modern collectors, such as T. James Clarke, Mrs. Emery May Norweb, and Richard Picker, to name just three.

Despite the prominence Massachusetts silver coins have always enjoyed among collectors, no book specifically studying the contextual numismatics of the coinage has appeared, until now. Crosby's came closest, as he usually seems to have done in things colonial, but his book had a wider focus than a single coinage. Crosby certainly appreciated the cultural and economic contexts in which Massachusetts struck its coins, however. Outstanding among his contemporaries, he included illustrated and transcribed source documents bearing on the history of the coinage. Crosby's die numbering system fell out of favor in the 1960's but a new generation of collectors is returning to it, attracted by its simplicity and flexibility. Sydney Noe's monographs on the four types are more modern. They attempt to create a chronology for the coinage based upon reconstructed die emission sequences. Noe's dating of the types assumed that each followed the other, starting with the NE's, but recent research has shown the assumption to be unsafe. Chronologies based upon dates of contract renewals, popularized by Breen and others, fall for the same reason. Noe sequentially numbered the die combinations of each type known to him without allowing for new discoveries, leading to such inelegancies as an Oak Tree threepence numbered higher than the twopence and a Pine Tree shilling numbered higher than the threepence. Noe's decision to give separate numbers to states of the same dies, a methodological flaw that has bedeviled collectors ever since, later led to the creation of new "Noe" numbers with decimal designations. Collectors were left with a cumbersome and arcane numbering system describing a coinage that was poorly understood unless one took the trouble to read the original documents printed by Crosby supplemented by studies of seventeenth century English economic and technological history.

Lou Jordan's study of the Massachusetts Mint is a long awaited and very welcome corrective to the literature on the series. It will certainly become the standard treatment. Beginning as a chronology of the known historical facts about the coinage posted on the Notre Dame colonial coins website, it grew into a study of the Massachusetts Mint, its technology, personnel, and operations. While it incorporates some familiar documents, it approaches them in an entirely new way. As a result, Lou has been able to deduce the most likely ways in which the mint operated, where it was located, how it was run, how its customers were served, and what its fate turned out to be over the 30 years it was in operation. Perhaps the single most important addition to our knowledge of the Massachusetts coinage to be found within these pages comes from Hull's ledgers. Lou is the first numismatic historian to look at this source. The mintage figures he derives from them may be subject to interpretation but what is not is the sheer size of the coinage over time. We tend to assume that a coin rare today was rare when it was made. The figures for the number of troy ounces of sterling silver accounted for in the incomplete ledgers for 1671-1680, more than 11,000, show a coinage whose economic impact must have been far larger than we ever thought it was. Contemporaries noted the large amount of silver coming out of Massachusetts but their observations seem to have been overlooked. The data Lou has developed will go a long way towards placing Massachusetts Bay in the forefront of late seventeenth century transatlantic trade. Perhaps we should not be so surprised that the crown took so long to close the Boston Mint: the economic dislocation might have rivaled that we have seen in our own time, following the collapse of the international banking system in the 1980's.

The 350th anniversary of the founding of the Boston Mint is the perfect time for Lou's book to be presented to its public. It just so happened that it was the same time I was asked to catalogue the Hain Family collection of Massachusetts silver, for sale by Stack's. I decided to put into the auction catalogue most of what I had learned about the coinage in the years I had been cataloging it, starting with the Norweb sale in 1987. I included my observations on the use of a rocker press as the primary technology for all types save the small planchet Pines, the ways in which planchets were prepared and handled after striking, the "assay office" nature of the mint's daily operations, and so on. My commentary was based principally on the evidence of the coins, themselves, supplemented by documentary source material. It was only after I had finished the cataloging that I received an email from Phil Mossman, asking if I would like to read a new manuscript on Massachusetts silver coins by Lou Jordan. Lou is a friend of mine, a fellow medievalist turned numismatic historian, so my answer was obvious. It wasn't until I read the book you now hold that I realized the real meaning of "serendipity." Lou had approached the coinage from a purely documentary standpoint and the conclusions he had drawn about it closely tallied with what I had written in the Hain catalogue and elsewhere. I felt we were on to something. I leave it up to the reader to decide if I was right.

Mike Hodder
Wolfeboro, NH
January 2002

Preface

The present project began as an exercise in chronology. Sylvester Crosby's long chapter on Massachusetts silver in his *The Early Coins of America* is structured topically, which is the best way to explain a large quantity of complex information. However, it sometimes prevents one from readily seeing connections between events. For example, the legislation of 1652, which Crosby explained on pages 31-44, is followed by a discussion of the coins and a summary of mint related events up to 1697. Yet, it is not until page 102 that we learn of John Mansfield's attempt to gain employment at the mint in 1654. Various proposals to revise mint standards are also treated as separate units. I felt a strict chronological presentation of the material would aid in understanding historical development. This was the initial reason for my chronology.

Soon I began adding several references to documents that were not in Crosby. Many documents had not been edited when Crosby's book was published in 1875.[1] Most importantly, the eight volumes of *The Calendar of State Papers, Colonial Series*, containing the minutes of the Committee for Trade and Plantations, for the period of the operation of the Massachusetts Bay Mint, were not published until 1880-1911. Firth's, *Acts of the Interregnum* did not appear until 1911. Further, the records relating to the Hull estate were not edited and analyzed until after Crosby's work. Several other significant primary sources were made available after Crosby's publication, such as the Reports of the Record Commissioners of the City of Boston, the *Records of the Suffolk County Court: 1671-1680* and Samuel Sewall's *Letter-Book*. Also, he did not have the advantage of numerous secondary works that analyzed and interpreted the documents nor did he have access to several major reference works as the extraordinary encyclopedic dictionary, *Colonial Massachusetts Silversmiths and Jewelers* edited by Patricia Kane.

Crosby, and his Boston Brahmin contemporaries, assumed the average reader had a fairly detailed knowledge of their Puritan past since at the time much research focused on Puritan studies and genealogy. One recent and widely read work that went through several printings was John Palfrey's, *A Compendious History of New England*, first published in 1873. It presented a detailed and sympathetic interpretation of Puritan politics and culture. In this climate Crosby was comfortable simply extracting citations to the mint from relevant documents and producing an excellent compilation of excerpts.

I went back to read the full text of the documents from which Crosby derived his excerpts. When reading the documents in their entirety, and in relation to related documents,

---

[1] Crosby probably completed writing the text in 1872. See the Centennial Foreword by Eric Newman in Crosby, pp. viii-x.

I began to realize Crosby's presentation did not give the full story. For example, if one limited one's reading to Crosby, one might think the mint was the central area of conflict between Massachusetts Bay and England. This is because Crosby included quotations from several individuals who made statements against the Massachusetts Bay Mint, such as the report of Edward Randolph. In doing so, Crosby was adding to the historical record. He did not have the benefit of Toppan's five-volume annotated edition of the Randolph letters that appeared in 1899 nor did he have printed editions for many of the other documents he cited. However, Crosby never intended his work to be used to the exclusion of other sources. He intentionally excluded significant information when it did not directly pertain to the mint and coinage. If one examines all the relevant documents, one soon realizes the seizure of New Hampshire and Maine by Massachusetts Bay was the center of the conflict between Massachusetts Bay and England. Crosby understood this. It simply was not his intention to give a complete history. But in twenty-first century America, the politics of Puritan Boston are not part of our general knowledge and we sometimes simply do not interpret the excerpts in their proper context.

Crosby's publication was a monumental achievement. Yet, some limitations have been imposed on it by over a century of additional research. Also, I believe we have overly emphasized some points in Crosby's text due to our general lack of familiarity with Puritan history. For these reasons, I decided to write some studies that would supplement and update Crosby. Initially, I took up the problem of the location of the mint. With the edition of Aspenwall's *Notarial Records,* the edition of Samuel Sewall's diary, the corrections to the diary by Estes Howe, Whitmore's edition of the *Book of Possessions,* and the twelve volume set of Suffolk County deeds I had access to several important sources that were not available to Crosby. Using these resources I was able to trace the history of John Hull's homestead.

The specific location of the mint has been a longstanding question with no definitive answer. From my initial investigations the best information I was able to uncover was a reference to Hull's shop in the posthumous property division document filed with the county court. Several other researchers had used this source but no one had analyzed it in relation to other surviving deeds and documented the research for others to follow. Essentially, a study of the surviving deeds allows us to locate Hull's shop, but there is no specific reference to the mint. The relationship between the shop and the mint has been a matter of conjecture.

It was about this time Phil Mossman saw my chronology on the web and offered to print a revised version in *The Colonial Newsletter.* In preparation for publication I tried to make the chronology as complete as possible. When rereading Clarke's 1940 biography of Hull for additional material to include in the chronology, I came upon the sentence, "In several of John Hull's account books, fortunately preserved, there are three ledger entries relating to 'ye shop' and its dealing with the mint house from November 18, 1671, to June 30, 1680" (Clarke, *Hull,* pp. 63-64). Sydney Noe also briefly mentioned the ledgers, in passing, in his 1942 book on the Castine hoard (Noe, *Castine,* p. 23). I knew I needed to see these ledger entries both for the information on minting and for the tantalizing relationship Clarke implied between the shop and the mint.

Many numismatists had read the passage concerning Hull's ledger in Clarke's biography as well as the passing reference in Noe's work. The ledger was a known source. Indeed, three of the four extant ledgers recorded the Commonwealth's expenses during King Philip's War and have been frequently consulted by historians. However, it appears no one used the ledger passages cited by Clarke to uncover the relationship of the mint to the shop. Patricia Kane went through the ledger rather thoroughly for citations to silversmithing but did not analyze the mint data. Although Clarke, Noe and others consulted these very passages, it appeared the ledger entries relating to the mint have never been transcribed and analyzed.

A close study of the ledger has been quite revealing. It proves the shop and the mint were, in fact, two terms used by Hull for a single structure. Moreover, the ledger shows how Hull interpreted and applied the regulations in the 1652 mint statute. Additionally, it allows us to gain some insights on production at the mint. Thus, what began as a search to resolve a single point on the relationship of the shop and the mint, grew into a major study on production and allowed me to include some new information on the application of mint charges and the wastage fee.

My investigations are presented in the following studies on the mint at Massachusetts Bay and the economic factors that impacted the mint. In addition to the use of the ledger, I have tried to update the documentation in Crosby by including the major edited sources and selected secondary research from the past 125 years. I have also tried to put the sources into an historical context for an audience that may not be conversant with seventeenth century economics and politics.

A note on chronology

There are two important factors that need to be considered when interpreting dates from British sources before 1752. One consideration relates to the change of the year. In modern times all western countries begin the year on January 1st, which was not always the case. In the Middle Ages, some cities, such as Rome, started the new year with the Nativity of Christ, so the new year began on December 25th. Other cities, such as Paris, began the year on the movable feast of Easter, whereas Venice retained the ancient Roman new year of March 1st. England and several other areas used the Feast of the Annunciation. This is when the angel Gabriel announced to the Virgin Mary that she would be the mother of Jesus. The feast is celebrated on March 25th, exactly nine months before Christmas. In Britain this was known as Lady Day. By the mid-sixteenth century most areas adopted the current practice of designating January 1st as New Year's day but Britain held onto its traditional new year until 1752. Consequently, in British and colonial American documents dated between January 1st and March 24th, the year designated in that date will be the previous year based on our current practice, while documents from March 25th through December 31st will have the correct year. In the seventeenth and eighteenth centuries this difference from the January 1st standard was sometimes quite confusing; consequently documents from the problematic months were sometimes dated with a dual date. For example, March 10, 1651/2, was used to show the date represented the British year 1651 but that elsewhere it represented 1652.   In this book all dates have been have been converted to the current or what has been designated as "new style" system except in quotations, where the words of the contemporaries have been preserved.

The second important consideration relates to the type of calendar used in Britain. Throughout the Middle Ages all western countries used the Julian calendar. This calendar was originally issued by Julius Caesar and then modified by the Emperor Augustus. The central problem with the Julian calendar was that it was based on a year of 365.25 days, whereas the astronomical year is actually 365.242199 days. Thus, each year the seasons shifted by 11 minutes and 14 seconds or 1.5 days in two centuries. By 1545, the vernal equinox, which was used to determine the date of the movable feast of Easter, had shifted by 10 days. At the Council of Trent, which opened in December of 1545, a request was forwarded to the pope that the calendar error be corrected. After much research Pope Gregory XIII issued a papal bull in March of 1582 that decreed the day following the Feast of Saint Francis of Assisi, which was celebrated on Thursday, October 4, 1582, would be Friday, October 15th, thus ten days (October 5th through the 14th) were suppressed.[2]

Between 1582 and 1584 most western nations adopted the Gregorian reform. However, several Protestant regions in Germany and parts of the Netherlands (but not the Province of Holland) held out. Prussia adopted the Gregorian system in 1610 while most other Protestant areas on the continent had converted by 1701. Britain was the last of the major western countries to convert. The only nations to hold out longer were the Eastern Orthodox states. The final areas to convert were Bulgaria (1917), Russia (1918), Greece (1923) and Turkey (1928). By the time Britain converted, in 1752, the discrepancy between the Julian calendar and Gregorian calendars had increased from ten to eleven days. The British Calendar Reform Act was passed in March of 1751 (24 George II, c. 23). It decreed the new year would commence on January 1, 1752, and that the day following Wednesday, September 2, 1752, would be Thursday the 14th, thus eleven days (September 3rd through the 13th) were suppressed.[3]

---

[2] In order to stop the problem from reoccurring Gregory declared that no centennial year would be a leap year unless it was exactly divisible by 400. Therefore, 1700, 1800 and 1900 were not leap years, while 2000 was a leap year. In this way the differential of 1.5 days every two centuries was addressed by suppressing three days every four hundred years.

[3] Phil Mossman reminded me, not only were eleven days suppressed, but additionally, three weekdays were lost. Since September 14, 1752, would have been a Monday on the Julian calendar, three weekdays, a Monday, Tuesday and a Wednesday, were lost, to allow the weekday to conform to the Gregorian calendar.

In converting dates to our current usage, historians do not compensate for the suppressed days. Thus, an event that occurred on May 27, 1652, would still be recognized as having occurred on that date, rather than converting for what was at that time a discrepancy of ten suppressed days and using the date of June 7th. Similarly, when we move the time forward or backward one hour for daylight savings time we do not convert the hour for events from the past six months to make up for the time change. An event that occurred at 8:00 PM on October 14th, will still be said to have occurred at 8:00 PM even after we have adjusted the clocks back one hour.

In dealing with British history one must recognize the implications of the date change, especially in the period between the calendar reform of 1582 and the British adoption of the reform in 1752. The date in Britain was ten and then, by the mid-eighteenth century, eleven days behind the date in the rest of Europe. As time passed the discrepancy between the Julian and Gregorian calendars increased at a rate of 1.5 days per two hundred years. To demonstrate a specific example, April 2, 1679, was a Wednesday in Britain and in their colonies. However, that same day was Sunday, April 13th in France and the rest of continental Europe. In fact, for the continent, April 2nd had been Easter Sunday, while that day had been recognized as Wednesday, March 22nd in Britain. Thus, during the period of operation of the Boston mint, the British date was ten days behind the continent. Obviously, the confusion this caused to international business and trade in Britain was a major reason for finally abandoning tradition and conforming to the predominant dating system.

The British use of the Julian calendar means one cannot use a standard calendar or the Gregorian perpetual calendar to determine the specific day of the week for a date in British history from this period. For this reason I have appended a British Julian calendar for the years 1671 to 1680 so one can easily determine the specific day of the week for any date in the surviving portion of the Hull ledger.

Acknowledgments

Special thanks are due to Phil Mossman, who carefully read several drafts of this work, made numerous helpful suggestions and edited this book for publication. He has meticulously checked grammar and punctuation, as well as content. His comments helped me to revise and clarify my assumptions and conclusions throughout the text. Without Phil's help this book would have been much poorer. Les Elam proofread the final draft and made numerous helpful suggestions on grammar and style. Les also offered some very helpful formatting suggestions based on his many years of experience as an editor at the American Numismatic Society. Ray Williams and Gary Trudgen read drafts and made several helpful suggestions on word usage and caught some typographical errors. Ray also reminded me of the eleven-day discrepancy between the Julian and Gregorian calendars. Eric Newman read an early draft and provided me with several very helpful suggestions. Jim Spilman and

Angel Pietri also took the time to read early drafts and provided encouragement. Angel sent an e-mail urging me to published the work with The Colonial Coin Collectors Club as soon as he received the draft. Michael Hodder did not see the text until late December of 2001, after his Hain catalogue was at the press. When I heard the Hain collection was to be sold and that Mike had produced a catalogue, I asked him for a copy and explained my monograph was in the final stages of preparation. Mike agreed to send me a catalogue as soon as it was available. He read a draft of my manuscript during the Christmas holiday and made some useful comments. In his study of Massachusetts silver, Mike came to very similar conclusion as I have from my analysis of the documents. I was very pleased he consented to write an introduction to this volume. Additionally, I am very grateful to Jim Rosen who helped expedite this volume through the press so it could be published during 2002 for the 350th anniversary of the establishment of the Massachusetts Bay Mint. Also, my daughter, Elizabeth Jordan, assisted me by formatting the ledger transcriptions so they closely reflect the spacing in the originals. She also assisted with scanning and various formatting issues, saving me weeks of work during the final push before publication. I am also grateful to Stack's for allowing me to reproduce images from their magnificent Hain auction catalogue and to The New England Historic Genealogical Society, Boston, Massachusetts, for furnishing me with a microfilm of the Hull ledger and allowing me to reproduce selected pages.

Louis Jordan
Notre Dame, Indiana
March 2002

❀❀❀❀❀❀❀❀

Part One

John Hull and the Massachusetts Mint

Chapter 1

The Hull and Sanderson Homesteads and the Location of the Massachusetts Mint

Regrettably, there are no surviving documents precisely locating the site of the Massachusetts Mint. Our most specific information concerning the location of the mint is found in an announcement recorded in the minutes of the Massachusetts Bay General Court's mint committee meeting of June 22, 1652. It specified "That the said mint howse shall be sett upon the land of the said John Hull." Clearly, to determine the location of the mint we must first ascertain the real estate holdings John Hull had acquired by June of 1652. Determining the property holdings of the 27 year-old John Hull must begin with an investigation of the Hull family and homestead.

The family and homestead of Robert Hull

Robert Hull was a blacksmith from Market Harborough in Leicestershire, England, who took the widow Elizabeth Storer as his wife. Elizabeth had a young son named Richard from her previous marriage to the late Paul Storer. Robert and Elizabeth then had two children of their own. The elder son, named John, was born about December 18th in the year 1624. The date of the birth of their second son, Edward, is not known. However, according the records of the local parish church, Edward was baptized on July 25, 1628, thus we may assume he was about three years younger than John. In July of 1629 Robert Hull sent his stepson, Richard, to London to apprentice under the goldsmith James Fearne for a period of ten years. Unfortunately, Richard was not able to complete his training since the entire Hull family departed England from Bristol on the ship *George* on September 28, 1635, arriving in Boston Harbor on November 7th.

During the early years of Massachusetts Bay, families newly arriving in Boston were usually given a house plot in the town and an allotment of farmland at Muddy River (now Brookline), which was about three miles to the southwest. The Boston town records state Robert Hull received his "great allotment" of farmland on December 12, 1636 (Whitmore, *Boston Records,* p. 14). The allotments were parcels of land assigned to newcomers by an Allotment Committee with the stipulation that the grantee become a member of the Puritan Congregation (at the time the only church was the First Church of Boston). New arrivals were also required to construct a dwelling on their house plot before March 1st of the following year. The specific location of the Hull allotment was not mentioned; the record simply stated the members of the allocation committee agreed:

> …that Edward Belchar, William Talmage, Thomas Snowe, and William Deninge, and John Aratt, the servants of William Brenton, shall have their great Allotments at Muddy Ryver, and also our brother Robert Hull and Thomas Wheelar. (Whitmore, *Boston Records,* p. 14)

This record indicates both Hull and Wheeler obtained acreage at Muddy River, but no mention was made of their house plots. However, from later sources we know their house plots were on the same street block.

The records of several later allocations assist in determining the location of the Robert Hull house plot. The general location of the Hull residence can be determined from its proximity to other allocations. For example, it is recorded that a house plot was allocated to John Hurd on January 31, 1642, "betweene the howse plats of Robert Hull and William Plantayne" (Whitmore, *Boston Records,* pp. 65-66). The specific location of these house plots is contained in a manuscript volume entitled, "Possessions of the Inhabitants of Boston," found in the Suffolk County Bureau of Records. The origin of this volume is unrecorded. However, an undated note referring to the work was made by the recorder of the General Court, Isaac Addington. Addington stated he had discovered the book in 1672 and frequently used it but that he "alwaies was in doubt of the validity of it as a Record." The book lists each landowner with a description of the parcels of land they owned in the town of Boston, covering the period 1645-1648 with some supplemental updates extending the coverage up to 1652. During the October 1652 session of the General Court it was legislated that verbal agreements for the sale of land would no longer be recognized by the law. From that time all transfers of land needed to be documented in writing with a deed that was validated by an official notary with the seal of the Commonwealth or the sale had to be acknowledged and recorded through the court (Shurtleff, vol. 3, p. 280). With the cessation of oral land transfers the *Book of Possessions* was replaced by the filing of written deeds.

The *Book of Possessions* is in the handwriting of William Aspinwall, who had been appointed by the General Court on November 13, 1644, to the positions of both Recorder for the Suffolk County Court and Public Notary for Suffolk County. His predecessor, Stephen Winthrop, who was a son of Governor John Winthrop, stepped down from the posts when he obtained permission to travel to England in September of 1644. Aspinwall wrote the majority of the text (pp. 1-111) by March of 1645. This has been determined because the book lists a parcel of land on School Street as belonging to Thomas Scottow, however a deed exists stating Scottow sold the land on March 31, 1645. Pages 112-49 amend and supplement the text by year, p. 112 for 1645, pp. 113-22 for 1646, pp. 123-34 for 1647, and pp. 135-49 for 1648, with marginal updates throughout covering up to 1652 (the final updates by Aspinwall are: October 27, 1651 in item 35 and November 11, 1651 in items 40 and 77; there is one addition by Edward Rawson, dated January - February 1652, which probably refers to 1653 in item 127). Aspinwall continued in his positions until 1651. In that year John Witherden brought charges against Aspinwall in the Suffolk County Court for overstepping his authority. The county court upheld the charges and, as a result, the Massachusetts Bay General Court removed Aspinwall from his posts during the session of October 14, 1651. His two positions were divided among three people. In the October 14th session of the General Court, Edward Rawson, who was Secretary of the Commonwealth, also assumed the duties as Suffolk County Recorder, while Jonathan Negoos took the title of the Clerk of Writs in

Boston (Shurtleff, vol. 2, pp. 257-58). At the General Court session of October 26th, Nathaniell Souther was appointed as public notary for Suffolk County (Whitmore, *Aspinwall* pp. i-x).

Item 96 in *The Book of Possessions* defined the Hull homestead as follows:

> Robert Hulls Possession in Boston. One house and garden bounded with John Hurd south; the high streete west: Job Judkin north: and Gamaliel Waite, east. (Whitmore, *The Book of Possessions,* p. 36)[1]

The location of the Hull homestead was determined in 1866 by William Whitmore who plotted each lot described in *The Book of Possessions* onto a map. The Hull house was designated on the Whitmore map as parcel F 60 [figure 1] (*The Book of Possessions,* p. 82 and map on p. 74). Since specific lot measurements are lacking, Whitmore could only plot the lots based on the adjacencies described in *The Book of Possessions* and the references to known landmarks (such as streets, hills, ponds or streams). Thus, although the general location of each plot is fairly accurate relative to other named lots within a specifically described geographic location (such as a town block), without exact measurements for each plot, the precise location of any plot within a specific block is only an estimate. Realizing this limitation, we can locate the Hull lot with some reliability since it was located on a central thoroughfare known as the highway or High Street (by 1700 it was called Newbury Street), which is now Washington Street in downtown Boston. Moving south on Washington from the intersection of Washington and Summer Streets (Summer was then called Mill Street or Seven Star Lane) the Hull homestead was the third parcel of land on the east side of the street. Following the Hull lot there were three other lots before reaching the intersection of Washington and Bedford Streets.[2] The lot owners, on the east side of Washington Street moving from the intersection with Summer Street to the intersection with Bedford Street, were: Elizabeth Purton, Job Judkin, Robert Hull, John Hurd, William Blantaine (or Plantayne) and Thomas Wheeler (Whitmore map, lots F 58 to F 63). This would put the Hull lot almost half of the way between Summer and Bedford Streets (due to recent redevelopment in downtown Boston as of the year 2000, Bedford Street stops a block east of Washington). The east side of Washington Street is the side where Macy's Department Store (formerly The Jordan Marsh Company) is now located.

John Hull is promised the homestead

John Hull's mother, Elizabeth (Storer) Hull, died on May 7, 1646. The widower Robert, then living with his twenty-one-year-old son John and his seventeen-year-old son Edward, made a deed of gift to John on December 15, 1646, five months before John was to marry. The agreement stated that since John was "now being upon his marriage, being about the one

---

[1] In the original manuscript each item is a separate page. In the Whitmore edition the original pages were treated as item numbers with page numbers referring to the pages in his edition.

[2] Bedford Street was simply called the road to the Watering Place because of the pond found there. In 1753 the pond was purchased by David Wheeler so the street was referred to as the road to Wheeler's Pond and later Pond Street. In 1820 the road was renamed Bedford Street (*The Book of Possessions,* p. 81).

and twentieth yeare of his age" his father, Robert Hull, promised to give to John,

> My dwelling House & garden, with all the fruit trees and Appurtenances, bounded on the north, with the land of Job Judkin; on the south with the land of John Hurd; on the east with the Land of Gamaliel Waite; on the north west with the high way. As also my Lott of ground at mudy river, given to me by the towne of Boston, of about 36 or 38 ackras, bounded with Cambridg line on the North; upon the south, with the Land of Edward Belsher; on the East, partly: with the Land of Robert Turner; on the west, with the Lotts of Thomas Wheeler, Thomas Scottow & Isack Perry. As also a Lott of 21 ackras given by the town of Boston unto my sonn, Richard Storer, & by me purchased off him, Lieing at Brantree, by Manatticott river, between Mr. Francis Loyall & Mr Ting. Said property, Robert Hull gave to his son, John, reserving to himself during life, the full enjoyment of it. (Trask, "Abstracts," vol. 15, p. 323 and Howe, p. 40)

Richard Storer had been given an allotment of twelve acres in Braintree on November 25, 1639, said to be enough for "three heads" (Whitmore, *Boston Records,* p. 43 and Clarke, *Hull,* pp. 30-31). Presumably he was married and had a child at the time. Storer subsequently acquired about nine additional acres but at some point before 1646 he sold the land to his stepfather and seems to have returned to England.

On May 11, 1647, the twenty-two-year-old John Hull married Judith Quincy, daughter of Edmund and Judith Quincy. In his diary John Hull wrote that he had been married in his own house. His exact words were, "Mr. John Winthrop married me and my wife Judith, in my own house,..." (Hull, *Private Diary,* p. 143). From passing references to the Hull house in his diaries and letters, as well as from later references to the house in the extensive diaries and letters of his son-in-law Samuel Sewall, we know the Hull house originally consisted of a single large room with a fireplace at one end. John Hull extended the structure, adding a room onto the other side of the fireplace, so that the hearth was now at the center of the house between two large rooms. At this time the original room was called the "Great Hall" or the "Old Hall" while John's addition was called the "Little Hall." John also extended the size of the kitchen (Clarke, *Hull,* p. 36 as well as p. 162 for later comments on the rooms made in reference to the marriage of Hull's daughter). When John Hull stated he had been married in his own house he was referring to the addition he had built onto his father's house. John's father continued to reside in the "Great Hall." Indeed, Robert Hull later remarried, taking as his second wife, Judith Paine, the widow of Edmund Quincy, that is, John's mother-in-law (through this marriage Judith's son Edmund Quincy, who had been John's brother-in-law, became his step-brother). Thus, although the estate contained John Hull's residence and the land had been promised to him, it did not legally revert to John Hull's ownership until after the death of his father. Since his father was still alive when the updates to the information in *The Book of Possessions* ceased, there was no mention of John Hull in that book as an independent property owner. However, it is clear that in 1652, when the mint was constructed on Hull's property, the 27 year-old John Hull and his wife of five years were settled on the Hull family homestead.

John Hull inherits the homestead

In 1657 Robert Hull recorded his last will and testament which, upon his death, would give his estate to his son John Hull. The document read:

> I, Robert Hull, being in good memory of body and mind doe [do] give to sonne, John Hull, my part of this house which was first bylt [built], and the orchard or garden, with all oppurttynances to it, and on lotte [one lot] at muddye river, of thurty Accores, which I promised to him at his marridge to give at my death, and doe make him my full executores of all oether goods, cattells [chattel] after my death, and to see this my will to be performed, that is to saye, I give to my sonne, Edmund Quinney [Quincy], that porsson [portion] which is due to me by my wife [the former Judith Quincy], that £20 in goods and corne, be it more or less, and to his sonne, John Quiney, on lote [one lot] at brantrye which was my sonne, Richard Storer; to the oether childrens [Edmund's other children], 12 pence a peece. To Richard Storer, £9, to be payed before or after my death, and to sonne Edward Hull, that peece of ground at the water mile [mill] and three core [score] poundes in money or goods. [signed below] Robert Hull (Trask, "Abstracts," vol. 15, p. 322-23 and Howe, p. 40)

Robert left the bulk of his estate to John, while offering far less to his son Edward and his stepson Richard. As we have seen, Richard had most likely returned to England by this date. Edward moved to Braintree in 1650 and by 1652 had married Elinor Newman. However, a few months after his marriage, Edward set sail on a frigate owned by the family. He joined Captain John Underhill in an expedition to seize Dutch ships, under the authority of a commission from the Rhode Island Assembly. Soon the sailors were not only raiding the Dutch but also preying on the French and any others they could overpower. Edward dragged the entire Hull family into a piracy charge, because both his father Robert and his brother John were listed with him as owners of the vessel. At the Essex County Court held in Salem on November 29, 1653, a Captain Kempo Seibada sued all the Hulls. The court record stated Seibada sued Robert and John along with Edward since they were all listed as partial owners of the frigate *Swallow,* "...under the command of Edward Hull, pirate, for damages of his estate in taking out of his house at Block Island by said Edward Hull, goods to the value of £96" (Dow, *Records,* vol. 1, p. 314). During the proceedings Robert and John produced several letters they had sent to Edward disapproving of his actions. Robert and John stated that they "did endeavour to improve all the interest wee had in him to gaine him from that imployment by letters & by message..." (Dow, *Records,* vol. 1, p. 318). Robert and John were acquitted of any wrongdoing while Edward, who did not appear at the trial, seems to have fled to England. There are several letters from Edward written in the 1650's from London (Clarke, *Hull,* pp. 73-75 and Morison, p. 152).

Robert Hull died on July 28, 1666. On February 12, 1667, John was appointed executor of his father's estate. The document stated John was "his Eldest & now only sonn." This clearly refers to natural sons, since Edmund Quincy was still living and probably Richard Storer was still alive in England. The inference is that Edward Hull had died by this date. On the same day John Hull was appointed executor of his father's estate, he filed a copy of his deed of gift from 1646. At this point John Hull became the sole owner of the Hull estate.

The homestead at the death of John Hull

When John Hull died on October 1, 1683, he owned numerous properties and was a partner in several businesses. Unfortunately, Hull died intestate, so there was no will detailing his holdings, but we have a document of almost equal value. An agreement was submitted to the court on March 12, 1684, for the division of John Hull's estate. The agreement was forwarded by the executors of the estate with the approval of John Hull's widow, Judith Hull, and the approval of the Hull's only child, Hannah,[3] along with Hannah's husband, Samuel Sewall. The document contains some important details concerning the Hull residence, which reverted to his wife Judith. The residence was described as follows,

> the mansion house of the said Mr. Hull, wherein hee dyed, with all the land thereto adjoining and belonging; and all tenements, shop, out houseing and buildings whatsoever on any part of said land standing; with a small orchard or parcel of land thereto neer adjacent late purchased of Mr. Edward Rawson. (Hull, *Diary,* addenda, p. 258)

The 1684 agreement also stated that upon the death of Hull's wife the property would revert to Samuel Sewall. For an excellent discussion of Hull and Sewall references to this property see the article of Estes Howe cited in the bibliography.

The Boston properties of John Hull

From a variety of sources we know Hull acquired several properties during his career. His holdings in Rhode Island and New Hampshire as well as his Massachusetts real estate outside of Boston have never been proposed as locations for the Boston mint, hence I shall limit my remarks to Hull's various holdings within Boston (for his land outside of Boston see Clarke, *Hull,* pp. 84-92). It has sometimes been suggested the mint could have been located on any of Hull's Boston properties. The central problem with this argument is that none of Hull's land acquisitions date back to the period of the construction of the mint in 1652 other than his father's gift of December 1646 promising he would inherit the family estate. Since the mint was constructed in 1652 on land said to be owned by Hull, it seems clear that land acquired after the mint was constructed could not be considered a likely location. The problem lies in that many of Hull's land holdings are listed in the 1684 agreement for the division of his estate, but no dates were given as to when he acquired the lands. It has sometimes been incorrectly assumed Hull held these lands from his earliest years. Indeed, the editor of the 1878 edition of Samuel Sewall's *Diary* mistakenly located the Hull residence (and thus also the Sewall residence) to Hull's land on Cotton Hill! Even though Estes Howe wrote an article in 1885 rectifying the numerous geographical errors in the 1878 edition, those using this source without recourse to Howe's article sometime perpetuate errors concerning Hull's properties.

---

[3] The children of John and Judith Hull were as follows: On January 23, 1653 twins, Elizabeth and Mary, were born but they lived barely a week. Mary died on January 30th and Elizabeth died on February 1st. On November 3, 1654, the Hull's had a son, named John, who died less than two weeks later on November 14th. On February 14, 1658, their daughter, Hannah, was born. She was the only child to survive to adulthood. On August 6, 1661, a son, Samuel, was born but he died within two weeks on August 20th (Hull, *Private Diary,* pp.143-44).

Hull's first acquisition of Boston real estate dates to 1653. On April 9, 1653, the widow, Sarah Phippen, sold to "John Hull of Boston Goldsmith,"

> ...[for] the some of fiveteene pounds ...one Howse and parcell of Ground therevnto belonging being bounded Vpon the South wth the Sea and vpon the North wth the Highway and vpon the west wth Richard Woodhowse his land and vpon the east wth Jonathan Negoose his land... . (*Suffolk Deeds,* vol. 3, pp. 69-70; also mentioned in, Hull, *Diary,* Addenda, p. 260 and again on p. 261)

This was a small parcel located about seven lots behind, that is, to the east of, the Hull family homestead. On the Whitmore map (figure 1) it is a portion of the parcel of land listed as lot F 26. Thomas Foster had owned the lot in the 1640's but apparently sold it to David and Sarah Phippen, who lived at the northern end of Boston near the Mill Creek (Whitmore, *Boston Records,* p. 84). The Phippen's also obtained lot F 25, which was the residence of Jonathan Negoos. Sarah Phippen sold a portion of the Foster lot to Hull following the death of her husband. Below, we shall see she sold the remainder of the land, including the Negoos homestead, to Robert Sanderson. On the Whitmore map lot F 46 was the home of Richard Woodhouse, which was defined as the western border of the Hull purchase. John Hull's land extended from the shore on the south to " the Highway" on the north, which, in this case, referred to Mill Street. The northern border of the Hull lot included some land listed on the Whitmore map as lot F 27, which had formerly been the location of a windmill owned by Richard Tuttle that had been moved to the fort in 1642 (Whitmore, *The Book of Possessions*, p. 78)[4].

The Phippen acquisition is mentioned in the 1684 agreement for the division of John Hull's property as "...a small close or pasture ground scituate in Boston adjoining upon Mr. Robert Sanderson formerly purchased of Sarah Phippen" (Hull, *Diary,* Addenda, p. 260 and mentioned again on p. 261). That the land was acquired for only £15 indicates it was not a residential lot. Clearly the house on this parcel was some variety of storage building or barn and not a home. On November 3, 1655, Richard Martin purchased a residential lot consisting of a house and a parcel of land 108 feet by 30 feet for £40 (*Suffolk Deeds,* vol. 3, pp. 60-61), also, we shall see Sanderson acquired a residential lot from Sarah Phippen for £40. The pasture was the first of Hull's several land acquisitions, followed in November of 1657 by the acquisition of 280 acres in Braintree and the purchase of 1,000 unspecified acres in Massachusetts from Governor John Endicott for £50 on March 9, 1658 (*Suffolk Deeds,* vol. 3, pp. 71-72 and 202-04).

In 1660 John Hull obtained a warehouse in Boston (*Suffolk Deeds,* vol. 11, pp. 55-57). ✓ He purchased a house with some land on Cotton Hill from Seaborn Cotton on September 24, 1664, for £200. Cotton Hill was located off Tremont Street north of the corner of Tremont and School Streets, up to Pemberton Square (*Suffolk Deeds,* vol. 6, pp. 225-26). Later, on May 29, 1682, Hull expanded his holdings in the area by purchasing the house and property

---

[4] The fort was located on a hill overlooking the ocean in the area near what is now the intersection of Franklin and Broad streets.

originally owned by the Reverend John Cotton, after the house had gone through several owners (Whitmore, *The Book of Possessions,* p. 3, item 9 and p. 111, item H 13; Howe, p. 316 and Clarke, *Hull,* pp. 86-87). Hull also acquired one-and-a-half acres of land on January 3, 1665/6, for £50 from Richard Dummer, the father of his apprentice, Jeremiah Dummer. This property was a section of what had originally been Christopher Stanley's pasture located in the North End of Boston near Cobb's Hill. About 1711, Hull's heirs, Samuel and Hannah Sewall, conveyed the North End land to the town of Boston with the proviso that the road connecting that land to the main thoroughfare be called Hull Street. The town agreed and the road still retains that name to this day (Whitmore, *The Book of Possessions*, p. 16, item 43 and p. 119, item I 1 and Clarke, *Hull,* p. 87).

In the last decade of his life Hull seems to have gone on a buying spree, acquiring several nearby lots to add to his estate. On November 6, 1676, John Hull purchased half of his neighbor's lot, acquiring the house and the southern half of the lot (which was the portion that abutted the north end of his own property) from Samuel Judkin, the son of Job Judkin; the northern half of the Judkin lot was acquired by Christopher Morse (Howe, p. 313 and *Suffolk Deeds*, vol. 10, pp. 12-14). In fact, the first thirty pages of the tenth book of the deeds of Suffolk County, which lists deeds recorded during January through February of 1677, is completely devoted to recording 22 deeds for land in Boston, Braintree, Muddy River and Milton recently acquired by Hull. In the agreement submitted to the court for the division of John Hull's estate following his death we learn among the properties Hull had purchased were:

> …ye little orchard or parcel of land bought of Mr. Rawson neer adjacent to ye Mansion house; with the dwelling house and land on the other side of the street purchased of Robert Walker... .(Hull, *Diary,* Addenda, p. 259)

The Walker property was acquired in March of 1680 and was described as bounded to the east by High Street, south by the land late of Robert Mason, west by the land of Hezekiah Usher and north by the land late of Peter Goose. This locates the property to the other side of Washington Street, two lots south of the Hull residence (Howe, p. 314). Hull purchased the Rawson property on June 30, 1683, just three months before he died. This orchard, acquired from Edward Rawson, Secretary for Massachusetts Bay, was on Summer Street, formerly the east end of the Widow Elizabeth Purton's lot and extended 100 feet down Summer Street (Howe, p. 313).

Moreover, in the agreement for the division of John Hull's estate, other Boston properties are mentioned in which Hull had an interest including half-interest in some warehouses and a wharf, a third-interest in three dwellings that were then occupied by William Hoar, Hudson Leveret, and the widow of Richard Woodde. The division agreement also explained Hull's Muddy River property was "in the tenure and occupation of Simon Gates." All of these properties were acquired long after the construction of the mint and could not be seriously considered as sites Hull could have selected in 1652 for the mint house.

In 1652, John Hull owned the section of the family home he had built for himself and his wife. John also had a signed promissory note from his father stating he was to receive the homestead upon the death of his father. This was the only real estate to which John Hull had a claim in 1652. Therefore, it seems quite probable the Hull homestead was the location referred to in the minutes of mint committee meeting of June 22, 1652, which stated "That the said mint howse shall be sett upon the land of the said John Hull."

Hull's shop and its relationship to the mint

John Hull and his wife Judith continually improved and expanded the family homestead, living at that location until they died. The description of Hull's estate at the time of his death in 1683 mentions several buildings located on the homestead in addition to the "mansion house." It mentions "all tenements, shop, out houseing and buildings whatsoever on any part of said land standing" but it does not specifically name any buildings except the mansion residence and the shop. Hull's surviving ledger gives some further information concerning the buildings on the Hull estate (for details on the ledger see Chapter Two). Among the numerous personal accounts in the ledger is an account for Hull's "dwelling house" detailing expenses Hull incurred in regard to his residence. In this account we find Hull incurred a debt of £18 on October 9, 1671, "To Building my little stone house of office" (New England Historic Genealogical Society, MS Cb 110, vol. 1, folios 24 verso - 25 recto). In addition to the construction of an office we find the "shop" was mentioned several times in the ledger as the location where his silversmith business took place. For example, there is an entry under the account of Mr. William Brenton from May 27, 1673, "To [be] paid ye shop for mending a pott & 3 spoons and silver added 10 · 6" [that is, 10s6d] (New England Historic Genealogical Society, MS Cb 110, vol. 1, folio 13 verso; illustrated in Jordan, "Mint," p. 2329). There are also other accounts that refer to payments for items needed for the shop such as coal and charcoal. In the account of John Winchester and Dorman Morean of Muddy River (now Brookline) are several payments for coal delivered to the shop. On February 28, 1674, [listed in the old style dating as 1673 since the new year began in March] is an entry: "By money of the shop for coals - for John Winchester · · 1 / 10 /· ·" [that is, £1 10s]. Also, under November 17, 1674, "By money of the shop for 73 bushels 1/2 coal - for John Winchester · · 1 / · 4 /· 6" [that is, 73.5 bushels for £1 4s6d]. And finally under December 3 [1674], "For charcoal to ye shop whose money for Dorman Morean · · 2 / 17 / · 8" [that is, £2 17s8d] (New England Historic Genealogical Society, MS Cb 110, vol. 1, folio 40 recto; also see Addenda to Appendix I, below; illustrated in Jordan, "Mint," pp. 2327-28). Clearly, the shop was the location where Hull and Sanderson kept their tools and made silver cups, bowls and other objects.

The ledger also contains an account relating to the shop. This is a three part listing beginning on folios 26 verso - 27 recto under the heading "Account of the shop..." (this account is fully transcribed in Appendix I). Several entries clearly related to the coining operation and demonstrate Hull used the terms shop and mint interchangeably. The first entry specifically mentions silver sent to the shop, rather than the mint house, to be minted into coins. The entry, from October 18, 1671, stated, "To 417$^{oz.}$ 1/2 sterling silver sent into y^e shop to be minted... ." On the other hand, two of the following entries use the term mint house rather than shop. Under August 25, 1673, Hull wrote, "To Put into y^e mint house to be Coyned 265$^{oz.}$ sterling at 6^s · 2d is £81 · 14 · 2" and again under December 12, 1674, "To Put into the mint house to Coyne 275$^{oz.}$ 1/2 sterling at 6 · 2^d £84 · 19 · 0." Other entries neglect to mention either the shop or the mint house as under October 24, 1671, which simply stated "To 208$^{oz.}$ sterling sent in to be minted..." and under June 29, 1672, "To Put into Coyne

179$^{oz.}$ 1/2." Although most of the entries in this section relate to sterling silver to be turned into coinage there are some entries specifically relating to silversmithing, for instance "4 Rings get in ye shop of mine. 1 · 12 · 74." [that is, February 1, 1675, as February was the 12th month in the old style calendar]. There are also entries relating to the purchase of items that could be used both in silversmithing and in minting, as an entry of December 26, 1671, concerning the purchase of 12 parcels of files.

That this account was listed under the heading of "Account of the shop," indicates Hull considered both the coining operation and silversmithing business to be activities of his shop. Hull listed mint expenses as shop expenses. Additionally, he sometimes used the term mint house when referring to coining, while at other times he use the word shop. Hull understood the General Court had authorized his silversmith shop to also function as a mint house. Therefore, he sometimes used the more legally appropriate term mint house when referring to the location of the coining function while at other times he simply used the term shop since that was the location where the minting was performed.

The Massachusetts Bay General Court mint documents of 1652 refer to a building on the Hull estate called a "mint house." These documents also mention the acquisition of the tools required for the melting and refining of silver as well as those needed for the stamping of the coins. It is clear the building constructed to house these items was the structure Hull and Sanderson used for all of their silversmith operations and was the structure they referred to as the "shop."

Contemporary references to the mint house

There are very few documents that actually describe the structure or structures where Massachusetts silver coins were minted. The following discussion analyzes the specific terminology used to refer to the mint house in contemporary government documents to determine if they provide any further information concerning the mint building.

1. Citations to the mint house from 1652

The earliest reference to a "mint house" is found in the undated draft legislation for establishing a mint brought before the May 1652 session of the Massachusetts Bay General Court. The legislation explained:

> That all persons what soeuer have liberty to bring in vnto the mint howse at Boston all bulljon plate or Spannish Cojne there to be melted & brought to the allay of sterling Silver by John Hull master of the sajd mint and his sworne officers, & by him to be Cojned into 12^d : 6^d & 3^d peeces... . (Crosby, p. 34)

The final part of the draft legislation ordered the mint committee:

> ...to Appoint the mint howse in some Convenjent place in Boston. to Give John Hull master of the mint the oath suiteable to his place. And to Approove of all other officers and determine what els shall Appeare to them as necessaryly to be donne for the Carrying an end of the whole order.

> & That all other orders concerning the valuation or coining of money past
> this Court shallbe repealed: (Crosby, pp. 34-35)

This wording is also found in the final forms of the legislation as passed by the House of Magistrates on May 26, 1652, and as passed by the House of Deputies a day later on May 27th (see the entries in the chronology in Appendix II). Thus, the idea of constructing a special mint facility in Boston was an essential part of the legislation and expediting the construction of that facility was one of the primary charges delegated to the mint committee.

Interestingly, the most detailed description of the mint house is not a description at all but rather reflects general building specifications issued by the mint committee dating to before the building was constructed! The reference is found in an undated and incomplete draft version of an action of the mint committee of the General Court that stated:

> …ffor melting Refining & Coyning of Silver ... thire shall be an howse built
> at the Countryes Charge of sixteene foote square tenn foote high,
> substantially wrought and further also, provide all necessery tooles &
> Implements for the same at the Countrjes charge... .(Crosby, p. 39)

The final version of this action is dated June 20, 1652. It used the same wording but slightly revised the spelling and punctuation presented in the draft; the final version stated that:

> …for melting Refyning and Coyning of silver... there shall be an howse built
> at the Countrjes charge, of sixteene ffoote square, ten foote high;
> substantially wrought; and further also, Provide all necessary tooles and
> Implements for the same, at the Countrjes charge... .(Crosby, p. 40)

The location of this structure was not mentioned but it is clear the committee was negotiating for a site that would meet the requirements of the legislation, namely "some Convenjent place in Boston." Two days later a site was announced and orders for the construction of a mint house were issued.

On June 22nd, the committee stated that, "there should be a mint howse & all tooles and Implements necessary thereto, built and procured At the Countrjes charge." To that end the committee stated a warrant had been issued to the Constables of Boston impressing Isacke Cullimore into the service of the state and another warrant had been issued to Cullimore allowing him to impress "other workmen Carpenters" to join him. Furthermore the document explained, "That the sajd mint howse shall be sett vppon the land of the sajd John Hull." This announcement is the first evidence we have that the committee had been negotiating an agreement with Hull on the use of his land for the mint house. The substance of that agreement is explained in a provision added to the announcement on the selection of the site. The provision explained if Hull ceased to hold the position of mintmaster, the Commonwealth had the option of purchasing the land from Hull or allowing Hull the option of purchasing "the sajd Howse" from the Commonwealth at a price determined by two impartial men, one of whom would be selected by the Commonwealth and the other selected by Hull (Crosby, p. 42).

From these documents we learn the mint was conceived to be housed in a single building erected on Hull's land where silver would be melted and refined into a sterling alloy and then stamped into coins. The Commonwealth impressed the carpenters and paid for the construction of the mint building as well as acquiring the tools necessary for refining silver and minting coins. Whether the building that Cullimore actually constructed varied from the specifications set forth in the memorandum of June 20th is unknown, because there is no similarly detailed description of the structure with specific dimensions from an eyewitness who actually saw the building. The June 20th statement predated the construction of the mint. It was intended as a general guide for the carpenters, explaining the kind of building the state anticipated would be required. However, it does seem quite probable the carpenters followed the committee's request as closely as possible, constructing a single structure with the intention that the building would be used for the entire process from melting and refining silver to stamping coins. Indeed, later General Court documents refer to a single structure called the "mint house."

Assuming Cullimore quickly found the additional carpenters for the job and the necessary building materials were available, it is quite likely the mint building was completed by mid-July, although the precise date is unknown. We do know that Hull took his oath as an officer of the mint on June 10th or 11th while Sanderson, who resided in Watertown at that time, waited until August 19, 1652. The construction of the building was not the only task that needed to be completed before coins could be minted. Presumably, Hull had a hearth in which to melt silver since he worked as a silversmith before this time, although it is quite possible he had been using his father's hearth, as he was a blacksmith. Minimally, some type of stone hearth would be required in the mint building. It is not stated whether Cullimore and the carpenters he impressed into service also built a hearth, or if a stonemason was later brought in to complete the structure. Additionally, Hull would need a variety of equipment for coin production (see Chapter Seven for details). He may have needed a furnace or foundry to melt larger quantities of silver, although it is possible at first only a hearth was sufficient. Hull would also need to set up a wet sand area to cast silver into thin strips. Additionally, he would need to acquire some type of rolling machine to press the strips to the desired coin thickness and metal cutting shears to cut out the NE coinage. Hull would also need punches for the NE and the denomination numerals as well as other equipment for coinage production such as crucibles or pots in which to melt the silver and ladles to remove the molten metal. Naturally, he would need equipment for assaying silver, which he presumably owned as part of his silversmith supplies. The construction of the building was an important visible sign of the establishment of the mint, but coins could not be produced until the structure was completed with a working hearth and filled with the benches and all the tools and special equipment required for minting.

If one assumes the equipment had to be ordered from England, then it is necessary to allow for a 6-8 week ocean crossing, in each direction, as well as some time in England to place the orders and have the items produced. Even if the mint committee had sent an equipment request from Boston on June 20th, the date of their action ordering the equipment to be procured, it would be unlikely any items could have reached Boston before the beginning of October at the very earliest.[5] On the other hand, if it is assumed the essential tools could have been produced locally by Joseph Jenks at the Hammersmith Ironworks, then it is possible to suppose the equipment was produced and made available during the summer months suggesting the mint could certainly have commenced operations by the start of September.[6]

Minting may not have started until after Sanderson moved to Boson and took his oath of office in mid-August. The legislation of May 26/27 stated Massachusetts silver coins were to become current money as of September first. This probably reflects the date on which the mint was to officially open. However it is possible Hull may have started experimenting with minting in August. Certainly it would take some time to test the new equipment and to formulate a production process that would be both efficient and economical, assuring the viability of the enterprise. It is possible Sanderson did not take the oath earlier that August 19th because he was still in Watertown until that date. We know Hull personally signed the undated mint committee draft of early June 1652 while Edward Rawson, the Secretary of the General Court and a member of the mint committee, added Sanderson's name to the document, indicating Sanderson may not have been available. In any event, it seems clear NE coinage was in production before mid-October since on October 19, 1652, the General Court passed legislation changing the coin design.

Unfortunately the pages in the account book of Richard Russell, Treasurer of Massachusetts Bay, relating to the period during the construction of the mint were excised from the surviving text at some point in the past and are now lost (Noe, *Silver,* p. 6). This source would have listed the specific mint expenses incurred by the Commonwealth. Although we have been deprived of the best source for financial information, we do have some verification that the expenses relating to the construction of the mint house had been paid by October. In the October 1652 session of the General Court treasurer Russell summarized the expenses incurred by the Commonwealth since the May General Court meeting. Unfortunately he did not give a detailed itemized account, rather he included the mint expenses along with prison costs stating:

> To several sums paid on the charge, - prisons and prisoners and keeper and
> executioner and mint house. All is £395. 12s. 2d... . (Hull, *Diary,* appendix,
> p. 289 and Shurtleff, vol. 4, pt. 1, p. 104)

The unknown portion of this sum reflecting the mint costs probably included both the cost of constructing the building as well as the cost of purchasing the necessary tools for soon thereafter, on October 26, 1652, the secretary of the Court recorded that the whole General

---

[5] This allows for a trip of six weeks in each direction and about two weeks in London to procure the items. Examples of ocean voyage time during the seventeenth century include the Hull family voyage from Bristol to Boston, mentioned above, which took from September 28 to November 7, 1635, or just a few days short of six full weeks at sea, while Edward Randolph's trip in 1683 from London to Boston that took eight weeks from August 20th through October 20th. For more on the Randolph voyage see the chronology entry in Appendix II.

[5] For additional information on Joseph Jenks and the Hammersmith Ironworks see below, Chapter 13.

Court voted to allow and approve the actions of the mint committee concerning the construction of a mint house and the acquisition of the necessary minting equipment at government expense (Crosby, p. 41, Hull, *Diary,* appendix, p. 289 and Shurtleff, vol. 4, pt. 1, p. 118). Thus, during the summer of 1652 a building called a mint house had been constructed and the needed equipment had been purchased. Further, the General Court subsequently approved both of these expenses at the October session.

2. Citations to the minting facilities from the 1660's

Although the 1652 references mention only a single building, some later references, made after the mint building had been constructed, but while the mint was in operation, suggest there may have been more than one structure involved in the production of coinage. On October 16, 1660, the General Court established a second mint committee in the hope of obtaining more favorable terms for the Commonwealth. On June 6, 1661, the committee submitted a report stating they felt that "the use of the mint & house required in justice some certaine part of the income received..." be paid to the government. The committee asked for 5% of the mint fee. However, Hull and Sanderson would not agree to give the Commonwealth an annual percentage but offered a yearly payment of £10 as a free gift (Crosby, p. 72). The use of the ampersand for the conjunction "and" in the phrase "the mint & house" is imprecise. It is difficult to know exactly what was meant by the phrase, "the use of the mint & house." Possibly the word "mint" referred to the privilege granted to Hull and Sanderson to mint coins, while the term "house" referred to the building constructed at the expense of the Commonwealth. It would be rather unusual for the General Court to use the phrase "use of the mint" in place of a more accurate phrase such as, "for the granting of the exclusive privilege to coin," but this is certainly a plausible interpretation. It is also possible the phrase referred to the use of two distinct structures. It should be remembered in early New England the word house not only referred to a home but was also used to refer to any building, thus we find the phrase, which we might consider to be a redundancy, namely, "dwelling House" used in Robert Hull's December 15, 1646 promissory deed of gift. Alternatively, we find the term "howse" and "mint howse" used in the General Court documents of June 20 and 22, 1652, to refer to a building for the mint. Based on the generic usage of the term "house" it is possible, in the present context, that the phrase "the use of the mint & house" could refer to the use of two separate structures, a mint building and a related building generically called a house. On the other hand the phrase could refer to a single edifice with multiple functions, namely a structure that functioned as a mint and had other unspecified uses as a house, building or shop. Alternatively, the phrase could simply be an awkward method of referring to a single structure that was used solely as a mint house. Interestingly, in the comments made on this report by William Torrey, the Clerk for the lower house of the court, the House of Deputies, there was no mention of a payment for the granting of the privilege of coining, rather the comments focused on money paid for the use of a structure, which he referred to as a mint house. In a codicil to the report, Torrey stated the Deputies felt the committee should accept the £10 "& what else they can gett by way of recompenc for the mint howse for the time past, & that[7] it be deliuered to the Treasurer to be bestowed in powder & oill,..." (Crosby, p. 72). This decision of the deputies was also added to the record of the General Court, backdated to the start of the court session on May 22nd, where the phrase referring to the structure was again transcribed as a mint house, "Recompence for the mint house," and stating the money would be used to acquire powder (that is, gunpowder) without mention of oil (Crosby, p. 72). Although the reference made by the mint committee is unclear if it referred to the minting privilege and a building or to the use of one or more buildings, it appears the General Court continued to refer to a single structure called the mint house.

Additional references to the mint building are found in relation to a third mint committee appointed by the General Court on May 15, 1667, to obtain "...some allowance annually, or otherwise, for & in Consideration of the charge the Country hath binn at in erecting a mint house, & for the vse of it for so many years without any Considerable sattisfaction, ..." (Crosby, p. 78). An agreement was reached with this third mint committee and a document was signed on October 4, 1667. The contract stated, "hauing duely weighed the Countrys Interest in the aediffices apperteyning to the sajd office, and Agitated the matter with mr. John Hull & mr. Robert Saunderson, the present mint masters..." that Hull and Sanderson agreed to pay £40 into the Commonwealth treasury within six months "In Consideration of the Countrys disbursments in the said aediffices, & for Interest the Generall Court hath therein." Presumably this payment was to reimburse the government for construction costs and appears to have been made to acquire the rights to the government's interest in the buildings associated with the mint. Further, Hull and Sanderson agreed to pay £10 annually to the Commonwealth for the next seven years (Shurtleff, vol. 4, pt. 2, p. 347 and Crosby, p. 78). That the 1667 agreement refers to "aediffices" in the plural implies there was more than one structure taken into consideration. Also, by this one time payment of £40 it appears the mintmasters acquired whatever interest the Commonwealth had in the buildings.

Thus, the documents of 1652 refer to a single structure where the entire refining and minting process would take place; this structure was an entity simply called a house or mint house. In the references made after the mint had been in operation and had expanded through the acquisition of more sophisticated coining presses, evolving from simply using punches to the acquisition of a rocker press and then to a screw press, we find the General Court continued to refer to a single building called a mint house. However, the reports of mint committees, who actually investigated the matter and presumably viewed the mint facilities, do not use the standard phrase "mint house." The 1661 report uses the ambiguous phrase "the mint & house" while the 1667 contract uses the word "aediffices." As the 1667 document details a payment made by the mintmasters to acquire the government's interests in the structures, I assume the wording was selected with more care than was the case in the document of 1661. Thus, it seems possible as Hull's businesses expanded, the minting operation may have been carried out in more than one building.

---

[7] The abbreviation yᵗ in the text is transcribed as "that" rather than "yet." See the General Court transcription of this text, which is also given on p. 72 in Crosby and the use of the abbreviation yᵗ by Sewall in Hull, *Diary,* p. 254, in the entry for March 21, 1677.

The reference to multiple buildings may reflect a separation of minting operations. Probably the assays, the processing of the silver strips and the engraving of the dies may have been performed in the shop where Hull conducted his silversmith business. It is also likely the shop contained a heat source. During the seventeenth century the most common heat source was an open hearth or forge as would be found in a blacksmith shop. Less prevalent, because they were more costly, was a forced air stone furnace called a wind oven in contemporary sources (See figure 2 for a wind oven and figure 4 for a large contemporary forge). A small forge or wind oven, supplemented with a bellows, could reach temperatures hot enough to shape metal, granulate small quantities of silver and then melt the granulated silver so that it could be refined to sterling and shaped into a small object such as a ring, cup or a bowl (see Lazarus Ercker's treatise, cited in the bibliography, for details on the granulation process, pp. 51-59, and for several illustrations of forges and wind ovens). A wind oven or open hearth forge would also be essential in several other silversmith related tasks such as baking wet clay to make an assay oven or baking cupels to be used in an assay, as well as keeping the staff warm during the winter months. It is possible a hearth or oven may have been the only heat source in the shop when the mint first opened.

However, as the mint became more successful and moved from the hammer technology used on the NE coins to the more sophisticated machine press technologies used for the later series, the production rates increased. This required more silver and larger melts. It is clear from Hull's ledger that large quantities of silver, sometimes over one hundred troy pounds, were consigned to the mint. Unlike most silversmiths who only melted small quantities of silver, Hull needed to melt much larger quantities of silver for coinage, often up to 25 troy pounds in a single melt. For melts of this magnitude he needed a larger foundry furnace. It did not need to be as large as the furnace constructed in the late 1640's at the Hammersmith Ironworks ten miles north of Boston in Saugus, but it certainly had to be much larger than the wind ovens and forges used in silversmith and blacksmith shops. These larger foundry furnaces reached temperatures of up to 2000° Fahrenheit and were often found at mining sites where they were used to extract minerals from ore. The foundry furnace was usually located outside, frequently in an open structure that could be described as a lean-to, or what we might now call a car port, consisting of a back wall and a roof giving some protection from rain and snow. Sometimes this structure was attached to an outside wall of a building or was free standing in the proximity of a building [figure 3] (Agricola's treatise on metals contains several plates of large furnaces in operation, see pp. 474-82). Only the most advanced facilities, such as the London mint and a few large London goldsmith operations, had the financial means to construct special foundry rooms within the confines of a building. If the Massachusetts Mint house was only about sixteen feet square and ten feet high there may have been room to include a wall hearth or possibly a wind oven along with the work benches and other tools Hull needed. But there would certainly not be sufficient room for a foundry furnace and the adjacent sand molds required to shape large quantities of molten silver into strips. Indeed, when such a furnace was in operation the heat would be so intense it would be difficult to remain nearby. Thus, it seems quite likely when a melting furnace was added to the operation it was not located inside the shop, although it may have been just outside the shop under a lean-to or in a nearby shed. Moreover, at least during the screw press period, and possibly earlier, it is likely the relatively noisy job of actually striking the planchets into coins may have been performed in another building where the coin press would have been kept.

In conclusion it seems a mint building was erected on the Hull estate in 1652 and was called both "the shop" and "the mint house" by Hull. As the coining operation expanded with the acquisition of a foundry furnace to melt large quantities of silver, the furnace was probably not located inside the shop. Subsequently, with the acquisition of newer, larger and more sophisticated minting equipment, mint production work was probably distributed so that more than one building was used for the coining operation. Also, it appears in 1667 Hull and Sanderson made a payment of £40 to acquire the Commonwealth's interest in the physical facilities used in the operation of the mint.

Robert Sanderson and his homestead

Unlike John Hull who had immigrated to America as a child with no professional training, Robert Sanderson came to America as a fully trained adult. Indeed, Sanderson began an apprenticeship in the goldsmith trade under Robert Rawlings (or Rawlins) a year before Hull was born. The London goldsmith's guild register for October 17, 1623 states:

> That I Robert Sanderson the sonne of Saundersonne of Higham doe put
> myselfe apprentize until William Rawlins Citizen & Goldsmith of London
> for the terme of nyne yeares. (Clarke, *Hull,* p. 57)

Following his apprenticeship Sanderson continued to work for Rawlings. In all Sanderson had sixteen years of experience as a goldsmith before he departed England for Massachusetts Bay. Upon his arrival in 1639 Sanderson and his wife Lydia first settled in Hampton, New Hampshire, where they were granted 80 acres of land. Sanderson took an oath as a freeman of Massachusetts Bay on September 7, 1639 (Shurtleff, *Records,* vol. 1, p. 376). Soon thereafter, on October 29, 1639, their daughter Mary was baptized at the Hampton church (*The New England Historical and Genealogical Register,* vol. 12, 1858, p. 79). By 1642 Lydia had died and Sanderson married Mary Cross, the widow of John Cross of Watertown, Massachusetts, which is just west of Cambridge. Sandersons's brother lived in Watertown, so Robert and his new wife soon moved there. The birth of their son, Joseph, was recorded in the Watertown register on January 1, 1643, followed by Benjamin in 1649, Sarah in 1651 and Robert in 1652 (*The New England Historical and Genealogical Register,* vol. 7, 1853, p. 282). In 1652 Sanderson joined John Hull as a partner in the Boston mint and presumably moved to Boston soon before he took his oath of office on August 19, 1652. Sanderson was admitted as an inhabitant of Boston on May 30, 1653, and in December of 1653 he purchased a house in Boston (Kane, p. 882, Clarke, *Hull,* p. 57 and Whitmore, *Boston Records,* p. 116).

On December 3, 1653, the widow, Sarah Phippen, sold to "Robert Saunderson of Boston Goldsmith,"

> ...[for] the some of forty pounds ...one house and parcell of Ground there
> vnto belonging being bounded vpon the south wth the Sea, & vppon the
> North wth the High way & vpon the west wth the land of Jn° Hull. and vpon
> the east wth the land of Thomas munt ... . (*Suffolk Deeds,* vol. 3, pp. 70-71)

The Sanderson lot was adjacent to the pasture acquired by John Hull from Sarah Phippen in April of that year; it was just two blocks east of the Hull family estate. That Sanderson lived so close to Hull is a further indication their joint silversmith and minting operations were located on the Hull estate.

On the Whitmore map (figure 1) the Sanderson parcel is listed as lot F 25, formerly the residence of Jonathan Negoos. Sanderson's land extended from the shore to "the Highway," which, in this case, referred to Mill Street. The lot directly east of the Sanderson property, lot F 24 on the map, was owned by Thomas Munt. According to the Boston town records for June 29, 1657, Robert Sanderson was allowed to rent "a Little 3 square strip of Land" from the Commonwealth for 18d per year. This land adjoined "...the upper end of his owne Garden, Coming from the upper Corner of Tho. Munt's pailes [i.e., his boundary stakes] unto stile [the entrance steps] of the said Robert Sanderson" (Whitmore, *Boston Records,* pp. 137-38). Later, on January 23, 1663, Thomas and Elinor Munt sold Sanderson sixteen and a half rods of land (Anderson, p. 1317). About a block east of the Munt and Sanderson lots were some windmills on a promontory overlooking the ocean called windmill point[8] (lot F 22 on the map), thus the main road connecting that area to High Street (i.e. Washington Street) was called Mill Street (now Summer Street).

Addendum to Chapter One

Massachusetts Bay Colonists Named John Hull

John Hull of Dorchester

There were at least two, or possibly three, individuals in Massachusetts Bay during the first half of the seventeenth century with the name of John Hull. The first settler with the name John Hull came to Massachusetts in 1632, becoming a freeman on August 7, 1632. He settled in Dorchester where he was granted a lot of sixteen acres on January 16, 1633. The last known reference to this individual was from March 9, 1642. Thereafter, he was no longer mentioned, suggesting he may have died, moved or returned to England. Another Hull from Dorchester, possibly a relative of John, by the name of George Hull, moved from Dorchester to Windsor, Connecticut, sometime after May of 1636 but before May of 1637 (Anderson, vol. 2, pp. 1040-44). The possibility exists that John Hull also moved from Dorchester. He may (or may not) be the same John Hull who settled in Newbury.

John Hull of Newbury

Regardless of the disposition of the first John Hull, what is especially important to remember when searching primary sources is that in the 1650's and 1660's there were two

---

[8] See, Whitmore, *The Book of Possessions,* p. 38, item 108b and p. 78, items F 23, 24, 25 and information on the mill in item 27. The University of Notre Dame Libraries, Department of Special Collections has a deed of sale concerning a windmill at windmill point that dates to November of 1645.

individuals residing in Massachusetts Bay with the name John Hull. In addition to the Boston mintmaster another John Hull, listed as living in Newbury, is mentioned in three General Court documents. He is first mentioned in the General Court records of May 18, 1653, in a description of the road from Rowley to Newbury. The road was described as going over John Hull's bridge then through the edge of his "plaine" and on to Mr. Woodman's bridge near the mill at Newbury (Shurtleff, vol. 3, p. 305 and vol. 4, pt. 1, p. 139). Then on May 14, 1654, a petition was forwarded to the House of Magistrates by this John Hull and his wife, Margaret, concerning some land they had sold to a John White. The documentation concerning the sale of the land had been destroyed in a fire and therefore the petition requested the oral recollections of the participants be recorded (Shurtleff, vol. 4, pt. 1, p. 190). Supplementary information on the petition is found in the May 15th record from the House of Deputies where the request was acted upon and entered into the record stating "Uppon the request of John Hull, of Newbery, & Margartt, his wife, this Court doth confirme & allow the sale of a parcell of land at Watertowne, sometimes in the possession of the said Margaret, unto John White & his heires for ever, the evidences being burned" (Shurtleff, vol. 3, p. 347). John Hull of Newbury is also mentioned several times in the records of the Essex County Court. In the court session held at Ipswich on March 29, 1670, it was stated that this John Hull had died intestate and that the administration of his estate was being granted to his widow, Margaret Hull (Dow, *Records,* vol. 4, p. 231).

It is unknown if the John White who acquired the land in Watertown was the same John White who was listed as an inhabitant of Kittery, Maine, in a document from a local court session convened in Kittery at the house of William Everett between 8:00 and 9:00 AM on November 16, 1652, requiring the inhabitants to submit to the government of Massachusetts Bay. This document and related reports were forwarded to the General Court and recorded in the session of May 18, 1653 (Shurtleff, vol. 4, pt. 1, p. 124). Also, a John White is listed in an annexation document of July 5, 1653, as an inhabitant of Wells, Maine, as recorded in the General Court session of September 7, 1653 (Shurtleff, vol. 4, pt. 1, p. 158 in the House of Magistrates and in the records of the House of Deputies under September 14, 1653, Shurtleff, vol. 3, pp. 332-33).

❀❀❀❀❀❀❀❀❀❀❀

Chapter 2
The Personal Ledger of John Hull and the Shop Account from 1671 to 1680

The personal ledger of John Hull

There are four large manuscript volumes written by John Hull now held at the New England Historic Genealogical Society in Boston, Massachusetts, designated as Manuscript Cb 110. According to a bookplate on the inside front cover of each volume, the set was donated to the society by Dr. Winslow Lewis of Boston on November 30, 1861; another bookplate in volume one states the volumes were bound on June 19, 1891. The microfilm of these manuscripts calls the volumes John Hull's *Colony Journal*. Actually, volume one is Hull's personal ledger from the 1670's while volumes two through four are the Massachusetts Bay accounts regarding all payments related to King Philip's War. Hull was treasurer of the War Committee, therefore, he maintained the official record of all debts incurred and payments received by the Commonwealth relating to this conflict. Clarke cited the ledger on pp. 63-64 in his 1940 biography of Hull as being in the New England Historic Genealogical Society but he did not list a shelfmark. Clarke briefly perused the work but did not attempt to analyze the contents and it appears since that time the numismatic information in the ledger has not been published.

The ledger is one of several varieties of accounting books described in seventeenth century English merchant manuals. Since the later Middle Ages merchants and accountants had been advised to retain a variety of records. Among the most common records was the letter book in which the merchant made copies of all the correspondence he sent out to others so he would have a record of what was sent should a controversy or misunderstanding arise. Also, there were various account books. One basic item was the journal or day book which included a listing of all transactions as they occurred arranged by day. Naturally, a journal would be cumbersome to use in settling an account with an individual, since payments to and from each client would be scattered throughout the journal. To alleviate that inconvenience, a merchant would transfer his journal entries to a ledger (seventeenth century spellings include leager and lieger), which grouped transactions by client, so one could easily discover the current and past balances for any party. The merchant might also have a factor book in which he recorded inventory, such as items he had imported for resale or items due to him and debts he owed as a partner in a specific trading venture. There were numerous other accounting options including a book recording petty expenses, a specie book containing the exchange rates for various coins, and a book called a memorial, used to record items that did not pertain to any of the other accounting books. Some merchants also kept a waste book, basically a notebook in which one recorded daily transactions as they occurred and then discarded the notes once the information was transferred into a journal at the end of the day. Additionally some merchants kept a cash book since journal and ledger entries may not be up to date and there was a need to keep track of cash that was immediately available (Dafforne, pp. 4-5).

During the seventeenth century, accounting practices in England were being streamlined, especially for smaller businesses. Because of the growth of paper receipts, emphasis was placed on the ledger. One merchant manual explained:

> ... If we should pay or receive any Monies, buy or sell any Commodities, remit or draw any Bills of Exchange, or otherwise receive any Bills, Invoices, Advice, Accounts, Certificates, Notes, from our Factors, Stewards, Correspondents, Friends, or others with whom we have to deal, either for matter of Money, as Exchanges, Principals and Charges, paid and laid out, or for Goods and Commodities as aforesaid bought or sold; then instead of a Journal or Memorial we take such Letters of advise, Accounts, Bills, Certificates, Invoices and Notes, and keep them from time to time in safe custody, until we may be conveniently at leasure (sic) to enter such original papers, one after another, very orderly and exactly into the Lieger... . (Liset, unpaginated, on signature Q1^v)

The ledger grouped transactions by account. An account could represent a client or customer, alternatively it may represent a shop or business, a piece of real estate or a specific short term business venture or partnership. It was even possible to use an account to track a commodity. One accounting book stated that some merchants:

> ...(because their monies are laid up or locked in a Chest which they call Cash) they will therefore imagine this Cash to be a person whom they have trusted, and make the said Cash a *Debitor* for the Money they put into it; and when they pay out that money or any part thereof, they will make Cash *Creditor,* and that party to whom it was paid shall be made the *Debitor,* ... . (Liset, unpaginated, on signature Q1^r)

As the quote implies, the ledger was a record of debts and credits by individual accounts. For each account there was a column recording the debits of that account in chronological order and a column showing the credits. The basic concept was explained as follows:

> It is observable that a man negotiating in this world must trust and be trusted. He that is trusted with any Goods, monies or other moveable things, is therefore called a *Debitor* or *Debtor* unto the Party that trusteth him therewith, and he calleth that Party his *Creditor,* because he gave him Credit for the same; ... . (Liset, unpaginated, on signature Q1^v)

In Hull's ledger each account is read across a two page opening, consisting of a left hand page, or verso, and a right hand page, or recto. The left hand page identified the specific account, listing the money, merchandise or services for which the account was indebted. On the opposite side of the opening, the right hand page, was a listing of the money, merchandise or services provided by the named account in payment of the debts, in other words, the credits. Ideally the two sides of the account would eventually be equal so the amount owed and the amount paid would cancel each other out, leaving a balance of zero. Simply stated the ledger was a balance sheet.

The majority of the entries in Hull's ledger were accounts with individuals. For example, in one opening on the left hand page, identified as folio 44 verso, is an account Hull had with his former apprentice, Jeremiah Dummer, under the heading, "Jerimiah Dummer as debtor" meaning Dummer as the debtor in his account with Hull, while on the right hand side of the opening, numbered as folio 45 recto, is the account of payments from Dummer to Hull entitled "Contra Creditor." Hull did not use a comma in this title, but from the standard merchant texts we know the phrase was "Contra, Creditor." In this context the Latin word *contra* means, on the contrary or on the other hand, in reference to the account name on the opposite page; thus the Latin could be paraphrased into English as "On the other hand, Jeremiah Dummer as creditor."

Each two page opening in the Hull ledger averages four to six accounts. Most of the entries in the various accounts date from 1671 through 1679. However, a few entries appear to represent transactions from earlier years that were postdated to this period while some other entries seem to have been added after 1679, dating to as late as 1683, the year John Hull died. Most of the accounts concern business dealings with specific individuals but some accounts refer to property income and expenses or corporate ventures in which Hull participated. A typical opening of individual accounts is the opening on folios 44 verso through 45 recto which contains the accounts of William East of Milford covering July 3, 1672 - May 6, 1675; Jeremiah Dummer covering July 3, 1672 - November 21, 1679; John Paine of Hogg Island covering July 2, 1672 - August 21, 1674 and Hull's cousin, Captain Daniel Henchman, covering August 27, 1672 - February 1, 1673. An interesting opening containing several property and corporate accounts is on folios 24 verso - 25 recto which includes the account for Hull's own "dwelling house" detailing three entries as follows: a debt of £203 19s10d brought over from folio 80 of ledger A; a debt incurred on October 9, 1671, "To Building my little stone house of office" at £18 and finally a debt incurred in November of 1672 "To John Dewey for claboarding £6 & nailes 40s" for a total of £8. Hull shows no payments against these debts. Another account on that opening is for lands and housing in Virginia detailing debts and payments from 1669 through 1681. This account is post-dated to the year without any month or day listed. The interest owed to Hull for the years 1669 - 1671 is combined as a single entry clearly added in 1671. The next account on that opening regards a house Hull purchased from the Cotton family detailing payments received and debts incurred from December 1, 1671 - June 1, 1683; following that is an account for shipments of goods to Virginia from 1671 – 1673. The opening concludes with an account for Henry and Richard Williams from 1673 (folio 24 verso is illustrated in Jordan, "Mint," p. 2326).

Several accounts were carried forward from an earlier ledger. For example, as mentioned above, on folio 24 verso Hull began the account relating to his house, "To Brought from Leg^r A. fol. 80" and on folio 56 verso he began the account for John Plumb and Joseph Butler, "To Ballance Brought from Leager B. fol. 179." From these annotations we can surmise the surviving ledger had at least two earlier volumes, called ledger A and ledger B. Sometimes the space allotted for a specific account was insufficient so Hull would continue the account on the next free page of the ledger giving a note as to where the next portion of that account could be found. For example, on folio 48 recto he ends an account with his cousin Edward Hull of London (this is not his brother, who had also been named

Edward), "By Ballance of this Account caried to fol. 78." The Edward Hull account is continued on the opening 77 verso - 78 recto and then carried forward again to folio 125. When all the spaces in the ledger had been allocated, Hull began a new ledger. However, Hull did not waste paper, as long as there was some free space under a specific account he would continue to use that space. Thus, for an account with few transactions the allocated space in the surviving ledger might suffice for all entries until Hull's death in 1683, while for more active accounts the balance would be forwarded to subsequent ledgers. Therefore, some accounts in the surviving ledger continue to the year of Hull's death while others fill the allocated space and conclude with the note that the account was continued in another ledger. For example on folio 68 verso the account with Joseph David ends with, "Bal. carried to Leg^r D. fol. 153." In other instances the allotted space was not used up until Hull had started ledger E, thus he concluded some accounts, as the account with Daniel Smith of Rehoboth on folio 79 recto, with, "Balance is carried to Leg^r E fol. 11." From these various notes we can surmise the present ledger was designated as ledger C. There were at least two fully allocated ledgers that preceded it and at least one fully allocated ledger followed it with an additional ledger called ledger E. It is unknown if ledger E was only partially or completely allocated at the time of Hull's death in 1683, or if there were any subsequent volumes. The designation of the surviving ledger as ledger C is confirmed in Hull's private diary. In the diary, below the entry for November 20, 1678, Hull added the comment: "James Elson was taken by the Algerines, where I lost only my eighth part of a ship; as see my ledger C, fol. 54, £113. 17s. 10d, through it might be worth more, £82. 2s. 2d" (Hull, *Private Diary,* p. 163). In the surviving ledger, on folio 54 recto, in his account for the ship called *The Blessing* Hull added the comment, "by Profit & loss for ball[ance] being taken by the turkes - 113 17 10." Certainly, this £113 17s 10d loss is the entry Hull referred to in his diary as being from ledger C.

Hull also seems to have had another series of accounts referred to as books rather than ledgers. In entries relating to shipments Hull occasionally refers to a Book H, which must have contained listings of shipping expenses. For example, on folio 24 verso under "Voyages to Virginia," Hull mentioned this book three times, "To disbursements on the ketch Friendship & victualling as Book H. Fol. 33 · 34 --- £53 19s1d," and "To disbursements victualling & Goods as in Book H fol. 37 --- £110 11s7d," and "To disbursements victualling & Cargo as Book H fol. 39 --- £130 3s3d." Book H is also mentioned in the entry for the ship *Blessing*, on folio 53 verso, "To my 1/8 of disbursements on ship & Cargo as B. H fol. 55 --- £106 15s5d." It seems this book H was what accountants of the time called a factor book or a memorial.

The shop account

Of special interest to numismatists is an account in the ledger at the bottom of the opening on folios 26 verso through 27 recto which is continued on 133 verso - 134 recto and 170 verso - 171 recto, representing the account relating to Hull's shop and the mint house. In Appendix I is a transcription of the account with a commentary on each entry. In these entries Hull specified the troy ounces of sterling silver deposited at the mint. Hull then calculated the return to his consignors based on the consignor receiving 74d (6s2d) in coins per troy ounce of silver. In June of 1675 the seven year mint renewal increased the return to

75d (6s3d) per troy ounce and then, by private agreement with his consignors, the return was increased again in 1677 and further increased in 1680. In his annotations Hull expressed the troy ounces of sterling giving the whole ounces followed by the abbreviation oz. and then added any fraction of an ounce as 255$^{oz.}$ 1/4 for 255.25 troy ounces.

Hull's personal ledger differs from a modern account book. For Hull, the ledger was a method of recording debts and payments that were owed to him or that he owed to others. One contemporary accounting book called the ledger a mirror of ones true estate, for it not only listed payments or income but also included debits (Dafforne, unnumbered, signature O2^r). We use an account book to record all assets and costs related to a business. Assets would include inventory, capital investments and other income beyond payments from customers while costs would comprise salaries, maintenance, capital depreciation and other items in addition to payments made to suppliers or creditors. We would then balance the total credits against the total costs to determine the profitability of the enterprise. Hull's goal was not to determine profitability but to understand just what he owed each client and what each client owed to him.

Hull recorded debts and payments in the manner that was the easiest for him to understand and in the way it was most convenient for him to track his dealings. Although we may wish Hull would have focused his ledger on his coining business and included every mint and silversmith related expense in his shop account, that was not the case. Certainly the shop was important to Hull but it was only one of many ventures in which he was associated. Indeed, all the mint entries would fill only one opening, the equivalent of two pages, in the surviving 320 pages of this ledger! Because of his diverse activities, Hull found it useful to record some shop related expenses in other accounts. For example, John Winchester and Dorman Morean of Muddy River (Brookline) rented sixteen acres of land from Hull for which they were required to make two payments per year; they were to pay £1 13s each March 25th and each September 29th. According to the debit side of their account with Hull this situation continued from 1672-1677. Then the amount owed was recorded as a single annual payment of £3 6s due each March 25th from 1678-1681 (New England Historic Genealogical Society, MS Cb 110, vol. 1, folio 39 verso). On the credit side of this account we discover Winchester and Morean sometimes paid their debt with deliveries of coal and in one case with 14 bushels of malt, while at other times they paid in cash. As mentioned earlier, the coal was delivered for use at Hull's shop. For example, one entry in the account stated "1674 November 17 by money of the shop for 73 bushels 1/2 coal - for John Winchester · · 1 / · 4 /· 6" [that is, 73.5 bushels for £1 4s6d] (New England Historic Genealogical Society, MS Cb 110, vol. 1, folio 40 recto, the full account is illustrated in Jordan, "Mint," pp. 2327-28). In this instance Winchester delivered the coal to the shop and Hull reimbursed himself, taking £1 4s6d in money from the shop account and then crediting Winchester with a payment of £1 4s6d against his annual rent due to Hull. Hull did not mention this delivery or payment in the shop account, rather it was simpler for him to keep track of the Winchester and Morean payments in a separate personal account with these two men. Thus, payments for coal, which we would expect to be on the debit side of the shop account, if one were intent of determining the profitability of the enterprise, are not even recorded in the shop account! It was easier for Hull to keep track of the Winchester/Morean account as a single unit rather than record payments under the various enterprises for which the two provided goods or services.

Just as the expense of coal was not added to the shop account there are instances where Hull neglected to add some shop income to the shop account. In Hull's account with Mr. William Brenton we saw in the previous chapter that on May 27, 1673, Brenton incurred a debit to the shop 10s6d for the mending of a pot and three spoons. The cost included a charge for some silver that was needed to repair the pieces (New England Historic Genealogical Society, MS Cb 110, vol. 1, folio 13 verso - 14 recto). This charge was only listed in Hull's personal account with Brenton and was not mentioned in the account of the shop. In the shop account Hull appears to have been most meticulous in listing jewelry and bullion deposited in the shop and verifying the annual payment to the Commonwealth. Apparently, Brenton's pot and spoons were not deposited in the shop; probably the items were mended while the customer waited. If that was the case then there would be no debit to be added into the shop account, rather when the mending was completed the repaired items would be returned to Brenton and then he would owe a debit to Hull. In these circumstances the debit would be included in the Brenton account, not the shop account, and would be cancelled when Brenton paid the charges which would be indicated by adding the payment to the credit side of his account. In fact this is just what happened. For the period up to May 27, 1673, Brenton had owed Hull a total of £88 11s4d and had paid Hull a total of £87 14s. Thus he owed Hull 17s 4d before the mending fee was incurred and with the 10s6d mending fee the total outstanding balance was £1 7s10d. The account shows that about ten days after the pot and spoons were mended Hull received a payment of £1 7s10d from John Newcomb on behalf of William Brenton. Hull added this payment to the Brenton account so that the total owed by Brenton of £89 1s10d was balanced by the total paid, which was also £89 1s10d (illustrated in Jordan, "Mint," p. 2329).

There are additonal examples in the ledger concerning silversmith charges from accounts with other individuals, see the *addenda* to Appendix I for details. It seems each silversmith commission awarded to Hull or Sanderson was treated separately. The commission was part of either Sanderson's or Hull's general business accounts. Each silversmith charged and collected from their own customers for work performed by them or their apprentices. Some work, such as funeral rings, needed to be made quickly, therefore the work was distributed and jointly billed to the shop. In a letter to William Vaughan from January 5, 1713, Hull's son-in-law Samuel Sewall explained, "The Business of the Mint was managed by it self, and the Account kept distinct..." (Sewall, *Letter-Book*, vol. 2, pp. 9-10). By this statement Sewall meant the joint enterprise of the mint as well as shared shop orders would be found in the shop account, however individual silver commissions would not be listed in the joint account. Thus, the vast majority of the shop account relates to minting.

That the ledger represents the joint mint account is clear because the account includes the full amount of the annual payments to Massachusetts Bay. The seven year contract renewal of June 3, 1675, stated: "... the sajd minters are to pay in to the Treasurer of the Country, in mony, twenty pounds per Anno..." (Crosby, p. 82). All these annual payments are reflected in full in the account. If there were two mint accounts, one for Hull and another for Sanderson, one would expect a sharing of the payment. Possibly each would pay half or they would alternate so one paid then the following year the other would pay. That all payments are recorded in full suggest this represents the complete mint account. Further, there is an entry by Hull dated December 4, 1677, stating he borrowed 24 oz. 3 dwt. 18 gr. in sterling silver from the account. Later, on August 24, 1678, Hull recorded that he paid back the account. If this represented Hull's private account there would be no need for him to pay himself back since he would simply have taken the silver as part of his share of the profits.

Interestingly, in the shop account Hull sometimes included the mint fees as income while at other times he did not reveal the fees. In balancing the shop account Hull made sure there was enough income to pay expenses. If income was more than expenses Hull would take some of the income off the books and only carry over the amount required to balance the account. On the credit side of the shop account at the bottom of folio 134 recto Hull had a credit balance of £75 3s, while on the debit side of the account, at the bottom of folio 133 verso, there was debit of only £9 18s. Hull only carried £9 18s forward in the next credit entry of the account, since that was all he needed to balance the debits. The remaining £65 5s was taken off the books as profit. Thus the ledger was used to record and verify when debits were incurred by the shop or when payments were made to the shop but it did not carry a record of profits paid out to Hull or Sanderson. In addition to verifying when outstanding debits had been paid, Hull used the ledger to confirm that all specie left on deposit had been returned to the consignors and that the annual payment to Massachusetts Bay had been made. However, it is clear the shop account did not include a detailed listing of all the expenses or income related to the business. For a transcription and commentary on the shop ledger entries see Appendix I. Although the ledger does not give us a full picture of mint profits and expenses, it does contain much useful information on mint activities. Insights from the ledger entries are discussed below in Parts Three and Four.

Part Two

The Massachusetts Mint and British Politics

Chapter 3

The Massachusetts Mint and British Politics after the Restoration

The 1652 backdating hypothesis

Perhaps the most widely held assumption pertaining to Massachusetts silver coinage relates to an explanation of the continued use of the date 1652 on the coins. It has been conjectured Massachusetts coins were dated 1652 because the colonists did not want to incur the wrath of the king. By backdating the coins to 1652, which is the date found on all varieties of Massachusetts Willow, Oak and Pine tree coinage except the Oak Tree twopence, Massachusetts Bay could claim the coins had been produced during the English Commonwealth, when there was no king. This explanation is still repeated in current editions of the *Red Book* (in the Willow Tree introduction), even though it has been demonstrated to be incorrect by several specialists in colonial numismatics including Mike Hodder in the October 1987 catalogue of the Norweb collection (p. 329) and Phil Mossman in his 1993 monograph, *Money of the American Colonies* (p. 84). In 1995 Hodder addressed this issue again in an article for *Coin World.*

If we examine the assumptions one must accept in order to consider this interpretation of the dating to be valid, it becomes clear the explanation is no more than a fanciful story. The Massachusetts Puritans were certainly pleased by the capture and execution of King Charles I and the establishment of the English Commonwealth in 1649. They felt freer to assert rights and liberties without fear of transgressing royal prerogatives or privileges. Massachusetts Bay aggressively asserted itself in numerous ways. During the General Court session that opened on October 14, 1651, Simon Bradstreet, Daniel Denison and Captain William Hawthorn were appointed as commissioners with the task of annexing Maine to Massachusetts Bay. Between 1652 and 1653 the towns of Kittery, York, Wells, Saco and Kennebunkport were annexed, then in 1658, Casco Bay (Portland) and the surrounding area was added. Maine became the county of Yorkshire in Massachusetts Bay. During this period Massachusetts also claimed settlements in New Hampshire as well as part of Connecticut and Rhode Island (Palfrey, vol. 1, pp. 402-4). In the General Court session that opened on May 27, 1652, a law was instituted requiring all inhabitants to take an oath of loyalty to Massachusetts Bay which previously only freemen had been required to take. Also, among other legislation passed during that session of the General Court was the expansion of the militia from a single company into four companies and the opening of a mint to produce silver shilling, sixpence and threepence coins.

This was a period of expansion. Indeed, the political situation could not have looked more favorable for the Massachusetts Bay Puritans than it did in early 1654. On December 16, 1653, Oliver Cromwell, who was Captain General of the British army, was named Lord Protector of the Commonwealth of England, Scotland and Ireland. The English Commonwealth was now under the complete authority and protection of a fellow Puritan. The above anecdote about the backdating of the coinage requires us to believe that during these very years of growth, the Puritans of Massachusetts Bay were apprehensive that at some future time the Commonwealth would dissolve and the monarchy might return. It is clear this anxiety did not affect their territorial expansion or their political decisions. However, we must believe that such fears did affect the way they dated coins. Through this entire period of expansion we must presume Hull and the Massachusetts Bay General Court were so distressed about an unknown future possibility that they did not dare date their coins to the current year.

What makes this explanation even stranger is that, even if one was convinced the Puritans did indeed fear that at some future date the monarchy might return to power and close the mint, such a fear still would not justify the continued use of the date 1652. Naturally, a coin with any date from the Commonwealth era (up to 1660) would work equally as well as 1652. Thus, the backdating argument would seem more appropriate if the coins were dated 1652-1660 with the continued use of those dates in the 1660's and 1670's.

A further difficulty with the backdating hypothesis is that it does not explain, and indeed, seems to be discredited by, the date on the twopence coin. In 1660, to the great disappointment of Massachusetts Bay, the monarchy was restored. One would suppose under these circumstances the Massachusetts Bay General Court would be even more cautious about the date on their coins than had been the case during the English Commonwealth. However, inexplicably, we must assume the General Court disregarded their carefully thought out plan that had been followed throughout the 1650's, for when Massachusetts Bay began minting twopence coins in 1662, the date of 1662 was displayed on the new denomination coins. Thus, the backdating hypothesis implies the Puritans fearlessly minted twopence in defiance of the monarchy, displaying a date that expicitly proved the coins were minted after the restoration. However, at the same time they continued to fear retribution for minting shillings, sixpence and threepence coins since those varieties continued to display the 1652 date.

Clearly, the strange assumptions one must advocate in order to accept the 1652 backdating story are untenable. As Hodder and Mossman have explained, it is far easier and simpler to suppose the date on each denomination represented the year a particular coin denomination was authorized by the Massachusetts Bay General Court. Indeed, the facts of the coinage legislation bear this out since the shilling, sixpence and threepence were authorized in the legislation of May 26/27, 1652, while the twopence denomination was authorized in the legislation of May 16, 1662.

Also, it should be noted the coins actually produced in 1652 were the NE silver series, which did not carry any date! The revision of the coin design, which was passed by the General Court on October 19, 1652, stated the revised design:

> ... shall haue a double Ringe on either side with this Inscription (massachusetts) & a tree in the center on the one side, And (New England) & the date of the yeare on the other side according to a draught herewithall presented... . (Crosby, p. 44)

Unfortunately the drawing of the coin, which the legislation referred to as a draft, only shows an obverse with a tree and a double ring. There is no illustration of the reverse with the date. This revised design first appeared on what is now known as the Willow Tree series, which most probably was not produced until after 1652 (below I suggest it may have been as late as 1654). Thus, it seems although the legislation was unclear as to whether "the date of the yeare" referred to the year of authorization or the year of minting, Hull took it to refer to the year of authorization and used 1652. This was also a pragmatic decision as dies could be used until they wore out and would never be outdated.

Presuppositions

When one considers the two differing interpretations it is clear the second explanation suggesting the use of the date of authorization more closely fits the facts. Given the problematic assumptions one must accept to agree with the backdating hypothesis and the unresolved difficulties presented by the 1662 date on the Oak Tree twopence, the question I would like to pose is - why would anyone consider such a supposition to have validity? I believe the answer lies in the fact that this theory assumes some presuppositions that are difficult to overcome. First, it presupposes the date on a coin represents the year in which the coin was minted. This is an instinctive numismatic assumption, because most coins minted during the past four centuries do contain the year in which they were minted. Rarely is the year of authorization found on coins, although paper currency frequently includes the date of the legislation that authorized the emission.

Another presupposition of the backdating story is that the restored monarch, Charles II, was opposed to the mint and tried to close it down. If one accepts this presupposition, the backdating theory suggests the Massachusetts Mint was quite successful. Hull was able to remain in operation into the 1680's due to his shrewd foresight in using the 1652 date on the coins and thereby tricking the monarch into thinking the coinage was from an earlier decade.

One problem with accepting this presupposition is that royal supporters in Boston did know of the continued operation of the mint. The mint was never a surreptitious operation, because the mint contract renewals were publicly available in the records of the General Court. These records were usually the first documents to be examined by royal inspectors sent to Massachusetts Bay. However, beyond the obvious problem that the mint was never a clandestine operation, the presupposition that the king wanted to close the mint seems to be a reasonable assumption from various points of view. As early as elementary school, Americans learn about the inequity of the mercantile system and the numerous acts of British oppression that impelled the colonists to revolt and declare their independence in 1776. Furthermore, we learn it was due to clever tactics and native ingenuity that the colonists were able to defeat the mighty British empire. There is certainly truth in these generalizations as well as oversimplification and some misconceptions. However, without debating the validity of this theory, I simply want to state that it has existed for several generations and is widely accepted. If this interpretation is accepted as true for the period of the American Revolution it seems quite reasonable to assume the situation went back to the earliest years of colonization. Thus, on one level Americans are predisposed to believe interpretations that validate their basic ideas on how and why America was founded.

From another point of view there are historical facts that could be used as evidence to show the British wanted to close the mint. On May 24, 1665, four commissioners of the king presented the Massachusetts Bay General Court with a letter requesting twenty-six articles of Massachusetts law be repealed or amended. Article twenty-two stated that the 1652 mint act be repealed "for coyning is a royall prerogative, for the usurping of which ye act of indemnity is only a salvo" (Shurtleff, vol. 4, p. 213 and Crosby, p. 77). Also, from 1676 through the 1680's a British informer named Edward Randolph spend much time in Boston reporting on illegal activities and urging the charter of Massachusetts Bay be revoked. As early as his first report to the Committee of the Lords for Trade and Plantations, which was dated October 12, 1676, and was read at the Committee meeting of November 16th, he stated:

> And as a marke of soveraignty they coin mony stamped with the inscription Mattachusets and a tree in the center, on the one side, and New England, with the year 1652 and the value of the piece, on the reverse. Their money is of the standard of England for finenesse, the shillings weigh three pennyweight troy, in value of English money ninepence farthing, and the smaller coins proportionable. These are the current monies of the colony and not to be transported thence, except twenty shillings for necessary expenses, on penalty of confiscation of the whole visible estate of the transporters.

> All the money is stamped with these figures, 1652, that year being the era of the commonwealth, wherein they erected themselves into a free state, enlarged their dominions, subjected adjacent colonies under their obedience, and summoned deputies to sit in the generall court, which year is still commemorated on their coin.

Randolph made similar comments in numerous other reports to the Committee and in several letter writing campaigns to top British administrators over the next decade (*Hutchinson Papers,* vol. 2, pp. 210-41 with the quote on pp. 213-14; also in Toppan, *Randolph,* vol. 2, pp. 225-59 with the quote on p. 229; Toppan, "Right to Coin," p. 221 and Sainsbury, *Calendar 1675-1676,* pp. 463-68, item 1067. Crosby, pp. 75-76 gives an incomplete quote which he attributes to a publication of 1769; undoubtedly Crosby is referring to the *Hutchinson Papers,* which is an anthology of documents on Massachusetts history first published in 1769 by Thomas Hutchinson).

In addition to the royal commissioners and Randolph there were also various individuals who characterized the Massachusetts Mint as an illegal operation in testimony they gave before the Committee of the Lords for Trade and Plantations. Finally, on June 27, 1683, the King's Bench issued a writ of *Quo warranto* against Massachusetts Bay. This was a legal action requiring the defendants to present themselves before the court and show by what authority they were permitted to exercise the liberties in question. Thirty individuals were named in the writ including John Hull. Thus, the evidence of the commissioners, the testimonies before the Lords for Trade and Plantations and the inclusion of Hull in the writ seem to indicate the British did indeed try to close the Massachusetts Mint.

Although it appears historical data support this position, a closer examination of the documents, without the preconceived notion of British opposition to the mint, leads one to a very different interpretation of the events.

Post-Restoration relations with Massachusetts Bay: 1660-1666

With the restoration of Charles II as king of England in 1660 the monarchy and its accompanying bureaucracy were reestablished to rule over England and the British possessions. In 1660, the Council for Plantations, also known as the Council for Foreign Plantations, was established to oversee England's colonial territories. Soon thereafter the Council began hearing complaints of irregularities and injustices in the colonies.

Between March 4th and the 14th in 1661 the Council heard several individuals complain how they had been mistreated in Massachusetts Bay. Among the complainants was John Gifford who has resided in Massachusetts Bay during the 1650's and had been the principal agent for the Hammersmith Ironworks in Saugus, Massachusetts, from 1650 through 1653, when he became involved in several lawsuits and ended up spending some time in jail. From October of 1658 through April of 1662, Gifford was in England bringing suits against just about everyone connected with the Ironworks enterprise. Another complainant was Samuel Maverick, an independent adventurer who had settled on Noddle's Island in Boston Harbor before the Puritans arrived. Maverick, an Anglican, refused to endure Puritan restrictions. He was fined and jailed several times for his open opposition to laws requiring all inhabitants to abide by Puritan teachings. For example, in 1646 he joined Robert Child in petitioning the General Court to recognize the legal privileges, civil liberties and religious freedoms due to Englishmen (Hutchinson, ed. Mayo, vol. 1, pp. 124-25). In 1649 Maverick was fined £150 for conspiracy and perjury. He protested that the accusations were baseless but the General Court did not agree, although they did reduce the fine in half (Shurtleff, vol. 3, pp. 166-67 and 200). Eventually Maverick was forced out of Massachusetts Bay and returned to England. Also, among the group of complainants was Edward Godfrey, who had been Governor of Maine until Massachusetts Bay annexed the province.

Indeed, Massachusetts Bay had several detractors. The Puritans of the General Court had little toleration for unorthodox behavior and even less toleration for non-Puritans. When some English Quakers settled in Rhode Island and Connecticut, the Massachusetts Bay General Court was alarmed. During the General Court session of August 22, 1654, a law was enacted requiring all Quaker books be burned. Not long thereafter some Quakers tried to settle peacefully in Massachusetts Bay. In 1656 they were arrested, placed in a workhouse, subjected to a whipping of twenty lashes and required to work at hard labor until they were transported out of the Commonwealth. If they returned to Massachusetts Bay they would be punished by having one ear cut off and, should they return a third time, they would have their tongue bored with a red hot iron. Over the next few years additional Quakers, not knowing the Puritan bias against them, came to settle in the Commonwealth. In order to stop this undesirable immigration it was decreed in 1658 that any expelled Quaker who returned to his Massachusetts Bay homestead was to be summarily executed by hanging. Several Quakers were whipped and banished with at least four hanged at the Boston Common (William Robinson and Marmaduke Stephenson on October 27, 1659, Mary Dyer on June 1, 1660 and William Ledea on March 14, 1661). In September of 1661 the restored monarch, Charles II, ordered a stop to capital and corporal punishment of English Quakers because of their religious beliefs (Hutchinson, ed. Mayo, vol. 1, pp. 167-75). There was even very little tolerance for members of the Church of England. Anglicans were treated as second class persons. They were not freemen, as all freemen were required to be members of the Puritan church, and thus they could not vote or hold public office. However, they were required to conform to all Puritan laws or they would be punished, even if they simply expressed the opinion that they should not be required to attend the Puritan Sunday service or that they should not be taxed to pay the salaries of Puritan ministers (Earle, pp. 294-95).

Numerous morality regulations known as "blue laws" were strictly enforced; they were even difficult for many committed Puritans to follow. For example, in 1656 the young sea captain Thomas Kemble, who would later be father to the diarist Sarah Kemble Knight, upon returning home from a three-year voyage, kissed his wife at the doorstep of their house on the Sabbath. The incident was immediately reported and Kemble spent two hours in the stocks for his offence (Earle, p. 247). Such punishments were handed out to non-Puritans as well. The laborers at the Hammersmith Ironworks were frequently summonsed to sessions of the Essex County Court in Salem where they paid fines for drinking, swearing and missing Sunday services.

The strict and uncompromising attitudes of the Massachusetts Bay Puritan government resulted is numerous complaints. Among the criticisms brought forward to the Council for Foreign Plantations was an undated petition, recorded into the Council record in March of 1661, which had been received from "divers persons who had been sufferers in New England on behalf of themselves and thousands there [i.e. in New England]" stating:

> Through the tyranny and oppression of those in power there, multitudes of the King's subjects have been most unjustly and grievously oppressed contrary to their own laws and the laws of England, imprisoned, fined, fettered, whipt, and further punished by cutting off of their ears, branding the face, their estates seized and themselves banished [from] the country.

Among the thirteen signatories were Gifford and Godfrey (Sainsbury, *Calendar 1661-1668,* pp. 15-19, items 42, 45, 46, 49-53, quote from item 49 on pp. 16-17).

On April 4, 1661, just a few weeks after the Council had heard several complaints against Massachusetts Bay, a petition from Ferdinando Gorges was read to the Council. In 1622 his grandfather, who had also been named Ferdinando Gorges (1566-1647), received a grant from the Council of New England for the province of Maine, while another individual, John Mason, received a similar grant for New Hampshire. In 1639 Gorges was granted a royal charter as Lord Proprietor of Maine. Massachusetts Bay believed they had the rights to the land and gradually annexed Maine between 1652-1658 during the English Commonwealth. Under the restored monarchy, Gorges's grandson petitioned the Council to restore the territory to his family. Soon thereafter on April 8th the Council drafted a letter to

Massachusetts Bay explaining the Council had been appointed to manage the colonies and Massachusetts Bay would need to respond to the charges that had been brought against them. It was also suggested that agents be appointed to represent their positions to the Council when requested (Sainsbury, *Calendar 1661-1668,* pp. 22-23, items 64 and 66).

By the end of April several additional petitions against Massachusetts had been forwarded, including a petition from John Mason's heir, Robert Mason, for the restoration of his Patent to New Hampshire. One of these letters is particularly interesting in relation to Massachusetts coinage. It is an undated and unsigned letter that accompanied a proposal signed by John Gifford. As both the signed proposal and the unsigned letter discuss ore and mineral mines in Massachusetts Bay, it is quite likely Gifford was the author of both documents. The unsigned letter detailed several problems with the laws of Massachusetts Bay. This document contains the earliest reference accusing the Massachusetts Mint of illegal acts. The summary of the letter in the Calendar of Colonial Papers states:

> ... they have acted repugnant to the laws of England ; they have allowed the King's coin to be brought and melted down in Boston to be new coined there, by which means they gain threepence in every shilling, and lessen his Majesty's coin a full fourth.

In this 1661 complaint it is not suggested that the minting of coins was considered to be an illegal activity. The complaint simply stated British sterling coinage was being melted at the Massachusetts Bay Mint to produce lighter weight Massachusetts coinage. The melting of the king's coin was the offence that was being disclosed. The weight reduction of Massachusetts Bay silver was mentioned because it explained why British coinage was being melted, although the complaint did not indicate the weight reduction itself was thought to be illegal (Sainsbury, *Calendar 1661-1668,* pp. 24-26, items 73-78 and 80; quote from item 78 on p. 26).

Once the April 8th letter from the Council reached Boston, requesting Massachusetts Bay defend its position, there were discussions about sending some agents to London. On December 24, 1661, a group of magistrates and church elders selected Simon Bradstreet and John Norton to be sent to the court of King Charles II in London as advocates for the Commonwealth's interests and liberties. Bradstreet was one of the Governor's nine Assistants and also one of two Commissioners for the Commonwealth to the United Colonies of New England, while Norton was the Minister of the First Church of Christ in Boston. William Davis and John Hull accompanied the agents as their aides. At a December 31, 1661 special session of the General Court, Captain William Davis was selected to be part of a four person committee allowed to make agreements to procure money for the Commonwealth with the authorization of the General Court.

The group arrived in London on March 24, 1662, and conducted several meeting with the Council. An interesting episode from the 1662 negotiations was related in a later document. In 1684 a committee of the Massachusetts Bay General Court was appointed to produce a response to King Charles II concerning the right of the Commonwealth to retain its charter. In a draft of a report by the committee dated October 30, 1684, outlining a proposed response to the king, there is a passage about the mint which included the following detail:

> For in 1662, when our first agents were in England, some of our money was
> showed by Sir Thomas Temple at the Council-Table, and no dislike thereof
> manifested by any of those right honourable persons: much less a forbidding
> of it.

Later retellings of this event embellished the Temple presentation to include the story of
Temple telling the king that the Massachusetts coins displayed the Royal Oak at Whiteladies,
where Charles had hidden on September 6, 1650, to escape capture following his defeat at
Worcester on September 3rd by Cromwell's forces. Unfortunately, the month and day of
Temple's presentation was not recorded in this 1684 document. The entire passage on the
mint was struck from the final version of the official 1684 response. Although Temple
arrived in London about a month before Norton and Bradstreet, the 1684 document stated
this specific presentation by Temple took place after the Massachusetts Bay delegation was
in London. It is interesting to note Temple was a friend of Hull, and, in fact, Hull was named
as one of four executors in Temple's will. Possibly Hull, who was an advisor to the
delegation, may have been present when this event occurred (Crosby, pp. 75-76; the
appendix to Hull's *Diary,* p. 282 and Hutchinson, ed. Mayo, vol. 1, p. 191).

That no council member disapproved of the coinage suggests the British government did
not object to the Massachusetts Mint. The mint was not a concern for the Council or the
king. In fact, on June 28, 1662, King Charles II sent a letter to the Massachusetts Bay
delegation of Norton and Bradstreet confirming the Commonwealth's patent and charter and
"all the privileges and liberties granted unto them in and by the same," along with an offer to
renew the charter whenever the Commonwealth desired it. The letter also pardoned subjects
for treasonous acts committed during the interregnum but required the Commonwealth's
laws to be reviewed and anything against the king's authority or government should be
annulled and repealed. The letter also required an oath of allegiance to the king be
administered and that freedom and liberty should be allowed to any individuals wishing to
follow the practices of the Church of England (Hutchinson, ed. Mayo, vol. 1, pp. 187-88; the
full letter is in *Hutchinson Papers*, vol. 2, pp. 100-104). Although the letter was conciliatory
and quite positive, the General Court of Massachusetts Bay was not pleased. They
understood their rights to govern and create laws for the colony were being questioned;
additionally they had little toleration for the Church of England or any other non-Puritan sect.

In was not until two years later, on April 23, 1664, that Charles II appointed Colonel
Richard Nichols, George Cartwright, Sir Robert Carr and Samuel Maverick as royal
commissioners with full power to examine and determine all complaints and appeals
concerning the liberties and privileges granted to the New England colonies in various
charters (Shurtleff, vol. 4, pt. 2, p. 157; Hutchinson, ed. Mayo, vol. 1, pp. 443-44). The
commissioners traveled to America and first turned their attention to the subjugation of New
Netherland. Following that task the commissioners traveled to Massachusetts Bay and on
May 8, 1665, requested that the General Court supply them with a copy of the
Commonwealth's laws so they could determine if any were "Contrary & derogatory to the
king's authority & Government" (Shurtleff, vol. 4, pt. 2, p. 194; Crosby, p. 77). Twenty-one
days later on May 24th the commissioners sent a letter to the General Court requesting
twenty-six articles be repealed or amended from the Commonwealth's laws. Article twenty-
two of their letter requested the repeal of the coining act stating, "coyning is a royall

prerogative, for the usurping of which ye act of indemnity is only a salvo" (Shurtleff, vol. 4, pt. 2, pp. 211-13 with the quote on p. 213; Crosby, p. 77). This was the first time British commissioners had formally stated the Massachusetts Mint was illegal in that it was usurping a royal prerogative.

On August 7, 1665, an order from the king was presented to the General Court requesting the Massachusetts Bay governor and other officials to travel to London and answer the charges brought against them. There was little desire on the part of the Governor and his Assistants to make such a trip. Certainly they were not eager to debate what they considered to be their rights by a charter from Charles I. Moreover, in April of 1665 the plague had hit London and a few months later the British declared war on the Dutch. Massachusetts Bay intentionally delayed in responding to the king's order. This turned out to be a shrewd policy for the longer they stalled the less likely it seemed they would be required to send any delegates. In September London was struck by the Great Fire, followed in 1666 by a revolt in Scotland. Soon thereafter France joined the Dutch in their war against Britain. In this climate Massachusetts Bay decided to send a gift of ship masts to Britain instead of sending delegates. During the 1666 fall session of the Massachusetts Bay General Court, it was ordered that two large masts were to be sent immediately to the king's navy and a ship load more were to follow in the spring. These gifts to the navy were gratefully accepted. Due to the pressing military issues no further discussion took place concerning the twenty-six contested articles of Massachusetts law.

In 1667 the war against the Dutch and the French ended with the Peace of Breda, signed on July 21st. But in that same year there was a major change in the King's Council with Lord Clarendon impeached. He was replaced by Lords Buckingham and Arlington who advised Charles to enter into several secret alliances. These actions resulted in another war with Holland in March of 1672 and another purge of the ministers in 1673. Soon thereafter, the second Dutch war ended with the Treaty of Westminster signed on February 9, 1674. A stable ministry and peace at home allowed for an opportunity to deal with colonial problems once again. To that end the Council for Trade and Plantations was dissolved on March 12, 1675, and replaced by the Committee for Trade and Foreign Plantations. This was a very powerful committee consisting of appointed members selected from the Privy Council (the King's Council). These Lords were to meet weekly and report concerns and recommendations back to the full Council, which could then initiate actions as needed to remedy any problems.

Thus for the most part, Massachusetts Bay had been left alone from the Restoration in 1660 through 1675. During this period the Council for Trade and Plantations had not objected to the mint. In fact, the only direct criticism of the mint was from the four appointed commissioners. They spent two weeks reading Massachusetts laws and based on their reading considered the mint to impinge on royal prerogatives. However, even they had not thought it to be a major problem, listing it at number 22 out of 26 contested articles.

Most unfortunately, when the British were finally ready to discuss the various problems identified in the Massachusetts Bay law, the Commonwealth became embroiled in a costly and bloody war against the Indian Sachem Metacom who was known to the colonists as King Philip. This war lasted from June of 1675 through February of 1677.

Renewed interest in Massachusetts Bay: the complaints of 1675-1677

Soon after the Committee for Trade and Foreign Plantations was constituted, both Robert Mason and Ferdinando Gorges brought petitions requesting restitution of their lands of New Hampshire and Maine from Massachusetts Bay. On December 1, 1675, Mason submitted a report to the committee by a Captain Wyborne who had visited Massachusetts Bay in 1673. Wyborne complained of several irregularities, arbitrary laws and resistance to the king's commissioners (Sainsbury, *Calendar 1675-1676,* item 721 on pp. 306-8). These petitions resulted in a royal letter being sent to Massachusetts Bay in March of 1676 requesting the Commonwealth to send agents to London to argue the case for Massachusetts against the claims of Mason and Gorges. The letter was to be taken to Massachusetts by Edward Randolph, a cousin of Robert Mason. Randolph was to question the Governor's Council, known in Massachusetts Bay as the upper house of the General Court, that is, the House of Magistrates. Randolph was also given supplementary instructions from the Lords of the Committee for Trade and Plantations detailing twelve areas of inquiry on which Randolph was to bring back intelligence. The areas of inquiry concerned the government and laws of the colony, the population, religion, military strength, economic resources, imports and exports, boundaries, taxes, relationships with other colonies and related information. Included was an abstract of information on Massachusetts which Randolph was to verify; there was no mention of coinage in this abstract, nor was it directly mentioned as an area of inquiry (Toppan, *Randolph,* vol. 2, pp. 196-201 and Sainsbury, *Calendar 1675-1676,* pp. 360-63, items 844-49).

In mid-June of 1676, about a week after landing in Boston, Randolph wrote a long letter to the British Secretary of State, Sir Henry Coventry, including much information on Massachusetts Bay but with no reference to minting. Soon after returning to London, Randolph sent a report to the king on September 20th detailing his meetings with numerous New England government officials in Massachusetts and New Hampshire. He explained the Governor of Massachusetts Bay,

> ... freely declared to me that the lawes made by your Majestie and your parliament obligeth them in nothing but what consists with the interest of that colony, that the legislative power is and abides in them solely to act and make lawes by virtue of a charter from your Majesties royall father.

Randolph went on to state he met several colonists who complained "...of the arbitrary government and oppression of their magistrates and doe hope your Majestie will be pleased to free them from this bondage by establishing your own royall authority among them..." (Toppan, *Randolph,* vol. 2, pp. 216-25 with quotes from pp. 219 and 223, also in *Hutchinson Papers,* vol. 2, pp. 240-51 with the quotes from pp. 243 and 247 and Sainsbury, *Calendar 1675-1676,* pp. 455-66, item 1037).

About three weeks later, on October 12th, Randolph send a lengthy report to the members of the Committee for Trade and Plantations detailing much information and presenting several criticisms of the government in Massachusetts Bay. The report was read at the committee meeting of November 16, 1676. Randolph answered each of the twelve areas of inquiry the committee had requested him to investigate. Part of his answer to their first inquiry, "Where the Legislative and Executive Powers of the Government of New England are seated," was a discussion of the structure of the government which included the comments quoted above on page 30, that "... as a marke of soveraignty they coin mony... ." Interestingly, at this point in time, Randolph did not include the coinage comments under his answer to the second point of inquiry which was "What Laws and ordinances, are now in force there, derogatory or contradictory to those of England, and what Oath is prescribed by the Government." To this question Randolph included ten points but nothing on coinage. Thus Randolph was either not aware of, or chose not to follow the comments in the 1664 report of the four royal commissioners where minting was listed as a law that needed to be repealed or amended (*Hutchinson Papers,* vol. 2, pp. 210-41; also Toppan, *Randolph,* vol. 2, pp. 225-59; Toppan, "Right to Coin," p. 221 and Sainsbury, *Calendar 1675-1676,* pp. 463-68, item 1067).

The Governor of Massachusetts Bay and his Assistants had originally told Randolph they were not able to send agents to London as the king had requested. However, by the October session of the General Court the Commonwealth had reconsidered and elected William Stoughton and Peter Bulkley to represent them at the king's court. The agents arrived in London in December and presented a letter to the king from the Massachusetts Bay Governor John Leveret and the General Court. The letter apologized for not sending agents earlier, stating the colony had been in the middle of a war against several Indian tribes and all their resources had been expended on defense, therefore they had not been able to address the king's request. However, now that the main enemy, the Indian Sachem known as King Philip, was dead, they were assigning William Stoughton and Peter Bulkley to be their agents defending the Massachusetts claims to New Hampshire and Maine (Toppan, *Randolph,* vol. 2, pp. 262-65 and Sainsbury, *Calendar 1675-1676,* p. 513, item 1186).

With the Massachusetts Bay agents present in London, Edward Randolph stepped up his campaign. On May 6, 1677, Randolph forwarded a brief memorandum to the Committee on Foreign Affairs entitled, "Representation of ye Affaires of New England," which was sometimes referred to as "The present State of the affaires of New England." This document listed eight accusations against Massachusetts Bay as follows: (1) they were usurpers without a royal charter, (2) they did not take an oath of allegiance to the king, (3) they protected Cromwell's confidants, Major General William Goffe and Lieutenant General Edward Whaley, who had participated in the murder of Charles I, (4) "They Coyne money with their owne Impress," (5) they had murdered some English Quakers because of their religious beliefs, (6) they opposed the king's commissioners in the settlement of New Hampshire and Maine, (7) they imposed an oath of fidelity to Massachusetts Bay on all inhabitants and, finally, (8) they violated the acts of trade and navigation robbing the king of his custom duties. This document was forwarded to the Lords for Trade and Plantations for discussion at their meeting on June 7th which led to further investigations (Hall, *Randolph,* pp. 33-36 and Toppan, *Randolph,* vol. 2, pp. 265-68 as well as Toppan, "Right to Coin," p. 221 and Sainsbury, *Calendar 1677-1680,* pp. 79-80, items 218-20. Also, under the date 1680 this list is found in *Hutchinson Papers,* vol. 2, pp. 264-65 and Toppan, *Randolph,* vol. 3, pp. 78-79).

The pronouncements of 1677

During the June 7, 1677 meeting of the Committee for Trade and Plantations, the Lords requested the cases of Mason and Gorges against Massachusetts Bay be expedited. Additionally, Randolph's memorandum to the Committee on Foreign Affairs was forwarded and read at this meeting. In discussing the memorandum the Lords decided they should seek legal opinions before acting on the memorandum. On June 8th an order of the king in Council stated the Lords for Trade and Plantations were to seek the opinions of such judges as they saw fit. Also, on the 8th, the Lords for Trade and Plantations issued a report stating the Massachusetts agents were to be notified that they would be required to answer the observations of Randolph as well as defend against the claims of Mason and Gorges (Toppan, *Randolph,* vol. 2, pp. 268-72 and Sainsbury, *Calendar 1677-1680,* pp. 102-03, items 289-90 and 294 for the events of June 7-12 and pp. 79-80, item 218 on the document of May 6th).

The Committee of the Lords for Trade and Plantations met a few days later on June 12th to discuss the eight point memorandum by Edward Randolph. The Lords decided Randolph's first and second points were to be referred to the judges and the King's Council, the committee would inquire into the third point and examine the Massachusetts charter on the fourth and fifth points, while the sixth, seventh and eighth points were to be "looked upon as matters of State." The fourth point, on the coinage of money, was mentioned in the same sentence in which they responded to the fifth point on the execution of some English Quakers in 1659. The committee stated:

> The Fourth Head concerning Coining of Money And The Fifth that they have put His Majesties Subjects to death for Religion are to be referred, and examination to bee made whether, by their Charter, or by the right of making Laws they are enabled soe to doe. (Toppan, *Randolph,* vol. 2, pp. 271-72; Toppan, "Right to Coin," p. 221, also Sainsbury, *Calendar 1677-1680,* pp. 103-4, item 294)

The discussion on the Massachusetts Mint and the execution of Quakers continued into July. On July 19th Randolph was brought in to testify before the Lords for Trade and Plantations. Then, the Massachusetts agents William Stoughton and Peter Bulkley were brought in and ordered to defend the Commonwealth against Randolph's charges. According to a report of the meeting made by the Lords for Trade and forwarded to the king by the Lord of the Privy Seal, the agents answered that they had not been authorized to speak on behalf of Massachusetts except in the land claim disputes. However, they consented to reply "...as private men, and His Majesties subjects, as far as they were acquainted with the occurrence and transactions of ye Government under which they had lived." Concerning coining the minutes report:

> That Upon the Article where they are charged to have coyned money, they confess it, and say they were necessitated to it, about the yeare 1652, for the support of their Trade, and have not, hitherto, discontinued it, as being never excepted against, or disallowed by His Majesty And doe therefore submit this matter to His Majectie and beg pardon if they have offended.

(Toppan, *Randolph,* vol. 2, pp. 274-77 with quote on 276, Toppan, "Right to Coin," p. 221 and Sainsbury, *Calendar 1677-1680,* pp. 122-23, items 350-51)

On July 27th the Massachusetts Bay agents were again called to a meeting of the Committee of the Lords for Trade and Plantations. According to the committee minutes the agents were told the decision of the committee on several points. The committee asked for a commission to look into the boundary disputes, they insisted the Navigation Act be "religiously observed" and explained that some Massachusetts Bay laws would need to be revised while any future laws should be sent to the Privy Council for review. As to the mint the minutes stated:

> That Whereas they had transgressed, in presuming to Coyne Money, which is an Act of Sovereignty, and to which they were by noe Grant sufficiently authorized, That tho' His Majesty may, upon due application, grant them a Charter containing such a Power; yet they must sollicit His Majesties Pardon for the offence that is past.

The committee assured Stoughton and Bulkley that "His Majestie will not destroy their Charter, but rather by a Supplemental one to bee given them, set all things right that are now amiss" (Toppan, *Randolph,* vol. 2, pp. 277-80 with the quotes on pp. 278 and 279-80; Toppan, "Right to Coin," p. 222 and Sainsbury, *Calendar 1677-1680,* pp. 135-36, item 371).

Thus after all the complaints by Randolph about the mint, the Lords of the Committee for Trade and Plantations had decided although Massachusetts Bay had not been authorized to open a mint they were recommending the privilege to coin be added to their charter! Clearly, this ruling shows there was no concerted governmental effort to oppose or close the mint. Although several individuals had listed the mint among their complaints against Massachusetts Bay, the British government acknowledged the problem but was ready to remedy the situation.

On August 2, 1677, Stoughton and Bulkley were again brought before the Committee of the Lords for Trade and Plantations where they were lectured on the errors of the Massachusetts government and told what they must do. As to the mint the Lords were rather lenient stating that the agents would need to discuss the matter with the Attorney General about soliciting the king's pardon for past offenses of coining money without authority. Also, the Attorney General was to attend to the action:

> That an Additional Charter bee prepared containing a Power from His Majestie to Coyn Money, and to make all forreigne coins current in that Country... . (Toppan, *Randolph,* vol. 2, pp. 281-84 with the quote on p. 283 and Toppan, "Right to Coin," p. 222)

The news of the pronouncements of the Lords for Trade and Plantations was gratefully received in Massachusetts because the charter had not been abolished and the Commonwealth hoped they would be granted a minting license. During the fall session of the Massachusetts Bay General Court, in October of 1677, a proclamation was issued that a day of Thanksgiving would be observed on November 15th. The preamble to the proclamation stated the reasons for the observance were because God had spared them from an outbreak of an infectious disease and because God had been on their side in the London proceedings,

> ... frustrating the hopes of our Malicious Adversaries and graciously considering us in the midst of our fears, giving us favour in the eyes of our Soveraign Lord and King, and his most horourable Council as Letters received from Agents do fully inform us ... .

Also, an order in the record of the General Court under this date stated the treasurer would provide the king with ten barrels of Cranberries, two hogsheads of their best samp [samp is coarsely ground Indian corn made into a porridge] and three thousand codfish. Additionally, two other laws were instituted. The General Court also resolved that "...the acts of Trade and Navigation be exactly and punctually observed by this his Majesties Colony." However, in partial defiance of another suggestion from the Committee for Trade and Plantations, the General Court revived the oath of fidelity formerly required of inhabitants of the Commonwealth, re-enacting a law "...requiring all persons, as well inhabitants as straingers, (that haue not taken it,) to take the oath of fidelity to the country" [the country refers to Massachusetts Bay] and extending the law to include an oath of allegiance to the king (Hall, *Randolph*, pp. 37-39; Palfrey, vol. 2, pp. 212-13 and Sainsbury, *Calendar 1677-1680*, pp. 140-42, items 380-81; Cushing, *Laws*, vol. 3, pp. 516-19. This preamble is found in the printed version of the law but it was not included in the record of the General Court, see Shurtleff, vol. 5, pp. 154-56; the preamble is summarized in Sainsbury, *Calendar 1677-1680*, p. 164, item 429).

During the fall session, on October 22nd, the General Court sent a letter to their agents in London, Stoughton and Bulkley, stating they were optimistic about the future and would forward an additional £1,000 to them so they could continue their work. The letter encouraged them to defend the Massachusetts patents to New Hampshire and Maine. The Court also stated "As for the coynage, or any other additionall priviledge offered, (not prejudiciall to our charter,) wee would not slight, but humbly accept." They also encouraged the agents to protect the shipping and fishing rights of the Commonwealth. The letter concluded that they hoped the men of Portsmouth would be able to send the king a ship load of masts if the king would send a ship to pick them up and from Boston, the General Court would send the king some codfish, samp and cranberries (Shurtleff, vol. 5, pp. 163-64; Crosby, p. 82 and Hall, *Randolph*, pp. 39-40). Further, on the 24th, Governor John Leveret, with the consent of the General Court, sent a letter to the British Secretary of State, Sir Joseph Williamson, thanking the secretary for his "...most friendly and christian rediness to promote the equity and righteousness of their cause," in the face of false representations made against them (Sainsbury, *Calendar 1677-1680*, p. 171, item 456).

Thus, in December of 1677 the situation looked quite good for the Puritans. Back on Februray 12, 1677, a treaty had been signed ending King Philip's war with a full victory for Massachusetts Bay. By December it also appeared as if Massachusetts would be victorious over their detractors in London. Indeed, the Massachusetts agents became bolder petitioning the king on December 16th that the towns of Dover, Portsmouth, Exeter and Hampton (all in

New Hampshire) remain under the jurisdiction of Massachusetts Bay and suggesting they be allowed to coin both silver and gold coins. The petition stated they had:

> ... received a signification of the King's promise of pardon to the Massachusetts Government, and particularly of the offence of coining money without the King's authority, with His majesty's license for setting up a Mint within said Colony for coining gold and silver with such impress as His Majesty shall think fit to pass current in said colony only... [the agents then went on to] implore His Majesty to add the grant of these four towns, with the land and royalties, and the liberty of coining money. (Sainsbury, *Calendar 1677-1680*, pp. 211-12, item 587 with the quote on p. 211)

A reversal of fortune: 1678-1684

This increased boldness soon turned against them. In January, Robert Mason put forward a counter petition to the king asking that the New Hampshire towns not be annexed to Massachusetts. Both petitions, along with a petition by Gorges for Maine were forwarded from the King's Council to the Lords of the Committee for Trade and Plantations with a request that a report on the matter be sent back to the Council (Sainsbury, *Calendar 1677-1680,* p. 211, item 456). While the Lords of the Committee for Trade and Plantations were conducting their investigation, the Massachusetts Bay agents, Stoughton and Bulkley, made an agreement with Gorges to purchase his claim to Maine and made a similar offer to Mason. Mason reported this to the Lords at their meeting of March 25, 1678 (Sainsbury, *Calendar 1677-1680,* pp. 224-26, items 629-32). The Lords were quite distressed that the Massachusetts agents were trying to bypass their authority. On the 28th Stoughton and Bulkley were asked to appear before the Committee for Trade and Plantations and explain themselves. During their explanation they stated they had obtained a copy of Randolph's extensive report against Massachusetts Bay (of October 12, 1676) and hoped to publicly discredit it by reopening the inquiry. Robert Mason appeared before the committee stating he had given the report to the representatives from Massachusetts Bay because he had been duped into believing a servant to the Lord of the Privy Seal had previously given them a copy (Hall, *Randolph,* p. 42; Toppan, *Randolph,* vol. 2, pp. 286-87; Palfrey, vol. 2, p. 216 and Sainsbury, *Calendar 1677-1680,* pp. 229-30, item 640).

Upon hearing of the breach in security, Randolph attended the April 8th meeting of the Lords for Trade and Plantations, explaining his October 1676 report had been confidential and that the Massachusetts agents could only have obtained it surreptitiously. Furthermore, Randolph explained Massachusetts continued to disregard the authority of the Committee. He informed the Committee that the October 1677 session of the Massachusetts General Court had only addressed the Lords request that the colony adhere to the Navigation Acts but the General Court had been silent on other areas of concern and had reimposed the oath of fidelity. Randolph also reported, "Nor had they even suspended their Coining of money (which they confess to bee a crime) until His Majesties Pleasure bee knowne." Following the testimony of Mason and Randolph the Committee for Trade and Plantations inquired of the Massachusetts agents if these events were correct. Once it was determined these events had occurred the committee changed their attitude and took a stern stance against Massachusetts Bay. They sent an inquiry to the Attorney General asking whether the Massachusetts charter could be nullified (Hall, *Randolph,* pp. 41-44; Toppan, *Randolph,* vol. 2, pp. 289-98 with the quote on coining money from p. 295 and Sainsbury, *Calendar 1677-1680,* pp. 233-36, item 653).

Between December of 1677 and April of 1678 the position of the Committee for Trade and Plantations was completely reversed. Rather than accommodating Massachusetts Bay, inquiries were started on nullifying their charter with numerous accusations made on both sides. Randolph became the champion of the nullification movement with the support of the Lords of the Committee for Trade and Plantations and the Privy Council. In fact, soon thereafter, on May 18th, Stoughton and Bulkley were called to the committee meeting of the Lords for Trade and Plantations where the opinion of the Attorney General was read, stating the offenses of Massachusetts Bay were sufficient to void their charter. This was the start of the process that would lead to the issuing of the writ *Quo warranto* against Massachusetts. Also, on this day the Lords for Trade and Plantations, with the consent of the king, directed that a commission be issued to Edward Randolph to make him Collector of Customs in New England (Hall, *Randolph,* pp. 44-45; Toppan, *Randolph,* vol. 3, pp. 2-6 and Sainsbury, *Calendar 1677-1680,* pp. 253-54, items 703-6).

From this point it was simply a matter of time before the charter was revoked. However, the General Court of Massachusetts Bay continued to believe they could prevail. During the 1678 fall session the General Court sent a letter to the Commonwealth's agents in London, William Stoughton and Peter Bulkley, asking them to continue to lobby for the minting privilege. The letter included an explanation that the mint was needed to keep up the colony's prosperity and that this prosperity increased the king's customs they paid annually. The General Court also stated they would change the "Impresse" on their coins (that is, the images and legends) if the king wished (Shurtleff, vol. 5, pp. 201-3, Crosby, p. 83 and Toppan, "Right to Coin," p. 222).

Additional petitions continued through the entire period of the Hull mint. Indeed, in a special February session of the General Court in 1682, instructions were composed for two new Massachusetts agents being sent to London. These instructions included information concerning the necessity of the mint, as follows:

> You shall informe his majestie that we tooke up stamping of silver meerley upon necessitie, to prevent cheats by false peeces of eight, which were brought hither in the time of the late confusions, and wee have been well informed that his majestie had knowledge thereof, yet did not manifest nay dissatisfaction thereat until of very late; and if that be a trespasse upon his majesties royal prerogative, of which wee are ignorant, wee humbly beg his majesties pardon and gratious allowance therein, it being so exceeding necessary for our civil commerce, & no way, as wee humbly conceive, detrimentall to his royal majestie.

The "time of the late confusions" is a reference to the period from the outbreak of civil war in 1642 through the demise of the English Commonwealth in 1660 (Shurtleff, vol. 5, pp. 333-34, 346-49 with the quote on p. 347; Crosby, p. 83 and Toppan, "Right to Coin," p. 223. The letter of instructions is dated February 15th, but it was included in the record of the General

Court under the date of March 17, 1682). Just three and a half months later, June 3, 1682, was the official expiration date of the final Commonwealth mint contract to Hull and Sanderson. Thus, during the entire life of the mint the Massachusetts Bay General Court continued to believe they could persuade the king to grant them the privilege of minting.

On June 27, 1683, the King's Bench issued a writ of *Quo warranto* against the Governor and Company of Massachusetts Bay. This was a legal action inquiring into the validity of their charter asking "By what authority" they exercised the liberties in question. The writ named thirty individuals including Governor Bradstreet, Deputy Governor Danforth and the Assistants as well as several other government officials. The writ listed Massachusetts officials as of the election of May 24, 1682, using the same order of names as is found in the General Court records. Since John Hull was one of the elected Assistants that year he was named in the writ. Thus, Hull was named in the writ because he was an elected official and not because of his position as mintmaster. Edward Randolph landed in Boston from London with the writ *Quo warranto* on October 26th. John Hull had died on October 1st and thus never learned of the action (Shurtleff, vol. 5, pp. 350 for the 1682 election results and pp. 421-22 for the text; Hart, vol. 1, p. 565 and Hutchinson, ed. Mayo, pp. 284-87).

From the abolition of the charter to Queen Anne's proclamation: 1684-1704

Massachusetts Bay continued to resist. The writ was overturned due to technicalities but a different writ of *Scire facias* (to show cause why the charter should not be revoked) was issued by the King's Bench on April 14, 1684, resulting in the abolition of the charter on October 23rd. Even after the charter was revoked Massachusetts Bay continued to hope for a new charter with the right to reestablish the mint. The question of a mint was brought up in November of 1684. The King's Council was establishing instructions for a newly appointed Royal Governor who would abolish the Massachusetts General Court. One question that was circulated to the Commissioners of Customs and the Commissioners of the Treasury was, should the king allow a mint to operate. The question reappeared in July of 1686 in a discussion of whether a mint should be reestablished in Massachusetts. The London mint was adamant that Massachusetts Bay should only be allowed to reopen a mint if they would conform to the British standard for both fineness and weight so the coins would be equivalent in intrinsic value to the coins of England.

There were no further requests to reopen the mint during the reign of the British appointed government. In November of 1688 William of Orange landed in England claiming his right to the throne. By December he had defeated James II and in January of 1689 William and Mary were pronounced King and Queen. The news reached Boston on April 4th. Then, on April 18th the inhabitants of Massachusetts Bay rebelled against the autocratic governor, Edmund Andros, who had been appointed by James II. Andros and his allies were jailed and eventually sent back to England for trial. The new king, William III, supported the colonists and began hearings to establish a new charter for Massachusetts Bay.

The colony's agents in London who were negotiating the specifics of the charter believed there was still the possibility of obtaining the privilege to coin and continued to request the reestablishment of the mint. On December 10, 1690, the Massachusetts Bay

General Court authorized the first emission of paper currency and on February 3, 1691, authorized an additional emission. Later that year, on October 7, 1691, Massachusetts Bay was granted a new charter but without the right to mint coins. The request for the right to reestablish the mint continued with a solicitation forwarded by the Massachusetts agents to the Royal Commissioners of the Mint on January 12, 1692. This request was countered by a letter from the Royal Commissioners on January 19, 1692, stating they did not feel such a mint was necessary but if it was approved the coins should be equal in intrinsic value to those of the London mint. Faced with what would be a prolonged campaign of lobbying, and then being required to mint coins equal in intrinsic value to the British, Massachusetts Bay decided to drop the idea of reestablishing a mint and concentrate on legislating the value of Spanish American silver. Soon after 1700 there were some attempts by independent merchants to produce small change tokens and in 1703 the General Court investigated the possibility of obtaining some copper "pence" from a British supplier. These initiatives were soon abandoned. On March 24, 1704, an act was passed authorizing a new emission of paper currency and on June 18 of that year Queen Anne issued a proclamation on coin values in the colonies. From this point on the Massachusetts Bay General Court focused its attention on printing paper currency and regulating Spanish American and other foreign silver and gold coinage. There were no further discussions on minting coinage.

British opposition to the mint in Massachusetts Bay: a summary

There was no concerted effort by the king and his ministers to crush the Massachusetts Mint. The central conflict was Massachusetts Bay's seizure of New Hampshire and Maine. The mint was simply listed as another area of concern. In 1662 British ministers did not object to the mint. In 1664 the royal commissioners listed the mint as an area of concern, but nothing came of their report for over a decade. When the Lords of the Committee for Trade and Plantations finally took up the charges in 1677 they again did not consider minting to be a significant problem. Indeed, the Lords immediately offered to assist by revising the charter so it would include the privilege to mint coins. When the situation turned against Massachusetts Bay, the focus of the British attack was the nullification of the charter. Even after the charter had been nullified, ministers in Britain continued to ask if the mint should be reestablished under the newly appointed royal governor. Four years later, after overthrowing the governor appointed by James II, the inhabitants of Massachusetts continued to believe the new king, William III, would grant them permission to reestablish the mint. From these actions it is clear, although the mint had detractors, the British government did not make an effort to shut it down; indeed they tried to accommodate the mint. Certainly the government of Massachusetts Bay believed the British ministers would support their mint since they continued to request for the reestablishment of the mint. The only impediment was that the Commissioners of the London mint required a reestablished mint to produce coins equal in intrinsic value to those of the London mint.

The Massachusetts Mint was not under political pressure, fearing that they might be closed down any day. In fact, during the life of the mint, there was no direct attack from British authorities. The most significant political problem faced by the mint was the potential nullification of the charter of Massachusetts Bay. This would not only close the mint but would nullify all laws passed by the General Court. However, before this event occurred the mint seems to have ceased operations when the seven year mint contract was not renewed in 1682.

This analysis of events is not new. Indeed, it was the view expressed in colonial Massachusetts. In 1764 Thomas Hutchinson wrote his famous work, *The History of the Colony and Province of Massachusetts-Bay,* in which he said of the mint:

> No notice was taken of it by the parliament, nor by Cromwell, and having been thus indulged, there was a tacit allowance of it afterwards even by King Charles the second, for more than 20 years; and although it was made one of the charges against the colony, when the charter was called into question, no great stress was laid upon it. It appeared to have been so beneficial, that, during Sir Edmund Andross's administration, endeavours were used to obtain leave for continuing it, and the objections against it seemed not to have proceeded from its being an encroachment upon the prerogative, for the motion was referred to the master of the mint, and the report against it was upon mere prudential considerations. (Hutchinson, ed. Mayo, vol. 1, pp. 151-52, part of one of Hutchinson's original footnotes to his text)

Certainly, British political events are factors that needs to be considered in the development and eventual decline of the mint. But political problems were not the central issues the mint had to overcome. Rather, I would suggest looking at economic factors. To understand the success and eventual decline of this business we must focus on the profitability and productivity of the mint.

Part Three

The Economics of Massachusetts Silver Coinage

Chapter 4

Mint Charges in Massachusetts Bay

The debate over mint fees in 1652

One point of contention in the mint act of May 26/27, 1652, concerned the fee a consignor was required to pay to the mintmaster. The mint fee originally included in the earliest extant draft version of the act was 1s6d (18d) out of every 20s minted. This was the fee assigned to Hull in the version of the act that was originally passed by the House of Magistrates on May 26th. However, the House of Deputies dramatically reduced the fee by one-third to 1s (12d) in the version passed by that house on May 27th. The Magistrates accepted the reduction and accordingly reduced the fee in their version of the legislation.

Mintmaster Hull had most likely proposed the 18d fee found in the original legislation and understandably was concerned about the significant reduction legislated in the House of Deputies. Hull did not have an opportunity to address the General Court on this matter because the semi-annual session ended a few days after the mint act was passed. However, a mint committee had been authorized to continue to meet and expedite the implementation of the mint act. The committee consisted of Edward Rawson, the Secretary to the General Court, Richard Bellingham and William Hibbens (or Hibbins) from the House of Magistrates along with John Leveret and Thomas Clarke from the House of Deputies. This group was busy planning the construction of a mint house and arranging for the appropriation of the necessary minting tools when Hull brought his complaints to them about the fee reduction. The committee members honestly explained they really did not know how to calculate a suitable and just fee for the mintmaster's service. The charge of the mint committee was to facilitate the implementation of the mint act, therefore they were disposed to accommodate Hull and open the mint as soon as possible. The sooner the mint opened the sooner their work would be completed. However, as representatives of their respective houses of the General Court, they had to consider the opinions and actions of their colleagues. This was a sensitive situation as it is clear the opposition to the original 18d mint fee in the House of Deputies was so strong that the majority of the members voted for a substantial one-third reduction in the fee.

Hull's concerns were addressed in the committee's action of June 20, 1652, announcing the construction of a mint house. The committee agreed to raise the mint fee to a maximum of 15d per 20s coined, that is, half way between the lower figure proposed by the House of Deputies and the original figure, probably proposed by Hull. This did not satisfy Hull.

Therefore to appease him, while at the same time not appearing to back down from the fee reduction, the committee also added "...a penny in euery ounce allowed for wast... ." While the mint fee was expressed in terms of pence per 20s coined, the waste supplement was expressed in terms of pence per troy ounce of sterling. As 20s was the equivalent of three troy ounces of sterling, in effect, this brought the total charges to the customer back up to the amount in the original request of 18d per 20s minted. Thus, the committee had appeased Hull but had worded the document so that it appeared they had negotiated a fee that was only halfway between the original fee and the reduction voted by the Deputies. From the surviving ledger we see Hull did not itemize fees, he simply collected a total of 18d per 20s as his commission, which he took at the end of the process from the newly minted coins.

The text of the mint committee document explained the central problem for the legislators was that they were unsure how to calculate an appropriate refining fee, since some silver objects brought into the mint would require more refining than others, while sterling silver items brought in would need no refining at all. Indeed, the document stated 15d plus 1d per ounce for waste was the maximum allowable charge. In some instances it was thought Hull should charge a customer less. Once the mint was in production it was hoped more information would be available on an acceptable fee and the legislators could revisit the question during the fall session of the General Court. The June 20th committee action explained a mint house was to be built and the necessary coining tools were to be acquired and that initial steps had already been taken towards these ends (or as they said, "all which is in Acting"). The committee then went on to discuss the mint fees:

> And that the mint master may not have Just Cawse to Complajne, wee cannot but Judge it meete [meete = what is suitable or sufficient] to Allow the said mint master, for Refyning and Coyning such bulljon, plate & mony, that shall be brought vnto them, what was in his Judgment and Conscience, on his experience he shall Judge aequall, so as he exceede not 15^d in twenty shillings ouer and besides a penny in euery ounce allowed for wast till the next sessions [that is, the October session of the General Court] Against which tjme, Itt is to be hoped such experjence will be had of what is necessary to be Allowed, as there will be no Just occasion of Complainte only wee doe desire and Advise the sajd John Hull, (there being a likely hood of seuerall sorts of worke: in which he is to be Imployed where there is no Refjning and so lesse labor, he would take lesse : and where both Refining and Coyning is necessary there; if he finde he Cannot subsist with lesse he may take fiveteene pence, for euery twenty shillings. (Crosby, p. 40) [Crosby does not include any closing parenthesis in the final section of this quote. For meete see the *Oxford English Dictionary,* volume M, p. 305, meaning 3.]

A comment was added to the document by Edward Rawson the Secretary of the General Court that on October 28, 1652, during the fall session of the General Court, it was agreed to approve the "Allowance of 15d per 20s" minted. The text read:

> Voted by the whole Court. that they Allowe ye Act of the Committee for minting of mony, Respecting the howse & Allowance of 15^d per 20^s. 28 8mo. 1652: Edward Rawson Secretary. (Crosby, p. 40)

A similar notation was made in the record of the General Court:

> The whole Courte by their Gennerall vote did Allow and Approove of the acte of the Committee about minting of money & Respecting their building of the mint howse at the Common charge, and allowance of the officers 15ᵈ in euery twenty shillings for their paines and Ordered the Committee to Continew in their power till the next Election. (Crosby, p. 41)

Since the statements did not specify that the Court approved a mint fee "up to" 15d, it appears the legislators believed Hull regularly charged the full rate. However, the two records of the endorsement were simple brief notes signifying the General Court agreed with the actions of the mint committee and cannot be taken to have revised or modified the committee decisions. For example, it is assumed the acquisition of the coining tools and the wastage allowance were also approved although not specifically stated in the endorsement. Indeed, the wastage allowance continued in force through the history of the mint. Even in the final contract renewal of June 3, 1675, where the mint fee was reduced, the wastage allowance was specifically mentioned and allowed at the same rate as it had been since 1652.

Hull's application of the mint fees

The 1652 mint act stated anyone consigning silver to the mint could watch the silver be refined to sterling fineness and would then be given a receipt for the weight of sterling silver consigned to the mint. The legislation went on to explain that at the end of the minting process the customer was to be paid the receipt weight in Massachusetts coins minus any mint fees or allowances authorized to Hull by the General Court. The text of the mint act, in the version passed on May 27, 1652, by the House of Deputies stated:

> & It shalbe in the liberty of any person who brings into the mint howse any bullian plate or spanish Coyne as afforsaid to be present and se [see] the same melted & refined Allayed & then to take a receit of the master of the mint for the weyght of that which is good silver allayd as aforesaid, for which the mint master shall deliver him the like weight in Current money viz. every shilling to weigh three penny Troy weight & lesser peeces proportionably deducting allowances for coynage as before exprest. (Crosby, pp. 37-38)

According to a strict reading of the statute, Hull should have deducted his allowances from the sterling weight on the receipt (at the conversion rate of six grains in sterling being equal to 1d in fees) and then delivered all coinage made from the remaining silver to the customer.

In Hull's surviving ledger there are several examples of how the mint fee, or more correctly, the customer's return, was calculated and collected from October of 1671 through September of 1680. From these examples we see the methodology specified in the statute was reinterpreted at the mint. Each ounce of sterling silver would theoretically yield 80d (6s8d) in full weight Massachusetts silver if there were no waste or loss of silver in the minting process. From this amount the maximum mint fee was 5d per troy ounce of sterling with a wastage allowance of 1d per troy ounce for a total of 6d in charges, leaving a return to the customer of 74d (6s2d) in Massachusetts coinage per ounce of sterling brought into the mint. In Chapter Seven we shall see Hull assayed the silver consigned to the mint to determine its fineness. He then weighed the silver. If the silver was not of sterling fineness he calculated the differential and then gave the consignor a receipt for all silver consigned to the mint. According to the 1652 mint act, Hull should have used the consigned silver to produce as many coins as possible at the authorized weight. Next, he should have calculated his mint fee based on the troy ounces of sterling deposited and then deducted his fee from the total coinage produced. Using this method any overproduction would go to the customer. However, from the ledger we see Hull multiplied the number of ounces of sterling consigned to the mint by 74d (6s2d) to arrive at the return to the customer; the unspecified remainder of the coins were retained by Hull as income. As an example of how Hull calculated a customer's return, in his ledger under the date of August 25, 1673, Hull noted: "To put in to ye mint house to be coyned 265$^{oz.}$ sterling at 6^s · 2^d is £81 · 14 · 2" (New England Historic Genealogical Society, MS Cb 110, vol. 1, folio 26 verso). At the rate of 74d (6s2d) per ounce of sterling the return to the individual would be exactly what Hull calculated £81 14s2d. Thus, Hull calculated the minimum amount he was obligated to give to the customer based on the ounces of sterling silver received and he retained whatever was left as his income. Technically, the mint act stated the opposite methodology, namely Hull should calculate his authorized fee and then the customer would retain whatever remained.

Later reductions of the mint fees

As the economies of the British colonies in the West Indies and along the Atlantic seaboard began to flourish during the later 1660's there was an increased demand for silver coinage. As a result, the value of silver and especially the value of eight reales coins increased. Many colonies legislated rates for Spanish American cob coinage that were above the British value for the silver content of the coins, in effect, overvaluing or as the colonials stated "crying-up" the value, so that the coins would have increased purchasing power at home with much less temptation that they would be exported as bullion. As the value of Spanish cobs rose closer and closer to the value of Massachusetts silver, which had been legislated at the rate of 80d per ounce of sterling, it became less profitable for individuals to bring Spanish cobs to the mint, resulting in declining production of Massachusetts silver coinage.

In order to make the transaction of converting Spanish cobs into Massachusetts coinage more profitable, there were several suggestions to lower the mint fees. Indeed, the situation became so serious, the goal of reducing customer fees became an objective of the General Court. Whereas the focus of the earlier General Court mint committees formed on October 16, 1660, and May 15, 1667, had been stated as negotiating additional revenue for the Commonwealth, the stated objective of the third renewal committee (this is the fourth mint committee, since the first mint committee was appointed in 1652), included in the record of the General Court under the date of May 12, 1675, was to make an agreement that "may be most encouraging to all persons who have bullion to bring in the same mint" (Crosby, pp. 71, 78 and 81). The result of these negotiations was the contract renewal of June 3, 1675, in which the mint fee was reduced from 15d per 20s, or 6.25%, to 1s (12d) per 20s, or 5%, while the allowance of 1d per ounce for waste continued, bringing the total charges down from 7.5 % to 6.25%. This represented a reduction in fees from 6d per ounce of sterling to 5d per ounce so that the return for the customer per ounce of sterling silver increased from 74d

(6s2d) to 75d (6s3d). Hull's surviving ledger includes a record of what may represent the first consignment calculated at the new rate. Under the date of June 17, 1675, is the following entry: "To 217^{oz} sterling silver dollars into ye mint house to be coyned. 6 · 3^d · £67 · 16 · 3" (New England Historic Genealogical Society, MS Cb 110, vol. 1, folio 26 verso). At the rate of 75d (6s3d) per ounce of sterling the return to the individual would be exactly what Hull calculated £67 16s3d.

The 1d increase to the customer's return did not bring much silver into the mint. Apparently the small increase was not a sufficient inducement. Also, just a few weeks after the reduced rates were put into effect, Massachusetts Bay became involved in a costly and prolonged struggle against King Philip, lasting from June 20, 1675, until February 12, 1677. Indeed, Hull was named treasurer of the War Committee and spent much time compiling three large ledgers of all Commonwealth payments relating to this war. The total mint production of Massachusetts coinage during this period listed in Hull's private ledger consisted of just two consignments. One consignment for 217 ounces of sterling was deposited on June 17, 1675, just a few days before the outbreak of hostilities. It was the first consignment at the higher customer return as agreed to in the renewal of June 3, 1675. The only consignment actually placed during the war was probably a personal consignment for Hull recorded in the ledger on June 14, 1676, as a consignment of 496.75 ounces of sterling (see the ledger commentary in Appendix I for details).

With the end of the war, shipments of silver began to increase. About six weeks after the war officially ended, several shipments totaling 1575.5 ounces of sterling and 282 ounces of Spanish plate were delivered between April 20-27, 1677, and on July 13, 1677, an additional consignment of 125 ounces of sterling was delivered. At this point Hull reduced his fee in the hope of attracting more customers to the mint. An entry in Hull's ledger stated between May 3 and August 29 several parcels of silver were delivered to the mint, but the weight of these parcels was not recorded. However, Hull calculated the return to the customer quite differently from what had been done in earlier entries. Hull explained the face value of the total amount of money minted from the silver was £671 12s and that his fee was to be 12d per £1, that is, 1s (12d) per every 20s (£1) produced, or 5% of the money coined. Interestingly, this was the exact fee proposed by the House of Deputies in 1652. Hull calculated his fee for these several parcels at £33 10s (although a full 12d per 20s would have entitled him to £33 11s 7.2d). By using this method Hull was limiting his income to a fixed sum of 5% of the total return; any overage above 80d per ounce of sterling would be split with 5% going to Hull and 95% going to the customer. This fee continued to be used for all shipments through the shipment received on December 26, 1679; in each instance Hull wrote in his ledger that by an agreement with the customer he was to receive 12d per 20s as his fee.

The return to Hull in terms of a fixed fee of 12d per 20s coined was lower than the June 3, 1675 agreement. Essentially his return was about equal to a 4d per troy ounce mint fee, while the customer benefitted by an increase of 1d per ounce in the return as well as acquiring 95% of any production over 80d per ounce. From an entry on February 24, 1679, we learn 400 troy ounces of Spanish sterling were brought into the shop and used to produce £133 18s in Massachusetts coinage, which equals 80.34d in coins per troy ounce. At 12d per 20s Hull took £6 14s as his fee (although strictly speaking he was only entitled to £6 13s 10.8d). Based on the June 3, 1675 rate Hull would have taken a mint fee of 4d and a wastage allowance of 1d for a total of 5d per ounce, giving the customer a return of 75d per ounce. This would have yielded Hull a mint fee of £6 13s4d and a wastage allowance of £1 13s4d for a total fee of £8 6s8d plus the entire extra 0.34d per ounce for an additional 11s4d bringing his total return to £8 18s, while the customer would have received £125. Certainly, in relation to the rate in the June 3, 1675 mint agreement, the revised rate of 12d per 20s was an incentive to the customer, since Hull's return dropped from £8 18s to £6 14s and the customer's return increased from £125 to £127 4s.

Although the new rates improved customer return it was not enough of a concession to keep a supply of silver coming into the mint. As previously mentioned, the last shipment received under the 12d per 20s fee agreement was on December 26, 1679. For the next eight months no new shipments were recorded in Hull's ledger.

During this post-war period several proposals were sent to the Massachusetts General Court to remedy the silver shortage at the mint. On June 2, 1677, a committee of the General Court in consultation with John Hull proposed two options: one option was to either raise the value of the current coins or reduce the weight of a shilling by nine to twelve grains, while the other option was to abolish mint fees. The proposal candidly stated both alternatives were "attended with Difficulty" but that they were worthy of further consideration. The difficulties referred to political problems Massachusetts Bay had with the British government concerning several issues, including the right to mint coins as discussed in Chapter Three. This was a very sensitive period. Indeed, the pronouncements of the Committee of the Lords for Trade and Plantations to resolve the problems in Massachusetts Bay were issued in June and July, just a few weeks after the June 2nd proposal was debated. Clearly the General Court could not take any action on devaluing their coinage for that would further strain their relations with Britain at this critical juncture. At the same time the General Court did not have the funds to pay for the mint from government revenue. It was suggested that until the difficulties were resolved, the General Court could double the tax on wine, brandy and rum and then use the money to partly finance the mint. A similar tax had been instituted in Britain in 1663 to finance the royal mint. However, Massachusetts Bay had severe financial problems and a general tax to support the mint was not popular. The 1677 proposal died in committee and never came up for a vote (Crosby, p. 108).

In May of 1680 several additional proposals recommending the abolition of mint fees were forwarded to the General Court. Basically, the proposals stated the mint should be a free service to the public with the mintmaster being paid a salary out of the government treasury rather than relying on customer fees (Crosby, pp. 109-11). Hull had served as treasurer of the Commonwealth from May of 1676 through May of 1680 and realized the Commonwealth did not have the funds to pay his salary. Indeed, Hull had loaned Massachusetts Bay money on several occasions and much of that money had never been repaid. On June 6, 1680, Hull, who had recently been appointed to the House of Magistrates, forwarded his own proposal to the General Court suggesting the government revalue Massachusetts silver in an attempt to make the minting concern profitable once again. Hull proposed reducing the authorized weight of a Massachusetts shilling from 72 grains sterling to 60 grains sterling. This would cry up the value of an ounce of sterling silver in Massachusetts money from 80d per ounce to 96d per ounce. As an eight reales of 408 grains was valued at 72d (6s), the value of a troy ounce of Spanish silver was 84d. At the new rate,

Massachusetts silver would once again be more valuable than Spanish silver. Hull suggested the customer would gain 7d to 7.5d by converting a full weight eight reales into Massachusetts shillings. Clearly, this would attract silver back to the mint (Crosby, pp. 111-12).

The General Court was forced to reject this proposal. At the time Massachusetts Bay had two agents in London defending the Commonwealth's actions to the Committee for Trade and Plantations against accusations put forward by several detractors who sought to have the Massachusetts Bay charter revoked. Many complaints had been lodged against Massachusetts Bay including the fact that they operated a mint without royal permission and issued coins that were below the British weight specifications. The General Court knew that on February 8, 1679, Henry Slingesby, Master of the London Mint, had made a presentation before the Committee for Trade and Plantations regarding the Earl of Carlisle's request to establish a mint in Jamaica. Slingesby was adamant that any coins minted in Jamaica must adhere to the British standards for both weight and fineness. On June 20th the earl wrote a reply to the committee (read at the committee meeting of October 9, 1679) that Jamaica would not be able to open a mint because they could not comply with Slingesby's restrictions. Moreover, the earl implied this ruling was unfair since Massachusetts Bay did not follow British weight standards. Faced with such opposition in London, the Massachusetts Bay General Court could not afford to further alienate the Committee for Trade and Plantations by allowing any additional reduction of the weight standard.

Hull's June 6, 1680 weight reduction proposal was quickly dismissed. Left with no alternative, Hull was forced to take matters into his own hands and further reduce his fee to attract silver into the mint. In his surviving ledger we see that a shipment of sterling in three installments totaling 1306.75 troy ounces was deposited in the mint on August 3-4, 1680. To attract this shipment Hull slashed his fee almost in half, from 12d per 20s coined to 6.6d per 20s. Unfortunately the ledger entry does not give the full information on the value of the coinage produced; Hull simply included the value of the coins returned to the customer, thus we are unable to determine if Hull continued to share overages with the customer. For specifics on this entry see the commentary on Hull's ledger in Appendix I.

The surviving portion of the Hull ledger stops at this point. The ledger did continue, for there are citations to accounts that were carried forward to subsequent ledgers, but those ledgers have not survived. We have no further records on minting activities for the final two years of the mint contract, which officially expired on June 3, 1682. The ledger entries for the mint that have survived cover the period 1671-1680. They show that during the years of the final mint agreement (a seven year agreement signed on June 3, 1675) Hull and Sanderson struggled to bring in new business by slashing fees and deeply reducing the profit margin in order to keep the mint in operation.

A comparison of the mint fees in Massachusetts and England

In the January 15, 1685 report concerning the Boston mint, produced by the London Mint Commissioners, Philip Loyd, Thomas Neale, Charles Duncombe and James Hoare, the topic of mint fees was briefly mentioned. The commissioners based their comments on a printed copy of the Massachusetts Bay Act of May 26/27, 1652, which stated the mint fee was to be 12d for every 20s coined, or 5%. The commissioners had no knowledge of the June renegotiations that increased the mint fee and added a wastage allowance bringing the total fees to 18d per 20s or 7.5%; nor did they know of the June 1675 negotiations reducing the total fees to 6.25%. Additionally, they were unaware of the private agreements Hull made with customers in the final years further reducing his income. Using the 5% allowance found in the printed version of the act, the commissioners commented that in Boston "a third more is allowed for the Coynage then what hath been allowed for the Coynage of his Maj^{sts} Silver Mints in England" (Crosby, p. 88). The commissioners used the past tense "hath been allowed" when they referred to English mint fees because on December 20, 1666, Charles II had abolished seignorage charges and decreed mint fees would be paid by the exchequer from a series of new taxes. This was done in an attempt to increase the quantity of bullion brought into the mint. Mint workers producing gold and silver coins were to be paid by the government from a customs duty imposed on liquor, wine, beer, vinegar and cider. Under this new system, the total mint charges came to 17.5d for every troy pound of silver (that is, per every 62 shillings coined) or about 2.35%. It should be noted the government mint subsidy only applied to the production of gold and silver issues. Regal copper coinage was just being initiated at this time and was produced under contract. During earlier periods of the century, when the London mint had collected fees, the charges had amounted to about 3.35%, hence the statement by the commissioners that Massachusetts fees at 5% had been about one-third higher. In 1623 mint fees in London were 25d per troy pound or just above 3.36% of which 10d went to the king and 15d to the mint. By 1663, this was down slightly to 24d (about 3.225%), of which 5d went to the king and 19d went to the mint (Craig, pp. 424-25). In comparison, the actual percentages allowed to Hull and Sanderson of 6.25% and later 5% seems quite generous, an amount that does not even include the 1.25% wastage allowance.

Of course, comparing mint fees between England and Massachusetts is not an equitable correlation. There was a more skilled labor force available in London through the guild of goldsmiths and the machinery was more advanced so that the London mint was certainly more efficient. Also, minting equipment was more difficult to obtain in Massachusetts since it needed to be special ordered or possibly imported, increasing the costs. Further, the quantity of coins minted in London was much higher than in Massachusetts. As has been often observed in modern numismatic discussions of colonial minting, the set up costs of coining, especially diecutting, were quite expensive. It has been said, if one did not amortize, the first coin minted from a die could cost twenty to fifty pounds or more while subsequent coins would cost only a fraction of a farthing to produce (excluding the intrinsic metal value). In such businesses the profits increase as production volume increases and undoubtedly the volume was much smaller in Massachusetts than in London, necessitating a higher fee for solvency. The London mint could certainly be profitable with lower fees than were required in Massachusetts. The real question was how much more did the Massachusetts fee need to be. This was the question the 1652 mint committee could not answer and so they accepted Hull's arguments which turned out to be quite adequate for Hull until the price of Spanish silver rose to the level that made it unprofitable to convert Spanish cobs into Massachusetts coinage. At that point Hull had to decrease his fees in order to stay in business. Certainly, as his income continued to dramatically decrease during 1679 and 1680, there was less incentive for Hull to remain in the minting business.

Chapter 5

Coin Weight at the Massachusetts Bay Mint

Coin weight as expressed in the legislation of May 26/27, 1652

For several centuries coin weight had been expressed in royal decrees in terms that were based on practical considerations of economics and the limitations of available technology. In terms of economics, the definition of coin weight had to address the value of the metal used, be it gold, silver or copper, while in terms of technology the definition had to be within parameters that could be reasonably and efficiently followed by artisans using available machinery. Working under the implicit assumption that minters would employ quality control techniques that would produce a product which was as standardized as possible, Ferdinand and Isabella of Spain decreed in 1497 that 67 reales would be cut from a *marco* of silver of a specific fineness; similarly, Elizabeth I of England decreed in 1601 that 62 shillings would be cut from a troy pound of sterling silver. By wording decrees in this manner the monarchs were actually legislating the value of silver; in the case of Elizabeth, a troy pound of sterling silver was rated at 62 shillings. In these promulgations there was no specific authorized weight for an individual coin, simply an average weight mathematically calculated from the number of coins authorized to be produced per unit of metal. Generally, any detailed specifications affecting coin weight, such as an allowance for wastage, were not a part of a public legal promulgation but rather were included in a private contractual agreement between the ruler and the minter known as a mint indenture.

In Massachusetts Bay the situation was different in that all aspects of the coining agreement were part of the public record and were included in the legislation passed by the General Court. Thus, the minter's fee was not part of a private mint indenture but rather, it was publicly stated in the 1652 Massachusetts law that the minter would be allowed to retain a fee of one shilling out of every twenty shillings produced. Also, the law did not define coin weight in terms of production per unit of silver but rather precisely defined the weight of an individual coin, stating "euery shilling to weigh three penny Troy weight & lesser peeces proportionably..." (Crosby, p. 38). Thus, it was quite clear a shilling was authorized at a weight of three pennyweight in the troy scale, which is equivalent to 72 grains. Undoubtedly, the legislators considered definitions based on a shilling would be more meaningful to the public than definitions stated in terms of a troy ounce. The same information on mint fees and coin weight could have been worded so that it stated the minter was allowed a fee of 4d per troy ounce of sterling minted and the coin weight defined by simply stating 80d in coinage was to be cut from a troy ounce of sterling, with no further elaboration. Neither of these statements are found in the legislation. By using the shilling rather than the troy ounce as the focus of the definitions, the May 26/27, 1652, Massachusetts Bay Mint Act may be the first English legislation to specifically authorize a weight for an individual silver coin.

Nevertheless, although the act specified an exact weight for a shilling, it is clear from Hull's surviving ledger, the application of the statute was based on the requirement of producing a full 80d in Massachusetts coinage from each troy ounce of sterling, rather than focusing on the requirement of producing every shilling at a uniform weight. It is also clear the legislators understood the concept of production per troy ounce even though they chose to express values in terms of shillings rather than in terms troy ounces. This concept had been used earlier by the General Court when defining the value of sterling for the 1640 Massachusetts Bay tax rate, where sterling had been rated at 5s per troy ounce.[1] Although the 1652 mint legislation did not specifically state the production rate of Massachusetts silver in terms of producing 80d in Massachusetts coinage per troy ounce of sterling, this relationship was clearly understood. Indeed, it was critical to the solvency of the mint since that rate defined the value of silver when minted into Massachusetts money. As long as Spanish silver cob coinage was rated below 80d per troy ounce it would be profitable to mint Massachusetts coinage. In practice, this meant Hull had to be sure he would always be able to mint the required number of coins from an ounce of sterling.

The mint committee wastage allowance of June 20, 1652

Immediately following the passage of the May 27th version of the mint act, Hull was greatly concerned about the reduction in the mint fee. We do not know the specific arguments he used to justify the higher fee. Possibly he was concerned about his ability to produce 80d in coinage at the authorized weight from an ounce of sterling and remain solvent. The legislated mint fee had been reduced from 18d per 20s in the original draft legislation to 12d per 20s in the final act, which equaled a reduction in fees from just over 6d per troy ounce to 4d per troy ounce. If Hull should miscalculate and produce shillings just one grain overweight (that is, 73 instead of 72 grains) he would be loosing 6.66 grains per troy ounce, which would reduce his income by just over 25% from 4d to slightly under 3d per ounce. A similar miscalculation of one grain per coin with 6d coinage would be twice as costly, since twice as many coins would be produced, so Hull's income would be reduced by just over 50% to slightly under 2d per ounce. If the same error were made with threepence coins, the result would be catastrophic resulting in a loss of slightly more than the entire 4d mint fee! Also, Hull may have been concerned about fineness, since any silver that happened to be refined even slightly above the sterling standard would reduce his income. Basically, unlike earlier acts which legislated an average weight but gave minters some tolerance in individual coin weight, the Massachusetts Bay Mint Act specified a precise weight as well as designating an exact fineness. A strict reading of the Massachusetts law could be interpreted as quite onerous to the minter, because there was no tolerance for error at any step in the coining process. Hull may also have been concerned that the time involved and the expenses incurred in assaying and minting coins required a higher remuneration than 12d per 20s. Certainly, Hull was rather vociferous on this issue, complaining to the mint committee that it would be difficult for him to make a profit from this venture based on the specification in the

---

[1] Additionally, the concept of pricing coins based on the value per ounce of silver was used later by the General Court in legislation of October 12, 1682, when the House of Magistrates issued an explanation of an earlier law of May 24th that had stated the eight reales "shall passe amongst us as Currant mony of New England, according to their weight in the present New England Coyne;" (Crosby, p. 84). An October clarification stated eight reales would be paid and received at "Six Shillings and Eight Pence the ounce, troy weight," that is, they were to trade by weight at 80d (6s8d) per troy ounce. Moreover, the concept of the value of coins based on the legislated value of a troy ounce of silver was central to the legislative debate concerning the acceptance of the Proclamation of 1704.

May 26/27, 1652 statute. The minutes of the mint committee from June 20, 1652, alluded to Hull's complaints in their answer to him stating "And that the mint master may not have Just Cawse to Complajne..." (Crosby, p. 40). The committee went on to increase his fee to 15d per 20s minted plus "...a penny in euery ounce allowed for wast...," which, as we have seen, brought his commission back up to 6d per troy ounce. These modifications to the May legislation made during the June 20th mint committee meeting were approved by a vote of the full court during the October 1652 session of the General Court and became amendments to the statute.

Production issues and the application of the wastage allowance

Once the mint went into production several issues surfaced that had not been anticipated in the original legislation. Some issues, such as the lack of legends and other designs on the coins to deter clipping, were legislated to be added to the coins during the October session of the General Court, while other issues, such as those related to consignment acceptance and allowable tolerances, were left to Hull to interpret. In regard to these concerns Hull seems to have made an effort to follow the minting statute but he appears to have modified specifics when he felt it to be necessary.

Hull had to tackle a significant problem that had not been anticipated in the legislation. In England, there was a wastage fee specifically related to the loss of sterling during the melting process. Even though the London mint employed professional melters who specialized in this process and performed their task in special rooms (one room was reserved for gold melts and another for silver melts), it was inevitable that some sterling would vaporize. Silver has a very high melting point (960.8° Celsius or 1761.4° Fahrenheit). It must be melted in an enclosed furnace using a bellows to produce what Georgius Agricola, in his 1556 work on metals, called a "fierce fire" and which Lazarus Ercker, in his 1574 treatise, called a "strong heat" (Agricola, pp. 486-87 and Ecker, 1951, pp. 54-56 and 1683, pp. 51-54). Naturally, there was no way to precisely regulate the fire to the melting temperature. In fact, until the mid-twentieth century the specific melting point of silver was not known because molten silver adsorbs large quantities of oxygen making it difficult to determine the precise moment of melting (Butts, pp. 105-6 and 304-9). However it had long been known that when the temperature rose above the melting point, silver began to volatilize in the form of a pale blue vapor. Although he does not specify the exact quantity of silver being used, Agricola mentioned silver would melt in about an hour (Agricola, p. 487). Undoubtedly, vaporization would begin before all the silver in the crucible was melted. Moreover, if the silver needed to be refined to sterling, it would remain on the heat longer thus causing additional vaporization. Volatization of silver was considered the largest unrecoverable loss in the entire minting process. The standard melting allowance at the London mint seems to have been 3d per pound of sterling or one farthing per ounce, a figure that was in use in 1422 when the pound was the Tower pound and also in 1591 when the pound was the troy pound (Craig, pp. 86 and 127). As this figure comes from the period when the shilling was 96 grains, the one farthing per ounce allowance was equivalent to a loss of two grains per troy ounce.

It was certainly well understood the melt was a critical operation and would be a potential problem in Massachusetts Bay since there were neither professional melters nor any special melting facilities. The original Massachusetts Bay legislation indirectly addressed this concern by stating the actual melting and refining process would take place in the presence of the customer at the time of the deposit. Immediately thereafter the customer would be given a receipt for the quantity of refined sterling resulting from the melt. In this chain of events the sterling loss from the melt would not be a factor, because it would be an unrecorded loss at the customer's expense before any consignment receipt had been written. However, as we shall see in the production section, Hull found it impossible to follow this procedure. Basically, we shall see from the ledger records it was not economical for Hull to do a melt on request. Rather, he simply performed sample or spot assays on the consignment, gave the customer a receipt specifying the weight and value of the consignment based on the fineness of the assay and then backlogged the consignment until there was enough silver to perform a more economical large melt (see Chapters Seven and Ten below for details). Since Hull had to change the order of operations from what had been directed in the statute, he had to consider how to recover the costs related to sterling loss during the melting process since the weight on the customer's receipt reflected the pre-melt weight of the consignment.

Concurrently, Hull needed to establish some guidelines in relation to acceptable weight variation for minted coins, because it was clear product loss would not allow an average weight of 72 grains per shilling if 80d were to be minted from a troy ounce of sterling. In England there were allowable tolerances in minting specifications issued in the regulations for the trial of the pyx. The pyx, derived from the Greek word *pyxis*, meaning a container or a vase, refers to a chest in which the mint secured samples of the coins it produced. The coins were submitted to an independent testing group who verified if they were within allowable parameters for weight and fineness. The official weights from the office of the Exchequer were used to test coin weight while members of the goldsmith guild tested the coins for fineness. From the period of Elizabeth in 1560 the tolerance, or as they called it, the remedy, was two pennyweight (24 grains) per troy pound (12 ounces) of sterling. This equaled a tolerance of two grains per troy ounce of coinage in both fineness and in weight (Craig, pp. 394-407 and Challis, *Tudor Coinage,* pp. 25-27, and 322-25). Although this was not meant to be a license to reduce the standards by that amount it was sometimes interpreted as such by the minters (Challis, *Tudor Coinage,* pp. 134-40). In Massachusetts Bay there was no independent testing of the coinage, thus no formal tolerances were set. However, it is clear Hull needed to have some tolerance guidelines. It would be impossible for him to make all shillings average 72 grains because of sterling loss during the minting process, so he needed some measure to determine if a coin was simply too light to issue.

It appears Hull dealt with both the tolerance issue and the melt loss problem by recourse to the wastage allowance. Hull's ledger confirms he understood the wastage allowance as an additional 1d supplement to the mint fee and that he charged the 1d fee to his clients (see Chapter Four for details). Hull did not consider this an allowance for waste but an actual fee to his customer that brought the mint charge up to 6d per troy ounce of sterling, which was the charge he had proposed to the Magistrates when the mint act was first drafted in May of 1652. He did not consider the 1d fee a remuneration for waste because, when we examine the production records in the ledger we see Hull dealt with remuneration for waste in a different manner. Hull not only collected the 1d for waste as part of his fee but he also interpreted the 1d per troy ounce wastage allowance as authorizing the mint a six grain wastage allowance per troy ounce of sterling minted (since six grains in sterling equaled 1d in Massachusetts coinage). That is, it appears Hull charged the allowance as an outright fee and secondly he used it as a guide to create an average tolerance standard that allowed the loss of six grains per ounce of sterling minted.

Hull did not use the six grains per troy ounce loss as an outside tolerance but rather took it to be the acceptable average weight. In effect, it appears Hull used the wastage allowance to justify a reduction in the legal average weight for Massachusetts coinage so that he could produce 80d in coinage that would weigh a total of 474 grains of sterling. This was a six grains reduction from the original May 26/27 statute, which required 80d to weigh a full troy ounce of 480 grains. Based on this revision whereby 80d in coins could be produced from 474 grains of sterling, the average weight of a shilling calculates to 71.1 grains (for the other denominations: 6d is 35.55 grains, 3d is 17.775 grains and 2d is 11.85 grains). This total six grains allowance was somewhat more generous than the British allowance, which equaled two grains per ounce for the sterling lost in the melt and an additional two grains per ounce tolerance or remedy during the trial of the pyx. The pyx tolerance was not specifically meant to be an allowance but some minters treated it as such. As shown below, this six grains weight reduction was slightly more (approximately 0.44d or 2.64 grains more) than what Hull needed to produce an average of 80d per troy ounce of sterling. It appears in using an allowance of six grains per troy ounce of sterling Hull set 71.1 grains as an average weight for each 12d in coinage. Thus, a shilling would average 71.1 grains with some shillings lighter and some heavier, however as long as Hull kept to this average it seems he felt he was working within the parameters of the coinage legislation.

Unfortunately it is not easy to verify production weight using surviving examples of Massachusetts silver. It has long been thought most Massachusetts silver was clipped or filed down after it entered circulation. Indeed, there are several examples that prove this to be true, especially "large planchet" shillings clipped down to small planchet size. There are also several examples of cut shillings used for small change (see Martin and Pietri). However, some past comments on post-emission clipping were based on any clipping mark found on a coin, since it was thought all coins had been minted from round planchets. We now know all varieties except the small planchet Pine Tree shillings were cut out of strips. It is also clear that weight control at the mint was accomplished by clipping. Thus, we find several examples, as in the Stack's catalogue of the Hain Family Collection by Michael Hodder, where it is apparent the clipping was performed at the mint. On just one page of the catalogue, page 79, we find two excellent examples, lots 89 and 92 are both Noe 1 Pine Tree "large planchet" shillings showing heavy clip marks on the sides but displaying some unstamped planchet at the top and bottom [figures 22-23]. Although they are clipped, the examples are actually heavy weighing 73.6 and 72.8 grains respectively. If this had been post-emission clipping surely the unstamped blank areas of the planchet would have been clipped off leaving the coin more round and less suspicious when being passed; further the coins would have been clipped below the 72 grains weight. It seems most probable the clipping was done at the mint when the coins were originally cut out from a silver strip as part of the weight inspection and control process. Thus, some examples of Massachusetts silver that exhibit clip marks may still reflect their original emission weight. However, there are many pitfalls in simply using the weight of surviving coins. In addition to wear from circulation and post-emission clipping, several surviving coins have been salvaged from the sea or have been uncovered after being buried underground, resulting in corrosion, pitting and other problems affecting coin weight. Additionally, many recorded weights for surviving coins have not been measured under exacting conditions and may be somewhat inaccurate. Realizing these problems it seems quite difficult to derive fully accurate information on the emission weight of surviving examples.

We must certainly be cautious when attempting to derive accurate emission weight from surviving Massachusetts silver. However, I assume survivors in the best condition will most closely approximate the original emission weight. Therefore, they can assist in determining if there is any correlation between the surviving coins and the 71.1 grains per shilling average weight derived from a six grains per troy ounce weight allowance. I have made a brief study of survivor weight limited to the coins from the 1991 American Numismatic Society exhibition organized by Tony Terranova and cataloged by John M. Kleeberg which was prepared in conjunction with the Coinage of the Americans Conference on Money of Pre-Federal America. These coins represent some of the best extant specimens of Massachusetts silver with fuller strikes and better details than most surviving examples. Also, this exhibition brought together a selection covering almost every die variety in each of the series from the NE to the small planchet Pine Tree coins. Thus the sampling covers the entire production period from the first coins to the last varieties minted. Excluding counterfeit and cut coins, the shillings in this exhibition were as follows: 11 NE shillings (items 1-11 at a total of 776 grains) with a mean average weight of 70.545 grains, the heaviest example was at 72.3 grains and the lightest was at 66.7 grains; 10 Willow Tree shillings (items 13-22 at a total of 698.7 grains) with a mean average weight of 69.87 grains, the heaviest example was at 71.7 grains and the lightest was at 67.7 grains; 51 Oak Tree shillings (items 26-55, excluding item 51 at a total of 2077.6 grains) with a mean average weight of 71.64 grains, the heaviest example was at 74.8 grains and the lightest was at 69.1 grains; 27 "large planchet" Pine Tree shillings (items 79-105 at a total of 1911.3 grains) with a mean average weight of 70.78 grains, the heaviest example was at 73.8 grains and the lightest was at 67.5 grains; and 22 small planchet Pine Tree shillings (items 108-129 at a total of 1549.6 grains) with a mean average weight of 70.436 grains, the heaviest example was at 75.5 grains and the lightest was at 66.7 grains. Overall this calculates to 99 shillings at a total of 7013.2 grains with a mean average weight of 70.84 grains per shilling. These COAC exhibition examples are among the best available coins and thus represent a sample that is about as close as we can come to survivors that retain their original weight. The average weight at 70.84 grains is quite close to the 71.1 grains based on a six grains per troy ounce wastage allowance. Thus, it seems probable shillings in the range of 71.1 grains may represent survivors at the original issuing weight.

When this book was in the final stages of proofing, Stack's catalogue of *The Hain Family Collection of Massachusetts Silver Coins* appeared. This is an extensive collection of premier examples from all varieties of Massachusetts silver. I have done a weight analysis of the shillings, excluding lots 16, 28, 35, 119, 129, 130 and 139 because they were holed, counterfeit, displayed what was clearly post-emission clipping or were otherwise suspect. This left 122 shillings for the sample reported below, of which 35, or close to 30%, were also in the COAC exhibition. The totals are as follows: 3 NE shillings (lots 1-3 at a total of 213.6 grains) with a mean average weight of 71.2 grains, the heaviest example was at 72.1 grains and the lightest was at 69.8 grains; 8 Willow Tree shillings (lots 4-11 at a total of 546.6 grains) with a mean average weight of 68.325 grains, the heaviest example was at 71.7 grains and the lightest was at 62.7 grains; 38 Oak Tree shillings (lots 12-52, excluding lots

16, 28 and 35, at a total of 2672.9 grains) with a mean average weight of 70.339 grains, the heaviest example was at 74.6 grains and the lightest was at 61.0 grains; 40 "large planchet" Pine Tree shillings (lots 88-130, excluding lots 119, 129 and 130, at a total of 2744.5 grains) with a mean average weight of 68.6125 grains, the heaviest example was at 73.8 grains and the lightest was at 63.7 grains; and 33 small planchet Pine Tree shillings (lots 131-164 excluding 139 as questionable, at a total of 2295.4 grains) with a mean average weight of 69.557 grains, the heaviest example was at 75.5 grains and the lightest was at 62.7 grains. Overall this calculates to 122 shillings at a total of 8473.0 grains with a mean average weight of 69.45 grains per shilling. This is just 1.4 grains below the COAC average of 70.85 grains. The difference may, in part, be due to circulation wear, since several Hain collection examples exhibit some wear and a few have scratch marks, but in almost all cases they are graded very fine or better. It is quite interesting to see the mean average weight of the shillings in both the COAC exhibition, at 70.85 grains and the Hain collection, at 69.54 grains, is much closer to 71.1 grains than it is to 72 grains. The coins in the COAC and Hain catalogues represent many of the best extant specimens and they corroborate the interpretation that Hull used the six grains per troy ounce wastage allowance to produce shilling with an average weight of 71.1 grains.

Actual wastage and the average coin weight from the mint production records

Assuming Hull did use 71.1 grains as the mean average weight for a shilling, we can then estimate the amount of silver per troy ounce that was actually lost or wasted in the minting process using the information provided in the surviving ledger. Hull interpreted the wastage allowance as authorizing six grains per troy ounce for waste and from the surviving coins it appears he took the full six ounces, reducing the average weight of a shilling from 72 grains to 71.1 grains. However, this does not necessarily mean Hull actually lost the entire six grains per troy ounce.

In the surviving ledger we can gain insights into just how much silver Hull actually lost during a production run. The mint production records for 1679 are more revealing in this regard than the records from any of the other years, since during 1679, Hull included in his ledger both the quantity of silver minted into coins and the total value of coins produced from that silver. During the final years of the mint Hull based his mint fee on a percentage of the value of the coins minted. He took a predetermined amount from each 20s of coins produced. That amount was his entire remuneration; it included his mint fee, the wastage allowance and any extra coinage from production over 80d per troy ounce. In earlier years Hull had simply recorded in his ledger the quantity of silver deposited and the return to be given to the customer without recording the quantity of coins produced or exactly what income he made from the transaction. Only in the later entries do we have the exact weight of the silver consigned and the precise value of the coins produced from that sterling.

I have used four of the six consignments recorded for 1679 in Hull's ledger in the following calculations. A small consignment from November 8, 1679, for coinage from 56 ounces of sterling has been excluded because the quantity of silver is questionable since Hull stated he was reducing the quantity by two troy ounces as the silver was not of sterling fineness. It is not clear if this reduction was an educated guess by Hull or the result of an assay. Also, I did not include a consignment from August 3-4, 1679, for coinage from 1306.75 troy ounces of sterling for Hull did not include the value of the coins produced from that silver. What I have included were the following: a consignment placed on November 20, 1678, and completed on February 18, 1679, for 1292.5 ounces of sterling used to produce £433 3s in Massachusetts silver; a consignment of February 24, 1679, that was completed on March 12th for 400 ounces of sterling used to produce £133 18s; a consignment of April 11, 1679, that was completed on July 21st for 564.5 ounces of sterling used to produce £189 2s; and a consignment of November 21, 1679, that was completed on December 21st for 770.5 ounces of sterling used to produce £258 11s. The combined total of these four consignments represents 3027.5 troy ounces of sterling used to produce £1014 14s in Massachusetts coinage. This averages out to a production rate of just under 80.44d (or more precisely 80.438645d) in Massachusetts coinage per troy ounce of sterling. From this it is clear Hull was producing more than 80d in coinage per troy ounce of sterling. Hull seems to have averaged 80.44d which would yield an additional .44d in income per troy ounce of silver minted into Massachusetts coinage. Obviously, Hull could not have consistently produced more than 80d per troy ounce of sterling unless he interpreted the wastage allowance as authorizing shillings at a weight that averaged below 72 grains.

I shall review the 1679 consignments to see what we can discover about average weight and actual sterling loss during the production run. For simplicity, I have assumed all of coins produced in these four consignments were shillings. If some portion of the coinage was in smaller denomination coins, the number of coins produced would differ but the per unit weight and wastage results would be the same, since all the denominations were proportional and the wastage actually refers to grains lost per 12d of coinage rather than specifically to a shilling. For example, the facts from Hull's ledger state 3027.5 troy ounces of sterling were used to produce £1014 14s in Massachusetts coinage. Precisely how that coinage may have been distributed between shillings and lower denomination coinage is unknown. If the entire amount were in shillings it would total 20,294 shillings, if in threepence the number of coins would be quadrupled, however the overall weight per every 12d in coinage would not change, as the weight per value figures are the known facts taken from the Hull ledger. Obviously, the weight per value would remain the same no matter what combination of threepence, sixpence and shilling coins were used, as long as the total added up to £1014 14s in coinage produced from 3027.5 troy ounces of sterling. Thus, for purposes of estimating the actual wastage and then calculating an average coin weight, it is simpler to assume the entire run was in shillings rather than create some artificial divisions among the three denominations of coinage. Essentially a shilling is used here to represent 12d in coinage. Furthermore, the four consignments under discussion were from 1679, during the final years of the mint, and certainly reflect the period when the majority, if not all of the coinage production, was in small planchet shillings produced on a screw press.[2]

Assuming only shillings were produced, the four consignments would combine to a total of 20,294 Massachusetts shillings from 3027.5 troy ounces of sterling. The next step is to calculate the weight of an individual shilling. If one assumes there was absolutely no waste or loss of silver at all during the entire minting process the 20,294 shillings produced from the 3027.5 troy ounces of sterling (that is, 1,453,200 grains), would yield an average weight

---

[2] Some additional comments concerning the time period when Pine Tree threepence and sixpence coins may have been minted are found below in Chapter Eight on page 96.

of 71.6 grains (or exactly 71.607371 grains) per shilling. We have seen the authorized weight of a shilling was 72 grains. Certainly, Hull was averaging less than 72 grains, because with absolutely no waste a shilling from the four 1679 production runs averaged only 71.6 grains. Further, the 71.6 grains average is undoubtedly too high, since contemporary technology did not allow for production with absolutely no loss of product. Interestingly, even this highest end weight estimate suggests Hull was allowing for over two grains of waste per troy ounce. At two grains per ounce the maximum acceptable loss from 72 grains per shilling would be 71.7 grains. It seems clear that Hull was using a wastage allowance well beyond two grains per troy ounce.

The 71.6 grains per shilling average assumes every grain of the 3027.5 troy grains of sterling consigned to the mint found its way into one of the coins and therefore must be too high for an average weight. Obviously, some quantity of silver was actually wasted in the minting process at Massachusetts Bay. By waste I mean sterling silver that was lost to the consignment during the production run. At each step in the processing of a consignment of sterling into coinage there was the possibility of some product loss. As we have seen, the most significant unrecoverable loss was from vaporization during the melting process. Some smaller amounts of sterling could also be lost at other steps. There was always the possibility of some loss when ladling the silver from the melting pot and pouring it into the wet sand molds or when rolling the molded strips to the specified thickness. Obviously a small amount of silver would turn to dust when the planchets were cut. Larger quantities of sterling would be lost if the sharp edges on the newly cut planchets were filed down and even more sterling would be removed from the production run from leftover planchet stock called scissel. Scissel could be remelted along with defective planchets in a second pass, but at some point there would be some scissel remaining that could not be used for the consignment but had to be put in Hull's inventory. Again there could be some small loss when the planchet was struck with the dies. Most of this loss, other than the vaporized sterling, was recoverable by treating the tools and work surfaces with mercury. Mercury will attract silver and over a few days it will form an amalgam. Once the amalgam is heated the mercury will vaporize leaving only the silver. We can assume Hull used this process since his ledger records the purchase of 21 pounds of mercury in 1677. However, even this recovered silver would be lost to the consignment, for the recovery process would only be performed after a production run had been completed. Basically, this recovered silver would simply be additional inventory for Hull; it would not be reflected in the weight of the coins produced from the consignment.

Certainly, like all other mints, the Massachusetts Bay Mint lost some silver as waste during the minting process. From the above ledger records the average weight of a shilling from the 1679 production runs was 71.6 grains if there was absolutely no silver loss. However, we have seen that Hull interpreted the wastage allowance of 1d per troy ounce as giving him a remedy or tolerance of six grains of sterling per troy ounce making the average weight of a shilling 71.1 grains. If we assume an average weight of about 71.1 grains per shilling we can surmise Hull sustained an actual loss of about three grains of sterling per troy ounce during the production run. At a loss of three grains per troy ounce the total amount of sterling lost from the four consignments would be 18.921875 troy ounces (that is, 9,082.5 grains). If that quantity of sterling was actually lost as waste it would not be present in the 20,294 shillings that were minted from the consigned sterling. In order to estimate the actual weight of an average shilling from these consignments, the lost or wasted sterling would need to be subtracted from the 3027.5 troy ounces of sterling (that is, 1,453,200 grains) that were originally consigned to the mint. The shillings would actually weigh 3,008.5718 troy ounces (that is, 1,444,117.5 grains) which yields an average weight of a shilling of just about 71.1 grains (or precisely, 71.159825 grains).[3]

Thus, if one assumes a 71.1 grains average weight per shilling, the 1679 production records indicate an estimated actual production loss of just a little more or less than three grains of silver per ounce. This assumes Hull produced as many coins as possible per troy ounce of silver while keeping the average weight close to what I suspect he interpreted as the minimum standard, based on a wastage allowance of six grains per ounce. Thus, from surviving examples it seems Hull used a six grains per troy ounce allowance, which meant 71.1 grains was his standard for an average shilling. Moreover, it appears that during production he actually lost about three grains per troy ounce, which allowed him a yield averaging 80.44d per troy ounce of sterling.

It should be remembered that an estimated loss of three grains per troy ounce at the Massachusetts Bay Mint refers to any sterling lost from the consignment, including silver that was recovered at the end of the production process. This represents all sterling that did not end up in the coins minted from a specific consignment of sterling deposited in the mint. I suspect some, if not most, of this waste was recoverable and found its way into Hull's inventory. Loss at the London mint referred to sterling that was vaporized or otherwise unrecoverable; it did not include recoverable sterling, which was simply added to the next melt. Since melts at the Massachusetts Mint were for specific consignors, sterling lost from one consignment could not be recovered by adding it to the next consignment. Thus, the loss of a little more or less than three grains of sterling per troy ounce at Massachusetts Bay is higher than the London melt allowance of a loss of two grains (the actual loss at London may have been less), but they do not measure the same thing.

If the average output of these four consignments from 1679 could be generalized as an estimate of production rates from earlier years, it appears Hull was able to produce coinage at a rate of close to 80.44d per troy ounce, allowing him an extra income of 0.44d per ounce. Furthermore, if we assume Hull tried to keep the average weight of a shilling close to 71.1 grains, we may speculate that during the production run on average Hull lost about three grains per ounce of sterling as waste.

In the previous chapter it was explained that Hull calculated his fee of 6d per troy ounce based on a total return of 80d per ounce of sterling. Any actual return above 80d per ounce was additional income for Hull, hence Hull's income was more than the total of the fees. Basically, the customer's return was a stable rate whereby the customer received 74d in coins per ounce of sterling. Hull would then receive the remainder, which would come to 6d if he produced 80d in coinage per ounce of sterling, but it could be higher or lower based on his production rates. The extant data show Hull was able to average about 80.44d in coinage per ounce of sterling, which would give him a total return averaging about 6.44d per ounce.

---

[3] Stated as a formula this would be: weight of the silver consigned to the mint = weight of the finished coins + weight of the silver lost in the minting process.

Chapter 6

The Relative Value of Massachusetts and British Silver Coinage

Fineness and weight: The "new" sterling alloy and the two pence per shilling reduction mentioned in the 1652 Mint Act

The minting specifications discussed in the Massachusetts coinage act of 1652 and in the related mint committee documents were based on three factors. First, and most obvious, was the face value of the coinage. Massachusetts silver coins were denominated in English monetary units of 3d, 6d and 1s (1s = 12d), with a 2d denomination added in 1662. Related to the face value of the coin were two crucial factors that defined the intrinsic value of the coin, namely fineness and weight. Pure silver is rather soft and not practical for coins since it would wear down quickly. In order to make silver more durable it is combined (alloyed) with other metals. During the seventeenth and eighteenth centuries each country, or sometime individual mints or cities, defined their own ratio of precious metal to alloy in minting silver and gold coins. Therefore, the weight of a coin alone would not give its precise value, for one needed to know the percent of alloy (sometimes called impurities) in the silver. The purity of silver is known as its fineness and is measured in millesimals.

1. Sterling fineness, debasements and coin weight

From the reign of William the Conqueror in 1066, and probably going back even earlier to the later Anglo-Saxon era, the alloy for British silver coinage had been set at a standard known as sterling fineness. Sterling referred to an alloy in which 925 parts pure silver were combined with 75 parts copper resulting in a product containing a 92.5% silver content expressed as 925 or .925 fine silver. Although we now measure silver content in millesimals, in earlier periods other measurement systems were used. During the seventeenth and eighteenth centuries the measurement system in use was the troy weight scale. The troy system was created at the medieval fairs in Troyes, France, where it was used for weighing precious metals. During the later Middle Ages the Troyes fair became the most significant gold and silver exchange in medieval Europe, consequently troy weight became the standard for the international bullion trade. During the early sixteenth century the British gradually adopted the troy weight system to facilitate international exchange. Between July 24th and November 5th of 1526, the London mint updated their measurement system from the Tower pound, which was equal to 5,400 troy grains, to the heavier and more widely used troy pound which equaled 5,760 troy grains. (Ruding, vol. 1, pp. 303-6 and Craig, pp. 102-3). The troy weight scale differs from the more familiar avoirdupois scale, which is used for copper and other non-precious metals. Although both systems use the pennyweight measure, at 24 grains per pennyweight, the avoirdupois weight system defines a pound as sixteen ounces while the troy system contains only twelve ounces per pound. The units in the troy scale are as follows:

01 blank	[approximately .0000043 grain]
24 blanks = 1 perit	[approximately .0001041 grain]
20 perits = 1 droit	[approximately .0020833 grain]
24 droits = 1 mite	[.05 grain]
20 mites = 1 grain (gr.)	
24 grains = 1 pennyweight (dwt.)	
20 pennyweight = 1 ounce (oz.)	
12 ounces = 1 troy pound (lb.)	

Using the troy nomenclature sterling fineness was defined as 11 ounces and 2 pennyweight of fine silver per troy pound. This assumed the additional 18 pennyweight would be copper to produce a troy pound of sterling silver.

During the reigns of Henry VIII and Edward VI both silver and gold coins were debased in an attempt to increase revenues. The process started with a mint indenture of May 16, 1542, debasing silver coinage from .925 to .771 fineness. As the debasement continued silver went far below the sterling standard with the lowest point occurring in an order issued on April 30, 1551, which remained in effect until September, authorizing silver coins that were only .250 fine silver. In other words the coins were three quarters copper! During the end of the reign of Edward VI the standard came close to sterling at 11 oz. 1 dwt. of fine silver per troy pound, that is a .9208 fineness. Under Mary silver coinage contained 11 oz. of fine silver per troy pound, which was a fineness of .9166 and then under Elizabeth silver coinage was restored to the sterling standard. On October 8, 1560, Elizabeth officially put her seal to a mint indenture for a new coinage that stated silver coins were to be of sterling fineness and were to be minted at 5s per ounce of sterling (or 60s per troy pound). This meant a shilling would contain 96 grains (or 4 dwt.) of sterling silver. Production of the new coinage commenced in February of 1561 and continued into 1578. In the mint indenture of April 19, 1578, the fineness was lowered slightly for the next four and a half years but it was returned to sterling fineness again in the indenture of January 30, 1583. By her order of July 29, 1601, the fineness remained at .925 sterling silver but Elizabeth reduced the weight of the shilling from 60 per troy pound by authorizing them to be produced at 62 per troy pound, effectively reducing the average weight of a shilling from 96 grains to 92.9 grains. This weight reduction was continued under James I and Charles I and was renewed by the new government created during the Commonwealth. A Parliamentary act of July 17, 1649, stated a Commonwealth shilling was to weigh exactly 3 pennyweight, 20 grains, 18 mites, 1 droit and 10 perits in sterling silver, which is very close to 92.90312 grains (Feavearyear, pp. 46-87, Craig, pp. 106-32, Challis, *Tudor Coinage,* pp. 44-198 and 303-25; Ruding, vol. 1, pp. 342-43, 349, 350, 357, 362-63, 410-11 and Firth, vol. 2, pp. 191-94).

In the final draft of the Massachusetts coinage legislation of May 1652 the third article stated:

> And further the sajd master of the mint aforesjd is heereby Required to cojne
> new
> all the sajd mony of good Silver and of the Just allay of$_\wedge$sterling English
>
> two
> mony, & for valew to stampe ~~three~~ pence in a shilling of lesser vallew then the p^{r}sent English Cojne & the lesser peeces p^{r}oportionably... . (Crosby, p. 34)

This article clearly required Massachusetts silver to be of sterling fineness but mentioned a just alloy of new sterling money. In the quote given above the word "new" is an interlinear insertion added to the original draft. The phrase "new sterling English mony" probably does not refer to the restitution of the sterling standard by Queen Elizabeth about a century earlier in 1560, nor does it refer to the mint indenture of January 1583 restoring the sterling standard after a four year hiatus. More likely, it refers to the weight reduction of 1601 that had been recently renewed by the new Commonwealth government on July 17, 1649, whereby silver coins were of sterling fineness but reduced in weight. If we interpret the word "new" to refer to the weight reduction renewal of three years earlier it would mean the standard used by the Massachusetts Bay legislators for the British shilling would have been 92.9 grains of sterling silver, as was then in use in Britain. The word "new" was added to clarify that they were not using the older, pre-1601, weight standard of four pennyweight (96 grains) per shilling.

2. The "two pence" reduction in Massachusetts Bay

However, rather than minting coins at the British standard of 92.9 grains of sterling per shilling, which priced a troy ounce of sterling silver at 62d (5s2d), the Massachusetts Bay act further explained the General Court would reduce the intrinsic value of the Massachusetts shilling. The text originally stated the Massachusetts shilling would be reduced by "three" pence but the word "three" was then crossed out and replaced by inserting the word "two."

The corrected "two pence" reduction has caused problems in interpreting how the legislators came to a decision on the ultimate weight of the Massachusetts shilling (for example, see Sumner, "Coin Shilling," p. 251). The London mint defined a penny as 7 grains, 14 mites, 20 droits, 2 perits and 12 blanks in sterling. This equalled 7.741926 grains of sterling. A two pence reduction per Massachusetts shilling would lessen the weight of a Massachusetts coin by 15.483852 grains resulting in a Massachusetts shilling of 77.416148 grains. Alternatively, if the Massachusetts Bay legislators had instituted a three pence reduction, the weight per Massachusetts shilling would be 69.674222 grains. On the other hand, based on the older British standard of 96 grains, there would be 8 grains of sterling silver per penny. A two pence reduction per shilling would calculate to a reduction of 16 grains which would give a weight of 80 grains per shilling; using the three pence reduction the weight per shilling would be 72 grains.

Interestingly, the two pence reduction as stated in the Massachusetts Bay Mint act of 1652 does not correspond to the weight specified for the Massachusetts shilling in article six of that act, where it stated [with the word troj inserted in the final draft to clarify the text]:

> to   troj:
> ...euery shilling weigh~~ing~~ ~~the~~ three penny_∧weight & lesser peeces
> proportionably. (Crosby, p. 34)

This explicitly specifies the shilling was to be minted at three pennyweight in the troy scale (72 grains) which does not reflect a two pence reduction at either the older weight of 96 grains of sterling per shilling or at the newer weight at 92.9 grains per coin. The only calculation that matches this weight is a three pence reduction based on the older weight of 96 grains per shilling. However, the legislation specifically stated they were using the new sterling standard, which was 92.9 grains. This lack of precision has caused confusion because it has been assumed these statements were an explanation as to how the General Court arrived at a valuation for their coinage. This assumption seems highly unlikely, not only because of the imprecision in the definition but also because silver was considered to be a commodity and was priced at a specific value per troy ounce. I suspect the weight of the Massachusetts shilling was derived by increasing the value of sterling from the then current British value of 62d (5s2d) per troy ounce of sterling to 80d (6s8d) [in Massachusetts money of account] per troy ounce. This crying-up of silver valued six grains of sterling at 1d or 72 grains per shilling. The terminology specifically stating a troy ounce of sterling would be valued at 80d is not mentioned in the 1652 legislation. However, as mentioned earlier (see Chapter Four), this concept had been used several times by the General Court. Also, in his personal ledger Hull calculated mint returns due to the customer and due to him in mint fees based on a troy ounce of sterling at 80d minus the mint fees and wastage allowance. Thus, although it was not specifically stated in the legislation, it seems fairly clear the General Court calculated the value of silver coinage based on the price per troy ounce of silver.

In the 1652 mint act it seems the three pence reduction, which was then revised to a two pence reduction, was simply a rough estimate of the relative value of the proposed Massachusetts shilling. At 72 grains (3 dwt.) per shilling the General Court calculated the Massachusetts shilling at about 10d in British coinage, hence the 2d reduction. When the Commissioners of the Royal Mint wrote a report concerning Massachusetts coinage on January 15, 1685, they stated they had examined 12d, 6d and 3d pieces of Massachusetts silver and found them to be of sterling alloy but discovered them to be lighter in weight that English coinage by about 21 grains per shilling,[1] which the commissioners estimated at nearly 2 pence and 3 farthings less per shilling (actually, it would be 2 pence and 2.8 farthings) or just about 22.5% below the value of British silver coins. The report stated:

---

[1] Based on examples at the full authorized weight of both an English shilling at 92.9 grains and a Massachusetts shilling at 72 grains, the Massachusetts shilling would be exactly 20.9 grains lighter.

Wee haue examened ye 12 pene, 6[d], 3[d] pieces coyned at ye Mint in Boston in N E aforesaid, for weight & allay, & do finde as to ye allay it is equal to his Majesties silver Coyns of England, but different in weight, being Less by about 21 grains upon the shilling, & so proportionally in the other Coyns from his Majestys shilling Coyne, which is near two pence three farthings upon the shilling, & is about 22 1/2 per cent;....(Crosby, p. 88)

There is no doubt the Massachusetts Bay legislators authorized the shilling at three pennyweight (72 grains). They certainly understood this was valuing sterling at 80d per troy ounce (or 1d = 6 grains of sterling) and realized this would be very close to a 22.5% reduction from the British standard of 92.9 grains per shilling, which equaled 62d per troy ounce of sterling (or 1d = 7.74 grains of sterling). However, the Massachusetts reduction was not derived by calculating a percentage reduction from the British standard, rather it was based on a revaluation of a troy ounce of sterling. Indeed, a value of 80d may have been accepted because the General Court was looking for a reduction in the area of 25% and 80d was the only valuation in that range that was evenly divisible into one troy ounce (480 grains). This valued six grains of sterling at a penny, making the weight of any denomination coin they wished to produce (either to a whole or even to a half penny) easily calculated in whole grains. However, the legislators understood the Massachusetts shilling would have an intrinsic value that was very close to 2 pence and 2.8 farthings (or 2.7d) less than a British shilling.[2] In the 1652 mint act the legislators expressed this differential to the whole penny. At first, in the original draft, they rounded the number up expressing the differential as a three pence reduction. However, after further consideration they amended the draft and rounded the number down to two pence, even though the actual intrinsic value of a Massachusetts shilling at 2.7d less than a British shilling, was closer to a three pence than it was to a two pence reduction. Apparently the Massachusetts Bay legislators felt that minimizing the magnitude of the reduction would be to their advantage, possibly helping to make the coins more readily accepted.

The 22.5% and 25% differentials

The lack of clarity in the pence reduction statement in the 1652 act has caused confusion in determining how contemporaries perceived and calculated the difference between the Massachusetts and British shillings. The 22.5% differential, based on a comparison of a British shilling of 92.9 grains and a Massachusetts shilling of 72 grains, was used by Edward Randolph, the British informer and the most vociferous critic of Massachusetts Bay. In a report to the Lords of Trade and Plantations made on October 12, 1676, Randolph stated concerning Massachusetts silver, "Their money is of the standard of England for finenesse, the shillings weigh three pennyweight troy, in value of English money ninepence farthing, and the smaller coins proportionable." Based on a British shilling of 92.9 grains, nine pence and one farthing would equal 71.610415 grains, or very close to the Massachusetts weight of

---

[2] An exact 22.5% reduction would yield a coin of 71.9975 grains of sterling which is just .0025 grain less than the fully authorized weight of 72 grains

72 grains. This was also the comparison made by the Commissioners of the Royal Mint in their report on an assay of Massachusetts silver, written on January 15, 1685. As mentioned above, they discussed the reduction as being nearly two pence three farthings, which yields a final value for the Massachusetts shilling of nine pence and one farthing. Thus, both Randolph and the Royal mint understood the differential to be 22.5%.

However, it appears Massachusetts silver regularly traded at a 25% reduction in relation to British silver. As early as May 12, 1654, there is reference to this differential in the deliberations of the General Court in relation to prohibiting the exportation of Massachusetts silver from the Commonwealth. The statement explained Massachusetts silver coinage was intended for internal use only and not for payments outside the Commonwealth of Massachusetts Bay, since outside the Commonwealth individuals would sustain a loss of 25%. The legislation further explained the only way an individual could recover such a loss was to sell the purchased goods locally at an oppressively high price, hence the need to prohibit exporting Massachusetts coinage. The text stated:

> Whereas, the end of Coyning mony within this Commonwealth is for the more easy managing the traficque thereof within itself, & not Indended to make returnes to other Countrjes, which cannot Advance any proffitt to such as send it, but Rather a fowerth part Losse Vnlesse such persons doe oppresse & extort in the sale of theire goods to make vp the sajd losse... . (Massachusetts Archives, vol. 100, p. 46, no. 350, Crosby, pp. 104-5, also cited in Davis, vol. 1, original edition p. 725, reprint p. 25)

This differential is also mentioned in a set of orders from Britain dated June 9, 1655. The British Commissioners responsible for managing expeditions to America, presented a set of orders and regulations to Robert Wadeson, Captain William Crispin and Thomas Broughton, who were charged with traveling to Massachusetts Bay to acquire £10,000 worth of provisions for the British army and fleet stationed at Jamaica. The fifth of the seven regulations stated:

> 5. You are to take notice that the intrinsic value of New England money is less in weight by one quarter than at London. As for example a shilling in New England is of the same weight as ninepence is at London. Which is mainly to be considered if you take up money. (*Manuscripts of the Duke of Portland,* vol. 2, p. 94 and Sumner, "Coin Shilling," p. 252)

In late April of 1661 we again find this 25% differential mentioned in a petition of John Gifford, who, residing in Massachusetts Bay during the 1650's, had been the principal agent for the Hammersmith Ironworks in Saugus, Massachusetts, from 1650 through 1653, when he became involved in several lawsuits and ended up spending some time in jail. From October of 1658 through April of 1662 Gifford was in England bringing suits against just about everyone connected with the Ironworks enterprise. The summary of an unsigned letter, attributed to him, details several problems with the laws of Massachusetts Bay and contains the earliest mention of illegal activities related to the Massachusetts Mint. Gifford accused the Boston mint of illegally melting British silver to make Massachusetts coinage. He assumed Massachusetts coinage had an intrinsic value that was 25% below the British standard. Hence, a Massachusetts shilling (that is, a 12d coin) was valued at 9d in relation to a British shilling with a value of 12d. By melting British shillings Gifford stated the mint was able to produce 25% more in face value in Massachusetts silver, or, 15d from each British shilling. The summary of the letter in the Calendar of Colonial Papers states:

> they have acted repugnant to the laws of England ; they have allowed the King's coin to be bought and melted down in Boston to be new coined there, by which means they gain threepence in every shilling, and lessen his Majesty's coin a full fourth. (Sainsbury, *Calendar 1661-1668,* item 78 on p. 26. For Gifford see, Hartley, pp. 139-64 and 215-43)

In a small notebook of the British Secretary of State, Sir Joseph Williamson,[3] covering the years 1674-1677 is a recapitulation of the Gifford statement that in Massachusetts Bay British shillings were melted to produce 15d in Massachusetts silver. In an entry called New England dated to May of 1675 Williamson stated:

> They melt down all English money brought in there into their own coin, making every shilling 15d to avoid the carrying it out... .(Sainsbury, *Calendar 1675-1676,* pp. 154-63, item 405 with the quote on p. 156)

The melting of British silver and the 25% differential are also mentioned in an account of Boston by Captain John Wyborne that was read at the committee meeting of the Lords for Trade and Plantations on December 2, 1675. Captain Wyborne had spent three months in Boston in 1673 while his ship, the H.M.S. *Garland,* was being resupplied and refitted. In his narrative on Massachusetts Bay, Captain Wyborne complained of several irregularities, arbitrary laws and resistance to the king's commissioners. Concerning money he stated:

> ...as soon as any English money is brought there, it is melted down into their coin, making of each shilling fifteen-pence to keep it from being carried out again. (Sainsbury, *Calendar 1675-1676,* item 721 on pp. 306-8, with the quote on p. 306)

Another statement referring to a 25% differential was made by the Earl of Carlisle, who had presented a request to the Lords of Trade and Plantations for the establishment of a mint in Jamaica. In reply to this request Henry Slingesby, Master of the London Mint, stated the Earl would need to abide by the British standards for fineness and weight. On June 20, 1679, the Earl replied to the Lords of Trade and Plantations:

> If we should make our coin of the same weight and fineness as the coin of England, we should never keep any money in the Island, which is our principal difficulty. In New England they raise money one fourth, a ninepence goes for twelvepence, which fills them full of money;... . (Sainsbury, *Calendar 1677-1680,* pp. 378-79, item 1030 with the quote on p. 379)

---

[3] Sir Joseph Williamson was a member of the Privy Council and Secretary of State, June 1674 - February 10, 1679.

Lord Thomas Culpepper also used the 25% differential, but he specifically compared the Massachusetts shilling to the old British standard of a shilling at 96 grains. At the conclusion of his tenure as Governor of Virginia, Lord Culpepper visited Boston for about seven weeks from August 24 through about October 15 of 1680 before embarking on his return voyage to London. About a year later, after settling back in London, Culpepper was asked to testify before the Committee of the Lords of Trade and Plantations regarding accusations made by Edward Randolph and others against the government in Massachusetts Bay. On August 9, 1681, Culpepper provided the committee with a list of complaints against the Massachusetts Bay Puritans which included criticisms of the Massachusetts Mint. Culpepper stated:

> As to the mint at Boston I think that, especially as it is managed, it is extremely prejudicial to all the King's subjects in what place soever, that deal with them. They call the piece that they coin a shilling, and it is current in all payments great and small, as, without special contract (in which no one can lose [sic] less than ten per cent.), equal with the English shilling; and this though it is not so fine in itself and weighs but three pennyweight against the English four. It is impossible to prevent the loss by bills of exchange, for they value their bills as they please and exact six per cent. coinage of all silver brought in their mint, to say nothing of loss of time. If therefore it be no longer connived at, it is absolutely necessary that the English shilling be made current there by law or proclamation at sixteenpence, and so proportionally, the coinage made more moderate and speedy.... (Fortescue, *Calendar 1681-1685,* pp. 99-100)

Culpepper felt the mint was poorly managed and slow in filling orders. He did not trust the fineness of Massachusetts silver which he incorrectly thought was "not so fine" as British coinage. However, he correctly stated the Massachusetts shilling was three pennyweight (72 grains) and understood the trading differential between British and Massachusetts silver to be 25% so he incorrectly concluded the British standard was four pennyweight (96 grains). Additionally, Culpepper mentioned the Massachusetts Mint fees, which he calculated at 6%. Actually, based on the negotiations of the June 3, 1675 mint contract renewal, which would have been the fees in effect when Culpepper visited Massachusetts, the total mint fees came to 6.25%, assuming the maximum wastage allowance. However, from Hull's ledger we know the mint fees had been reduced in 1677 by private agreement with the customers to approximately 5% and were further lowered to about 2.5% in 1680. Culpepper also mentioned the value of the British sterling shilling in Massachusetts. The intrinsic value of Massachusetts silver was based on the scale of 6 grains of sterling being equal to 1d in coin, hence a full weight British shillings at 92.9 grains of sterling would have a value of 15.483d in Massachusetts coin. Above, in his discussion of melt value, we have seen John Gifford implied a British shilling would produce 15d in Massachusetts coins. I suspect Gifford had not calculated the grain equivalents of the two coinages but based his statement on the trade value of a British shilling in Massachusetts. At 15d the British shilling was trading at just under a halfpenny (actually, it would be 0.483d) below its intrinsic value. Interestingly, Culpepper claimed the two currencies traded at face value. I suspect this was not usually the case, although it is quite possible some Bostonians took advantage of travelers. As Culpepper incorrectly believed the British standard to be 96 grains of sterling per shilling he calculated the intrinsic value of a British shilling at a full 16d in Massachusetts coinage and felt the Commonwealth of Massachusetts should set the value at that rate.

We also find the 25% trading differential in a paper from the Royal Mint. On September 23, 1686, a document written by the Commissioners of the Royal Mint was sent to the Lords of Trade and Plantations replying to an earlier memorandum that had enumerated reasons for the continuance of a mint in Massachusetts. The fourth point of the earlier memorandum stated, "The Renters of Houses and Land have been paid, and all Goods bought & Sold for many years in New England, by this measure." The measure had been mentioned in the previous point as "the shilling being in value nine pence farthing," (which would be a 22.5% reduction). In their reply the mint commissioners answered the fourth point as follows:

> That their Rents, Houses and Lands, and all Goods, have been negotiated at
> 9^d for a shilling (wch is about 25 per cent less then the money of England,) ...
> as to former Rents & Debts care may be taken that they may be discharged
> at 15^s per pound, wch holds proportion with the current money of England... .
> (Crosby, p. 93)

Thus, the commissioners of the mint, who in January of 1685 had explained Massachusetts coinage was 22.5% below the weight of British coins were stating less than two years later that Massachusetts silver traded 25% below British silver. The memorandum on behalf of a Massachusetts Mint had accurately followed the January 1685 mint paper in calculating the value of a Massachusetts shilling in British coinage at nine pence and one farthing. However, the mint commissioners in their 1686 response to the memorandum calculated a Massachusetts shilling at only 9d, explaining 15 British shillings would equal 20 Massachusetts shillings (20s = £1). The reason for this shift from a 22.5% to a 25% differential seems to be that in their January 1685 document, the Commissioners were explaining precisely how much Massachusetts silver was worth in terms of British coinage based on the authorized weights of the two coinages, so they accurately gave the differential as 22.5%. However, in the September 1686 response they were discussing the differential at which Massachusetts silver traded in daily commerce thus, instead of accepting the actual 22.5% differential they had earlier determined and that had been used in the pro-mint document, the mint commissioners used the 25% differential.

The 25% conversion rate appears to have been the standard rate used in colonial times; it was certainly much easier to calculate than a 22.5% differential. If circulating Massachusetts silver was accepted at face value rather than by weight, the 25% conversion rate may have somewhat offset disparities related to underweight Massachusetts coinage, that had been clipped, filed or washed. Indeed, based on Hull's ledger we can calculate Hull produced an average of 80.44d per troy ounce, which, assuming an actual minting wastage of three grains per troy ounce, yields an average weight of 71.1 grains per shilling for a differential of almost 23% (22.9%). In any event, the 25% differential was not based on an assay of the silver content of newly minted coins but rather was based on the accepted rate at which Massachusetts and British silver were exchanged. Since most Massachusetts transactions did not involve British silver this relationship was not a daily concern. Generally, local cash transactions were made using Spanish American cobs or Massachusetts silver coins. The exchange rate between the British and Massachusetts Bay coinage only came up when there was a necessity to convert from one coinage to the other. This usually occurred when dealing with overseas transactions that were effected through bills of exchange denominated in sterling. Based on the sources cited above, apparently in most transactions requiring a rating of Massachusetts and British silver, a Massachusetts shilling was calculated at nine pence in British coinage (a 25% differential) rather than calculating it at its fully authorized weight which yielded an intrinsic value of nine pence and one farthing (a 22.5% differential). Culpepper insinuated that sometimes the two coinages traded at face value as equals; this was probably a rare occurrence, if it ever happened at all. Obviously, conversion rates were taken to reflect the intrinsic values of these coins. Clearly, as most transactions were calculated at a 25% differential the misperception persisted, and is sometimes found in modern numismatic literature, that Massachusetts silver was authorized and minted at a 25% weight reduction from the British standard.

Part Four

Production Issues at the Massachusetts Mint

Chapter 7

Minting Procedures in Massachusetts Bay

The London mint during the 1660's

There is very little extant documentation concerning the specific procedures followed in producing coins at the Massachusetts Bay Mint. Many basic questions remain unanswered. Therefore, in order to interpret production related information in the Hull ledger, or to deduce production information from the surviving coins, we need to have a basic understanding of the processes used in minting silver coinage during the third quarter of the seventeenth century. Fortunately, the procedures followed in producing silver coins at the London mint during the reign of Charles II are fairly well documented. With the restoration of the monarchy in 1660, Charles was determined to replace Commonwealth era coinage and the older misshapen hammered coinage of his predecessors with a new royal milled coinage. Up to his reign only a few small runs of milled issues had been produced. Charles modernized the mint by implementing state of the art automated screw press technology to produce milled coinage; he first issued his royal milled shillings in 1663.

With the advent of this new technology Charles needed to increase his supply of silver. During the early Stuart era the London mint purchased silver at discounted prices, usually from 4s4d (52d) to 5s (60d) per troy ounce of sterling and then minted 5s2d (62d) in hammered coins from the silver to produce a profit. Government regulations required individuals to sell to the mint a portion of any silver imported into England at the reduced mint rates. Individuals brought in the required minimum amounts, but they did not readily sell additional silver to the mint. Some individuals consigned silver and split the profits with the mint, but in general the mint had problems acquiring enough sterling. Charles II transformed the London mint. In 1666 he instituted a series of tariffs on imported alcoholic beverages to subsidize the minting process. These custom duties were sent to the Exchequer where the money was reserved for the mint. The funds were used to pay mint employee salaries and to purchase silver. To attract as much silver as possible the mint paid the full price of 5s2d (62d) per ounce of sterling. Basically, an individual would bring silver to the mint where it was assayed and weighed. The mint then gave the individual a receipt for the value of the silver and the customer took the receipt to the Exchequer where it was redeemed for cash. In this way the London mint greatly increased its supply of silver and undertook a major initiative to produce milled silver coinage.

The minting process began by melting the purchased silver in a large iron crucible that was placed over a wood charcoal fire in a furnace. The melted silver was assayed and refined to insure it was of sterling purity. Obviously, if it was not of sterling fineness it was adjusted up or down accordingly to achieve the sterling standard of 11 dwt. 2 gr. of pure silver per troy ounce. Next, the molten sterling was ladled out of the crucible and poured into molds that shaped the silver into thin strips. Traditionally wet sand molds had been used but during the late sixtenth and seventeenth centuries, sand was being replaced by stackable cast iron molds. The molten sterling was allowed to cool. Molten silver adsorbs up to ten times its volume in oxygen, however, as it cools the oxygen is vigorously expelled in a process known as "the spitting of silver." Once the temperature of the silver falls below the 960.8°C (1761.4°F) melting point, it begins to spit, usually starting at about 951°C (1744°F) and continuing until solidification at 930°C (1706°F) (Butts, pp. 304-9). Once the silver strips had hardened, they were extracted from the molds and cleaned. The strips were then further flattened to the specific thickness of the coin that was being produced by sending each strip between a pair of wrought iron rollers. The two rollers were set at a measured distance from each other so that when the strips were sent between the two rollers they would be drawn to a predetermined thickness. Usually several passes through the rollers were necessary, each pass gradually reducing the strips until they were the precise thickness required.

The prepared strips were then used to produce planchets in a punch press. The strips were laid flat on a sturdy base plate and fed into the press. A sharp circular cutter with the precise diameter of the coin denomination to be minted was mounted on the central screw shaft of the press. The cutter did not drop down by gravity but was forced down by turning a horizontal bar on top of the press, bringing the cutter down with a rotating motion. This action cut a circular blank planchet out of the strip. The cut planchet immediately fell through a hole in the base plate that was aligned directly under the cutter and landed in a container placed below the hole. Once a planchet was punched out, the sterling strip would be pushed forward and the process would be repeated. After the strip had been completely fed through the cutter some excess sterling remained on the strip between the holes where the planchets had been extracted. This excess, or scissel, was remelted. The force used to punch out the coin blanks pushed the metal around the edge of the blank. This caused the blank to bow somewhat so that the top face took on a slightly convex shape. Also, the metal that was forced down left a sharp extruding edge on the underside of the planchet. In order to make the coins stackable the bowed planchets had to be flattened. A column of blank planchets was lined up in a drop press which simply struck the column with force straightening the planchets. Each flattened blank planchet still had a sharp edge. To remove this sharp surface the planchets were sent for rounding and edge markings.

Edge marking was an early pre-collar process whereby the edge of each blank was set between two parallel straight bars of an edge marking machine. The planchet was laid on the flat surface of the apparatus and the two parallel bars were brought together so that the edge of the planchet was secured tightly between them. One bar was held in place by a strong spring and could move sideways so that as the bar was moved, the planchet edge rotated along the bar and was impressed with whatever secret edge markings or grain lines had been engraved on the bar. This process also confirmed the circularity of the planchet and smoothed the edge. Occasionally this process was replaced with early experimental trials that employed a collar. A collar was a small round strip of iron secured to the bottom die at the time of minting. When the planchet, resting on the lower die, was struck by the force of the upper die the planchet was somewhat flattened, forcing the metal to expand outward. The collar acted as a retaining wall, stopping the flattening or outward expansion of the metal; it made the edge straight and smooth as well as giving the coin a perfect circular shape and impressed the edge with any letters or grain lines engraved in the collar. Edging was not added to Massachusetts silver, nor did later colonial or Confederation era minters adopt the use of collars, as edge markings were considered an unnecessary expense.

Once the planchets had been rounded and edged, they were individually weighed. Overweight planchets were "adjusted" by filing them down on the face, while disfigured or severely underweight planchets were remelted. The planchets were then annealed (that is, they were heated and then gradually cooled in a process that softened the metal and made it flow better during striking). The sterling planchets were then whitened by soaking them in a solution of alum and water. Next, they were dried in sawdust. Finally, the finished planchet was laid on a stationary lower anvil die in a coining press, the upper hammer die was affixed to a central screw shaft and was brought down with great force, striking the planchet and forcing the metal to flow into the engraved areas of the dies. This action impressed an image in raised relief on the planchet, transforming the planchet into a coin. The coining press was operated by five people, four pressmen, working in teams of two, each team turning one side of the heavily weighted horizontal bar on the upper screw shaft that forced the upper die downward impressing the planchet. Also, one other person was the planchet feeder. With a single motion this individual knocked off the finished coin with his middle finger and placed a new planchet on the lower die with his thumb and first finger. The actual stamping of the planchet and the positioning of a new planchet was a fast process that took about two seconds when working at top speed. Most planchet feeders at the London mint had lost at least part of one finger due to the constant, repetitive motions they had to perform at the point of impact in the one or two seconds between strikes (Craig, pp. 161-64).

Consignment acceptance at the Massachusetts Mint

Production at the Massachusetts Bay Mint was certainly on a far smaller scale than at the London mint and the procedures were less rigorous. The Massachusetts Bay Treasury did not have the funding to purchase silver. Also, as there was very little silver in Massachusetts, the General Court was not in a position to impede silver importation by requiring some portion of imported silver be offered to the mint at a reduced price. Since no minting could take place without a supply of silver, the mint had to resort to alternatives other than the purchase of silver. As we have seen, the General Court increased the value of Massachusetts silver coinage by 22.5% over its sterling value. This differential allowed the mint to make a profit and allowed a mint customer to benefit as well. With this incentive the mint was able to induce individuals to deposit silver at the mint on consignment, with the profit being distributed between the consignor and the mint.

We can derive some information on the method by which the mint accepted consignments from the details in Hull's ledger concerning a very small consignment for 56 troy ounces of sterling accepted on November 8, 1679. Whereas smaller consignments were usually backlogged for several months, this consignment was processed within a few weeks. However, it seems the consignment was put in the backlog when it first arrived but was taken out of the backlog around November 18th or 19th and processed within a few days, since the finished coins were delivered to the customer on November 21st. Very interestingly, on the same day this small consignment was completed and delivered, the mint accepted a rather large consignment for 770.5 troy ounces of silver that went into production within a week. This set of circumstances suggests the mint realized there was going to be a rather large consignment arriving on November 21st and therefore processed the smaller consignment in order to free up staff time for the larger consignment. These events suggest a potential mint customer would visit the shop and negotiate a mutually agreeable date on which to deliver a consignment. This insured that Hull or Sanderson would be available to accept the shipment so they could assay the silver and offer the customer a receipt. Thus, it appears the first step in processing a consignment was for the mintmaster and the customer to arrange a date for delivery of the consignment to the shop.

In the 1652 mint act, the legislators specified that mint customers would have the right to be present while the silver they consigned to the mint was melted and then refined to sterling fineness. The customer was to be given a receipt for the weight of the consignment after it had been refined to sterling silver. The text of the mint act, in the version passed on May 27, 1652, by the House of Deputies stated:

> & It shalbe in the liberty of any person who brings into the mint howse any bullian plate or spanish Coyne as afforsaid to be present and se [see] the same melted & refined Allayed & then to take a receit of the master of the mint for the weyght of that which is good silver allayd as aforesaid,.... (Crosby, pp. 37-38)

The legislators who composed this text probably understood some sterling would be lost during the melt and thus thought the most accurate weight to include on a customer receipt would be the post-melt weight in sterling. However, the legislators were not metallurgists and may not have understood the production issues involved in melting and refining consignments in the presence of the customer. They might not have understood the various economic problems and production inefficiencies attendant with numerous small melts. In addition, one might wonder - did they intend Hull to weight the molten sterling in the crucible or was the customer to wait until the sterling had been poured out of the crucible and cooled? Apparently, the constraints this regulation imposed on production methods had not been fully considered. Possibly the lawmakers were remembering the situation at the London mint from the time before they traveled to America. From an account of the London mint by Gerard Malynes during the hammered coinage era, which was printed in 1622, the author related he had brought his silver to the mint where it was assayed. He went on to say,

> ...we stayed to see our silver molten and cast into ingots, for to be deliuered to the moneyers to sheire [that is, shear or cut] the same by weight into small peeces for twelue pences & six pences ... and the Assay-master made another Assay of it (called the pot Assay) and found the same to be standard, whereupon we tooke our leaue and departed. ... The next weeke following I went to receiue my satiffaction in coyned moneys, ...(Malynes, pp. 280-86, with the quote from p. 286)

Since the London mint did two large melts a day when they were coining, it was sometimes possible for an individual to bring silver to the mint and then spend a few hours and actually see the silver melted on the very day it was deposited. The main reason for staying would be to insure the pot assay confirmed the fineness of the silver, thus verifying there would be no reduction in one's return. The Massachusetts legislators may have remembered this practice but confused the issue as to when the consignment was weighed. In any event the Massachusetts regulation did not precisely follow the London practice nor did it take into consideration the implications this regulation would have on the Massachusetts Bay Mint, where much less silver would be minted than was the case in London.

In this situation, as in others, we know Hull did not always precisely follow the instructions in the legislation. We have seen the methodology he used in calculating the customer's return and his mint fees differed from what was stated in the mint act. It is also clear from the ledger that when Hull accepted a consignment of silver he did not melt and refine the consignment in the presence of the customer, but he did give the customer a receipt for the quantity of sterling consigned. Clearly, the sterling weight on the receipt was not derived from the refining process. Rather, it appears Hull accepted British silver plate brought to the mint as being of sterling fineness, probably because British silver contained a silversmith's mark, which was a legal assurance by the London goldsmiths's guild of the quality of the silver as sterling. This was actually a series of marks stamped into the silver consisting of the goldsmith's initials, a crowned leopard's head representing the guild, a lion passant for sterling and the fourth mark being a letter that represented the specific year the item was produced. For example, the letter I was used for 1676 (*News,* pp. 4-5 and *Touchstone,* with the marks illustrated on the plate opposite page 1, item 5 and pp. 19-24). Also, as was common practice in Britain and Massachusetts Bay at the time, Hull accepted Spanish cobs as sterling (see below pp. 170-71). For instance, on May 8, 1675, he accepted 369.5 troy ounces in "sterling silver dollars," while in other consignments he sometimes simply used the phrase "sterling dollars" (as on June 14, 1676). Thus, it seems Hull accepted Spanish eight reales "dollars" and silver objects bearing a silversmith mark as equal to sterling, possibly without making an assay. He may have simply weighed the consignment and given the customer a receipt for the weight of the silver as sterling weight.

In other cases Hull seems to have conducted an assay to determine the fineness of the silver. Ledger entries demonstrate Hull did not melt and refine consignments as soon as they entered the mint. The consignments were usually backlogged for several weeks or months, in the hope additional silver would be available before another melt had to be undertaken. However, on the deposit date Hull regularly recorded the weight of the consignment in sterling ounces and calculated the customer return. When silver was below sterling fineness Hull recorded the weight and calculated a return per troy ounce based on the degree of fineness below sterling. He then gave the customer a receipt with the weight and the rate of return. What must have occurred is that, in lieu of a full melting and refining process, Hull made an assay of the silver to determine its fineness. In a consignment from April of 1677 Hull accepted some silver he referred to as "Spanish plate." While Hull offered customers a return of 6s3d (75d) per troy ounce for sterling silver at that time, he only offered the customer 6s (72d) per ounce for the "Spanish plate." Hull determined each troy ounce of the Spanish plate was deficient from the sterling standard by 3d. As 1d equaled six grains in

Massachusetts sterling coins, apparently Hull assayed the silver and discovered a troy ounce of the Spanish plate had 18 grains less of pure silver (and therefore 18 grains more of impurities) than sterling, thus a troy ounce of the Spanish plate would equal 462 grains of sterling and would therefore only yield a customer return of 6s per troy ounce.

From the ledger entries it appears Hull either accepted a consignment as sterling fineness or performed an assay on the silver and used the result of the assay to determine the sterling value of the silver consigned to the mint. He then issued a receipt to the customer for the quantity of silver based on the assay performed in the customer's presence. At that point the silver was probably secured in a box bearing the customer's name. Then the customer departed and the box was put aside for processing at a future date. It is clear melting and refining were not performed until the consignment was ready for production.

Assaying silver in the seventeenth century

We do not know specifically how Hull conducted an assay, but we do know how assays were performed in England and Germany. The assay was critical in all silversmith work since it determined the purity or fineness of silver. The purity, along with the weight, was used to arrive at the price a shop would pay for a specific consignment of silver. The assay also determined the degree of refining performed by a silversmith and therefore determined the purity of the silver in the items produced by the shop. Seventeenth century assays were not as precise as individuals would have wished. Even as late as March 6, 1696, the masters of the London mint, Thomas Neale and Thomas Hall, wrote to the Lords of the Treasury stating assays at the mint and assays at the Exchequer "...often differ, and sometimes as much as two pennyweights 'and better'" (Redington, p. 492, item 40). Although the standard by which the two pennyweight difference was measured is not mentioned, it is clear this statement refers to a two pennyweight differential per troy pound. The troy pound was the standard measure used in British legislation and in the official pyx coinage trials. A two pennyweight differential per troy pound would equal four grains per pennyweight (480 grains), which in fineness would translate to a variation of 8.2% from the standard .925 sterling, this results in a fineness range from a low of .9168 fine to a high of .9332 fine.

This disparity in the results of assays was partly due to the inability to accurately measure small differences. Assay equipment was made by the individual rather than purchased from a factory producing standardized products, so there were no two assayers with precisely the same equipment. Similarly, no two assayers had the same raw materials, nor did any assayer have a constant supply of the exact same raw materials as he used previously. The equipment used and the accuracy of the final measurement depended on the skill, ability and knowledge of the assayer to handle a variety of materials. Even the act of regulating the heat during an assay was a difficult task which demanded constant vigilance to insure the fire was neither too low nor too high. Considering the quantity and placement of fuel was never precisely the same for any two assays and there was no way to measure several significant factors such as changes in humidity, air temperature or pressure, the individual performing the assay had to rely on experience to insure the heat was correct and consistent. The ability to perform an assay was truly an art that took many years to perfect; the necessary skills went far beyond perfecting the procedures one followed during an assay.

Before an assay could be performed an individual had to construct an assay oven and prepare the necessary equipment. These tasks required skill in both selecting the best raw materials as well as in producing the necessary items. Lazarus Ercker, Chief Superintendent of Mines and Assay Master General of the German Empire, wrote a detailed work in German on metals and assaying in 1574. A second edition was published in 1580 with reissues in 1598, 1629, 1672, 1673, 1684, 1703 and 1736. The work was translated into English by John Pettus and published in London in 1683 (with reissues in 1685 and 1686). This work goes into great detail on every aspect of an assay. It was the standard text in seventeenth century Germany and, with the translation by Pettus, it became the most detailed discussion available to the English goldsmith. That Pettus found it worthy to translate in the 1680's and that it quickly went through three printings, demonstrates it was still considered quite useful in later seventeenth century England. Undoubtedly, by the time of the Pettus translation Ercker's treatise would not be the most recent word on the subject. In contemporary illustrations of the London goldsmith's guild, as is found in the frontispiece of the 1677 book, *A Touch-stone for Silver and Gold Wares,* by the London goldsmith William Badcock [figure 4], we find the guild had equipment that was superior to the apparatus discussed by Ercker. However, in relation to the facilities in London, the equipment described in Ercker would probably be closer to the equipment and procedures used by provincial English goldsmiths and most likely by American goldsmiths as Hull and Sanderson.

After describing several varieties of silver ore, Ercker gave detailed instructions on making an assay oven. He stated some ovens were made from iron plates or tiles but the most common variety of oven was one made of baked potter's clay [figure 5]. The base was about 11 inches square. The walls went straight up for about eight inches and then tapered inward for a total height of about 16 inches with a hole at the top about 7 inches wide, giving the oven a shape somewhat like a beehive or a pyramid with the top of the cone cut off. The walls were about one and a half inches thick, with the base about three quarters of a inch thick. There was a semicircular arch opening in the front at the base of the oven about three inches high and four and a half inches wide that was used to view the assay. About two inches above this was a second opening three and a half inches high and four inches wide that was used to gain access to and move the coals that were put in the oven. A plate was placed on the top opening and adjusted to regulate the heat by increasing or decreasing ventilation. In the back of the oven were two chutes for removal of ashes. The stove was strengthened with iron strapping (Ercker, 1951, pp. 19-23 and 1683, pp. 8-14).

The most critical item for an accurate reading was the cupel. This was a single use filter in the shape of a very small bowl or ashtray about three inches in diameter [figures 6 and 7]. The cupel was molded from a mixture of ashes. The ash of light wood or vines was washed in boiling water several times, then it was strained and dried. A mixture of two thirds washed wood ash was combined with one-third bone ash made from bones without marrow. Fish bones were best but sheep and calf bones were also very good; these bones were baked and then ground to a powder called bone ash. The wood and bone ashes were mixed together and then a liquid was added. Sometimes beer or an egg white acted as an added medium to promote cohesion but one usually used a binder called "glue water." Once the ashes were moistened they were shaped into balls and coated with an outer layer of bone ash, preferably made of the bones from a calf's head. The balls were then placed in metal collars and molded with a pestle into the shape of small bowl-like holders called cupels. The cupels would then be stacked on a tray and baked in an oven for about an hour. The directions stated the quality of the cupel depended on the purity of the ashes, the completeness of the outer coating and the proper baking temperature and time. Unless each step in the production of the cupel was meticulously followed, the final product might not filter properly (Ercker, 1951, pp. 26-34 and 1683, pp. 18-26).

The specific steps in an assay differed somewhat depending on the nature of the item to be assayed. Various silver ores were treated in different ways depending on the type of silver present in the ore and the other metals mixed with them. Also, refined silver items of different finenesses needed to have differing amounts of lead added during cupellation. Ercker has over thirty pages of instructions for assaying different ores and various refined products of differing finesses. However, in every case, when someone came into a shop with silver to be assayed, the silversmith made a small cut in the item. For this example, I shall use a coin as the item being assayed since one of Ercker's chapters dealt specifically with assaying coinage. For a larger coin, such as a thaler, Ercker stated the coin was beat thin on an anvil so it could be easily clipped into pieces. The precise weight of the clipping was recorded, and as Ercker stated, there should be two equal mark samples (the mark being a unit of weight). This would be enough for two assays. For smaller coins clippings were taken from several coins; Ercker said for two kreuzer coins, one would cut pieces from two or three examples, while for silver pennies, clippings would be taken from twelve coins. Hull probably clipped small samples from more than one coin when he performed an assay on a consignment since it would yield a better average fineness. The weighed clippings were then melted in the assay oven with some lead, resulting in an alloy, which cooled into a blob called a lead bead or button. During this process the lead fused with any impurities in the silver. It was very important that the lead used in the assay was pure, containing no silver. As most lead did include some silver, this meant the lead had to be filtered, or, in contemporary terms, proofed, several times before it could be used for an assay. The quantity of pure lead used in the process differed based on the assayer's estimate of the kind of silver being assayed. Ercker stated for thalers, which the British called rix dollars, the ratio was nine parts lead to one of silver, and for kreutzers and silver pennies the ratio was eighteen to one. Malynes said the ratio used at the London mint in 1622 for assaying sterling items was five parts lead to one of sterling (Ercker, 1951, pp. 45-46 and 60-63; 1683, pp. 40-41 and 59-62; Malynes, p. 285).

The silver and lead button alloy was then placed on a cupel with some flux. Ercker called the flux Clar, which was a clear by-product of a mixture of white pebble stone powder and a lead oxide called red litharge that had been heated with salt. Some individuals skipped the button alloy step. They simply cut the piece of the silver to be assayed, covered it with lead foil and placed it directly on the cupel with some flux. The cupel was then placed in the oven. Next a protective covering, known as a muffel, was placed over the cupel. The muffel was a baked clay cover in the shape of an igloo [figure 8]. The cover over the cupel was a small dome with slits to allow heat to enter, this was connected to an arched tunnel, like an entrance way to an igloo. The tunnel was lined up with the lower open arch in the oven so one could look inside the oven opening and have an unobstructed view the cupel. Next, hot charcoal was poured into the oven surrounding the muffle. A plate or lid would be placed over the top opening in the oven to stop the heat from escaping and to regulate the fire. The assayer would use some small tools to move the charcoal and further regulate the intensity of the fire. After about an hour the button in the cupel would melt. Generally an assay took about an hour if the impurities in the silver consisted of copper, lead or other metals with low melting points, but it could be longer it the silver contained iron or other impurities with higher melting points. Once the substance was liquefied, a filtering process called cupellation occurred. The lead and the impurities from the silver were absorbed into the bone ash cupel as lead oxide while only the pure silver remained unfiltered on the top of the cupel. The difference between the weight of the test sample before and after the assay, revealed the weight of any impurities in the item being assayed. In sterling the impurities were 7.5% of the total weight since sterling was 92.5% or .925 fine silver. Any variation over 7.5% determined the percent of deficiency from the sterling standard.

There were several possibilities for error in the assay. If the cupel was too small or did not contain either a sufficient quantity of ashes or ashes that were sufficiently pure, some lead might remain with the silver. If the fire was not regulated properly the cupel would become soggy and silver would drain to the cupel. Alternatively, if not enough lead was used in the cupellation some impurities might remain in the silver. Finally, if the lead used in the cupellation process was not completely free of silver the assay would show a higher silver content than was actually present in the object being assayed, for any silver that had been in the lead would remain in the cupel. Of course, there were additional possibilities for error in accurately weighing these small quantities of metal. Accuracy required diligence in insuring the balance was in no way out of alignment, that the weights were accurate and that the scales were used precisely with objects placed in the center of the pans. The weighing was to take place in a box with an open front so no wind or breeze would affect the measurement. Given the lack of standardization in equipment, supplies and procedures, it is astonishing there was not even greater disparity in assay results (on assaying see; Ercker, 1951, pp. 19-92 and 1683, pp. 8-69; Challis, *Tudor Coinage,* pp. 25 and 38 and *Encyclopaedia Britannica,* 11th edition, volume 2, "Assaying," Cambridge University Press, 1910, pp. 776-78).

Production issues in the Massachusetts Bay Mint Act: the shape of the coins and privy marks

In addition to changing melting procedures so that the mint performed an assay rather than a full melt upon acceptance of a consignment, there were other aspects of the mint act that had adverse effects on the production process and were revised. The text of the mint act, in the version passed on May 27, 1652, by the House of Deputies stated all silver consigned into the mint was to be:

> ...brought to the Allay of Sterling siluer by John Hull master of the said mint, & his sworne officers & by him to be Coyned into twelue pence Six pence & three pence peeces which shalbe for forme flatt & square on the sides & Stamped on the one side with N E & on the other side with xii^d. vi^d & iii^d according to the value of each peece together with a priuie marke which Shalbe appoynted euery three monethes by the governo^r & knowne only to him & the sworne officers of the mint,....(Crosby, p. 37)

This passage has two points directly related to production efficiency that never went into practice. The mint committee expressly reversed one point while the other seems to have been simply dismissed by Hull as impractical.

It seems almost as soon as the mint committee was formed, the shape of the coins was modified from square to round. This was an easy decision for the mint committee and was quickly made. In a document dated June 11, 1652, the mint committee drafted an oath of office for Hull and Sanderson. Immediately following the oath the committee added a passage revising the coin shape from what was stipulated in the original legislation. The committee stated:

> Whereas: by order of the Gennerall Courte It is Appointed that all monies Coyned heere, for forme should be flatt and square, wee, whose names are heere vnder written, Appointed by the Gennerall Court, as a Committee to Consider and determine of whatsoeuver wee should Judge necessary for the Carrying an end of the order Respecting minting of monyes doe hereby determine & declare that the office^{rs} for the minting of mony shall Coyne all the mony that they mints in A Round forme till the Gennerall Courte shall otherwise declare their minds. (Crosby, p. 43)

The second point, concerning a privy mark, is not mentioned in any surviving mint committee document. Apparently the problems related to adding a privy mark were not considered until production was started and the specification was simply not put into practice. A privy mark or mintmark refers to a small letter or numeral or a special design such as a cinquefoil, pellet or cross, that was added to every coin from a specific mint to differentiate the coins from similar coins minted at other locations. Such marks had been used on English coinage since the 1330's during the reign of Edward III. This allowed officials to identify any mint or mintmaster who produced and emitted coins below the authorized standards.

The secret privy mark, which was to be added to the coins and changed every three months, appears to be an anti-counterfeiting device. Certainly, there were administrative problems with this concept, in that there was no agency appointed to monitor coinage in circulation. Moreover, because the marks were secret, they would not assist the public in identifying counterfeits. As concerns the mint, the addition of such a mark added another step to the coining process. Since each NE coin was hammer punched this would not be a major inconvenience in processing time, but it would mean creating a series of punches to be used in some rotation that could put a secret mark on the coins. Since punches were expensive this would increase production costs. When the mint changed to a rocker press the privy mark would have been even more problematic, because it would require cutting a mark on each die every few months. This would be a time consuming process and it would wear out the dies more quickly. This is quite significant since the dies were the single most expensive expendable supply in the production process.[1] Thus, it appears that Hull, possibly

---

[1] By expendable supply I mean a periodically replaced non-capital expense. A capital expense such as a press or other major machinery or even the shop itself, was more costly than dies.

in consultation with the Governor or certain of his Assistants, who comprised the House of Magistrates, decided against implementing the statutory requirement to include a privy mark.

There are certainly no privy marks on surviving NE coinage. However some numismatists have suggested variations in the geometric dot designs, spelling variations and occasional backward letters (usually a backward N and sometimes an S) on the Oak and Pine Tree coins represented privy marks. I suspect these variations were probably not intentional but rather demonstrate Hull and Sanderson did not spend the time required to precisely copy every detail of a previous die, but rather, they simply kept to the same basic design. Indeed, there are no two varieties with the exact same tree design, lettering or spacing. Further, the lettering errors represent the kind of mistakes made by diecutters throughout the colonial period. A backward letter was an easy mistake to make since diecutters actually engraved the mirror image of the design onto the die. Thus, they had to engrave backwards but sometimes mistakenly forgot to reverse the letter they were adding. The letter N seems to have been particularly problematic for the Massachusetts Mint since in the obverse legend the N in IN is backwards on several die varieties, such as Noe, Pine Tree shilling varieties 2, 4, 5, 8, 11 and 12 [see figures 17, 18, 19, 24 and 25 for N and 25 for a backward S]. The frequency of this error makes it an unlikely candidate for a mark that could be used to distinguish a unique production period. Furthermore, these designs and lettering mistakes were not changed every three months, but rather are found on all coins minted from those dies. The recutting of dies seems to have been done to strengthen the design in order to extend their life. From the extant coins we know dies with inverse letters and other errors would not be corrected until the dies were worn down from use.

Processing consignments at Massachusetts Bay

When it was time to process a consignment, the silver would be removed from storage and placed in a melting pot or crucible. Ercker shows that the crucible was covered. Next, a pair of iron tongs with long handles were used to put the crucible into and take it out of the furnace [figure 2] (Ercker, 1951, pp. 180-81 and plate 25 on p. 179; 1568, pp. 200-203 and plate 25 on p. 200). A wood charcoal fire[2] was started in the furnace and a bellows would be used to get the fire hot enough to melt the silver (1761.4°F). The heat was extreme; usually there was an iron door on the furnace to protect the melter. When the melter had to open the door to see the molten mixture, he used a wooden paddle that had a slit in the center (Ercker, 1951, plate 19 on p. 139 and 1583, plate 19 on p. 153). The paddle protected his face from the heat and he could view the crucible through the center hole. Once the silver was melted, the molten mixture would be refined if necessary, to bring previously identified inferior silver up to the sterling standard. I suspect no specific pot assay check was performed at this point on consignments that had been accepted as equal to sterling, for Hull had already given the customer a receipt for a specific weight in sterling which promised the customer a predetermined return. Once the sterling silver was melted, the crucible was removed from the furnace and placed in a brace or stand to stabilize the vessel. The molten silver was then ladled out and poured into either wet sand molds or preformed molds made of ceramic or cast

---

[2] See the addenda to Appendix I for information on the cost of charcoal at the mint.

iron that shaped the sterling into strips. We do not know which type of molds were used at the mint, however we do know the Hammersmith Ironworks in Saugus used wet sand molds. A template would be carved from wood and then impressed into the wet molding sand to produce designs for fireplaces and other uses. Quite likely a similar process used at the Massachsuetts Bay mint. The benefit of sand molding was that it was more versatile and could be formed into any shape desired. Thus one could make narrower strips for smaller denomination coins or wider strips for shillings. Wet sand molds took up more space, had to be prepared before each use and required that the hardened silver strips be cleaned after extraction. Ceramic or cast iron molds were cleaner and could be stacked so they took up less space. But since they only made strips of a predetermined length and width, one needed molds for each length and width of strip desired. Further, preformed molds cost more than sand and unlike sand they eventually needed to be replaced. Probably the strips at the Massachusetts Bay Mint were cast in wet sand molds. As we shall see in Chapter Twelve, the 1666 inventory of the tools of Robert Sanderson's son, Joseph, included patterns, a sandbox and molding sand. This clearly indicates some silver items were cast in sand at the Hull shop. After the strips cooled they would be extracted from the molds and cleaned. The cleaned strips were probably heated and then rolled to make them thinner and give them a specified uniform thickness. These steps in accepting and assaying consignments as well as the processes used in melting and casting the silver into strips were probably fairly consistent during the life of the mint. However the methods and processes related to stamping coinage underwent substantial changes.

Minting coins in 1652

When the mint opened in September of 1652 Hull followed the assaying and melting processes just discussed. He then cut the rolled silver strips into coin size square planchets. Next, he simply used a punch to impress the raised letters NE on the top of the obverse. Hull then turned the square over and used another punch to impress the denomination, such as XII, on the reverse at the opposite end (this would be the 6:00 o'clock or the 180° position). The squares were then cut to a round shape with shears.[3] Transforming the silver squares into coins required the use of a hammer, punches and shears, no dies were used [figures 9-10]. In an e-mail of December 14, 2001, Michael Hodder concisely described this process stating that the silversmith Hull treated the planchets "as if they were cups or spoons needing a hallmark" (also see Hodder, *Hain*, pp. 20 and 26). However, it was soon apparent the simplicity of this process and the starkness of the design resulted in coins that could be easily

---

[3] The 1652 mint act stated Massachusetts coins were to be square but the mint committee amended the text so the coins would be round. I suspect Hull realized he would be cutting flat strips of sterling into squares and wanted to emit the coins that way as it was the most efficient method of production. Probably the unusual square shape mentioned in the legislation was included at Hull's suggestion. However, the mint committee considered the sharp corners would be problematic and therefore revised the coins to the more user friendly round shape. That Hull used square planchets is also indicated by the elongated planchet illustrated as figure 10 below. The description of that figure gives further details demonstrating the square planchet was stamped and then trimmed to a round shape. Michael Hodder suggested the use of a "cookie-cutter" style planchet cutter for some NE Noe III-D shillings, but suspects those examples may have been produced very late in the history of the mint as souvenirs or commemoratives (Hodder, "A letter," p. 20 and *Hain*, pp. 20 and 26).

clipped and then passed without detection. Therefore, only about seven weeks after the mint opened the General Court passed legislation, on October 19, 1652, to prevent clipping by changing the coin design from a round planchet with NE on one side and the value on the other, to a more complex design with a rim inscription within a double ring and a center design with a tree on one side and the date on the other.

The acquisition of a coining press

It is doubtful that a coining press was available on October 19th allowing the minters to immediately begin producing coins with the newly authorized design, now known as the Willow Tree coinage. It is far more probable that production of NE coinage continued until the minters could acquire the equipment needed to conform to the new regulations. Indeed, from surviving NE shilling coins we know the mint used at least three obverse punches (I-III) and four reverse punches (A-D), found in at least six combinations.[4] This number of punches suggests the coins were minted for more than seven weeks! NE coinage may have been produced until 1654. It seems some type of press was obtained by 1654, since there are some indications the mint was exploring the possibility of hiring a diecutter in that year. In 1654 Joseph Jenks at the Hammersmith Ironworks in Saugus corresponded with John Hull's brother, Edward Hull, who was in London, about bringing a diecutter to Massachusetts Bay. In the same year John Mansfield petitioned the General Court for a position at the mint but neither initiative seems to have been successful (Morison, p. 152; Crosby, pp. 103-4). That inquiries were made concerning a diecutter and that Mansfield, who said he had apprenticed in London as a goldsmith, applied for a position at the mint suggests Hull and Sanderson were seeking an experienced diecutter. Obviously, they would not have sought a diecutter unless they had acquired some type of coin press requiring dies.

There has been some debate as to the specific variety of press Hull may have acquired. During the early seventeenth century coins were stamped using a variety of methods. Some coins were produced using the traditional hammered method of placing a planchet between a stationary lower die and an upper die and then striking the upper die with a hammer. Other coins were impressed mechanically. One mechanical method, the hammer press, basically imitated hammer technology except the hammer was operated by a machine rather than by an individual. Drop presses were also employed, whereby a falling weight replaced the hammer. In some larger cities, screw presses with cylindrical dies were already in use. Another category of mechanical coining presses were those using roller or rocker dies.

It should be noted Richard Doty, expanding on information Michael Hodder had included in several auction catalogs, surmised the Willow and Oak series, as well as most, if not all, "large planchet" Pine Tree varieties, may have been stamped onto metal strips fed through a rocker or a roller press, with the impressed coins then cut out of the strips. These coins are slightly bent or wavy, which was probably a result of the metal being impressed as it passed between two curved surfaces supporting the suggestion of a rocker or a roller press since both utilized sets of curved dies. Curved dies also produced coins that have an oval or

---

[4] See Noe, *New England*, pp. 10-11 (rpt. pp. 24-25) and Newman, *Good Samaritan*, pp. 66-67 (rpt. pp. 226-27).

elongated appearance. This is because the greatest pressure is exerted when the two curved centers of the dies press against the stock. Many Massachusetts silver coins exhibit this elongated shape. To remedy this situation the die cutters actually needed to produce oval images on the curved dies. The elongated engravings distributed the pressure better and gave the final product a rounder appearance.

The presses used for the two minting methods, rocker and roller presses, were very similar; each had a hand crank and two adjustable adjacent shafts. The crank moved toothed wheel gears called cogs that were connected to flywheels. These gears modified the turning motion so that the two parallel shafts rotated in opposite directions. Also, the gear ratios reduced the turning force or torque required to rotate these shafts under pressure. Dies were affixed to the shafts, aligned and brought close together so that when a strip of metal was fed through the machine the images engraved on the top and bottom die would be impressed simultaneously into the metal.

With the roller press, the dies were engraved on rollers. Roller dies were available in two basic varieties. Sometimes a die was engraved directly on the cylindrical shaft. With this variety of press each time a new type of coin was to be minted the shafts were removed and replaced with other shafts that had the appropriate engraving (Cooper, figure 67). The other type of roller press had square shafts so that a three or four inch wide roller with a square hole in the center could be firmly positioned on the shaft (Cooper, figure 73). In both varieties a series of images would be engraved on the roller dies. The Richmond farthing tokens produced during the reign of Charles I, were made on a roller press that contained rollers dies with nine coin engravings. There were nine obverse engravings on one roller die and nine reverse engravings on the opposite roller die. When the two dies were aligned, each rotation of the dies would produce a strip of nine farthings. A description of the Edinburgh mint from 1637 described a roller press being used for larger denomination coins. In Spain roller dies were used at the Segovia mint for most denominations including the half real of 1652. For the large centiventa coin of Charles V, minted in 1682, the roller survives. There was only one engraving per roll; thus for each full rotation only 38% of the strip was impressed (Cooper, pp. 61-71).

The other variety of hand-cranked coining press had a hole in the center of each shaft for the insertion of a rocker die. A shank extension or handle on the die would be inserted into the hole and secured in place with a pin or bolt. The curved outer face of the die was engraved with a single coin image [figure 11]. An obverse die was affixed to one shaft and a reverse die was affixed to the other shaft. A strip of metal was placed between the dies. A rotation of the handle would turn the shafts and bring the rocker dies together so that aligned impressions were produced on each side of the strip of metal. The rocker dies and the metal strip would be repositioned so a second coin could be impressed. There were many varieties and sizes of rocker presses. Some presses had wheel gears that only contained teeth over half of the circumference, thus limiting the movement of the dies to a narrow reciprocating motion. For this variety of press the strips of coin stock had to be cut into squares that were individually fed between the dies. Most varieties of rocker presses had wheel gears that contained teeth over the entire circumference, thus allowing for a more extensive reciprocating motion which allowed a strip of stock to be fed through the press. Smaller presses were about two feet tall and could be bolted onto a table whereas other models were over twice that height. The larger presses were quite heavy and were permanently bolted into the floor. Several examples of rocker presses and rocker dies dating to 1661-1753 survive from the Kremnica mint in the Czech Republic [figures 12-13] (Cooper, pp. 61-71).

The benefit of the roller press was that it could produce coins more quickly than the rocker press. However, the major disadvantage was that one had to engrave several identical coin dies on a roller. Since much engraving time was involved there were several opportunities for errors; also, rusted or damaged dies were very costly to replace. The rocker press was slower in producing coins as each turn of the handle produced only one coin, but dies were easier to produce and if a die was damaged, only one engraving was lost.

Another variety of press was the sway press. A single example of a sway press is known (Cooper, figure 74). This press was acquired by the British Museum from Seville in the early twentieth century. Cooper believes the press was produced during the 1500's. The sway press is a variety of a rocker press in that it uses two curved rocker dies. However, rather than turning a handle that activated gears, this machine was much simpler. A frame held and aligned the two rockers in place. A long handle or lever was attached to the upper rocker allowing the minter to push down and impress a strip between the two dies (Cooper, pp. 73-74).

As stated above, Massachusetts silver from the Willow through the "large planchet" Pine Tree varieties display the characteristics of coinage produced by being impressed between two curved dies.[5] However, since coins produced with roller dies have the same characteristics as those minted with rocker dies it is possible the Massachusetts Mint used a rocker press, a roller press or some variety of sway press.

Rollers and gears for roller presses were certainly available in Massachusetts Bay. From the late 1640's there was a roller press at the Hammersmith Ironworks that was used to shape one-inch square iron bars into "flats" (Clarke, *Pioneer*, illustrations on pp. 59 and 61; also Carlotto, photograph on p. 50). Replacement rollers and gears for this machine were made locally at the ironworks. It is likely Hull had a roller press to draw silver strips to the required thickness for coinage. However, the evidence we can glean from the coins suggests Hull used a rocker press for impressing coins (see the numerous points made by Hodder throughout the Hain catalog; some specific examples from the Hain coins are described in the figures of Massachusetts silver at the end of this book).

---

[5] The number of surviving Willow Tree shillings is quite small. Noe lists only 23 examples and most are well worn. Some examples, as Noe plates 8, 9 and 11 do show an oval shape that would suggest a rocker press but others seem more round. Noe, in his *Oak Tree*, pp. 5-7 (rpt., pp. 111-13) compared the Willow and Oak series, noting the Willow Tree coins were somewhat rounder than the Oak. From this observation he suggested a more circular die for the Willow series. Based on Noe's comments Eric Newman has suggested the use of a drop press for the Willow series (in a public lecture at the C-4 convention in Boston, November, 2001 and in a letter to me dated December 27, 2001).

One especially significant clue pointing to the use of a rocker press, rather than a roller press, relates to the Oak Tree twopence. On May 16, 1662, a twopence coin was authorized with the stipulation that during the initial year of production the mint was to produce fifty pounds in twopence for every hundred pounds coined. For the following six years, twenty pounds of twopence were to be produced for every hundred pounds coined.[6] This meant half of the silver minted into coins for a year was to be made into twopence. Therefore, much more time would be spent actually impressing coins. For example, before this date a consignment that was turned into £50 of Massachusetts silver may have been minted into 800 shilling coins and, say, 200 sixpence and 400 threepence for a total of 1,400 coins. Hull was now required to mint half that amount into twopence or 3,000 twopence and no more than 500 shillings, increasing the number of coin impressions to a minimum of 2,500. If he also produced threepence and sixpence in the same proportions as assumed above, he would produce 400 shillings and 100 sixpence, 200 threepence and 3,000 twopence for a total of 3,700 coins. Thus, for the same profit Hull would need to impress somewhere between just under double to slightly more than two-and-a-half times more coins! Undoubtedly roller dies would be the most efficient way to produce these large quantities of small denomination twopence coins, just as roller dies had been used for Richmond farthings in London under Charles I. However, all Oak Tree twopence were produced from a single pair of dies,[7] not from a series of dies on a roller. This strongly suggests the Massachusetts Mint was limited to the use of a rocker press.

As rocker dies would be easier and therefore more economical to produce it seems probable this was the more appropriate choice for the Massachusetts Mint. If the mint produced vast quantities of coinage on a daily basis then a roller die press would be more economical in the long run. The additional daily production from roller dies would eventually make up for the extra time spent in die preparation. However, if production was not an ongoing daily activity, and this appears to be the situation at the Massachusetts Mint, die damage or rust might occur before enough coins could be minted to make the added time spent on die production profitable.

It seems likely the Massachusetts Mint used rocker dies. But what type of rocker press was used? They may have used a hand-cranked gear press or some version of a sway press. As hand crank gear technology was commonly used in seventeenth century England and was available in the Boston area at the Hammersmith Ironworks, it is probable the Massachusetts Mint used gear technology rather than the more primitive lever technology of the sway press. Identification of the specific variety of rocker press that may have been at the Massachusetts

---

[6] Although the statute does not specify, I suspect Hull interpreted it as referring to troy pounds rather than monetary pounds. The mint regularly based production on troy weight. However, as Massachusetts silver coins were proportional, £50 in twopence should be equal in weight to £50 in shillings. See Crosby, pp. 73-74.

[7] This die pair had a long life. It was well worn and was recut several times. Noe, *Oak Tree*, listed six states and assigned each state a separate variety number, Noe, Oak Tree 29-34, see pp. 10-12, 22-23 and plates 6-8. In 1976, Picker, p. 83 mentioned there were several additional intermediate states that he hoped to publish at a later date. Also see, Hodder, in his 1994, "A plea," and his 2002, *Hain*, p. 74 on the classification problems that result from assigning unique numbers to variations detected in surviving coins from a single die pair.

Mint is a topic for future research. For now, it seems probable to surmise the Willow, Oak and "large planchet" Pine Tree series, as well as the Pine Tree threepence and sixpence coins, were produced with rocker dies on a hand-cranked rocker press [see figures 14-25 and 28-29; also, Hodder, *Hain*, pp. 21 and 26 and throughout the catalogue].

Modifications in production methods during the rocker press era

During the period of the use of a rocker press (probably from about 1654 until sometime during the late 1660's), a strip of sterling silver would be directly fed into the press. The press stamped the coin images on each side of the metal strip by literally squeezing the strip between two engraved curved rocker dies. The coins were then cut out of the silver strip using metal cutting shears. Quality control of individual coin weight occurred after stamping by clipping overweight examples. During this period there appear to have been several improvements made in the minting process.

We distinguish the early impressed coinage as two distinct series, the Willow Tree and the Oak Tree. However, it is not certain this same distinction was made in Puritan Boston. The October 1652 legislation simply stated the coins would include a tree, without naming a variety. Our current designation of Willow Tree is first found in a catalog by Joseph C. Mickley from October of 1869 (Noe, *NE and Willow*, pp. 12-17 and *Silver Coinage*, pp. 26-31). Neither do we have a contemporary document mentioning an Oak Tree variety. In 1684, a committee of the Massachusetts Bay General Court was appointed to produce a response to King Charles II concerning the right of the Commonwealth to retain its charter. In a draft of a report by the committee dated October 30, 1684, outlining a proposed response to the king, there is a passage about the mint which included the following detail:

> For in 1662, when our first agents were in England, some of our money was showed by Sir Thomas Temple at the Council-Table, and no dislike thereof manifested by any of those right honourable persons: much less a forbidding of it. (Crosby, pp. 75-76)

Later retellings of this event embellished the Temple presentation to include the story of Temple telling the king that the Massachusetts coins displayed the royal oak at Whiteladies, where Charles had hidden on September 6, 1650, to escape capture following his defeat at Worcester on September 3rd by Cromwell's forces. Whether Temple actually told this story is a matter of conjecture. However, even if the event did occur in 1662, it was clearly an argument of opportunism and not meant as an accurate description of the generally accepted classification of the tree portrayed on the coins. Whereas we have no contemporary reference for the Willow or Oak Tree names, we do know the Pine Tree coins were referred to as "New England pines" in a contemporary source from May of 1680 (Crosby, pp. 109-11).

The coins we designate as the Willow Tree series appear in many ways to be experimental. The scarcity of the coins suggests they were only minted for a brief period. They are rarer than the NE series and may have had a shorter production period. The appearance of multiple striking that is prevalent on several of the few surviving examples of the Willow Tree series is probably due to inexperience in engraving and inexperience in controlling the reciprocating action of a rocker press (see Hodder, "A letter," p. 20 and *Hain*, pp. 21 and 29). It took practice to accurately align the dies in the press and it took time to develop the techniques needed to proficiently feed the stock between the reciprocating rockers to produce a strip of fully impressed coins. Moreover, many examples, especially those from dies 1-A, display significant radical but unique errors that were not in the die [see figures 14 and 15]. If the problems had been due to engraving errors the same radical errors would be replicated with each impression made from the die. However, that each error is unique demonstrates the errors are due to problems related to impressing the images on each individual specimen. These errors are certainly due to inexperience. Further, the dramatic nature of these errors, such as the erratic alignment of bead segments and the presence of fully double letters and numbers, suggests there was some slippage of the dies during minting. Possibly, the tolerance of the die shank was not accurate so that there was not a tight fit when it was inserted into the opening in the shaft of the press. It is also possible the pins fastening the die shank to the press did not fully stabilize the die. Any instability would be accentuated as soon as the press was operated and the dies began rocking back and forth on the shaft. That the errors appear more dramatic on the reverse or date side leads me to speculate the reverse die was in the upper position. The upper die would be more prone to slippage or "give" as the weight of the die worked to destabilize it, unlike the lower die where the weight of the die worked with gravity to make it more secure. Dies that were not fully stabilized on the shaft of the press could produce the dramatic and unique errors displayed in the Willow Tree series. The reduction of these errors in the later part of the series (generally, Noe 3-D and 3-E specimens exhibit fewer dramatic errors) suggests that as the minters gained experience with the press they were able to stabilize the dies more securely on the shaft.

In the Oak Tree series the tree was transformed into a series of branches without leaves, making it easier to engrave. The loss of the erratic doubling with the Oak series [figures 16-17] does not necessarily require one to assume the refinements were due to a new variety of press. The improvements may be due to increased proficiency in engraving and in minting techniques. It is also clear the mint learned to control die shank tolerances and were able to stabilize the dies in the press.

With a rocker press, thinner stock was more desirable than thicker stock because it would move more easily through the press and the coins would be easier to trim out from the strip. If the sterling was thinner, the coins needed to have a somewhat larger diameter, since a shillings was to weight close to an average of 71.1 grains. A larger surface was also an advantage as it was frequently difficult to properly align the obverse and reverse images on the rocker dies. Since each side of the coin was independently impressed on the strip, the two sides did not always line up perfectly. The smaller the surface the less room there was for a mistake. Errors in alignment were more perceptible on smaller surfaces as is evident from extant twopence, threepence and sixpence coins, which are often missing a portion of one side. Naturally, both sides had been fully struck but were out of alignment, so when the coin was cut out of the strip the cutter had to work from one side thereby defacing the other side. Usually the cutter retained the reverse because that side included the denomination of the coin; many surviving smaller denomination coins are missing significant portions of the upper part of the obverse legend [figures 18-21 and 28-29].

With the start of the Pine tree series the mint decided to further expand the diameter of the shilling from about 27 mm. in the Oak Tree series to about 29-30 mm. in the Pine Tree issues [figures 22-25]. These thinner and broader early Pine Tree shillings are now somewhat inaccurately known as the "large planchet" Pine Tree varieties. However, they were still made directly from strips of sterling rather than planchets. They represent another of the continuing attempts to facilitate production and improve product quality.

Technological change at the Massachusetts Mint during the late 1660's

With the arrival of a screw press at the Massachusetts Mint, the minting process was completely transformed. Coins were stamped using the downward force of a die as it collided with a planchet resting on a stationary lower die.[8] This process was quite different from earlier production practices whereby a rolling motion of two cylinders squeezed a design on a strip. The new process required the creation of planchets and relied on greater uses of force, both in planchet cutting and in stamping. It was a far more automated process, since the dies on a screw press would automatically align each time; neither the obverse nor the reverse would be off-center. Additionally, the use of a screw press required a large supply of ready-made planchets. As we shall see below, between Monday, January 20th and Thursday, January 30, 1679, the mint processed 600 troy ounces of silver and produced at least 4,024 planchets (assuming all the coins were shillings). In order to melt, process and coin the silver in that nine day work period it seems quite likely the Massachusetts Mint, like the London mint, used some type of planchet cutting device rather than hand held shears as had been used during the rocker press period (also see, Hodder, *Hain*, p. 100).

Indeed, it is possible the shift to smaller and thicker coins was the result of the introduction of a planchet cutting device.[9] Planchets cut from thicker strips of silver would better withstand the force necessary for automated planchet cutting. We have seen the London mint needed to straighten out planchets, for they were somewhat bowed by the force of the cutter. Thicker stock would hold up better when being cut and therefore would not require the added step of planchet straightening. Also, the thicker planchets would hold up better under the force of the screw press. In Massachusetts, as the stock, and therefore the shilling planchet, was made thicker, it was necessary to reduce the diameter of the planchet since the weight per coin continued to average 71.1 grains at sterling fineness. As the dies

---

[8] Mike Hodder has noted the obverse dies were probably the hammer dies and the reverse dies were the anvil dies. This is because the obverse dies wore out faster; for example, Noe 16-22 all share the same reverse. Hodder, *Hain*, pp. 100-101.

[9] The planchet cutting device may have been a smaller version of the planchet cutting machine used in London or possibly it was a "cookie cutter" punch that relied on hammer power. Based on surviving examples it is difficult to determine the degree of uniformity in the shape of Pine Tree coins when they left the mint, as examples may have been clipped, filed or worn while in circulation. However, small planchet varieties that are close to full weight are far more circular in appearance than full weight examples of earlier varieties, suggesting a more uniform planchet production process in the later period [see figures 26-27]. It should be noted some surviving "large planchet" Pine Tree shillings have been cut down and rounded to the small planchet diameter. Probably this practice began after the introduction of small planchet shillings. It appears some individuals made a profit by trimming down "large planchet" shillings and then passing the lightened coins as full weight small planchet varieties.

always aligned in the screw press there was no longer a need for a wider surface area to reduce misalignments. The new machinery required thicker and sturdier planchets rather than the thinner and broader surfaces that were more helpful with rocker press technology. During the screw press period the mint produced what are now called the "small planchet" Pine Tree shillings. In this later period, weight control was more likely performed before stamping, probably soon after the blank planchets were cut out of the sterling strips. In addition to weight control some additional preparation of the planchets, such as smoothing the sharp edges probably took place before they were stamped in the press.

Screw presses came in several sizes; many smaller models could be operated by one or two individuals. It is quite probable the screw press acquired by the Massachusetts Bay Mint was much smaller than the massive screw presses at the London mint. It seems likely the Massachusetts Mint acquired a screw press sometime near the end of the 1660's when the mint was still receiving large consignments of silver. Possibly Hull purchased the new press during his final trip to England from November of 1669 through August of 1670. As explained below, during the period 1672-1676 there was a dramatic reduction in the quantity of silver brought into the mint. It would not have been prudent, and it would have been out of character, for Hull to make the considerable financial investment necessary for the acquisition of screw press technology during this period when the mint was receiving very little sterling and was struggling to survive. One must remember the technology required the acquisition of both a screw press and a planchet cutting device; together they automated coin production, allowing more coins to be produced in less time. Thus, I suspect the screw press was in operation by the time the extant portion of Hull ledger entries on the mint were written dating from October of 1671 to August of 1680.

It should be noted the shift from broader and thinner shillings to smaller and thicker shillings might not have simply occurred overnight. That is, there was probably no designated day when all procedures were modified to optimize the use of screw press technology. More likely, this transformation was a gradual process based on techniques learned from trial and error. Naturally, there may have been a transitional period when both a rocker press and a screw press were in operation.[10] Moreover, there may have been some transitional period during which the coin dimensions were adapted in response to the production changes related to the use of a screw press. Indeed, it is possible the first dies prepared for the screw press may have imitated the large shilling coinage that had been minted up to that time. It is also possible the first stock produced for the planchet cutting device would have been the same thin strips that the mint had been producing for the rocker press. Possibly the thinner strips of silver that were preferable for rocker press technology did not work well with a planchet cutter, because thinner stock would produce planchets that warped or bowed. This was certainly a problem in London, where the mint had to add an additional step to flatten out the planchets. Also, it is possible the considerable force of the die strike on the screw press caused excessive damage to thinner planchets (and possibly to

---

[10] Here I am referring to the production of shillings. Certainly any Pine Tree sixpence and threepence coins produced at the mint continued to be struck on the rocker press with the existing dies. See figures 28-29.

the dies themselves). Such problems may have caused the mint to experiment and adopt a thicker sterling stock that was more compatible with the machinery related to screw press technology. Naturally a thicker stock would necessitate a reduction in the diameter of the coin, for the weight had to remain constant. Of course, this is only speculation but it suggests the possibility there may have been some transitional period in moving from one technology to another. Thus, we cannot assume all rocker press coining ceased on the day a screw press entered the mint, nor can we be absolutely sure every "large planchet" shilling was produced on a rocker press. However, it seems safe to assume all small planchet shillings were products of the screw press.

There is no direct information on the presses owned by the Massachusetts Bay Mint but it is possible a coin press listed in the estate of John Coney may represent a press formerly owned by Hull. Coney, who died on August 20, 1722, was one of Boston's leading silversmiths and was the engraver of the three plates used for the November 21, 1702 paper currency emission and several subsequent emissions. Unfortunately, it cannot be determined if Coney's coin press was a rocker or a small screw press because the description is too brief. The itemized inventory of Coney's estate, dated October 15, 1722, included, "An Engine for Coining with all Utensils belonging thereto" valued at "£10 10s" (the third item on the second page of the inventory). Although there is no evidence as to the origin of this coining engine, it is sometimes thought the machine may have passed down from Hull to his former apprentice Jeremiah Dummer and then to Coney, for Coney was related by marriage to Dummer. On November 8, 1694, Coney married his third wife, the former Mary Atwater, with whom he had six children. Mary's sister, Hannah Atwater, had married Dummer in 1672. The disposition of the Coney press is unknown. Apparently Coney's executors began selling off the estate soon after the inventory was completed, since an advertisement in the *Boston Gazette* for November 5-12, 1722, stated, "This evening the remaining part of the Tools of the late Mr. Coney are to be sold. About 5 a Clock." The notice implies that by early November all of Coney's tools had been sold (Clarke, *Coney,* pp. 12-13, with plates).

❀❀❀❀❀❀❀❀❀❀❀

Chapter 8

Consignments at the Massachusetts Bay Mint: 1671-1680

Interpreting the consignment information in Hull's ledger

The entries in Hull's surviving ledger provide us with the opportunity to extrapolate some information on production issues at the mint for the years 1671-1680. Most of the ledger entries for the shop recorded the troy ounces of sterling consigned to the mint along with both the date on which the silver was deposited as well as the date on which the consignment was ready for delivery to the customer in the form of Massachusetts coinage. Because of a change in the way Hull calculated his fee, only the final records in Hull's ledger, primarily those from 1679, include the total monetary pound value of the coinage produced from the consignment, which averaged 80.44d in coins per troy ounce of sterling. For the consignments from other years, Hull only included the weight of the silver and the quantity of coinage given to the customer, which Hull calculated at 74d per ounce of sterling (and from June 1675 at 75d). The coinage given to the customer was not the entire production run since it did not include Hull's fee or mint charge for waste nor did it reflect any production overruns due to producing coins that averaged less than 72 grains. For the pre-1679 consignments listed below I have estimated the total monetary pound value of each production run using 80.44d per ounce as an average yield. This value has been estimated to the nearest farthing.

One must remember the money value assigned to each consignment before 1679 is an estimate based on Hull's average output of 80.44d in coins per troy ounce of sterling. From information on specific consignments in 1679 we know the monetary yield varied from 80.417d to 80.537d per troy ounce. Clearly, production fluctuated somewhat depending on the individual weight of the coins produced. By assuming an average output for those consignments before 1679, where Hull does not reveal the specific number of coins produced, the value calculated in each of those consignments listed below is only an estimate of the actual output for the consignment. However, based on the more precise information given in the 1679 consignments, a production yield of 80.44d in coins per troy ounce of sterling fluctuates no more than 10d above or 2d below the actual monetary output of the coins produced from 100 troy ounces of sterling in the various 1679 consignments. That the fluctuation above the estimated monetary output of 80.44d per troy ounce can increase by up to about 10d more in coinage shows Hull was more likely to produce somewhat lighter coins and thereby increase his yield per troy ounce. He rarely produced heavier coins so the downward fluctuation in production per troy ounce is much smaller and never went below 2d less than the average yield. Specifically, 100 troy ounces of sterling at 80.44d per ounce yields £33 10s4d in coinage, while at the highest known production rate of 80.537d per ounce would produce £33 11s1d3f in Massachusetts silver; using the lowest know production rate of 80.417d per troy ounce the output would be £33 10s1d3f. Thus, the actual output in coins per 100 troy ounces may vary from the estimated average by up to 9d3f above the estimated value to 2d1f below the estimate.

For purposes of comparing the relative size of consignments, I often refer to the troy ounces per consignment and the average troy ounces produced per day. The weights in troy ounces are exact numbers that are recorded in the ledger. The next best measure is the estimated monetary value of the coins produced from the consignment using 80.44d as the average production rate, as is explained above. Additionally, I have converted the total monetary value of the coins produced from each consignment into shillings, rounding the value to the nearest shilling. In this way one has a quick estimate of the possible number of coins produced per consignment. I assume shillings were the predominant, if not the only, denomination minted in this period. Pine Tree sixpence were certainly contemporary with the earlier "large planchet" shillings because the obverse of one of the Pine Tree sixpence dies was married with an Oak Tree reverse, leading one to suspect it was put in use at the end of the Oak Tree series and the start of the Pine Tree series. The threepence Pine Tree varieties need further study to determine specifically where they come in the emission sequence relative to other series. As there are only two die combinations for the sixpence and four die combinations for the threepence, it seems the threepence coins had a longer minting history. However, it is unknown precisely when they were produced. If one assumes a specific portion of the coins minted in the 1670's were threepence, it would not alter the troy ounces or the monetary value but it would increase the number of coins per consignment. Interestingly in the 1679 consignments where Hull actually gives the full monetary value of the coins produced from each consignment, the values are always to the shilling, they are never calculated to the nearest 3d. Of course, that does not necessarily mean threepence coins were not produced. However, neither do I know when threepence coins were made, nor do I have any evidence in what quantities they were produced. We know the Oak tree twopence were produced at a proportional ratio.[1] If Pine Tree threepence were being minted during the later Pine Tree era and some proportional production quota system existed, then the number of coins per consignment would increase from the shilling estimates given here but the ratios between consignments would remain stable since all consignments would be altered proportionally.

Also, I have used Hull's deposit and delivery dates to calculate the number of workdays each consignment was in the mint. This does not imply a consignment was actually being processed on all of those days, rather, it represents the number of days a consignment was in the shop including production time as well as any time the consignment was backlogged. I counted the number of workdays exclusive of the date of deposit and the date of delivery since I assumed a consignment might have arrived later in the day so that work on the consignment could not start on the same day the consignment arrived. Furthermore, I assumed production of each consignment was completed by the end of the workday preceding the pick up date so that the consignment could have been picked up on the morning of the delivery date.

---

[1] The ratio for Oak Tree twopence in 1662 was fifty pounds in twopence per every hundred pounds coined and for the following six years it was to be twenty pounds in twopence per every hundred pounds coined. I suspect the order is worded in production terms and therefore pounds would refer to troy pounds of sterling consigned to the mint, see Crosby, pp. 73-74.

In the entries discussed below Hull included the deposit and delivery dates but he did not mention the day of the week, which I have supplied. Interestingly, the dates in Hull's ledger recording the deposits of silver consigned to the mint as well as the dates for the deliveries of coinage produced from those consignments contain examples that date to every day of the week. I take this as an indication the mint was open Monday through Saturday and thus I have counted six workdays per week. Sunday was a day of rest for the Puritans, but in Hull's ledger there is one consignment with a Sunday pick up date (the Truesdall consignment is dated to Sunday, December 3, 1671). Hull was very religious and strictly observed the Commonwealth of Massachusetts Bay laws prohibiting any work on Sunday, which was observed from dusk on Saturday evening to dusk on Sunday. This pick up may have occurred on Monday morning and was simply misdated to December 3rd instead of the 4th or it may have occurred as the sun was setting on Saturday or after dusk on Sunday.

Finally, on the debit or receipt side of his ledger, Hull typically recorded the consigned ounces of sterling. He then calculated the return due to the customer based on a standard 74d (and later 75d) per ounce payment with the unspecified remainder of the coinage being retained by Hull as his commission. Additionally, on the delivery date, Hull included an entry on the credit or right hand side of his ledger showing a payment for the amount of coinage owed to the customer. In some consignments no return was calculated and there is no indication of a payment to a customer. In these instances I have assumed Hull deposited the silver, thus he retained the entire return. Quite probably these consignments represent bulk silver purchases of eight reales made by Hull and any surplus stock from the shop. For further details see the ledger commentary in Appendix I.

Mint consignments in Hull's ledger

The following represent the consignments for Massachusetts Bay coinage recorded in Hull's surviving ledger:

On Wednesday, October 18, 1671, Hull deposited 528.5 troy ounces of sterling at the mint. At a rate of 80.44d per ounce the consignment would yield £177 2s8d2f. Assuming the entire consignment was produced as shillings there would be approximately 3543s. Since the consignment was delivered on Monday, November 13, 1671, the mint took 21 working days (Oct. 19 - Nov. 11) to complete the consignment.

On Tuesday, October 24, 1671, Richard Truesdall deposited 208 troy ounces of sterling. At a rate of 80.44d per ounce the consignment would yield £69 14s3d2f. Assuming the entire consignment was produced as shillings there would be approximately 1394s. The consignment was delivered on Sunday, December 3, 1671, giving 34 workdays (Oct. 25 – Dec. 2) to complete the consignment.

On Tuesday, January 2, 1672, a shipment of 255.25 troy ounces of sterling was deposited at the mint. This was probably a personal consignment for Hull. Part of this consignment went to coinage and part was turned into plate, that is, some type of bowls, cups or dishes. The ratio of plate to coinage cannot be determined. If the entire consignment were minted at a rate of 80.44d per ounce the consignment would have yielded £85 11s1f. Assuming the entire consignment was produced as shillings there would be approximately 1711s. The consignment was delivered on Tuesday, February 6, 1672, so mint personnel had 30 working days (Jan. 4 - Feb. 6) to complete the consignment.

On Saturday, June 29, 1672, there was a shipment of 179.5 troy ounces of sterling deposited at the mint. This was probably a personal consignment by Hull. If the entire consignment was minted at a rate of 80.44d per ounce the consignment would yield £60 3s3d. Assuming the entire consignment was produced as shillings there would be approximately 1203s. Since the consignment was delivered on Friday, August 23, 1672, the mint took 47 working days (July 1 - Aug. 22) to complete the consignment.

On Monday, August 25, 1673, a customer deposited 265 troy ounces of sterling. If the entire consignment was minted at a rate of 80.44d per ounce the consignment would yield £88 16s4d2f. Assuming the entire consignment was produced as shillings there would be approximately 1776s. Since the consignment was delivered on Saturday, October 25, 1673, the mint took 51 working days (Aug. 26 - Oct. 24) to complete the consignment.

On Saturday, December 12, 1674, there was a deposit of 275.5 troy ounces of sterling at the mint, probably made by Hull. If the entire consignment was minted at a rate of 80.44d per ounce the consignment would yield £92 6s9d1f. Assuming the entire consignment was produced as shillings there would be approximately 1847s. No delivery date was listed.

On Saturday, May 8, 1675, there was a deposit of 369.5 troy ounces of sterling, probably made by Hull. If the entire consignment was minted at a rate of 80.44d per ounce the consignment would yield £123 16s10d2f. Assuming the entire consignment was produced as shillings there would be approximately 2477s. Since the consignment was delivered on Saturday, May 22, 1675, mint personnel took 11 working days (May 10 - May 21) to complete the consignment.

On Thursday, June 17, 1675, there was a deposit of 217 troy ounces of sterling at the mint. If the entire consignment was minted at a rate of 80.44d per ounce the consignment would yield £72 14s7d2f. Assuming the entire consignment was produced as shillings there would be approximately 1455s. Since the consignment was delivered on Thursday, July 8, 1675, the mint took 17 working days (June 18 - July 7) to complete the consignment.

On Wednesday, June 14, 1676, a consignment of 496.75 troy ounces of sterling was deposited at the mint, probably by Hull. If the entire consignment was minted at a rate of 80.44d per ounce the consignment would yield £166 9s10d2f. Assuming the entire consignment was produced as shillings there would be approximately 3330s. Since the consignment was delivered on Wednesday, July 12, 1676, mint personnel took 24 working days (June 15 - July 11) to complete the consignment.

Between Friday, April 20 and Friday, April 27, 1677, a total of 1575.5 troy ounces of sterling and 282 ounces of Spanish plate (at 6s per ounce) was deposited at the mint. I have estimated the total consignment as yielding 1846.925 troy ounces of sterling. If the entire consignment was minted at a rate of 80.44d per ounce the consignment would yield £619 6d3f. Assuming the entire consignment was produced as shillings there would be approximately 12,381s. No delivery date was included.

On Friday, July 13, 1677, a customer deposited 125 troy ounces of sterling. If the entire consignment was minted at a rate of 80.44d per ounce the consignment would yield £41 17s11d. Assuming the entire consignment was produced as shillings there would be approximately 838s. No delivery date was listed.

Several parcels were deposited between Thursday, May 3 and Wednesday, August 29, 1677, that Hull stated were minted into £671 12s value in coinage. Assuming the entire consignment was produced as shillings there would be 13,432s. Unfortunately the exact quantity of silver was not given and no delivery date was specified. However, the consignment was most probably completed sometime before Tuesday, December 4, 1677, which was the date of the next entry in the ledger. Based on a production rate of 80.44d per troy ounce, I estimate the consignment to have consisted of about 2005 troy ounces of sterling.

On Wednesday, November 20, 1678, a customer deposited 159.75 troy ounces of sterling. On Monday, January 20, 1679, a consignment of 1132.5 ounces was deposited. It is unknown if these two deposits were from a single individual or from two different customers. Mint personnel processed the deposits together as if they were a total consignment of 1292.25 ounces. The coins were delivered in four installments, where each of the first three installments consisted of 300 ounces of sterling. Hull stated each of these installments was minted into £100 12s in coins (if it was all in shillings this would be 2012s per installment). The installments were delivered to the customer as soon as they were available, the first on Monday, January 27, 1679, the second on Thursday, January 30th and the third on Thursday, February 6th, 1679. Hull stated the fourth and final installment of 392.25 ounces of sterling produced £131 7s in coins (if all shillings this would be 2627s) and was delivered on Tuesday February 18, 1679. The final installment no doubt consisted of the 232.5 troy ounces remaining from the January 20th deposit and the 159.75 troy ounces from the November 20th deposit. It is unlikely mint personnel began work on this consignment before the second installment was received on January 20th. It is impossible to know precisely which delivery contained the sterling deposited on November 20th. However, it is more likely mint personnel began working with the second larger consignment dividing it into three installments of 300 ounces each and then adding the November 20th consignment in with the remaining 232.5 ounces of the January 20th consignment to produce the final installment which equaled 392.25 ounces. It is clear the mint used the 1132.5 troy ounces of sterling deposited on January 20th to produce coinage equal to £379 14s (if all shillings this would be 7,594s) by February 18th. It seems the 159.75 troy ounces deposited earlier on November 20th were used to create additional coinage equal to £53 9s (if all shillings this would be 1,069s) delivered on February 18th. Thus, according to Hull the total consignment produced £433 3s in coins. Assuming the entire consignment was produced as shillings there would be a total of 8,663s.

On Monday, February 24, 1679, a customer deposited 400 ounces of sterling in the mint. Hull stated the consignment was turned into £133 18s in Massachusetts coinage and delivered in just over two weeks time, on Wednesday, March 12, 1679. Assuming the entire consignment was produced as shillings there would be a total of 2678s. From February 25th through March 11th there were 13 workdays (excluding Sundays) to complete the consignment.

On Friday, April 11, 1679, a customer deposited 286.5 troy ounces of sterling silver at the mint which was delivered in two installments. Hull stated the first and smaller installment of 96 ounces produced £32 2s in coins. Assuming the entire installment was produced as shillings there would be a total of 642s. No delivery date was given for the installment but presumably delivery occurred between the date of the previous entry in the ledger on the credit side of Hull's account, which was Wednesday, July 16, 1679, and the date of the second installment of this consignment, which was dated to Wednesday, July 30th. Hull stated the second installment of 190.5 ounces produced £63 17s in coins. Assuming the entire installment was produced as shillings there would be a total of 1277s. These two installments equaled the total 286.5 troy ounces of silver brought in on April 11th. Assuming the total production was in shillings, it took mint personnel a little over three-and-a-half months, or more precisely, 93 workdays (April 12 - July 29), excluding Sundays, to produce 1919s in coins. About the time the April 11th deposit was ready to be picked up the same customer delivered another almost equal shipment of sterling to be coined. This second shipment of 278 troy ounces was deposited on Monday, July 21st and Hull stated it produced £93 3s in coinage. Assuming the entire consignment was produced as shillings there would be a total of 1863s. The consignment was delivered to the customer on Saturday, October 18th, which is a total of 76 workdays (July 22 - Oct. 17), excluding Sundays, or a wait of just a few days less that three months.

On Saturday, November 8, 1679, a customer deposited 58 ounces of plate which was accepted as equivalent to 56 ounces of sterling. Hull stated this plate was turned into £18 14s in coinage. Assuming the entire consignment was produced as shillings there would be a total of 374s. The consignment was delivered about two weeks later on Friday, November 21st. This was a total of 10 workdays (Nov. 9 - 20), excluding Sundays, to complete the consignment.

On Friday, November 21, 1679, a customer deposited two quantities of sterling, one lot of 445 ounces and a second lot of 325.5 ounces. Hull stated the 445 ounces was turned into £149 5s. Assuming the entire consignment was produced as shillings there would be a total of 2985s. This lot was completed in about two weeks, on Tuesday, December 9th, which is a total of 14 workdays (Nov. 22 - Dec. 8), excluding Sundays. Hull stated the second lot of 325.5 ounces was turned into £109 6s in coins. Assuming the entire consignment was produced as shillings there would be a total of 2186s. This second lot was ready in about two additional weeks on Friday, December 26th for a total of 15 workdays for the lot (Dec. 9 - 25, since Christmas was not a holiday for the Puritans), excluding Sundays. The two lots combine to a total of 29 workdays for completion of the entire consignment.

On Tuesday, August 3 - Wednesday, August 4, 1680, a customer deposited three quantities of sterling, a lot of 220.75 troy ounces, another of 538.75 troy ounces and a third of 547.25 troy ounces. The first installment to be completed was the lot of 538.75 ounces which was ready in about a month on Sunday, August 29th with the second installment of 220.75 ounces ready about a week later on Saturday, September 4th. The third lot consisting of 547.25 ounces was delivered on Monday, September 27, 1680. Hull listed the value in coinage delivered to the customer but he did not include his mint fee to reveal the total coinage produced. In the ledger commentary, I explained how I calculated Hull's mint fee. Including his fee I have estimated the total value of each installment as: £179 18s4d for the 538.75 ounces, £73 14s6d for the 220.75 ounces, and £182 9s8d for the 547.25 ounces of sterling. Assuming the entire consignment was produced as shillings there would be a total of 3,598s from the 538.75 ounces, 1,475s from the 220.75 ounces and 3,650s from the 547.25 ounces for a total of 8,723s. Overall the entire consignment took a total of 45 workdays, (Aug. 5 - Sept. 25) excluding Sundays.

Chapter 9

Estimated Mint Productivity as Reflected in the Hull Ledger

Productivity rates found in ledger entries: the consignment of January 1679

Generally, sterling consigned to the mint did not receive immediate attention. Therefore, for the most part, it is impossible to determine exactly when production work began on a specific consignment based on the information in Hull's ledger. Fortunately, there is one consignment from January of 1679 that appears to have been given top priority from the moment it entered the shop with installments being delivered to the customer as quickly as possible. Mint personnel immediately began to work on the 1132.5 troy ounces of sterling that were deposited on Monday, January 20, 1679. They divided the consignment into three installments of 300 ounces each, with a final installment of the remaining 232.5 troy ounces that was combined with an earlier shipment of 159.75 troy ounces. The first installment of 300 troy ounces of sterling produced £100 12s in coins and was delivered to the customer on Monday, January 27th, just one week after the consignment had been delivered to the mint. The second installment, also consisting of 300 troy ounces of silver was ready three workdays later on Thursday, January 30th. The third installment of 300 troy ounces was delivered on Thursday, February 6th. Hull stated each installment yielded £100 12s in coins. Thus, each installment would equal 2,012s if the entire amount was minted into shillings.

Hull did not leave any records stating on which day and at what hour the mint began processing a specific installment of sterling, nor did he record the date and hour when an installment was completed. The closest we come to such a statement is the record for the first installment of the January 1679 consignment. We know the sterling arrived at the mint on Monday, January 20th and that 300 troy ounces had been processed, turned into coins and delivered to the client by Monday, January 27th. We do not know at what time of the day the consignment arrived on Monday the 20th. It is possible Monday was to devoted to weighing and assaying the consignment. Perhaps production did not begin until Tuesday. However, since this was clearly a rush order, it is also possible work began on the first installment on Monday. Further, it is possible the installment was completed by the end of the day on Saturday, January 25th and was picked up by the client early Monday morning. However, it is also possible work continued into Monday with the consignment being picked up in the afternoon. There seems little doubt the installment was in production from at least Tuesday, January 21st through Saturday, January 25th. This five day period represents the minimum number of production days available. However, if we include a half-a-day on the date of deposit and half-a-day on the delivery date, it is possible the consignment was in production for six days. This represents the maximum number of production days available.

Although each of the three equal installments has a definite completion date only the first installment has a fairly firm start date as well as a specific completion date. Therefore, the first installment must be used as the standard by which to judge the number of production days for the second and third installments. Since it must be used as the standard, I believe it is more prudent to allow as much time as is reasonably possible, using the outside limit for the production run. By assuming the maximum number of production days, in this case six days, we can say without a doubt the mint was able to process the consignment within that time period. As a consequence of this, the average daily production rate will be the minimum rate. We can say without a doubt the mint could achieve this minimum average production rate. It is possible the number of processing days could have been slightly less and therefore the daily production rate may have been slightly higher but the ledger records show the work could not have taken any longer. Work may have progressed somewhat faster than what I have estimated, but that is a matter of speculation.

It is quite likely the minters started working on the January consignment as soon as it entered the shop. In fact, in this case I am assuming half-a-day was devoted to processing the first installment on the day it was deposited, that is, on Monday, January 20th. I am also assuming there would be a half-day available for work on the date the installment was delivered to the customer, that is, Monday, January 27th. This gives a maximum of six workdays available (half-a-day on Monday the day of the deposit, all day on Tuesday, Wednesday, Thursday, Friday and Saturday and half-a-day on Monday the day of delivery). Clearly, mint personnel worked on the first two installments simultaneously, since the second installment was finished and delivered only three workdays after the first installment. That the three installments were produced so quickly, and that they were all for equal amounts of sterling, allows us to extrapolate some valuable information on production runs. For example, it is quite likely each installment was in production for no more than six days. If we assume the second installment also took up to six days, production on that installment would have begun on Thursday, January 23rd.

I suspect the 300 troy ounces of sterling from the first installment was melted on the date of the deposit, Monday, January 20th, and the melt was then poured into the molds where it cooled into sterling strips. This process of melting, refining and pouring the sterling would only require a few hours of work. On Tuesday the hardened sterling strips were probably taken out of the molds and cleaned. Over the next few days the planchets would be prepared. The molded sterling strips would be rolled to the required thickness and then planchets would be cut out of the strips. The sharp edges of the newly cut planchets would be smoothed and the planchets checked for weight and defects. Inspected planchets would be annealed. At this time the screw press would be prepared and dies would be affixed. If the obverse and reverse die axes were accurately positioned in relation to each other, the die alignment process would take several hours (Challis, *New History*, p. 395). The obverse and reverse axes of existing Massachusetts Pine Tree small planchet shillings are fairly accurately aligned for a medal turn. The reverse die is often at 0° (12:00 o'clock) or within 30° of alignment, indicating that the mint did spend some time aligning the die axes.[1]

---

[1] Many Willow, Oak and "large planchet" Pine Tree coinage, which were made using some variety of rocker dies, align based on a medal turn, with the reverse axis at 0° (12:00 o'clock). An exception is the Noe 1 Oak Tree shilling which aligns as a coin turn with the reverse axis at 180° (6:00 o'clock).

Planchet preparation would probably take several days. Certainly, the steps were sequential; the stock was sent through one step in the production process and that step was completed before the minters started the next step in the process. Possibly the stock was rolled out on one day, the planchets may have been cut on the following day, while smoothing, weight control and annealing may have been performed on the next day. The actual stamping of the coins did not take as much time as planchet preparation. During the Confederation era, copper coins were stamped at a rate of one coin every two to three seconds. Assuming the Massachusetts silver mint had a smaller press, possibly operated by only one or two people, and even allowing time for breaks, we can certainly assume at least one coin could be stamped every twenty seconds. At the rate of one coin per twenty seconds it would take a little over 11 hours to stamp 2,012 finished planchets into shillings. Thus, the actual stamping of the coins probably occurred on the day before delivery, while on the delivery day the coins may have been inspected, counted and bagged or boxed for the customer. Following this time line, it would appear the melting of the sterling, as well as the molding and cleaning of the strips for the first consignment were steps performed on Monday and Tuesday, January 20-21. Possibly the molds would be readied for the next installment on Wednesday and work on the second installment would have begun on Thursday, January 23 with a few hours spent melting the silver and pouring it into the molds.

Although some work may have been performed on each installment of 300 troy ounces on every one of the six days each installment was in production, it did not take six full days of work by all of the mint employees to process each installment of 300 troy ounces. This is clear, for work on the first two installments overlapped, so that in effect 600 troy ounces of sterling were prepared over nine workdays. Thus, between the date the consignment entered the mint on Monday, January 20th and the delivery date of the second installment on Thursday, January 30th the mint processed a total of 600 troy ounces of sterling in a period of not more than nine workdays for an average production rate of not less than 66.66 troy ounces per day.

Work on the third installment probably began on Thursday January 30th, the date on which the second installment was delivered, with a few hours spent on melting the silver and pouring it into the molds. This third installment of 300 troy ounces, which also produced £100 12s in coins, was delivered to the customer on Thursday, February 6th. Again, allowing a half-day of work on the initial day of Thursday, January 30 and a half-day of work on the delivery date of Thursday, February 6th, there were a total of six workdays available for the production of this installment. Thus, it is quite likely each of these three installments of 300 troy ounces of sterling took no more than six days for the mint to process. This gives an average daily production rate per installment of not less than 50 troy ounces of silver per day.

**Estimated maximum production time for the first three installments
of the consignment deposited on January 20, 1679**

Date	Installment 1 300 troy ounces	Installment 2 300 troy ounces	Installment 3 300 troy ounces
Monday, Jan. 20	half day - melt		
Tuesday, Jan. 21	full day		
Wednesday, Jan. 22	full day		
Thursday, Jan. 23	full day	half day - melt	
Friday, Jan. 24	full day	full day	
Saturday, Jan. 25	full day	full day	
Sunday, Jan. 26	--------------------	--------------------	
Monday, Jan. 27	half day - delivery	full day	
Tuesday, Jan. 28		full day	
Wednesday, Jan. 29		full day	
Thursday, Jan. 30		half day - delivery	half day – melt
Friday, Jan. 31			full day
Saturday, Feb. 1			full day
Sunday, Feb. 2			--------------------
Monday, Feb. 3			full day
Tuesday, Feb. 4			full day
Wednesday, Feb. 5			full day
Thursday, Feb. 6			half day – delivery

If each of these three installments were minted completely as shillings this would mean, combining the first and second overlapping installments, a total of 4,024 shillings were produced over a period of nine days for a production rate of not less than 447.11 shillings per day. While, for the six days during which the third installment was in production, a total of

2,012 shillings would have been produced for a production rate of not less than 335.33 shillings per day. Naturally, the average production rate encompasses the time taken for the entire process. Thus, there would be no finished coins for several days during which the silver was melted and the planchets were prepared, while on one or two days at the end of the process an entire installment might be stamped, counted and boxed.

Actually, what we have in the January 1679 consignment is an installment of 600 troy ounces followed by an installment of 300 troy ounces. In no other consignment was the mint so anxious to deliver the coins to the customer. There were other consignments where Hull recorded large installments close in size to 600 troy ounces. In those instances we know the installments were processed by the mint as single production runs (such as consignments and installments of 547.25 troy ounces, 538.75 troy ounces, 528.5 troy ounces and 496.75 troy ounces of sterling), since in each case there was just one delivery date when the entire installment was completed. In order to deliver the coins from the first 600 troy ounces of the January 1679 consignment to the customer as soon as possible Hull processed the lot as two individual production units, so each unit could be delivered as soon as it was completed. In recording this pragmatic decision in his ledger, Hull gave us some additional insight as to how larger consignments were processed. It seems likely the maximum capacity of the melting furnace was 25 troy pounds of sterling (which is equal to 300 troy ounces). This will be explained in more detail below. Thus, large individual installments in the range of 400 to 600 troy ounces were most likely divided into two melts that were only a few days apart, allowing just enough time for the first melt to be hardened in the molds. Then, once the strips were removed from the molds, the molds would be prepared for the second melt and the staff would proceed with the second melt, as was the case with the installment of 600 ounces of January 1679.

Further, it seems 600 troy ounces was the maximum quantity of sterling the mint could handle in a single production run. Certainly, two or three days after the second melt of 300 troy ounces the molds would have been free for the third installment of 300 ounces. However, that installment was not started until the first two installments of 300 ounces were completed and delivered to the client. Possibly there were not enough employees or work space to simultaneously process three installments. Thus, in the nine days the mint processed the 600 troy ounces of sterling, it appears the mint was working at full capacity. Another installment could not be handled until the 600 troy ounces was completed.

Full capacity does not mean all mint employees worked on minting for the entire nine days. Undoubtedly, there were space and equipment limitations; for example, it seems two-and-a-half days were required before the molds were free and a second melt could occur. Thus, out of that nine day period, the first two-and-a-half days were devoted to melting and molding strips from the sterling of the first installment. During that time no work was performed on the second installment. Further, once the first installment was completed and delivered to the customer, the remaining days in the nine day cycle were devoted to the completion of the second installment. Therefore, the two installments would only be in simultaneous production for the middle four days of the nine day production period and only in simultaneous full production for two of those days. The average daily processing rates for the nine days would be 33.33 troy ounces per half-day per installment and 66.66 troy ounces per full day per installment. The daily processing rates would be a bell curve: 33.33 oz. on the January 20th; 66.66 oz. on January 21-22; 99.99 oz. on January 23; 133.32 oz. on January 24-25; 99.99 oz. on January 27; 66.66 oz. on January 28-29 and 33.33 oz. on January 30. Thus, if production of 600 troy ounces over a period of nine days is defined as full capacity, then clearly some of the time full capacity did not involve as many mint employees as at other times. On the first and last day just one installment was in process and then only for half-a-day, while during the middle of the production run both installments were simultaneously in full-time production. Thus, it seems at some points during the eight days not all employees were working full-time on minting. Hence, the average daily production level for 600 troy ounces is not double the rate for 300 ounces. Rather, the installment of 600 troy ounces, at 66.66 troy ounces per day, is only slightly more than 33% higher than the production rate for 300 troy ounces, at 50 troy ounces per day.

Precisely what full capacity mint production meant in terms of man-hours or full-time work cannot be determined. The estimates given above represent the maximum number of days each 300 troy ounce installment was in production. However, we simply do not know how many man-hours were required to process an installment of 300 troy ounces. It certainly appears that limitations of space, equipment and staffing did not allow production to proceed at a faster pace. However, even though much time was devoted to the installments, we cannot say that an installment was in production every minute of each day it was in process. The only mint employee we can track during this period is John Hull and it appears that even during the highest periods of production for these three installments of January 1679, Hull did not spend his entire day devoted to the minting process. Indeed, in Chapter 12, we shall discover Hull may have had very little to do with the daily operation of the mint during the later years of the partnership. From Hull's ledger we see Hull participated in several business dealings during the very days the first two installments of the January 20th consignment were being processed, namely from January 20th through 27th, 1679. On January 21st, Hull agreed to purchase 103 quarts of codfish from Charles Lidget for £66 19s; on the 22nd he collected £7 9s from Thomas Wheeler; on the 27th he received £200 from John Alcock and £600 in bills of exchange from John Paige of London (New England Historic Genealogical Society, MS Cb 110, vol. 1, folios, 166 recto, 167 verso and 168 recto). There are also transactions recorded during the production of the third installment, as the payment of £4 by Thomas Wheeler and a payment of £133 1s by Alcock, both on January 30th (New England Historic Genealogical Society, MS Cb 110, vol. 1, folios 166 recto and 167 verso). It should be noted these business transactions were found by looking through just three folios in Hull's ledger, namely the folios listing new accounts or accounts that were forwarded in the ledger with opening entries in late 1678 or early 1679. Additional business transactions dating to late January 1679 might be located anywhere throughout the ledger; I have not examined the first 160 folios for other entries from this period. Thus, it is quite likely other business was conducted on these specific days. Additionally, it is probable Hull attended the Thursday church lecture. As late as 1840 a descendant of the Sewall family owned a series of small notebooks in Hull's handwriting containing summaries of over two hundred Sunday sermons and Thursday lectures delivered at the First Church of Boston between 1655 and 1661 (Hull, *Diary,* Memoir, p. 123). These notebooks are now lost but they were probably part of a larger series. Patricia Kane remarks that notes Hull wrote on sermons delivered between 1671 and 1679 reside in the Massachusetts Historical Society (Kane, p. 571, footnote 2). The fact that Hull compiled such a work indicates he regularly attended both the Thursday lectures as well as the required Sunday services. Also, Hull was Treasurer for Massachusetts Bay at this time (1676-1680) and may have had meetings relating to that position. It seems clear Hull performed several non-mint duties during the fourteen days when the first three installments of the January 20th consignment were minted.

Although Hull may not have been available for full-time mint work during the weeks these installments were processed, we simply do not know what roles other individuals may have performed. It is certainly possible some individuals, probably apprentices, performed functions each day that were related to the various sequential steps that needed to be followed in producing planchets and processing the installments. However, each installment probably did not require six full days of uninterrupted work devoted solely to that installment. Thus, we cannot say precisely how many man-hours were devoted to processing an installment. Nevertheless, it seems the processing of 600 troy ounces over nine work days was the highest daily rate of production the mint was willing to sustain. The mint was unwilling to begin an additional installment until the 600 ounces was completed. Thus, although we cannot precisely define full capacity in terms of man-hours per day required for full capacity production, we may assume when the mint was working at the highest capacity it was willing to undertake, it could sustain an average production rate of not less than 66.66 troy ounces of silver per day.

The fourth and final installment of the January 20th consignment consisted of 392.25 troy ounces of sterling that yielded £131 7s in coins. If the entire installment was in shillings this would equal 2,627s. This installment was delivered on Tuesday, February 18, 1679. From Thursday, February 6th, which was the date on which the third installment was delivered to the customer and thus was the day work could commence on the fourth installment, there were a total of ten workdays before the delivery of the fourth installment (counting a half-day each on the 6th and the 18th). This yields an average production rate of

39.225 troy ounces per day (or 262.7s per day if the installment was entirely in shillings). Since this is a considerably lower production rate than we find in the first three installments (of 66.66 and 50 troy ounces per day), it seems likely mint personnel temporarily turned their attention to other duties after the third installment was completed before taking up the final installment. Thus, we cannot use the final installment to help derive production rate data. From the January 1679 consignment we have extrapolated much production related information. Most helpful in assisting with estimating the actual mint processing time for other installments is that a production run of 600 troy ounces took nine days for an average production rate of 66.66 troy ounces per day and a 300 troy ounce installment took six days for an average daily production rate of 50 troy ounces per day.

Productivity rates found in ledger entries: the consignment of August 1680

Some related production information may be gleaned from the final consignment recorded in the Hull shop account ledger, a consignment in three shipments totaling 1306.75 troy ounces of sterling deposited at the mint on August 3-4, 1680. As usual, the consignment was backlogged when it first arrived. The consignment was processed in three units, in the same quantities as the three shipments delivered to the mint; the first installment was for 538.75 ounces, the second was for 220.75 ounces and the third was for 547.25 ounces of sterling. The first installment was delivered to the customer on Sunday, August 29th. Because we do not know the start date for this installment we cannot calculate a daily production rate. However, we find the 220.75 ounces was delivered just a few days later on Saturday, September 4th. Clearly, the first installment was a large quantity of sterling, requiring two melts, which means the mint would be working at full capacity and would not be simultaneously processing any other installments. It seems, as soon as the mint delivered the first installment on August 29th, they immediately began work on the small 220.75 ounces installment. Allowing half-a-day for the melting of the installment on Monday, August 30th, and half-a-day for inspection and counting of the final coins on the delivery date of Saturday, September 4th, there was a maximum of five workdays to process this second installment, for an average daily production rate of not less than 44.15 troy ounces per day. I have estimated the total yield of the installment as £73 15s. Assuming the entire amount was in shillings this would equal 1475s, for an average production rate of 295s per day. As was usually the case with installments, there was a waiting period of a few weeks before the third installment was finally delivered on Monday, September 27th, which means the final installment was backlogged for some period. Therefore, of the three installments in the August 1680 consignment only the smaller 220.75 ounces installment can give us an indication of production time.

It should be recognized these averages are from 1679-1680 and certainly pertain to the period during which the mint was using a screw press. Average daily production output would have differed in the 1650's and 1660's when a rocker press was in use, since the coining procedures would have been different. Also, the rates are limited to the time required for planchet production and stamping, and do not reflect all the work related to the mint. The critical and time consuming job of diecutting is not included nor is any maintenance, repair or clean up of the machinery, tools or the building. These duties would be performed before or after a consignment was completed and therefore time spend on such activities would not be reflected in the data we find in Hull's ledger.

The number of days spent minting coins from October of 1671 through September of 1680

From Hull's ledger we have discovered an individual installment of 600 troy ounces of sterling took a maximum of nine workdays to be turned into coins for a minimum average production rate of 66.66 troy ounces per day. Furthermore, a 300 troy ounce installment took a maximum of six workdays to be turned into coins for an average minimum daily production rate of 50 troy ounces per day. And finally, an installment of 220.75 troy ounces took a maximum of five workdays to be turned into coins, for an average minimum daily production rate of 44.15 troy ounces per day.

In calculating the number of production days per year one cannot simply use a single average daily production rate, since we have seen the production rate differed depending on the size of the production run. Basically, installments within a certain weight range took a specific number of workdays to complete. Larger installments within a specific range took more time per day to complete and therefore yield a higher daily production rate. For instance, taking 600 troy ounces through the entire minting process would take up to nine days from the start to finish. If the installment was 575 troy ounces the consignment would still take nine days to complete, but each stage in the process would be completed a little more quickly than would be the case for a consignment of 600 troy ounces, so that slightly less time per day would need to be devoted to minting. As minting was a process in which each step had to be completed before proceeding to the next step, we must look at the number of days that were required for processing installments of various sizes. We cannot simply take the total weight of the annual consignments and then average them by a single daily production rate.

First, we must identify the troy ounces for each production run and determine whether the run is a complete consignment or an installment from a larger consignment. Then, we must treat each production run as an individual unit. A further complication is that from the Hull ledger we can only identify the number of production days for three different size production runs, namely a run of 600 troy ounces, a run of 300 troy ounces and a run of 220 troy ounces. Therefore, the number of production days assigned to each production run must necessarily be an estimate based on the available figures. The upper limit of an individual production run is 600 troy ounces. As with the installment of 600 ounces from January 1679 discussed above, I suspect production runs in this range were divided into two melts and processed as a single unit within nine work days. We have seen a day's work on a larger consignment averaged to a production rate of at least 66.66 troy ounces. Rather than simply subtract precisely 66.66 troy ounces from the upper limit of 600 troy ounces, to arrive at a lower limit of 534.33 troy ounces for a nine day production run, I believe it is more reasonable to round the lower limit down to around 525 troy ounces. A few ounces more or less per production run would not extend or decrease the number of workdays but would only extend or decrease the number of hours per day devoted to minting. Thus individual production runs from an upper limit of 600 troy ounces down to about 525 troy ounces will be considered to have taken no more than nine production days. Consignments just below 525 troy ounces to about 450 troy ounces will be considered to have been in production for no more than eight days. Consignments that are just under 450 troy ounces to those that are about 350 troy ounces will be listed as in production for no more than seven days. We know 300 troy ounces took no more than six production days, so production runs from about 350 troy ounces to 250 troy ounces will be considered to have taken no more than six production days. Production runs just below 250 troy ounces to about 150 troy ounces will be considered to have taken no more than five production days, similar to the installment of 220.75 troy ounces. By determining the number of production runs and then estimating the maximum number of days each run was in production we can estimate the maximum number of days the mint was actually producing coins each year.

These numbers do not represent entire days spent minting coins, but rather they represent the maximum number of days during which a consignment or installment was in production at the mint. Certainly, somewhat larger quantities of sterling would require more hours per day than somewhat smaller quantities. To give some relative indication of the quantity of time expended on minting for each production run, I have calculated the average production rate per day in troy ounces of silver for each production run by taking the total troy ounces of sterling in production and dividing it by the number of days in production. For comparison, we have seen the maximum production rate found in the Hull ledger averaged 66.66 troy ounces per day, although as mentioned above, this probably does not represent continuous full-time mint work by all shop personnel for the entire production period.

Notes to the table that follows:

Each row across represents all the consignments in the ledger sent to the mint during that year. In the column detailing the troy ounces of sterling per production run, each consignment for the year is separated by a blank line. For example, in October – December 1671 there were two separate consignments, one for 528.5 troy ounces and another for 208 troy ounces of sterling. Each consignment listed as a single installment was processed as a single production run and had a specific delivery date. Some larger consignments were divided into several installments, with each installment representing a specific production run that had its own delivery date. In these cases the quantities of sterling for each individual installment, that is, for each production run, are listed directly below each other without any blank lines. For example, under 1679 the first consignment was processed in three installments of 600, 300 and 392.25 troy ounces. These three production runs are individually listed but they are not seperated by a space as they represent a single consignment. The 400 troy ounces that is listed below these entries, but is separated from the above three entries by a space, represents another consignment and a different production run.

Under the year 1677 Hull gave no indication in his ledger how the three consignments from that year were apportioned into production runs. I have simply divided the 1677 totals using what would be the most efficient production schedule. It is purely speculation. There was a consignment from April 1677 for 1846.925 troy ounces that I treated as consisting of four production runs. Later in the year, there were two other consignments. I have combined those two consignments into a single series of four additional production runs. The two combined consignments consist of a large consignment that was delivered to the mint in several parcels between May 3rd and August 29th, altogether they yielded £671 12s in coins, which I have estimated as consisting of 2005 troy ounces. During this period another smaller consignment for 125 ounces of sterling was received on July 13th. I have combined this with the May-August consignment for a total of 2130 troy ounces in a single series of production runs. Also, two very small production runs from 1679 had to be estimated since they were outside the parameters discussed above for assigning the number of days one could reasonable expect the consignment to have been in production. An installment for 96 troy ounces which yielded £32 2s in coins (if the consignment was all in shillings this would be about 624s), was estimated as a three day run and a 56 ounce consignment, yielding £18 14s in coins (if only shillings this would be about 374s), was estimated at a two day production run. For these much smaller quantities I have assumed several different processes in planchet production could be completed in one or two days.

The number of days the Massachusetts Mint actually processed coinage consignments and average troy ounces produced per day

Year	Troy ounces per production run	Number of days in production	Average troy ounces produced per day
Oct.-Dec. 1671	528.5	9	58.722
	208	5	41.6
1672	255.25	6	42.5416
	179.5	5	35.9
1673	265	6	44.166
1674	275.5	6	45.916
1675	369.5	7	52.785
	217	5	43.4
1676	496.75	8	62.093
1677	500	8	
	500	8	
	400	8	
	446.925	8	
	500	8	
	500	8	
	565	9	
	565	9	
1678	none	none	
1679	600	9	66.666
	300	6	50
	392.25	7	56.035
	400	7	57.142
	96	3	32
	190.5	5	38.1
	278	6	46.333
	56	2	28
	445	7	63.571
	325.5	6	54.25
August 1680	538.75	9	59.861
	220.75	5	44.15
	547.25	9	60.805
TOTALS	11,161.925	÷ 204	= 54.715

Having identified the individual production runs and the maximum number of days each run was in production we are now in a position to present a summary table with yearly totals. The following summary table contains the quantity of sterling consigned to the mint per year as recorded in the Hull ledger with an estimate of the total number of shillings produced from all production runs that occurred during the year. This estimate assumes all production was in shillings. Next is the number of operational days per year, derived from the previous chart. This number represents the maximum number of days each consignment was actually in production. Operational days represent days during which some work was performed on a consignment; they do not necessarily represent days of full-time work on a consignment. To give an indication of the equivalent in full-time days per year that were devoted to minting I have estimated the number of full capacity days per year. As discussed above, we have seen full capacity work, as reflected in the nine day production run from January 1679, yielded a minimum average production rate of 66.66 troy ounces per day. This level of production clearly did not require full-time participation by all mint employees at all times. However, it is the highest production rate documented in the Hull ledger and was probably the highest sustainable rate, and thus I refer to that rate as "full capacity." Sustained higher rates, such as 100 troy ounces per day, would require larger single melts. As larger melts are undocumented, they were probably beyond the capacity of the mint. Therefore, the number of full capacity days per year has been derived by taking the total ounces of sterling consigned to the mint per year and dividing that number by 66.66, assuming a production rate of 66.66 troy ounces per day as full capacity. This reflects the number of days per year it would take to complete the entire year's consignments if the mint could have sustained full capacity work. Obviously, this rate could not be regularly attained, as it required 600 troy ounces of sterling to be available for each production run and presumably required most of the shop staff to be focused on mint production. However, this estimate gives some indication of the difference between the number of operational days used and the minimum number of days needed if the maximum amount of sterling that could be processed was available for each production run and most shop employees could focus on the mint consignment.

Summary of annual productivity at the Massachusetts Mint with equivalent full capacity days per year

Year	Quantity of sterling minted in troy ounces	Estimated number of shillings	Number of operational days	Equivalency in full capacity days at 66.66 troy oz. per day
Oct.-Dec. 1671	736.5	4937s	14	11
1672	434.75	2914s	11	6.5
1673	265	1776s	6	3.975
1674	275.5	1847s	6	4.1
1675	586.5	3932s	12	8.79
1676	496.75	3330s	8	7.45
1677	3976.925	26,651s	66	59.65
1678	none	none	none	none
1679	3083.25	20,668s	58	46.25
August 1680	1306.75	8723s	23	19.6
TOTALS	11,161.925	74,777s	204	167.4

From this table it is clear that during most years of the decade of the 1670's very little silver was brought to the mint for conversion into Pine Tree coinage. For the nine year period from October 18, 1671 through September 26, 1680, there were 930.16 troy pounds of sterling consigned to the mint that were transformed into approximately 74,777 shillings, if the entire production was in shillings. The period from October 18, 1671 through September 26, 1680 totals to approximately 2800 workdays, excluding Sundays; during this period the mint was in production a total of 204 days or just over 7.25% of the time. However, production was not equally distributed over these years. In fact, most years had a very low annual mintage with almost two-thirds of all coinage production concentrated in the two years 1677 and 1679. Interestingly, even in these higher production years, the mint was in operation for only about 60 days per year. At six workdays per week this is equivalent to a total of ten to eleven weeks per year during which consignments were in production. The above production figures assume no new technological innovations occurred during the period, so that production rates from 1679 would be valid for earlier years in that decade. In other words, this assumes the shift from a rocker press to a screw press had occurred before October of 1671.

Silver shortages at the Massachusetts Mint in the 1670's

Several contemporary sources indicate the 1670's was a period of reduced production with less silver brought into the mint than during previous decades. For example, the 1675 mint contract renewal documents from the General Court specifically addressed the need to consider ways of "Incouraging ... persons that haue bulljon, to bring the same to the mint" (Crosby, p. 81) and a proposal to the General Court from May 19, 1680, which stated, "little of late yeares ... hath been coyned" (Crosby, pp. 109-11). Clearly, the production numbers from the 1670's in Hull's ledger support such statements. There are several reasons for this situation. In 1670, the West Indian island of Montserrat increased the value of the eight reales cob to 72d (6s), and other islands soon followed. Since the eight reales was valued at 60d (5s) in Massachusetts Bay it was more profitable for individuals to export Spanish coins out of the Commonwealth rather than bring them to the mint. From Hull's ledger we see far fewer coins were minted during the entire year of 1672 than had been produced in the last three months of 1671. On October 8, 1672, the Massachusetts Bay General Court passed a law raising the value of the eight reales to 72d (6s). This legislation took away the economic advantages of exporting Spanish silver and thus stopped the depletion of Spanish cobs from Massachusetts Bay. However, it did not help the mint because the legislation rated Spanish silver at just over 84d (7s) per troy ounce while Massachusetts silver was only 80d (6s8d) per troy ounce thus, one actually lost money when converting Spanish cobs into Massachusetts coinage! The situation was compounded by the hoarding of silver that occurred during the war against King Philip (June 1675 - February 1677). Very little Massachusetts silver was produced through 1676, even after the mint fee was reduced in June of 1675. Indeed, from Hull's extant ledger we find from the first surviving entry, which dates to October of 1671, through the end of the war on February 12, 1677, there were only nine consignments of silver deposited in the mint and six of the nine consignments were personal consignments from Hull's inventory. During this five-and-a-half year period customer deposits were reduced to a total of 690 troy ounces of sterling which were turned into an estimated £231 5s in Massachusetts coinage, while Hull, himself, deposited 2,109.5 troy ounces of sterling which produced an estimated £678 11s in Massachusetts coinage.

On April 20, 1677, about two months after King Philip's War ended, a larger consignment of silver was brought to the mint, but further consignments were not forthcoming. In order to attract more silver to the mint, in May of 1677 Hull reduced his mint fees to 12d per troy ounce of sterling, just two years after the June 1675 reduction. This second fee reduction worked temporarily, bringing in some additional consignments through August 29th. Overall, during 1677, customers deposited approximately 3,977 troy ounces of sterling that produced an estimated £1,332 11s in Massachusetts coinage. However, for the next fifteen months, from September of 1677 through November of 1678, no consignments were placed with the mint. In fact, there was probably no minting in 1678; the only silver consignment in that year was a small shipment of 159.75 troy ounces of sterling received on

November 20th. Possibly this was a preliminary shipment to the 1,295.25 troy ounces of sterling consigned in January of 1679 which was soon followed by a consignment from another customer for 400 troy ounces of sterling on February 24th; altogether the November through February consignments produced £567 1s in Massachusetts coinage. Additionally, two smaller consignments were placed during the year, one on April 11th for £95 19s and another on July 21st for £93 3s with one very small consignment on November 8th for £17 14s in Massachusetts coinage. Then there was a larger consignment for 770.5 troy ounces of sterling deposited on November 21st that produced £258 11s in coinage. This was followed by a nine month hiatus in new consignments. Undoubtedly, Hull's inventory was very low during this period. Hull had not personally consigned any silver to the mint since June of 1676. Further, we see in the ledger that on May 6, 1679, Hull was apparently out of silver and needed to purchase 131.5 ounces of plate for £139 9s from his former apprentice, the silversmith, Jeremiah Dummer. In 1680, with little inventory and no consignments Hull was forced to further reduce his fee to 6.6d per troy ounce, which brought in a consignment in August of 1680 for £436 3s in Massachusetts coinage. At this point the ledger ends.

Even though productivity increased during the 1670's with the advent of screw press technology, silver shortages at the mint caused by overvaluing Spanish American silver cobs, resulted in reduced mint fees that decreased profitability. Now that we have an estimate for the number of days per year the mint was in production, we can determine the average daily income from minting operations. The earliest entries in the extant portion of the shop account are for the final months of 1671, before the 1672 General Court legislation raised the value of the eight reales to 72d. It has been estimated that during October through December of 1671 there were 4937 shillings minted over a period of fourteen workdays. Based on the then current customer return of 74d per troy ounce of sterling, an estimated 4541.75s (£227 1s 9d) would have been delivered to the consignors while the mint would have retained the remaining 395.25s (£19 15s 3d) as income. Averaging this income over the fourteen workdays yields an average return of 338.785d (£1 8s 2.78d) for each day of minting. As one of the two consignments from this period was for Hull, it is possible the actual mint income varied, since Hull may not have subtracted mint fees. However, in general, the average income during this period from a day of minting would be in the range of £1 8s, with a slightly higher daily income for larger consignments because they could be processed more efficiently. By the end of the decade the average daily income had dramatically declined. In 1679 the recorded mintage came to a total of 20,668 shillings. By that time the mint return had been reduced to 12d per £1 of coins produced. Therefore, during that year the mint obtained 1033s 4.8d (£51 13s 4.8d) as income. Since it has been estimated the mint was in operation for 58 workdays in 1679, there was an average return of 213.8d (17s 9.8d) per day of minting. Thus, the average income for a day of minting declined by more that one-third from £1 8s 2.78d per day in 1671 to only 17s 9.8d by 1679. Further, from the one consignment in the ledger from 1680, we see Hull reduced his mint fee from 1s to 6.6d per £1 of coins produced. This indicates that in 1680 mint income on a per workday basis plummeted to just slightly more than one-half of the 1679 level!

Chapter 10

Consignment Turnaround Time at the Massachusetts Bay Mint

Lord Culpepper's complaint

In his testimony before the Committee of the Lords of Trade and Plantations on August 9, 1681, Lord Thomas Culpepper criticized the Massachusetts Mint for requiring customers to wait an inordinate length of time for their silver to be turned into coins. Culpepper, who had served as Governor of Virginia and had visited Massachusetts Bay for about seven weeks from August 24 through about October 15 of 1680, suggested regulations be enacted requiring the mint to produce coinage "speedy" (Fortescue, *Calendar 1681-1685*, pp. 99-100, the full quote is given above, p. 71).[1] This is the only comment I have uncovered on what may be called the "turnaround time" which reflects both the processing time and the time a consignment of sterling was backlogged at the mint.

Whether backlogged consignments had been a persistent problem at the mint is unknown. However, from the entries in Hull's surviving ledger we can glean some information on turnaround time. We know the size of the various production runs for most consignments or installments and are able to estimate the number of days each run was actually in production. Also, we have the date each consignment was deposited at the mint and the date on which the completed coins were delivered to the customer. The difference between the processing time and the length of time a consignment was in the mint represents the length of time the consignment sat in the shop, in a backlog, before it was processed.

Turnaround time from the consignments in Hull's ledger

The mint consignments listed in Hull's ledger, which included both a deposit and a delivery date, combine to a total of 6,908.5 troy ounces of sterling that remained at the mint for approximately 601 workdays and produced an estimated 46,280 shillings, if the entire production was in shillings. Unfortunately four consignments, including the two largest consignments from that decade, documenting an additional 4,252.425 troy ounces of sterling that produced an estimated 28,506 shillings, did not list a delivery date and therefore a turnaround time cannot be determined for those consignments (these are the consignments deposited on December 12, 1674; April 20-27, 1677; July 13, 1677 and May-August 1677).

---

[1] Phil Mossman reminded me that in 1679 Governor Culpepper had speculated in Spanish American silver as a profiteer, buying up lightweight eight reales at 5s each and then issuing a proclamation raising the value of the coins to 6s. However, when Culpepper realized his salary would be paid at the inflated rate, he restored the eight reales to the 5s rate. Clearly Culpepper's comments on the Massachusetts Mint were not those of an unbiased outsider, but rather were the comments of an individual who sympathized with and participated in profiteering (see Mossman, p. 47).

In the following charts I have included the date of the consignment giving the month of the deposit and the month of the delivery; for the precise dates see the summary of the consignments given above in Chapter Eight. Next, in order to compare the sizes of the consignments, I have included the troy ounces of sterling deposited per consignment and an estimate of the number of shillings produced from each consignment. This is followed by the total number of workdays each consignment was in the shop and available for processing, based on a six day work week. It does not include the day of deposit or the day of delivery. I then give the maximum number of days each consignment was actually in production based on the data found in the chart discussed above labelled, "The number of days the Massachusetts Mint actually processed coinage consignments and average troy ounces produced per day." Since the present discussion focuses on the length of time a consignment was at the mint, any time a partial installment for a consignment was in production has been counted as a day during which the consignment was in process. The number of days the consignment, or any installment of the consignment, was in production has been subtracted from the number of workdays the consignment was in the shop to determine the number of workdays the consignment was in the backlog. Thus, consignment backlog time represents the number of days when no work was being performed on any installment of a consignment. Furthermore, I have calculated the percentage of time a consignment was in production based on the total number of workdays the consignment was at the mint. Additionally, I have included the percentage of time a consignment languished in the mint backlog, based on the total number of workdays a consignment was at the mint. I rounded the production and backlog percentages to the nearest tenth of a percent. Generally, the period of backlog would precede the production period, for when a production run was completed the coins would be delivered to the customer. However, in a few cases larger consignments were divided into installments and initial installments may have been produced in a more timely manner while there might have been some waiting period before the final installments were delivered. In the chart below in the entries for the larger consignments I have totalled the work days for every installment from the consignment, thus the backlog represents all of the non-production days from the time the silver was consigned to the mint to the time the final installment was delivered to the customer.

The consignments are arranged from those with the shortest periods of backlog to those with the longest backlogs. I have divided the data into two groups. The first group has the quicker turnaround times; since the mint worked on these consignments at least 30% of the time the consignments were on deposit in the shop (this is to say, they were backlogged less than 70% of the time). The second group has the slower turnaround times; as these consignments were in production less than 30% of the time they were at the mint (that is, they were backlogged more than 70% of the time they were on deposit).

Consignments in production at least 30% of the time they were in the mint

date of consignment	troy ounces	estimated number of shillings	number of workdays the consignment was in the shop	days in production	days in backlog	percent of time in production	percent of time in backlog
Jan. - Feb. 1679	1,132.5	7,594	24	22	2	91.7%	8.3%
May 1675	369.5	2,477	11	7	4	63.6%	36.4%
Feb. – March 1679	400	2,678	13	7	6	53.8%	46.2%
Aug. - Sept. 1680	1,306.25	8,723	45	23	22	51.1%	48.9%
Nov. - Dec. 1679	770.5	5,171	29	13	16	44.8%	55.2%
Oct. - Nov. 1671	528	3,543	21	9	12	42.9%	57.1%
June - July 1676	496.75	3,330	24	8	16	33.3%	66.6%

Consignments in production less than 30% of the time they were in the mint

date of consignment	troy ounces	estimated number of shillings	number of workdays the consignment was in the shop	days in production	days in backlog	percent of time in production	percent of time in backlog
June - July 1675	217	1,455	17	5	12	29.4%	70.6%
Jan. - Feb 1672	255.25	1,711	30	6	24	20%	80%
Nov. 1679	56	374	10	2	8	20%	80%
Oct. - Dec. 1671	208	1,394	34	5	29	14.7%	85.3%
Aug. - Oct. 1673	265	1,776	51	6	45	11.8%	88.2%
June - Aug. 1672	179.5	1,203	47	5	42	10.6%	89.4%
Nov. 1678 - Feb. 1679	159.75	1,069	76	7	69	9.2%	90.8%
April - July 1679	286.5	1,919	93	8	85	8.6%	91.4%
July - Oct. 1679	278	1,863	76	6	70	7.9%	92.1%

Expediting larger consignments

The tables show larger consignments were processed more quickly than smaller consignments. The entries are organized by consignment, starting with the consignment having the highest percentage of time in production and therefore the lowest percentage of time in the backlog. However, although the tables were not arranged by consignment size, we see all the consignments above 300 troy ounces of sterling are found in the first table and all those consignments below 300 troy ounces of sterling are in the second table.

Totaling the consignments from the first table we arrive at 5003.5 troy ounces of sterling that was in the shop for 167 workdays and was used to produce an estimated 33,516 shillings. This yields a daily production average of 200.69s and an overall average turnaround time for all the larger consignments combined, consisting of 89 days in production and 78 days in the backlog. This means, on average, larger consignments were in production for 53.3% of the time they were on deposit at the mint and were backlogged for 46.7% of the workdays they spent on deposit. Thus, on average, a larger consignment spent less than half of the time it was in the shop in a backlog. All the smaller consignments, under 300 troy ounces of silver, are found in the second table. Totaling the consignments from this second table we arrive at 1905 troy ounces of sterling that were in the shop for 434 workdays and were used to produce an estimated 12,764 shillings. This yields a daily production average of 29.41s and an overall average turnaround time for all the smaller consignments combined, consisting of 50 days in production and 384 days in the backlog. This means, on average, smaller consignments were in production 11.5% of the time they were on deposit in the mint and were backlogged for 88.5% of the workdays they spent in the mint. From this evidence it is clear larger consignments were expedited[2].

If we look at the average daily production rate we see, on a per unit basis, the larger consignments, at an average of 200.69s per day, were produced about 6.824 times more promptly than small consignments, which only averaged 29.41s per day. As a point of comparison, a consignment from April of 1679 totaling 1,919 shillings was in the shop for 93 days of which it was in the backlog for 85 days. However, a few months later in November of 1679 a consignment totaling 5,171 shillings was completed in 29 days with only 16 days in the backlog. The November consignment appears to have been produced three times more quickly, since it was completed in 29 days instead of 93. However, when we allow for the fact that it was over 2.5 times larger than the April consignment we see, on a per unit basis, the turnaround time was over 7.5 times faster. Clearly, when a larger consignment was deposited at the mint Hull and Sanderson would give it special attention but smaller consignments would remain at the shop unprocessed for longer periods. Most likely it was hoped additional small consignments or a large consignment would arrive before the shop staff would need to turn their attention back to minting. For example, we see the small consignment delivered on November 20, 1678, was backlogged for two months, but when a large order was consigned on January 20, 1679, the smaller order was taken out of the backlog and processed with the larger consignment. Interestingly, the January consignment has the fastest recorded turnaround time while the November consignment has a much slower turnaround time.

Unfortunately, the consignments from 1677 are not represented in the above tables. On February 12, 1677, the Indian war against King Philip was concluded. During the conflict very little silver had been consigned to the mint but once a treaty was signed, larger quantities of silver were deposited; in fact the quantities were even larger than the

---

[2] Three of the larger consignments were for Hull, namely, those of May 1675, October 1671 and June, 1676 as well as two of the smaller consignments, namely, those of January and June 1672.

consignments from the years preceding the outbreak of hostilities. In 1677 Hull recorded the quantity of silver deposited at the mint but he did not record completion dates for the consignments. Between April 20 and August 29, 1677, Hull listed three deposits totaling 3976.925 troy ounces of sterling that I have estimated to have yielded about 26,651 shillings. Certainly, 1677 was a time of increased production.

The turnaround time for consignments during Lord Culpepper's stay in Boston

Based on the entries in Hull's ledger the only consignment for coinage during the period of Culpepper's visit was the consignment of August 3-4, 1680, for coinage from 1306.75 ounces of sterling. This consignment was delivered in three installments at what would be considered an average rate for a large consignment. It was at the mint for 45 days during which it was in production for 23 days (51.1% of the time). Thus, in relation to other large consignments at the Massachusetts Bay Mint it was not delayed and in relation to small consignments it was processed rather quickly. In an account of a consignment of silver at the London mint from 1622, we learn Gerard Malynes deposited an unspecified quantity of silver at the mint and was able to return the next week to receive his coinage (Malynes, p. 286). By the 1660's the London mint was purchasing silver rather than accepting consignments, thus Culpepper could not compare processing rates between London and Boston. However, it is possible Culpepper was measuring the Massachusetts Bay Mint against the efficiency of the much larger early Stuart London mint, rather than analyzing how quickly a specific order was being processed at the Massachusetts Mint during the time he was in Boston relative to other production rates achieved at the Massachusetts Mint.

I assume the August 3-4, 1680 consignment was not placed by or for Culpepper, since he did not arrive in Boston until August 24th. However, the consignment may have been placed by a friend or an associate who complained to Culpepper about the wait. Of course, it is possible Culpepper's comments may have been anecdotal, based on complaints from others about past waiting periods rather than based on a personal experience or a contemporaneous event. Indeed, Culpepper mentioned the Massachusetts Mint fee was 6%. Actually, based on the negotiations of the June 3, 1675 mint contract renewal, the total mint fees came to 6.25%, assuming the maximum wastage allowance. However, from Hull's ledger we know the mint fees had been reduced in 1677 by private agreement with the customers to approximately 5% and were further lowered to about 2.5% in 1680. That Culpepper used 6% suggests he was referring to consignments placed before 1677 or that he was simply repeating stories he had heard and assumed the mint fee was unchanged.

❀❀❀❀❀❀❀❀❀❀❀

Chapter 11

The Size of a Melt and its Relation to Production Runs

at the Massachusetts Bay Mint

A sterling melt at the London mint in the 1660's

Every production run started with the melting of silver. At the London mint a large iron crucible or pot holding 800 troy pounds of silver was placed in a very large, specially constructed, furnace over a wood charcoal fire. The furnace was heated with a bellows to about 2,000°F in order to melt the silver. At these high temperatures the iron crucibles, which were two to three inches thick, would last for approximately 120 melts, during which time they would shrink in capacity by 15% or more. The first melt of the day took five hours, while the second melt took only four. If necessary, the mint could work overtime and produce a third melt. It was observed that one should use as small a crucible as possible because the larger the crucible the more copper was lost during the melt. The melted silver was assayed and then, if necessary, adjusted to sterling fineness. Once the mixture was confirmed to be molten sterling it was removed from the pot using a ladle that looked like a large iron skillet affixed to a six foot long wooden handle. This molten sterling was poured through a funnel into molds which shaped the sterling into thin strips. A melt of 800 troy pounds could be extracted from the crucible and poured into the molds within twenty minutes (Craig, p. 161).

The estimated size of a melt at the Massachusetts Bay Mint

Some insights on the size of a melt at Massachusetts Bay can be gained from the production information in the Hull ledger. As discussed above, the consignment of 1,132.5 troy ounces of sterling from January of 1679 suggests the preferred size of a melt was 25 troy pounds (that is, 300 troy ounces). I suspect the capacity of the mint furnace was 25 troy pounds of silver. This probably meant the maximum size crucible the furnace could accommodate was one that held 25 troy pounds of silver. Possibly two or more smaller crucibles were put into the furnace at one time, but it is more likely a single larger crucible was used, since that would save time if any refining was needed. In any event it appears the capacity of the furnace was 25 troy pounds of silver. It has been estimated that the clipped eight reales circulating in Massachusetts Bay averaged about 360 grains or 15 dwt. (Mossman, p. 57), at that weight a melt of 25 troy pounds would consist of 400 eight reales.

The maximum production rate recorded in the Hull ledger was the concurrent production of two melts of 25 troy pounds, which together took a total of nine days to complete. One melt of 25 pounds was started immediately upon arrival of the consignment and a few days later, presumably once the molds were available again, a second melt was performed so that for four of the nine day production period, two installments were being processed simultaneously. When these two installments were completed the mint immediately started a third melt of 25 pounds. Undoubtedly, the mint was trying to maximize production and elected to produce three full melts as quickly as possible. The installments from this January

1679 consignment demonstrate the Massachusetts Bay Mint was either limited to, or preferred to do, a melt of 25 troy pounds (that is, 300 troy ounces). For maximum productivity the mint performed what might be called a staggered double melt with a weight limit for the combined two melts of a total of 50 troy pounds (that is, 600 troy ounces).

Interestingly, when we look at the turnaround time for the consignments listed in the Hull ledger, we find all consignments above 25 troy pounds were expedited. In fact, four of the seven consignments over 25 troy pounds were backlogged less than 50% of the time they were at the mint. Of the three other consignments, two were backlogged just slightly over half the time with backlog rates of 55.2% and 57.1%. Only one order was backlogged somewhat longer, a consignment personally placed by Hull in 1676 for 496.75 troy ounces of sterling which was backlogged 66.6% of the time it was in the mint. Yet even this consignment was produced at a faster rate than any consignment below 25 troy pounds. The most responsive production rate among the smaller consignments, under 25 troy pounds, is a consignment from 1675 for 217 troy ounces of sterling that was backlogged 70.6% of the time it was at the mint. Eight additional smaller consignments were backlogged for an average of 80% to 92.1% of the time they were on deposit. This suggests a production run under 25 troy pounds was not considered efficient. It seems quantities of sterling under 25 troy pounds were put aside in the hope more silver would arrive so a more productive full melt could be performed.

The preference for the single melt of 25 troy pounds or the double melt of 50 troy pounds also holds up when looking at actual production runs. When possible, an entire consignment would be processed in a single production run, but larger consignments had to be divided into installments. What could be considered the largest single installment was the double run, which actually consisted of two melts of 25 troy pounds each from the January 1679 consignment. It is only because Hull needed to deliver coins to the consignor as quickly as possible that he recorded the product of each melt as soon as it was available as coinage. Because of this fortunate situation we can discover how larger installments were handled. If Hull had not needed to deliver the consignment as quickly as possible he would certainly have documented a single installment of 600 troy ounces that was delivered at the end of the nine day production run and we would not have known how the run was produced.

Unfortunately, Hull did not include the production runs for the 1677 consignments in his ledger. However he did detail the individual production runs for most other consignments, listing specific production runs in the following quantities of troy ounces of sterling: 547.25, 538.75, 528.5, 496.75, 445, 400, 392.25, 369.5, 325.5, 300, 300 [these two are the double installment], 300, 278, 275.5, 265, 255.25, 220.75, 217, 208, 190.5, 179.5, 96 and 56. All of the larger production runs, at least those down to about 400 ounces, were probably consecutive double melts as was done in the production run for the 600 troy ounces processed in January of 1679. It is possible the two production runs of 369.5 and 325.5 troy ounces of sterling were also double melts, consisting of a larger melt of 25 troy pounds (that is, 300 troy ounces) and a much smaller ancillary second melt of 69.5 and 25.5 ounces respectively, which were probably undertaken while the larger first melts were still in production. There is evidence from other consignments that Hull sometimes melted small quantities of silver in this weight range, however, there is no evidence as to how these two consignments were specifically handled other than Hull listed them as if each were processed as a single production run. The smaller melts listed above, that are below 300 troy ounces, represent the full amounts of the smaller consignments except for the melt of 220.27 ounces.

This was an installment from the August 1680 consignment which was produced in three installments of 538.75, 220.75 and 547.25 troy ounces. The smallest 220.75 installment was produced immediately after the completion of the 538.75 installment, but then production stopped for at least two weeks before the final 547.25 installment was put into production. The sizes of these three installments were the same as the size of the three shipments sent to the mint that comprised this consignment. By rearranging the sizes of the installments Hull would not have gained any advantage, since he would still need to perform two double melts and a single melt, so he retained the units as they had been consigned to the mint.

The two very small production runs of 96 and 56 troy ounces need some explanation. The 96 troy ounces was a preliminary installment from a consignment of 286.5 troy ounces and was delivered to the customer before the second installment consisting of the remainder of the consignment. This was an unusual occurrence and probably represented a mint customer who quickly needed some coins (the 96 ounces produced £32 2s or 642s). The consignment of 56 troy ounces was also anomalous, in that this was the smallest consignment accepted by the mint. The next smallest consignment was over three times as large, a consignment for 179.5 troy ounces which was a personal consignment placed by Hull in 1672.

Based on the production runs listed by Hull and the turnaround times calculated in the previous section, we see, when possible, the mint would put through an individual run consisting of up to 600 troy ounces of sterling. I suspect these larger quantities were produced as a double melt production run. When there were only smaller amounts of sterling available it seems the mint would expedite consignments in the range of 300 troy ounces. I suspect these consignments represented a full single melt. Smaller consignments were backlogged for longer periods in the hope more sterling would become available so a more efficient full or double melt could be performed. Of course, if no additional silver came into the mint within a few months Hull would need to satisfy the waiting client and process the smaller consignment. Additionally, the mint occasionally performed very small melts of under 100 troy ounces upon request.

We do not know the various sizes of crucibles or pots available at the mint. In his ledger Hull noted in his account for the shop that on July 17, 1675, the shop purchased twelve iron pots and three pounds of "small" wire for £5 6d. Unfortunately, Hull neither specified the size (or sizes) of the pots, nor did he state how the pots were to be used by the shop and the mint. The melting pots used in the furnace were probably made of cast iron and would need to be quite thick, like the melting pots used in London, because the furnace temperatures were quite high, about 2000° Fahrenheit. From the evidence in his ledger, it appears the furnace at the Massachusetts Mint would accommodate a melting pot that held up to 25 troy pounds of sterling (that is, 300 troy ounces). The mint may also have had some smaller pots available for smaller melts. It seems a single melting session at the Massachusetts Mint in the 1670's consisted of up to 25 troy pounds of sterling with a double melt producing up to 50 troy pounds. Thus, a Massachusetts melt was only 3.125% of a contemporary London melt of 800 troy pounds. However, by performing a double melt the Massachusetts Mint could maximize its production capacity, as two 25 pound melts could be processed in nine days instead of performing two independent 25 pound melts that would take six days each to process. Whenever the opportunity arose the mint tried to process sterling in production runs that were as close to 50 troy pounds of sterling as possible. However, even at the full 50 troy pounds, a Massachusetts production run was only 6.25% of a London production run.

The disposition of odd lots

Interestingly, almost all the consignments listed in Hull's ledger, including the smaller consignments, consisted of sizable quantities of sterling that contemporaries would have considered to be of significant value. Very rarely were consignments under 200 troy ounces, or, to state this in monetary terms, the minimum acceptable consignment was about £70 in Massachusetts silver. There were a few exceptions in the 160 - 180 troy ounces range, but only one consignment was substantially smaller, a consignment equal to 56 troy ounces of sterling, having a monetary value of £18 14s. Based on these figures Phil Mossman has asked the question as to whether Hull accepted small consignments of under 50 ounces. There is no direct evidence in Hull's ledger concerning his acceptance of small odd lots of silver. However, there were at least six consignments in the ledger that were probably deposited by Hull; these were the 528.5 troy ounces deposited on October 18, 1671, the 255.25 troy ounces deposited on January 2, 1672, the 179.5 troy ounces deposited on June 29, 1672, the 275.5 troy ounces deposited on December 2, 1674, the 369.5 troy ounces deposited on May 8, 1675 and the 496.75 troy ounces deposited on June 14, 1676. Much of this silver came from Spanish American eight reales Hull purchased through his trading ventures in the West Indies; several purchases are recorded in his extant letters. Additionally, it is quite likely these mint consignments included some sterling from Hull's shop inventory. Apparently, when an individual came into the mint with a small odd lot of sterling Hull immediately paid the person for the silver. As to what value Hull may have given the customer is unknown; he may have offered the same rate as offered for larger consignments or a somewhat reduced price, since the individual would not need to wait to receive payment. Because the customer was paid immediately no receipt would be issued, and since there was nothing due back to the customer at a future date, Hull would not have included such transactions in his ledger. Hull would probably simply pay the individual from cash on hand and add any small lots he acquired to his stock. However, when his stock became sizeable it appears Hull would convert it to coinage and reap his profit (depending on what he had paid for the silver), as well as benefiting from his mint fee and any extra income from coinage over 80d per ounce.

We have some evidence of an over the counter purchase in the records from the Suffolk County Court session of July 28, 1674. At that session Andrew Edmunds and Joseph Waters were convicted of stealing a silver bowl from Benjamin Gibbs and then selling the item, "at mʳ Hulls Shop valued at twelue Shillings." There is no record of this purchase in Hull's ledger. It appears Hull simply paid 12s for the item and placed it in his stock. The court ordered the bowl be returned to Gibbs. Waters was required to pay triple damages to Gibbs as well as court costs. Further, we learn the sentence against Edmunds was overturned when Waters confessed and cleared Edmunds (*Records of Suffolk County Court 1671-1680*, pt. 1, pp. 486, 490 and 493). Additionally, in Hull's account with Leonard Hoar, we see Hull loaned Hoar £8 on December 12, 1677, which was partly repaid on January 28, 1678, as Hull recorded that he received £6 of the money due to him "by mony out of the shopp for Plate 6 · 0 · 0" (ledger, folio 74 recto). Thus, it seems Hoar deposited the plate at the shop and the £6 value of the plate was credited as a partial payment against Hoar's debit to Hull. Again, there is no record of this transaction in the shop account as there was nothing consigned against a future return. The only bookkeeping needed was in Hull's account with Hoar. In Chapter 12 we shall discuss a letter of 1712 from Samuel Sewall to William Vaughan concerning an outstanding claim from Vaughn "...of twenty odd pounds due from the Mint ever since the year 1677, or 1678." Sewall's response indicates this transaction probably also related to an over the counter purchase of silver (Sewall, *Letter-Book*, v. 2, pp. 9-10).

Chapter 12

John Hull and Robert Sanderson as Silversmiths and Coiners

Hull as an apprentice

The blacksmith Robert Hull seems to have encouraged his children to enter the goldsmith profession (contemporaries used the term goldsmith for both goldsmithing and silversmithing). As previously mentioned, Robert Hull married Elizabeth, the widow of Paul Storer. At the time of the marriage, Elizabeth had a young son named Richard, who became Robert's stepson. When John was a child of about four-and-a-half years old, Robert Hull encouraged his stepson, Richard, to apprentice as a goldsmith. In the records of the London goldsmith guild on July 21, 1629, it stated,

> I Richard Storer, the son of Paul Storer of Harborrow in the County of Leicester (deceased) Barber do put myself apprentice unto James Fearne of London Goldsmith for the term of ten years to begin at the Feast day of the Nativity of St. John Baptist last past. [that is, June 24, 1629] (Clarke, *Hull,* p. 30, footnote 2)

Certainly, Richard was able to complete no more than six years of his apprenticeship because the family left England for Boston on September 28, 1635. At the time of their departure John Hull was ten years old and had not entered any profession. Hull's postdated diary entries describe the family's early years in Boston. John mentioned he had briefly attended school and then spent seven years assisting his father in planting corn on the family acreage at Muddy River and learning the trade of a goldsmith from his stepbrother Richard Storer. Hull stated:

> After we arrived here, my father settled at Boston; and, after a little keeping at school, I was taken from school to help my father plant corn, which I attended for seven years together; and then by God's good hand, I fell to learning (by the help of my brother), and to practising the trade of a goldsmith, and, through God's help, obtained that ability in it, as I was able to get my living by it. (Hull, *Private Diary,* p. 142, a transcription more accurately reflecting Hull's original spelling and capitalization is found in Clarke, *Hull,* pp. 26 and 30)

When the Hull family arrived in Boston on November 7, 1635, John was about a month away from his eleventh birthday (Hull stated he was born "in the year 1624, about December 18" Hull, *Private Diary,* p. 141). As discussed above, Robert Hull received his allotment of farmland on December 12, 1636. Therefore, it is likely John Hull began attending school in late 1635 or early 1636 soon after the family arrived in Boston and he remained in school until early in the spring of 1637 when the family had their first opportunity to begin clearing their newly acquired farmland and planting their first crop. This would have afforded John the opportunity to attend school from the time he turned eleven until a little beyond his twelfth birthday. Probably by March or April of 1637 John left school to assist the family with clearing the land and planting as well as beginning to learn his trade. As mentioned above, Richard Storer appears to have married and moved to Braintree by November or December of 1639, just as John was turning fifteen years old. Thus, John had no more than three years, at the most, to learn goldsmithing on a regular basis from his stepbrother. Presumably, from January of 1640 and for the next few years, Storer resided in Braintree (then called the Mount) and possibly was able to continue to instruct John on occasion. We do not know how long Richard Storer remained in Braintree. All we can say with certainty is that in the December 15, 1646 promissory deed from Robert Hull to his son John, it stated Richard Storer had sold his Braintree holdings to his stepfather. It is presumed that Storer returned to England following the sale of his Braintree homestead (some years later John Hull's English cousin Edward Hull wrote to John that he had been unable to persuade Richard to return to America, see Clarke, *Hull,* pp. 30-31). Storer's departure may have occurred soon after the death of his mother on May 7, 1646, or he could have left a few years earlier. Storer seems to have spent at least a few years on the Braintree allotment, for at some point after receiving his initial twelve acres allocation on November 25, 1639, he acquired nine additional acres. It seems Storer sold his acreage and departed the area sometime between the time John was around the age of eighteen and twenty-one (that is, between about 1642 and December 15, 1646).

Once Storer left Braintree, John had to rely on the assistance of his father, a blacksmith, for any further instruction. Interestingly, just about the time Storer left America the silversmith Robert Sanderson moved from Hampton, New Hampshire to Watertown, Massachusetts (the move occurred after 1639 but before 1642). Since Watertown is only a few miles west of Boston, it is possible Hull may have had an association with Sanderson. When Hull wrote about the founding of the mint in his private diary he stated "…and I chose my friend, Robert Sanderson, to be my partner, to which the Court consented" (Hull, *Private Diary,* pp. 145-46). This wording suggests their friendship may have predated the mint partnership. The only other local inhabitant that may have had training as a goldsmith was John Mansfield of Charlestown who was said to have apprenticed in London before immigrating to Boston in 1634. However, as discussed below in Chapter 13, there is no evidence Mansfield ever practiced the goldsmith trade.

Hull and Sanderson as silversmiths

In his informative biography of John Hull, Hermann Clarke has suggested Hull began practicing the silversmith trade about 1644 or 1645, when he was about 19 or 20 years old. That is about the same time his stepbrother moved away and about two years before he married Judith Quincy (Clarke, *Hull,* pp. 30 and 114). We do not know when Hull started business dealings but it may have predated 1650, for we have documents regarding a bill of exchange from that year which could be interpreted as showing Hull to be active in business. On April 17, 1650, John Parriss of London drew a bill of exchange for £20 to be paid to John Hull [Thomas Parriss was John's uncle and became his London agent; John Parriss is thought to have been a relation to Thomas]. When Hull received the bill he directed it to the sea captain, James Cranedg of London, who regularly traveled from England to the colonies. Hull requested that Cranedg pay the £20 to Hull's cousin in London, Daniel Hoare. When the bill was presented at Cranedg's house, Captain Cranedg was at sea and his wife refused to pay, resulting in a formal written protest by the notary Hoare hired to collect the funds. The final disposition of this affair is unrecorded. Hull is also mentioned in another bill of exchange from this period. In a document dated March 26, 1651, from Barbados, John Allen of Charlestown, who was commander of the ship, *William and George*, promised to pay "John Hull gould smith of Boston in New England,... thirty pounds sterling in good & lawfull moneys of England." The document stated Hull had the option of accepting the funds within ten days of the arrival of the ship in Boston or he could assign the money to someone in London. The subscriptions show Hull requested the funds be paid to "Tymothy Proute" and that Allan promised to satisfy the debt within thirty days after the arrival of his ship in London (Clarke, *Hull,* p. 45 and Whitmore, *Aspenwall,* pp. 336-38 and 381-82; Clarke dates the second document to 1652, but as the British new year began on March 25th, the year given in the document of "the 26th of March 1651" refers to 1651 and not 1651/2). The precise nature of these payments cannot be determined but it is possible among Hull's pursuits was some goldsmith work since Captain Allan referred to Hull as a goldsmith.

Clarke has suggested one fairly simple silver cup that bears only Hull's identification mark stamped on it may predate the Hull and Sanderson partnership, Kane dates the cup to ca. 1650. All of the thirty-four other surviving objects with Hull's mark also contain the mark of Robert Sanderson. Therefore, they are considered to date to the period of the partnership which is generally assumed to have commenced with the coining venture. Thus, this one cup, lacking the Sanderson mark, is considered to be before the inception of the June 1652 coining partnership (Clarke, *Hull,* pp. 115-16, updated in Kane, pp. 569-71).

Sanderson entered his goldsmith apprenticeship in 1623 in London under William Rawlings (also Rawlins). Nine years later, in 1632, he completed his aprenticeship and his name was entered as a freeman in the Goldsmith's Company. Sanderson continued to work for Rawlins for the next six years. In 1638 Sanderson was supervising the training of William Rawlings, Junior, when he transferred his apprentice to the goldsmith George Dixon since the Sanderson family was preparing to leave for America. There are three communion cups, two patens and one salver bearing Sanderson's mark that date from this period. Sanderson settled in Hampton, New Hampshire, in 1639, later he moved to Watertown, Massachsuetts and then came to Boston in 1652. Whereas there is one item by Hull thought to predate the partnership, three more intricate caudle cups, two wine cups and a tankard survive with the mark of Robert Sanderson and his son Robert Sanderson, Junior. This is actually Sanderson Senior's mark included twice, representing work in which Robert, Junior, assisted. These six items are thought to date to after the partnership ended. Kane dates the caudle cups and tankard to ca. 1685 with the two wine cups dated as ca. 1692 (Clarke, *Hull,* p. 126 and Kane, pp. 884-86). Based on the one early piece of silver by Hull and the several later extant pieces of silver by Sanderson, Clarke suspected Hull was the first person to practice the silversmith trade in Boston and as such was "...one of the prime movers in the establishment of the mint." Additionally, that author felt that Sanderson, a fully trained goldsmith, was the more skilled craftsman and took the more active role in the daily operation of the partnership, both in the mint and in the silversmith shop where he continued practicing the trade after the partnership ended (Clarke, *Hull,* pp. 67 and 114).

It is not know exactly how long Sanderson continued to operate the shop after Hull's death on October 1, 1683, but from the extant objects it appears he worked with his son Robert Sanderson, Junior. Robert Sanderson, Senior, lived ten years and one week longer than Hull, departing this life on October 7, 1693, at about age 85 (Kane, p. 882). The shop building was on Hull's property and was owned by the Hull family. An interesting note by Hull's son-in-law, Samuel Sewall, was added to an account in the extant Hull ledger. On folio 85 verso the account with Joseph Eliot showed a balance due on July 7, 1680, of £23 8s8d which was carried forward to ledger E on folio 11. Apparently as late as 1687 the debt had not been completely paid. Sewall added a note to the account in the surviving ledger C as follows: "Note – May 11, 1687. I paid mr. Saunderson 36s 6d & so ye whole shop – Debt for ye Gold, is mine. S.S." This note implies in May of 1687 Sewall paid Sanderson for the outstanding balances owed to the shop and thereby became the party to whom the shop debts were owed. Thus it seems in 1687, when Sanderson was 79 or 80, he retired and sold the remaining shop account assets to Sewall, who supervised the Hull estate for his mother-in-law, Judith Hull. Robert Sanderson, Junior, may not have continued as a goldsmith after his father's retirement since the only articles attributed to him are the six objects that also contain his father's mark (Kane, pp. 880-81).

Hull as a soldier, politician and entrepreneur

In addition to his silversmith and mint businesses, Hull participated in several other activities throughout his career. Hull joined the militia as a corporal in 1648, rising to a sergeant on June 28, 1652, just eight days after the mint committee had taken action to erect a mint house. Hull was commissioned as an ensign in 1655 and became recorder for the military company in 1656. In 1660 Hull was admitted into the prestigious artillery company, where he was promoted to ensign in 1663, lieutenant in 1664 and held the rank of captain from 1671 until his retirement in 1678.

Hull also held numerous political positions. He was elected as one of the seven Selectmen for Boston from 1657-1663, except for 1662, which he spent in England as an advisor to the two agents sent to defend the rights and privileges of Massachusetts Bay. During three of his terms as selectman (1658, 1661 and 1663) Hull was also appointed treasurer for Boston. In 1668, he accepted the position as the representative for Wenham in the House of Deputies, which was the lower house of the General Court, and from 1671-1674, he held the same position for the town of Westfield. In 1675, Hull was appointed a member of the committee for the war against King Philip and was named treasurer for the war. In May of 1676 he was appointed Treasurer of Massachusetts Bay and held that post until May of 1680; during this period he also held the seat in the House of Deputies from Concord in 1676 and the seat from Salisbury in 1679-1680. In May of 1680 Hull was chosen as one of the eighteen Assistants sitting in the upper house, the House of Magistrates. He continued in that position until his death. On September 6, 1683, he attended his last meeting, a preparatory meeting before the fall session of the General Court. Hull became too sick to return and died on October 1st, nine days later the fall session of the General Court was called to order.

Hull was also an entrepreneur involved in several major endeavors. He was a partner in numerous shipping ventures. As early as November of 1653 Hull mentioned in his diary that two ships were seized by the Dutch in which he lost £120 value in beavers and other furs bound for London (Hull, *Private Diary*, p. 156 and Clarke, *Hull*, p. 45). Hull avidly acquired real estate as well as investing in speculative land deals. In addition to his Boston holdings on Cotton and Copp's Hills, Hull owned about 500 acres in Braintree, some 300 acres in Muddy River, about 1,000 acres in Boxford, some 1,150 acres in Wilmington as well as interests in a lumber mill in New Hampshire (on the Piscataqua River at Salmon Falls) and a horse raising venture in Rhode Island (at South Kingston). Hull also participated in an unsuccessful mining operation and was in a partnership that purchased warehouses and a wharf in Boston. Moreover, Hull exported and imported commodities on some fifteen different vessels and was a merchant of hats, shoes, rugs, cloth and numerous other commodities using his uncle, Thomas Parriss, and then his cousin, Edward Hull, as his agents in London. In his surviving personal ledger from the 1670's, Hull lists ongoing accounts with well over three hundred individuals and several business partnerships (Clarke, *Hull*, pp. 71, 76, 85-92, 102-10, 164-65, 170, 176 and 185; Noe, *Silver*, p. 145; Hull, *Diary*, Memoir, see pp. 121-29, Hull's ledger as discussed above and Kane, pp. 567-72). Due to these numerous military, political and business commitments, as well as the higher quality of Sanderson's attributable silver, Clarke suspected Hull's major contributions to both the silversmith and the coining partnerships were primarily political and financial while Sanderson was the more skilled craftsman.

Hull and Sanderson at the shop

It is clear Robert Sanderson had a major role in the silversmith shop and mint. He certainly ran the operation while Hull was away in England from February through September of 1662 and again from November 1669 through August 1670. Sanderson was also responsible for the operation while Hull was diverted with his numerous other duties and commitments.[1] However, Hull was called a goldsmith in several documents and he took on apprentices. In fact, the most accomplished Boston silversmith of the next generation, Jeremiah Dummer, apprenticed with Hull and became his lifelong friend. Further, it is clear Hull kept the account books for the business. Hull continued to practice silversmithing at least until the mid-1670's. In the surviving ledger there are entries for silversmith work that

---

[1] It should be noted Sanderson also performed duties outside the shop. On March 9, 1663, he was elected as one of five constables for Boston for the year. In 1665 Sanderson became a member of the First Church of Boston and was made a deacon in 1670. He also invested in a powder mill at Canton in 1673 and in the 1670's Sanderson purchased and sold property, wharves and at least two shops in Boston. At his death Sanderson owned real estate valued at £535 and possessions valued at just over £718, including £20 worth of old tools (Kane, p. 883 and *Records Commission, Boston Records from 1660-1701*, p. 14).

may have been performed by Hull for various clients including repair work for William Brenton in 1672, and small silver items sold to Brenton in 1672, to Thomas Temple in 1673 and to Joseph Eliot in 1674. However, it does appear Sanderson had a central and expanding role in the daily operations of the shop as the business grew. As early as the initial oath ceremony from the summer of 1652, it was stated that Hull and Sanderson were to be equal officers in the mint, "...the Oath here unde^r written shall be the oath that John Hull and Robt Saunderson shall take as aequall office^{rs} In the minting of mony..." (Crosby, p. 41). Since the mint was on Hull's property, Hull was regularly named first and the business was generally referred to as Mr. Hull's shop, as in the 1674 Suffolk County Court case discussed in the previous chapter. But, by the final contract renewal of June 1675 Sanderson preceded Hull; the text stated "That the former masters of the mint, vizt, Robert Saunderson & John Hull, doe Continue to mint what Siluer bulljon shall Come in..." (Crosby, pp. 82-83).

A very interesting account of mint operations in the late 1670's is found in a letter of Samuel Sewall, Hull's son-in-law. In 1712, William Vaughan of Portsmouth, New Hampshire asked his son, Colonel George Vaughan, to present Judge Sewall with a demand "...of twenty odd pounds due from the Mint ever since the year 1677, or 1678." Since Sewall could not find a record of this debt in Hull's ledger he replied to Vaughan on January 5, 1713, that:

> The Business of the Mint was managed by it self, and the Account kept distinct; by which means I can find no footsteps at all of this latter [i.e. the £20 debt], in the Books of my honoured Father-in-Law Capt. John Hull, who died in the Fall 1683. The chief part of the Shop's Business went through Mr. Daniel Quinsey's hands; He was a very honest carefull Man. Mr. Saunderson and all that wrought in the Shop under him, used to be very diligent in paying for the Silver taken in. (Sewall, *Letter-Book*, v. 2, pp. 9-10)

From this account, discussing events from 35 years earlier, it appears that during the late 1670's Robert Sanderson supervised the daily operations and Daniel Quincy was the business manager. Kane has determined that Hull's nephew, Daniel Quincy, apprenticed at the shop between 1665 and 1673. On January 10, 1674, Hull gave Daniel £10 to pay for a box of tools Hull had ordered for him from London and he also gave Daniel £15 and continued to support him in subsequent years (ledger, folio 73 verso). Possibly Hull made Quincy the business manager in 1676 when Quincy returned from a trip to London. Sewall married Hull's daughter, Hannah, in 1676 and moved into the Hull house at that time. He did not know how the mint had operated in earlier periods. From the Sewall description it does seem that by the mid-1670's Sanderson was the shop supervisor while Hull produced his ledger entries for the shop account from Quincy's receipts or day book (Kane, pp. 788-90).

We find confirmation of a shift in Hull's profession in legal documents. Frequently documents included an individual's profession along with their name. In several dozen documents from the 1650's through the early 1670's Hull was designated as a goldsmith. I know of only three exceptions from this period where Hull was called a merchant rather than a goldsmith; namely, in two deeds for land in Braintree dated to October 20th and December 10th in 1663 (*Suffolk Deeds*, vol. 4, pp. 155 and 165) and one deed from September 17,

1666, that was not recorded until February 19, 1676/7 (*Suffolk Deeds*, vol. 10, pp. 18-19). However, one notices a shift in professions taking place in documents from 1672 through 1674. In documents of March 28, 1672; April 10, 1673; July 13, 1673 and September 13, 1674 Hull is called a merchant (*Suffolk Deeds*, vol. 8, pp. 269-71; 120-21; 232-33 and 28-30). Yet in several other contemporary documents he is listed as a goldsmith, as in deeds of August 9, 1672, October 2, 1672, July 22, 1673, September 15, 1673 and May 14, 1674 (*Suffolk Deeds*, vol. 10, pp. 15-16; vol. 12, pp. 174-75; vol. 10, pp. 26-27; vol. 12, p. 73 and vol. 10, pp. 20-21). In extant deeds later than the deed of May 14, 1674, Hull is no longer identified as a goldsmith. When a profession is listed, Hull is exclusively classified as a merchant in all legal documents between a deed of December 9, 1676, through a deed of April 14, 1681 (*Suffolk Deeds*, vol. 10, pp. 11-12, 29-30; vol. 11, pp. 27-28, 128-32, 271-72 and 275; vol. 12, pp. 69-73, 175-76, the April 1681 document is in vol. 12, pp. 70-71). In 1680 Hull was elected as an Assistant sitting in the House of Magistrates and thus in most later documents until his death in 1683 Hull was addressed as esquire and sometimes by his military rank of Captain (*Suffolk Deeds*, vol. 12, pp. 216-17, 264-75 and 337). Unfortunately the County Court records are not as helpful as recorded deeds. In the twenty-five Suffolk County Court cases that mentioned Hull between 1671 and 1680 only one case lists a profession, a case from the session of January 30, 1671/2 which lists Hull as a goldsmith; all other cases simply call him Mr. Hull or Captain Hull (*Records of the Suffolk County Court: 1671-1680*, pt. 1, pp. 65-68). Interestingly, during this entire period Sanderson was listed as a goldsmith, as in deeds of December 3, 1674 and August 24, 1681 (*Suffolk Deeds*, vol. 9, pp. 71-73 and vol. 12, pp. 125-26).

Over the thirty years during which the mint was in operation both Hull and Sanderson performed assays and refined silver to the sterling standard. Indeed, the legislation of October 8, 1672, regarding the value of Spanish silver, specifically stated that as to the evidence concerning the alloy and weight of Spanish coins, "...m^r John Hull & m^r Robert Saunde^{r}son, or either of them, be the persons for the tryall..." (Crosby, p. 80). It is also probable they both produced or supervised the production of the silver strips that were fed into the rocker press and, in the later period, were cut into blank planchets from which the coins were made. In the Massachusetts Bay Mint, the fineness of the silver and coin weight were critical to the solvency of the operation since any over-calculation would reduce the profit margin. Skill and precision in refining silver and in regulating coin weight (and in regulating planchet production during the screw press era) directly impacted mint profits; thus it is likely the partners would have performed these critical operations themselves or, if apprentices participated in these functions, they would be closely supervised. It is also likely the partners engraved most of the inverse images and letters onto the steel rocker and cylinder die blanks to create the dies. Probably advanced apprentices assisted with engraving, especially with recuttings or with the initial engraving of the legends, as in the Pine Tree shilling Noe 11 (and possibly engraving entire dies as for the Oak Tree threepence Noe 24). These were the most time consuming operations and required the greatest skill. Quite likely both Hull and Sanderson were proficient in all of these operations.

It is clear that as Hull spent more time away from the shop, Sanderson became the primary, if not the sole, supervisor of operations and production, especially after 1675. The surviving ledger entries corroborate Hull's reduced role during this period for the few silver pieces Hull billed to individuals between 1670 and 1680 all date to 1674 or earlier. When

Hull became Treasurer for the Commonwealth in 1676 he took an even more passive roll in the shop, appointing his cousin Daniel Quincy as business manager. However, Hull continued to keep the ledger and doubtless was interested in the shop profits.

Interestingly, the task most often associated with the mint, that of stamping the coins, was the noisiest and least important part of the process. I suspect apprentices may have stamped the coins. Also, as mentioned above in Chapter One, it is possible the stamping of the coins was performed in a nearby storage building rather than in the shop. It is also likely for the earlier varieties, made on a rocker press, that the apprentices cut the finished coins out of the silver strips and trimmed them down to the authorized weight, a process which would have been closely supervised since miscalculations could be costly.

Apprentices and journeymen at the shop

1652-1660

The first apprentices at the shop were Robert Sanderson's two sons, John and Joseph. John's birth is not recorded so we do not know his age. Most likely he was born in Hampton, New Hampshire, and was the oldest son. Under the date of September 1, 1658, John Hull stated in his private diary, "My boy, John Sanderson, complained of his head aching, and took his bed. A strong feaver set on him; and, after seventeen days' sore sickness, he departed this life" (Hull, *Private Diary,* p. 148). His death was recorded on September 17th (Kane, p. 879).

Joseph was born in Watertown, Massachusetts, on January 1, 1643. Kane has suggested his apprenticeship would have started when he was about 13 years old, that is, ca. 1656 and lasted for about seven years until ca. 1663, when he was about 20 years old. Joseph witnessed a deed for Hull in 1663 and thus was probably apprenticing in the shop at that time. However, within a few years Joseph had married, indicating his apprenticeship had been completed. A daughter named Mary was born to Joseph and his wife on July 6, 1666. Joseph died just about five months later on December 24, 1666, just before his 24th birthday. An inventory of his property at his death indicated Joseph was an active silversmith. His tools included "pattarns Sandbox & sand" valued at 9s, which proves the shop did cast objects in sand molds. The inventory also included "Chasing towles & small towles in a box" valued at 11s. Chasing tools refers to engraving tools which could be used to engrave designs on silver or used to incise images and letters on dies. Since the complete tool list is rather modest, totaling tools valued at only £9 3s, it is most likely Joseph continued to work in the Hull shop using the forges, anvils and other expensive items he was unable to afford. Joseph was clearly working as a silversmith at the time of his death for he had outstanding orders for silver (Kane pp. 24 and 879-80 with the full inventory of tools). Thus, Joseph continued working at the shop as a journeyman until his death in 1666.

During the first years of the shop and the mint John and Joseph Sanderson were the apprentices. John may have been at the mint during the NE period, which I suspect lasted until 1654. Certainly he was at the mint during the Willow Tree period. Joseph many have started work during the Willow Tree period and certainly was at the mint during the start of the Oak Tree era. In fact, he may have supervised two later apprentices, Jeremiah Dummer and Samuel Paddy, with the Oak Tree twopence in 1662.

1660-1665

A little less than a year after John Sanderson died, the shop took on two more apprentices. Under the date of July 1, 1659, Hull added in his private diary,

> I received into my house Jeremie Dummer and Samuel Paddy, to serve me as apprentices eight years. The Lord make me faithful in discharge of this new trust committed to me, and let his blessing be to me and them! (Hull, *Private Diary,* p. 150)

Jeremiah Dummer, who many years later engraved the plates for the first emission of Connecticut currency in 1709, became one of Boston's leading silversmiths. Dummer seems to have remained at the Hull shop as a journeyman when his apprenticeship ended in July of 1667. He may have stayed with Hull until about 1670, when he probably opened his own shop. A Suffolk County Court document from March 4, 1671, suggests Dummer has his own shop at that time (Kane, pp. 385-86 and 1028).

Samuel Paddy remained at the Hull shop until the end of his apprenticeship. In his private diary Hull noted that Paddy went back home to his mother for three weeks in January of 1667 because he contracted smallpox (Hull, *Private Diary,* pp. 156-57). In 1666 Paddy inherited £60 when his father died. It seems he used the funds to set himself up as a goldsmith when his apprenticeship ended in July of 1667. In October of 1668 he was identified as "of Boston Gold Smith" when he sold his interest in a warehouse. Later, Paddy moved to Port Royal, Jamaica, where he was known as a merchant and a goldsmith. In 1681, Hull wrote a letter to Paddy in Jamaica stating,

> Had you abode here and followed your calling you might have been worth many hundred pounds of clear estate and you might have enjoyed many more helpes for your sole [soul]. Mr. Dummer lives in good fashion hath a wife and three children and a good estate, is a member of the church and like to be very useful in his generation. (Hull, *Private Diary,* p. 150, footnote 2)

Although this seems to be a stern reprimand by modern standards, it is less offensive given Puritan sensibilities. In fact, Hull had several dealings with Paddy and following Hull's death his son-in-law, Samuel Sewall, settled the account with Paddy (Kane, pp.748-49).

As mentioned above, Joseph Sanderson probably completed his apprenticeship in 1663, while Dummer and Paddy were in the middle of their training. It is quite likely his younger brother, Benjamin Sanderson, started his apprenticeship in that same year. Benjamin was born in July of 1649 and thus would have been fourteen years old in 1663. Kane has suggested he apprenticed from 1663 through about 1670. Benjamin was married in about 1672 and resided in the North End working as a silversmith. He died in late 1678 or early 1679. Two dram cups, one caudle cup and a wine cup survive with his hallmark (Kane, pp. 878-79).

Thus, during the 1660's, Joseph Sanderson completed his apprenticeship in 1663 and then worked as a journeyman until he died in 1666. Dummer and Paddy apprenticed from

1659-1667; also Benjamin Sanderson was at the shop from about 1663-1670. Dummer may have remained at the shop as a journeyman until about 1670. The first half of that decade saw the production of the Oak Tree coinage with the Oak Tree twopence authorized in 1662.

1665-1675

In 1665 Joseph Sanderson was continuing at the shop as a journeyman, his brother Benjamin was a few years into his seven-year apprenticeship, while Dummer and Paddy had about two years left in their apprenticeships. At that time Hull took Daniel Quincy as an apprentice. Daniel was born on February 7, 1651, the son of Edmund Quincy and Joanna Hoar. Edmund was the brother of Hull's wife Judith Quincy, therefore, Daniel was John's nephew. They became even more closely related when John's father, Robert Hull, married Judith Paine Quincy, John's widowed mother-in-law, making Edmund, who had been John's brother-in-law, his half-brother. Daniel lived with his uncle and aunt, John and Judith Hull, from at least the time he was seven. In his private diary under September 1, 1658, John Hull mentioned his apprentice, John Sanderson, had come down with a fever. In the very next entry, dated September 8, 1658, Hull mentioned that, Daniel Quincy, became sick "…within a week after the other…" but recovered by October 18th. This suggests Daniel, like John Sanderson, was in the Hull household. Patricia Kane has suggested Daniel apprenticed at the shop between 1665 and 1673 (from ages 14 to 22) since he acted as a witness for Hull in various legal documents during those years. On January 10, 1674, Hull purchased a box of tools for Daniel from London for £10 suggesting his apprenticeship had ended. However Hull continued to pay for Daniel's room and board. There is an ongoing account for Daniel in Hull's ledger, showing several payments for board and daily expenses (ff. 73v-74r; 129v-130r and 161v-162r). In 1676, when Daniel was 25, he travelled to London. Upon his return he worked in the Hull shop. Samuel Sewall married John Hull's only surviving child, Hannah, in 1676, and moved into the Hull residence in that year. As we have seen above, Sewall stated Daniel Quincy was the business manager for the shop and the mint. Quincy continued at the shop after the mint closed. He was a close friend to Sewall and Robert Sanderson until his death on August 10, 1690 (Kane, pp. 788-90 and Hull, *Diary*, p. 276).

A year after Daniel Quincy began his apprenticeship, Robert Sanderson, Junior, probably started at the shop. He was born around October 1652, about the time the mint was opening for business. Thus he was very close in age to Daniel and may have started his apprenticeship with him or soon thereafter. Patricia Kane has suggested Robert Sanderson, Junior, apprenticed from about 1666 until about 1673. He was listed as a lodger with his older brother Benjamin in 1674, thus it is possible his training was completed and he was working as a journeyman in his brother's shop by 1674. After Benjamin died in late 1678 or early 1679, Robert probably went back to work with his father. The two Robert Sandersons continued to work together after the Hull and Sanderson partnership dissolved with the death of Hull in 1683. As mentioned above, some surviving silver items bear the mark of both Robert Sanderson, Senior and Junior, and thus are thought to post-date the Hull shop.

Around 1668 Timothy Dwight came to the shop. He had been born on November 26, 1654, and so would have been about fourteen at the time he entered the shop. His apprenticeship would have continued until about 1675. There are some deeds and a bill of sale from Hull dated between 1672 and 1674 which were witnessed by Dwight; some of these deeds were also witnessed by Daniel Quincy. It seems Dwight stayed at the Hull residence until about 1680 as there are several references to him in Samuel Sewall's diary up to that time. In his *Commonplace Book,* Sewall stated that Dwight paid £6 rent for use of space in the Hull shop for 1677. A silver tankard and a salver survive with Dwight's hallmark attesting to his work as a silversmith (Kane, pp. 29, 398-400).

Sometime during the mid to later part of this decade the shop produced the "large planchet" Pine Tree shillings. The final years of the 1660's were probably the period when the mint converted from producing large planchet Pine Tree shillings on a rocker press to minting small planchet shillings on a screw press. At that time it is likely Jeremiah Dummer was completing his tenure as a journeyman and Benjamin Sanderson was completing his apprenticeship. Daniel Quincy and Robert Sanderson, Junior, were well into their apprenticeships, with only two or three years remaining while Timothy Dwight was probably in his second year.

1675-1683

In 1673, when Daniel Quincy and Robert Sanderson, Junior, probably completed their apprenticeships, the shop took on a new apprentice, Samuel Clarke (or Clark). In a diary entry for November of 1673 John Hull wrote "November, I accept Samuel Clark, son of Jonas Clark, as an apprentice for eight years" (Hull, *Private Diary,* p. 162). Samuel Sewall's diary shows that Clarke remained at the Hull home for over ten years. Clarke witnessed deeds for the Hull estate and for Samuel Sewall in 1683 and 1684. From the Sewall diary it seems there was not much work for Clarke during the final years of the shop. Sewall wrote, "Sam. Clark keeps on Board his Brother's Ship, intending a Voyage to Sea, having no work in the Shop" (*Diary,* vol. 1, p. 77 as quoted in Kane, p. 287). Clarke died at sea in 1705 (Kane, pp. 286-87).

During the mid to late 1670's Daniel Quincy continued at the shop, performing the duties of business manager. Timothy Dwight completed his apprenticeship in 1675 and stayed on until about 1680 as a journeyman. Robert Sanderson, Junior, may have returned as a journeyman after the death of his brother Benjamin in late 1678 or early 1679. In late 1675 Samuel Clarke was two years into his apprenticeship, which continued until November of 1681, but he stayed at the shop until about 1684. As we have seen, the shop probably closed with the retirement of Robert Sanderson, Senior, in May of 1687.

Three other individuals have been mentioned as possible apprentices at the Hull shop: John Hall, Thomas Savage, Junior, and Richard Nevill. However, there is no evidence any were associated with either the mint or the shop. John Hall was born in Salisbury, Massachusetts, in 1641. He departed for England in the early 1660's and never returned. In his will of April 1691, he called himself a goldsmith of London, although other documents refer to him as a merchant or a gentleman. There is no record or evidence related to his apprenticing with Hull and Sanderson (Kane, pp. 523-24). The second individual, Thomas Savage, was a Boston silversmith born in 1664, whose training would have started about

1678. Because he married a cousin of Timthy Dwight and his uncle married a sister of Daniel Quincy, it has been thought he must have been associated with the Hull shop. Kane pointed out there is no evidence he trained with Hull. It is more likely he apprenticed with Jeremiah Dummer or another silversmith of the period (Kane, pp. 887-89). Finally, concerning Richard Nevill, the minutes of a meeting of the Boston Selectman from January 25, 1675, stated certain individuals were to return to the County Court including "Richard Neuill formerlie Aprentice to Robt Sand^rs now seru^t to John Whalie..." (*Record Commissions, Boston Town Records 1660-1701*, p. 90). Two days later, on January 27,1675, Nevill was listed as a goldsmith in a list of individuals who were returned to the County Court since they were not admitted or approved by the Selectmen to be inhabitants of Boston (*Record Commissions, Miscellaneous Papers*, pp. 55-56). No other evidence supports Nevill's claim to be a goldsmith. The attribution of goldsmith may be due to a misunderstanding. Quite likely the Robt Sand^rs mentioned in the January 25th document is not Robert Sanderson the goldsmith, but the name may have been mistakenly interpreted as referring to him (Kane, pp. 727-28).

Patricia Kane has also suggested some of the work from the Hull shop may have been outsourced. Specifically she felt that some of the dies may have been cut by Boston craftsmen in related occupations. She identified a clockmaker named Richard Taylor, who worked in Boston from ca. 1657 to 1673. There was also John Hatton who was identified as a watchmaker around 1663 and Robert Punt, a watchmaker from about 1670. Additionally, there was the gunsmith Thomas Matson who worked in Boston from 1654 until 1690 and the armorer John Odlin, who was active for half a century from 1635 through 1685 (Kane, p. 46). These individuals may have assisted the Hull shop and mint with various tasks, such as machine repair and possibly some toolmaking. However, I suspect the special skill needed for diecutting (and recutting) was a task mastered over time and performed by the silversmiths, with assistance from the apprentices and journeymen at the shop.

❀❀❀❀❀❀❀❀❀❀❀

Chapter 13

Other Individuals Mentioned in Connection with

the Massachusetts Bay Coining Operation

John Mansfield

In addition to Robert Sanderson, at least one other individual in the Boston area stated he had trained in the goldsmith profession, namely, John Mansfield of Charlestown. Mansfield immigrated to Massachusetts Bay in 1634 at the age of 33. References to him are sparse. He was listed as a witness to the Suffolk County will of Jonathan Waymouth, dated November 19, 1639 (*The New England Historical and Genealogical Register,* vol. 2, 1848, p. 261). He was also listed as taking the oath of a freeman on May 10, 1643 (Shurtleff, vol. 2, p. 293, column 2).

As mentioned above, it seems likely that by 1654 the mint had obtained a coining press and was seeking to hire a trained diecutter. Indeed, based on the work of Michael Hodder and Richard Doty, it seems likely the first press was a rocker press rather than a screw press. Clearly, the process of cutting dies on steel rocker die blanks, with a curved surface, was more challenging than engraving images on the flat surface of a hammer or screw press die blank. We know Joseph Jenks of Hammersmith wrote to John Hull's brother in London in 1654 asking him if there was an experienced diecutter available who would be willing to move to Boston. At that time Mansfield was in serious financial difficulties and apparently heard the mint was looking for an experienced diecutter. Being desperate for employment the 53-year-old Mansfield begged the General Court to allow him to be employed in the government coining operation run by Hull. His petition to the General Court requested that they "take into considderation the poore Estate of John Mansfield, of charlestoune." His plight had been brought to the attention of an earlier General Court that ordered the family to be put on relief. However, Mansfield protested when he discovered the family could not obtain relief,

> ...unlesse wee part with our Children ... which Children, being young, will pine away, to the greate hassordinge of there lives, if wee should give them away; besides, they are the greatest comfortt in this world, and doe learne there bookes & thrive better with us, & are soe loveing to us, & wee to them, that wee can not till [tell] how to part One from other. And I, for my part, do verryly beleeife my wife would runne quite Madd if anny of them should be taken from hir [her].

Mansfield then asked for some assistance and that he be allowed to work at the mint as an employee of the Commonwealth (or as he stated, a servant of the country) since he had eleven-and-a-half years's experience as a goldsmith apprentice and had sworn the oath of allegiance to Massachusetts Bay,

And alsoe your poore humble petitioner most humbly desires your worshipps would be pleased to graunt me to be the Country searvantt for helping to quine [coin] & melt & fine silver with mr. Hull & good man Saundres, in the country howse withe them, for I served 11 yeares & 1/2 prentiz [apprenticed] to the same arte, & am a free man of London, and am also sworne to be trew to the Country, as I hoope I shall, which, if soe greate a favor be now graunted me, your poore Supplicants, my selfe, my wife, & Children, shall have Cause Ever after to pray for your Worshipps' health, peace, & prosperitie heare in this life & everlast reward with God above.

He then continued,

...our howse do take fire manny times because it wants mendings, is like to fall uppon our headds before we be awarr, & wee are not able to mend it; but it is great want of foode & other nessessaries both for ourselves & Children, my selfe broaken bellied, my Wife much troubled in hir Mind because of som Wrongs & to see how hard it is with us and how wee run our selves in debt & all for the belly, and No worke stirring; nor are wee respected heare [here] because we are soe poore & can not have imployment in our callings; & we have both ben Wronged both in our Estats & good Name, & noe healpe [help] as yet, but patiently abide the Lord's pleasure. Your poore petitioners, John Mansfeilld, & Mary Mansfeilld his wife. (full text in Crosby, pp. 103-4)

There is no evidence Mansfield ever worked at the mint. He was not mentioned in Hull's diary, ledger or letters nor was he mentioned in any documents from the mint. It appears this petition was rejected. Apparently Hull did not believe Mansfield had the required diecutting skills and concluded it would be more economical for the two partners to assume the diecutting duties. Interestingly, Mansfield did not apply directly to Hull for a position, or if he did so, his request had been denied. Rather, Mansfield hoped the Commonwealth would appoint him as a mint employee. However, the mint had not been set up as a government operation but rather was subcontracted to Hull, a distinction Mansfield may have not understood. Mansfield stated he had eleven-and-a-half years experience as an apprentice, which was somewhat longer than the usual eight to ten years for a London apprenticeship, but did not specify that he had ever practiced the trade after his apprenticeship. Based on the desperation of his plea one would suppose he would have included any relevant experience in the profession as a journeyman or master. There is no record in London of his apprenticeship. Since Mansfield had been born in 1601, if he actually had apprenticed, his apprenticeship would had to have ended ca. 1625, some thirty years before he made his petition.

Based on the surviving evidence it appears John Mansfield did not work as a silversmith. The evidence suggests he was a misfit. He accompanied his sister and brother-in-law on the voyage from London to Boston and apparently lived off their charity. In 1653 his brother-in-law, John Keayne bequeathed a cow to each of the two Mansfield children. He stated the profits from the cow were to be used for the children's maintenance but that the profits should not be given to either of the parents. Keayne stated that he had bailed John Mansfield from jail, had paid his debts, paid his passage to America and lent him money but that Mansfield "…lived idlie & spent what he gott in drinke & company keeping & so spitefull & envious he was to me, notwithstanding all my former care over him in seeking & endeavouring his good, that he would have cutt my throate with his false accusations if it had lyen in his power" (*Record Commissioners; Miscellaneous Papers*, pp. 25-26). Mansfield was often in trouble. In 1650 he was jailed for debts and in 1655 he was charged with being drunk. In 1656 Mansfield and his wife Mary were forced to give up their eight-year-old twin children. It appears they had some funds in the early 1660's for on July 26, 1662, John Mansfield purchased some land in Charlestown from Peter Nash (*Record Commissioners; Charlestown Land Records, 1638-1802*, p. 159). However from 1664 through 1671 the Mansfields almost annually petitioned the town for better living conditions. Mansfield died on June 26, 1674, with an estate that was valued at only £8 9s6d (Kane, pp. 677-79).

Joseph Jenks

Although Hull and Sanderson were trained silversmiths and presumably skilled engravers, we do not know if they made their own steel punches and die blanks. Undoubtedly, when the mint opened in 1652 there were few people in Massachusetts Bay who had the ability to make hardened steel punches for the NE coinage. The most logical place to look for such skilled labor was to the master ironsmith at the only iron foundry in the colonies. That was Joseph Jenks (sometimes spelled Jynks or Jencks) who worked at the iron foundry in Hammersmith, which is now Saugus, Massachusetts (see Hartley, pp. 126, 184 and 208-10 and Kenny, p. 13).

Joseph was the son of John Jenks, a cutler, and John's second wife, Sara Fulwater, the daughter of a German family who had moved to England. On November 5, 1627, Joseph Jenks married a woman whose name is recorded as Jone (probably Joan) Hearne. In October of 1628 their first child, John Jr., was born and soon the family moved to Isleworth, Middlesex, where Jenks gained employment as a swordmaker at the steel factory of Benjamin Stone in Hounslow, Middlesex. Stone had imported several German master swordmakers to help build his business. Jenks was adept at his trade and became one of only two Englishmen that were able to rival the German craftsmen in producing steel blades. In fact, an example of his work from this period still survives, a 38 inch broadsword signed "Ioseph Ienckes." In 1635, his wife died and three years later his daughter Elizabeth died. Soon thereafter, during the summer of 1639, Jenks left Middlesex with his son for Northumberland. By 1641 the two had immigrated to Maine where Jenks operated a blacksmith shop on the Agamenticus River at York (Carlson, pp. 2-5). By 1646, Jenks was in Boston, where on May 10th he petitioned the General Court for a fourteen-year monopoly, "…to Build a Mill for making of Sithes; and alsoe a new Invented Saw Mill, and divers other Engines for making of divers sorts of edge tooles" (Carlson, Appendix B, pp. [21-23]). On June 5th, the General Court stated they had been "sufficiently informed of the ability of the

Petitioner to perform such workes" and granted his petition (Shurtleff, vol. 2, p. 149 and vol. 3, p. 65). By December of 1647, Jenks was living in Saugus, the site of the Hammersmith iron foundry.

The Hammersmith foundry operated the only blast furnace in Massachusetts Bay and regularly produced both cast iron items such as pots, anvils and various tools as well as wrought iron bars for the colony. The furnace was a massive granite lined pit 21 feet deep with walls two feet thick. The internal configuration of the furnace was such that the top blast hole opening had a diameter of about 30 inches across. The furnace gradually widened to a diameter of about six feet at the center. Its dimensions then gradually tapered down like a funnel, with the furnace base for the crucible narrowing to about 18 inches across, allowing for a total internal volume of 340 cubic feet. The furnace was located near the side of a slope. From the upper area at the top of the slope, day laborers loaded the blast hole with wheelbarrows full of charcoal, iron ore and flux. Bog iron ore (limonite) was available locally and gabbro (a granular igneous rock composed of ferromagnesian mineral), transported about five miles by sea from Nahant, was used in place of limestone as the flux. A fully charged furnace held 265 bushels of charcoal, three tons of iron ore and two tons of gabbro. The materials were alternately loaded into the furnace in measured units or layers of charcoal, iron ore and gabbro with each grouping represented about a twelve hour melt. A full furnace would contain six groupings of three layers per grouping that was tapped at twelve hour intervals. A full load would last for three days but the furnace was continually replenished so that it operated day and night without stop, except when the water froze during the winter or when the furnace needed repairs. At the base of the furnace was a large crucible that was 3.5 feet high and tapered from 21 inches square at the top to 18 inches square at the bottom. An opening at the bottom of the furnace allowed access to the crucible so it could be tapped.

A large wooden shed at the base station protected the crucible, the open hearth, the workers and the molten iron from rain and wind. It also housed two enormous eighteen foot bellows. These bellows were operated by a water wheel attached to a camshaft. The cam pushed the arm of the bellows up, while a box of stone weights attached to the top of the arm forced the bellows arm back down expelling the air from the bellows into the fire. The two bellows were in alternate positions so one bellows was always blowing into the fiery furnace. The furnace regularly held a temperature of 3,000°F, hot enough to melt iron, which has a melting point of 1,538°C or 2,800°F. Every twelve hours the slag was raked off the top of the molten iron. Then a clay plug at the base of the crucible was broken allowing a production run of between a half-ton to one ton of molten iron to flow out of the crucible into V shaped furrows that had been made in the sand floor. This iron was cast iron, sometimes called pig iron, because the main furrow was said to be a sow and the tributary or offshoot furrows were said to represent suckling pigs. A main sow iron bar was about four to five feet long, about six inches deep and about nine inches across at the top of the V, while a pig was about four feet long and about five inches wide at the top. Sows weighed from 300-400 pounds. In addition to bars some molten cast iron was ladled out of the furnace and poured directly into molds to produce pots, tools and other items.

Cast or pig iron is an alloy containing more than 1.5% carbon and is somewhat brittle, shortening the life of cast items. For example, the 500 pound hammer heads used at the ironworks forge were made of cast iron but needed to be replaced about six times a year. Large or intricate items had to be cast, but smaller, plain items like horseshoes and hinges could be shaped from more durable iron bars that had been refined. The refined iron was produced from cast iron bars in a nearby building called a finery. In one-half of the finery building were two open-hearth furnaces, each of which had a set of two seven foot bellows operated by a water wheel. The cast iron sows and pigs were fed into the forge and reheated until the iron was malleable. This refining process burned off much of the carbon producing wrought iron, which contains less that 0.5% carbon and is much stronger than cast iron. The malleable iron was heated three times and then kneaded with long metal hooks into a batch of about 75 pounds called a loop; one could get about 4 to 6 loops per sow. Each loop was beaten with a sledgehammer into a four inch square rod called a bloom. The bloom was cut lengthwise into two pieces. Each half-bloom was taken to the other side of the room where finishing work was performed, shaping the metal into merchant bars. The half-bloom was held in a pair of tongs and heated once again. Once it was hot, the iron was beaten with a 500 pound water powered hammer into lengths of about five feet long and from one to two inches square. The two inch square merchant bars represented about 75% of the output on the ironworks and were sold to blacksmiths to be reheated and shaped into horseshoes and other items. The one inch bars were sent on to the rolling and slitting mill.

At the rolling and slitting mill the bars were heated again and then passed through two or three sets of rollers that were powered by water wheels. The one inch square bars were gradually flatted to about two inches wide and half-an-inch thick and were appropriately called "flats." Some flats were sold to be used to make saws, iron rims for wagon wheels or barrel hoops, while others flats were sent on to the nearby slitting station. In this operation the flats were fed through a pair of sharp grooved rollers that slit them into small rods about a quarter of an inch square called nail rods. Any blacksmith could heat these rods and quickly make a supply of nails (about 1,200 nails could be produced per day). Orders for merchant bars, flats and nail rods as well as for finished cast metal objects produced at the foundry were taken by the Hammersmith company agent stationed in Boston and products were distributed through him. No doubt John Hull's father, the Boston blacksmith Robert Hull, acquired some items from Hammersmith (on ironmaking at Saugus see, Hartley, pp. 165-84 and Mary Clarke).

Jenks, who was actually an independent contractor associated with the foundry, made the more difficult special order requests. In January of 1648 Jenks obtained permission from Richard Leader, the agent for the Company of Undertakers of the Iron Works in New England, to build a private toolmaking shop near the forge. The document stated Jenks had:

> ...libertie to build & erect a mill or hammer for the forging and making of sithes or any other ware by water at the taile of the furnace & to have full benefit of the furnace water when the furnace goes provided he damnifies not any works that may hereafter be erected... .(quoted in Hartley, p. 208)

Jenk's shop was completed by June 24th. Archaeological excavations of the site from 1952 revealed the structure was located just east (to the left) of the blast furnace, near the Hammersmith boat landing on the Saugus River. He had three waterwheels, a hearth, an anvil block, water powered grindstones and possibly a water powered tilt hammer (Carlson, p. 10 and footnote 25). Jenks began his business as an independent master craftsman accepting special orders for all kinds of items. Since he had been a master steel swordmaker in England, he most likely forged some steel for some locally made steel articles have been discovered on the Hammersmith site. Steel is the strongest iron alloy, containing between 0.5% to 1.5% carbon. In the seventeenth century, steel was made by cementation, a process whereby wrought iron bars were packed with charcoal and sealed in clay. The mixture was heated at 900°C for several days, diffusing sufficient carbon into the wrought iron to convert it to steel. Typically, steel was used for swords, knives and scythes. It was also possible to make case hardened wrought iron, with a hard "outer skin" of about 0.05" thickness, by limiting the cementation process to eight hours (Tylecote, pp. 105-6).

Jenks could make steel, case hardened wrought iron and more intricate iron items. He did some work for the Hammersmith Company making saws, broadaxes and repairing iron fixtures on the company's boat. However, it appears the bulk of his business was for other clients since records show for the years 1648-1653 he received £18 10s for work performed for Hammersmith but during that same period he paid Hammersmith £32 for one-and-a-half tons of wrought iron bars. Unfortunately, we have no surviving records of his customers outside of Hammersmith except for an order from John Winthrop for several saws in February of 1653 (Carlson, p. 11). However, we do know Jenks was sought out for his skill. For instance, it was agreed at the Boston town council meeting of December 1, 1653, that "The select men have power and liberty hereby to agree with Jospeh Jynks for Ingins [engines] to Carry water in Case of fire, if they see Cause soe to doe" (Whitmore, *Boston Records,* p. 118). Just what these engines were or how they transported water was not mentioned, nor is it known if they were actually produced.[1] However, it does demonstrate how Jenks was called on when a difficult special order item was needed. Also, we discover in May of 1655 the General Court granted Jenks a seven year monopoly to produce an engine "for the more speedy cutting of grasse" (Shurtleff, vol. 3, p. 386 and vol. 4, pt. 1, pp. 233-34).

While there is no document directly linking Jenks to the mint, some suggestive evidence exists. A letter written in 1654 in London by John Hull's brother, Edward Hull, to Joseph Jenks survives in which Edward Hull told Jenks he knew of a German die cutter willing to immigrate to Boston, but there is no evidence this person ever came to Massachusetts Bay (Morison, p. 152). Interestingly, the master craftsmen at the sword factory in Hounslow, Middlesex, where Jenks had been employed, were Germans who had been brought from the

---

[1] At some point an engine was produced. In a meeting of the Boston Selectmen on May 28, 1683, Ralph Carter and seven other men were to "..take care and charge of the water Engine, to keepe it in good ord^r & be readie vpon all occasions, to attend the vse & seruice there of, when the said Carter shall require it, or there be any noyse or crie of fire..." *(Record Commissioners, Boston Town Records, 1660-1701,* p. 162).

continent specifically to develop the English sword industry. It seems unlikely that Jenks would be trying to open an illegal competing mint when he was busy with his own business and it is even more unlikely he would correspond with Hull's brother about such an enterprise. However, if Jenks was making the tools or die blanks for the mint it would seem quite logical for him to pursue leads on a diecutter among his former acquaintances in the profession. That he was corresponding on this topic with Hull's brother strongly suggests the request was made in relation to the recently opened mint. Jenks may have been pursuing a diecutter as a personal favor to John Hull, who was probably one of Jenks's customers, or, if Jenks produced items for the mint, he may have been doing this as part of a business deal.

In addition to this letter from the early years of the mint, there is a document from the later period. In the proceedings of the Massachusetts Bay General Court there is a record from May 15, 1672, stating the Court denied a petition brought forward by Joseph Jenks in which he requested permission to be allowed to open a mint (Crosby, pp. 79-80). It is generally assumed Jenks would not have gone through the expense and trouble to submit a petition unless he knew the trade and felt he could have successfully competed with Hull. This was during the final decade of the mint when the operation was less profitable and less silver was being brought in for minting into Boston shillings. It was also the time when the Hammersmith foundry was shutting down. Exactly when the Hammersmith ironworks ceased operation is unknown but records show production sharply declined in the 1660's. The demise of the plant seems to have occurred sometime between the last recorded use of the blast furnace in 1668 and a document of June 1676 where it stated that there were "neither utensils nor stock" at Hammersmith (Hartley, 258-62 with the quote on p. 262). With the demise of Hammersmith, Jenks seemed to have been searching for a new profession and felt he could be successful as a coiner. If Jenks had produced the steel die blanks or possibly some of the tools necessary for the continued operation of Hull's mint he would certainly be in a position to enter the coining business. Based on his reputation as a master ironsmith and interpreting both his 1654 inquiry to Edward Hull about a diecutter and his unsuccessful 1672 petition in the manner stated above, it is probable Jenks made some items for the Hull mint.

Specifically what Jenks may have produced for the mint is entirely conjectural. Various metal objects are possible candidates such as wrought iron rollers to roll out the molded sterling strips and possibly metal tools such as crucibles, ladles, tongs and metal parts for the furnace. However, the items most frequently suggested are punches and die blanks. Punches would refer to sets of hardened punches used to impress the letter grouping NE on the obverse and another punch for the reverse used to impress the denomination in Roman numerals directly onto each of the NE coins. Based on surviving examples we know there were at least three obverse and three reverse punches for the shillings and at least one set of obverse and reverse punches for the sixpence and threepence coins. These punches had to have been made of steel. Both Hull and Sanderson also had punches of their initials that were used to impress their mark into the bottom of the silver items they produced (primarily cups and bowls, see illustrations in Clarke, *Hull*, p. 115 and plate IX). The letters, numbers and images on the Willow, Oak and Pine Tree varieties of Massachusetts silver were hand cut into the dies. This hand cutting required hardened steel engraving tools, which could have been produced at Hammersmith or imported from England. Dies, or more properly die blanks, refer to the metal blanks provided to the mint for use in the minting press; these would be blank rocker dies for a rocker press and blank cylinder dies for a screw press. Both rocker and cylindrical die blanks could have been cast or possibly made of case hardened wrought iron. Die blanks would be engraved with an incuse mirror image (sometimes called a reverse or negative image) of the coin design to impress a positive image in relief on the coins. The engraving of the coin images onto those die blanks, turning them into usable dies, was most likely performed by Hull and Sanderson at the mint based on evidence they recut several of the dies to extend their life. There is likewise evidence they created the original designs since there are four sketches for the design of the Massachusetts coins found on the back of a sheet containing the minutes of a mint committee meeting from June of 1652, signed by John Hull. It is quite likely Hull was responsible for the sketches [figure 30].

Many long held assumptions concerning the minting and emission of colonial coins have been modified or overturned in the past few decades. It is no longer assumed that the smaller St. Patrick coins were considered farthings and we know that some New Jersey coppers dated 1786 were produced in 1787. In this climate, the question of who made the die blanks for Massachusetts silver is often passed over without comment. Sometimes, as in the recent editions of R. S. Yeoman's guide, popularly known as the *Red Book*, it is stated Jenks may have made the punches, without commenting on the dies. If we assume the partners did the recutting of the dies, it is also possible they did the original engraving on the die blanks. However, they needed to acquire the blanks that would be engraved into dies. If it is assumed the partners did not have the skill or did not have access to the necessary blast furnace needed to produce the punches for the NE coinage, it is also likely they needed access to a reliable supply of die blanks and the various metal items needed in melting and refining silver. Jenks is identified as the otherwise unknown craftsman who could have produced the punches for the NE coinage as well as the die blanks and the engraving tools that were necessary to impress the letters and images into those blanks for the other varieties of Massachusetts silver. He may also be the source of several other metal tools and supplies needed by the mint.

Interestingly, Hartley, in his book on the Saugus Ironworks, mentions Jenks had been credited with making dies for the Pine Tree shillings as well as constructing the first fire engine, but he was suspicious of those claims (Hartley, p. 11). Certainly, John Hull and Robert Sanderson knew silversmithing for they melted down and refined foreign silver plate and bullion in order to produce the correct fineness of silver needed for minting coins. It also seems quite probable they did the original engraving and were the ones to recut the dies. Further, Hull may have acquired some engraving tools through his London contacts or during his two voyages to London. However, during the 1650's, when the mint was first in operation, the only blast furnace in the colonies hot enough to melt iron to make either steel or case hardened wrought iron punches and die blanks as well as wrought iron rollers for a rolling machine, crucibles for melting silver and other iron products needed by the mint, was the furnace located at Hammersmith.

Part Five

The Eight Reales and its Value in Britain and Massachusetts Bay

---

Chapter 14

The Significance of the Eight Reales Cob Coinage

in Massachusetts Bay

British restrictions on exporting silver and gold

Due to Britain's limited supply of precious metals, various laws had been instituted making it illegal to export any silver or gold, including coins. Restrictions were first legislated during the reign of Edward III, when a law was passed in the Parliament of 1351 prohibiting the export of gold and silver coinage (Ruding, vol. 1, pp. 226-27). The prohibition was renewed several times up through the reign of Henry VI in 1423 with a proviso that money could be exported for payment of military expenses (Ruding, vol. 1, p. 270). However, merchants continually tried to circumvent the law so in 1477, Edward IV established a commission to look into the matter. The result was a new regulation making it a felony to export gold or silver coinage, either English or foreign, unless one had previously been granted a special license from the king (Ruding, vol. 1, p. 288). In 1553, Edward VI renewed this prohibition but included a provision that a merchant could export £4 in coinage, undoubtedly for expenses, as well as any gold or silver signets or rings worn on the fingers (Ruding, vol. 1. p. 325). The export prohibition was renewed by Elizabeth in 1559, by James I in proclamations of July 9, 1607, and June 11, 1622, and by Charles I in a proclamation of May 25, 1626 (Ruding, vol. 1, pp. 333, 365, 377 and 383-84).

During the Commonwealth several royal regulations were reversed, however it was difficult to get a consensus on allowing the exportation of silver. On September 23, 1648, an ordinance was passed to prevent the exportation of bullion, stating that Edward Watkins and others had been appointed under the seal of the Court of the Exchequer as "Commissioners for Discovery of Transporters of Coin and Bullion" (Firth, vol. 1, p. 1218). Additional legislation against exporting gold or silver was brought forward in 1649 and read twice but no vote was taken; the bill was resurrected on April 12, 1653, but again the legislation did not come up for a vote (Ruding, vol. 1, p. 417). However, on January 9, 1651, a law was passed to encourage the importation of bullion. This relaxed some export restrictions by allowing merchants to export "two third parts of such Bullion or Foreign Coyn as shall be so imported..." and that bullion could be sent "...to any part of Flanders or Holland, or to ship it away at their pleasure..." (Firth, vol. 2, p. 495). Thus, merchants were allowed to export two thirds of any bullion they imported. But in the last days of the Commonwealth, under Richard Cromwell, a motion was referred to the council of State on July 11, 1659, to investigate allegations of illegal exportation of bullion and to seize any bullion being illegally exported. Finally on May 21, 1660, it was voted to prohibit any exporting of bullion without the approval of Parliament (Ruding, vol. 1, p. 422). During this more liberal period some limited export of foreign bullion was possible but several lawmakers continued to believe that specie should remain in the country.

Soon after he was restored to the throne, Charles II issued a proclamation on June 10, 1661, confirming and reactivating previous royal commands against exporting coins or bullion (Ruding, vol. 2, pp. 3-4). However, his advisors quickly came to the realization that these restrictions were detrimental to the British economy, since British merchants could not easily participate in international agreements and such export restrictions made foreign merchants reluctant to bring specie into England. Accordingly, in 1663 the Act of June 10, 1661, was modified so that as of August 1, 1663, it became legal to export foreign specie coins as well as gold and silver bullion (Ruding, vol. 2, p. 11). This act allowed individuals to legally export foreign silver from England but it did not allow English coinage to be exported. The intention of the law was to both encourage trade and increase the specie supply in London without any concern for the welfare of the British colonies in North America where the inability to legally import British coinage caused serious problems.

Obviously, some British silver circulated in America. The British military was permitted to pay for items with British sterling. The military, especially the navy, purchased supplies in the colonies. For example, in Chapter Six we saw in 1655, Robert Wadeson, Captain William Crispin and Thomas Broughton, were given £10,000 sterling and charged to acquire provisions for the British army and fleet stationed at Jamaica. They were authorized to make purchases in Massachusetts Bay and were cautioned about the differing value of British and Massachusetts silver. Also, the navy regularly purchased masts at a cost of £95 to £115 each from Massachusetts Bay (see Carlton). Most likely the majority of these purchases involved the exchange of credit. It is quite likely the £10,000 sterling did not refer to boxes of coins but the equivalent value in credit. Colonists selling items would most likely receive credit in the form of bills of exchange. We have seen some bills of exchange that involved Hull (Chapter 12, pp. 129-30). The bills could be used to pay debts due in England for manufactured goods that had been shipped to the colonists. It is also possible some military payments involved Spanish cobs, even before the export ban was lifted in August of 1663. Further, some military transactions in Massachusetts Bay may have included British sterling coinage. Additionally, some sterling coinage was carried to the colonies in the personal belongings of immigrants and travelers. However, the supply of sterling in Massachusetts Bay was far too small to sustain daily commerce. The colonists needed to look elsewhere for coinage. The most abundant supply of silver coinage was found in the Spanish colonies.

Spanish and Spanish American coinage in the seventeenth century

During the seventeenth century silver from the rich and seemingly endless mines in Spanish America was transformed into substantial quantities of crude cob coinage that was then sent to Spain on treasure ships. At the Spanish American mints, small cigar shaped ingots of refined silver were simply cut into chunks of the appropriate weight. In fact, the term cob is derived from the Spanish word, *cabo*, which means the end; in this instance, the clump of silver clipped off the end of the bar. Each small silver clump was then hammer struck between dies. The size and shape of these cob coins were highly irregular as were the impressions. Many cobs were quite thick and disfigured with large cracks. If a cob was overweight the minter simply clipped a piece off, further disfiguring it [figure 31]. The intention in minting these crude but accurately weighed cobs was to produce an easily portable product that could be sent to Spain where they would be melted down to produce silver jewelry, coins, bars and other items. Cob coinage also circulated in Spanish America and became the standard coinage of the British West Indies. Massachusetts Bay and the other British colonies along the Atlantic coast regularly traded with the British possessions in the West Indies such as Jamaica and Barbados, and therefore significant quantities of Spanish American cobs found their way to these mainland colonies. Spanish, and particularly Spanish American silver, quickly became the predominant coinage throughout the British colonies in North America.

Since the Spanish American cobs were crude, misshapen chunks of silver, it was quite easy for colonial settlers to clip or file some silver from a coin and then pass the lightened coin off at full value. Obviously as a coin went through various hands and was repeatedly clipped it became lighter and lighter. Also, because of their crude shape and design it was easy to make lightweight counterfeit cobs using the clipped silver. Indeed, the reason most often given in contemporary sources for the opening of the Massachusetts Mint was to produce a uniform coinage to replace the numerous clipped, lightweight Spanish American cobs then in circulation.

The survival of the Massachusetts Mint was contingent upon the public bringing Spanish American silver cobs to the mint to be transformed into Massachusetts coinage. This process was dependent on the rate of exchange between Spanish American silver and Massachusetts silver. The Massachusetts Mint would continue to operate as long as it was profitable for individuals to convert Spanish silver into Massachusetts coinage. To understand this relationship we must review the history of the most prominent Spanish American silver coin to circulate in Massachusetts Bay, the eight reales.

❀❀❀❀❀❀❀❀❀❀❀❀

Chapter 15

The Intrinsic Value of the Spanish Real and the Eight Reales

The origin of the real

In 1474, Isabella succeeded as the ruler of Castile and soon initiated a coinage reform. In a decree of February 20, 1475, she proclaimed a standard value for each of the various local medieval coins then in circulation. Soon thereafter, on June 26, 1475, Queen Isabella sent a letter to the mint in Seville ordering the mint to produce 67 reales from a Spanish mark of silver (which equalled 8 Spanish ounces) that was 11 *dineros* and 4 *granos* in fineness.

In 1479, Isabella married Ferdinand of Aragon uniting the two most powerful Catholic kingdoms in Spain. Over the next twelve years the monarchs consolidated their power, finally driving out the Moors and Jews in 1492. Once they had united all of Spain under their rule, the monarchs undertook a series of new initiatives, one of which was a coinage reform. Essentially, the minting specifications issued by Isabella in 1475 became universal for all of Spain and the entire Spanish Empire, which had significantly expanded in late 1492 when Christopher Columbus claimed the West Indies and all of the Americas for Spain. The coinage reform was promulgated at Medina del Campo, the site of the largest silver and gold exchange fair in medieval Spain. In the *Pragmática* of Medina del Campo issued on June 13, 1497, it was declared that a Spanish mark of silver at a fineness of 11 *dineros* and 4 *granos* would be minted into 67 reales. The first article of this law discussed gold coins, then article two began:

> Otrosi, ordenamos e mandamos, que en cada una de las dichas nuestras casas de moneda se labre otra moneda de plata, que se llame reales, de talla e peso de sesenta e siete reales en cada marco, e no menos; e de ley de onze dineros e quatro granos, e no menos. E que destos se labren reales e medios reales e quartos de reales e ochavos de reales; los quales todos sean salvados uno a uno, porque sean de ygual peso; e que de la plata se labre el un tercio de reales enteros, e el otro tercio de medios reales; e el otro tercio se labre de quartos e de ochavos por meytad, e que los ochavos sean quadrados; e que en los reales se pongan de la una parte nuestras armas reales, e de la otra parte la divisa del yugo de mi rey, e la divisa de las flechas de mi reyna; e que diga enderredor continuando en ambas partes: FERDINANDUS E ELISABET REX E REGINA CASTELLE E LEGIONS E ARAGONUM E CECILIE E GRANATE: o lo que dello cupiere.   (Calbetó de Grau, vol. 2, p. 536, Gil Farrés, p. 231 and Heiss, vol. 1, pp. 322-24)

> [Furthermore, we order and mandate that in each one of our said mints that another money be made of silver, to be called reales, of size and weight of sixty seven reales in each mark and not less, and by law of eleven *dineros* and four *granos* and not less. And that from these be made reales and half

reales and quarters of reales and eighths of reales; all of which be proportional one to the other so that they may be of balanced weight; and that a third of the silver be worked into whole reales, and from another third half reales; and the other third equally divided between quarters and eighths, and that the eighths be square; and that on one side of the reales our royal arms be put, and on the other side the device of me the king, the yoke, and the device of my queen the arrows; and that it may say around the rim continuing from one side to the other: FERDINAND AND ISABELLA KING AND QUEEN OF CASTILE AND LEON AND ARAGON AND SICILY AND GRANADA : or that part which will fit.][1]

The law went on to explain that a Spanish mark of silver at eleven *dineros* and four *granos* fineness was worth sixty five reales but was to be minted into 67 reales. One of the two extra reales was to be retained by the mint and the other given to the owner of the silver.

During this period the largest denomination silver coin was the real, with fractional coins called a half, quarter and an eighth real; these were the only coins specifically mentioned in the *Pragmática*. The weight of these silver coins were proportional to each other and the fineness remained constant. Later, when higher denomination silver coins such as the two, four and eight reales, began to be minted, they too conformed to the authorized standards. The first eight reales coins carried the inscription, shield and devices of Ferdinand and Isabella but it is now believed these undated coins were struck posthumously during the reigns of Charles I (1516-1555) and Philip II (1556-1598). The minting of these posthumous eight reales probably did not begin much earlier than the *Cédula* of Charles I of November 18, 1537, authorizing the Viceroy of New Spain to mint eight reales coins and they cannot be after the *Pragmática* of Philip II of November 23, 1566, which called for his own name to be used on future coins (Tomás Dasí, vol. 1, p. 49; Calbetó de Grau, vol. 2, p. 552; Gil Farrés, pp. 236-37 and Heiss, vol. 1, pp. 161-62). Significant quantities of eight reales were minted in Spain and Spanish America during the reign of Philip II (1555-1598) and production continued under his successors. However, although Philip had his name added to coins in 1566, a date was not included until 1589. Thus, we do not know if the undated issues were minted sporadically, or, if they were produced annually like the later dated varieties (see Calbetó de Grau, vol. 1, pp. 32-34 and vol. 2, pp. 406-8, 432-36, 552-60).

There was actually no specific authorized weight for the eight reales. Rather, the *Pragmática* of Medina del Campo had only stated that a Spanish mark of silver at a specific fineness would be used to produce 67 reales in coins. We can calculate the average weight of an eight reales assuming a Spanish mark of silver was precisely weighed to the authorized standard and that all the coins from that mark of silver were exactly equal. Also, we must assume no silver was lost as waste during the minting process. Obviously, precise standardization in the minting process was not possible, so that the "authorized weight" was

---

[1] A double yoke or collar, as used to harness oxen to a plow, was adopted by the king as his emblem or device. The queen's emblem was a bundle of arrows tied together in the center of the shafts, similar in appearance to the arrows held in the eagle's talon in the Great Seal of the United States of America.

only a mathematical average. Individual examples could legitimately be above or below this weight because the only stipulation in the law was that 67 reales be produced from each mark of silver.

According to the Spanish weight system a Spanish mark equaled eight Spanish ounces which equaled 4608 Spanish grains. At 67 reales to a Spanish mark the authorized weight of a real was 68.776119 Spanish grains, thus an eight reales was authorized at 550.20895 Spanish grains. In the troy weight system, a Spanish mark was equal to 3550.16 troy grains which put the "authorized weight" of a real at 52.987462 troy grains and an eight reales at 423.89969 troy grains, which Phil Mossman has rounded to 423.9 troy grains.

To calculate the sterling value of an eight reales at the full authorized standard we also need to know the silver content or authorized fineness of the coin. The Spanish fineness scale was based on the *dinero*. *Dinero* is a Spanish word for money, originally silver money, derived from the Latin *denarius*. In the present context, as a measurement of fineness, the closest English equivalent is the troy ounce, where 12 troy ounces equaled a troy pound of pure silver. In this system the British defined sterling (.925 fineness) as 11 ounces and 2 pennyweight (11 oz. 2 dwt.) of silver per troy pound, the other 18 pennyweight being copper. Rather than use the misleading translation of "Spanish troy ounce" which would be the closest equivalent but could be confused with the Spanish ounce or the troy scale, numismatists simply leave the measurement in Spanish as *dinero*. Keeping with this practice, I have not translated the fineness terms. In the Spanish fineness scale, 12 *dineros* is pure silver or, as it would be currently expressed, a 1.000 millesimal fineness. The basic unit, a *dinero*, is just a fraction over .083333 fineness. The *dinero* is divided into 24 *granos*, so that one *grano* is just a fraction over .0034722 fineness. Therefore, Spanish silver coinage with a fineness of 11 *dineros* (just a fraction over .916663) and 4 *granos* (just a fraction over .0138888) calculates to a total fineness of .9305518, which Aloïss Heiss rounded up to .931 fine. Thus, according to the specifications in the *Pragmática* of Medina del Campo, an eight reales coin should average close to 423.9 troy grains of .931 fine silver (see, Mossman, p. 55, Gil Farrés, pp. 18-23, 226-27 and 230-31 and Heiss, vol. 1, pp. 413-18 for similar results, but Sumner, "Spanish Dollar," pp. 607-9, gives slightly different numbers).

The intrinsic value of Spanish and Spanish American eight reales in the seventeenth century

The specifications in the Spanish coinage law of 1497 remained the official standard for all Spanish American silver coinage until 1728, when the eight reales was reduced to 417.6 troy grains of .9166 fine silver. However, silver coinage minted in Spain had been reduced in weight back in 1642. The *Pragmática* of December 23, 1642, authorized 83.25 reales to be cut from a Spanish mark of silver at .93055 fineness. In relation to the earlier laws authorizing 67 reales per mark, this law increased the number of reales per mark by 16.25 or almost 25% (a full 25% increase from 67 would be 16.75 reales). The new real was authorized at 42.644564 troy grains and the new eight reales at 341.15651 troy grains. Since this law was limited to coins produced in Spain, the relationship between Spanish and Spanish American silver shifted. The Spanish American eight reales, at its fully authorized weight of 423.89969 troy grains, was equal to just a fraction over 9.94 reales of the new lighter Spanish coinage, called new plate, and traded at ten new plate reales (Calbetó de

Grau, vol. 2, pp. 578-79 and Heiss, vol. 1, pp. 186-87). In the *Pragmática* of October 14, 1686, mainland Spanish coinage was reduced once more but only slightly, so that 84 reales were to be cut from a Spanish mark (42.2638 troy grains per real with the eight reales at 338.1104 troy grains). This small reduction did not affect the exchange rate of Spanish American silver, which continued to trade at eight Spanish American reales for ten Spanish reales. The Spanish American eight reales went from 2.54594 grains below the equivalent of ten new plate reales at the 1642 rate to actually being 1.26169 grains more than ten Spanish reales at the 1686 rate (Gil Farrés, pp. 242-46 and 326-28 and Heiss, vol. 1, pp. 382-84).

These laws reducing the weight of Spanish reales did not affect the acceptance of Spanish silver in seventeenth century Britain or British America. Throughout the century all Spanish eight reales put into circulation were crude cob coins. The only fully struck coins were the rare presentation strikes produced at the royal mint in Segovia [Figure 34]. Fully struck coinage for general circulation was not produced until 1700 in Seville and 1709 in Madrid. All the circulating coinage made between the 1642 weight reduction and the introduction of fully struck coins continued to be crude cobs. Because these lighter cobs were of the same fineness as the pre-1642 cobs, they continued to be accepted and were simply traded by weight, just as if they were examples of pre-1642 underweight clipped cobs that were so common in colonial America.

Spanish American silver cobs continued to be authorized at the 1497 standards throughout the seventeenth century. These standards were closely followed at the central mint in Mexico City and at most other Spanish American mints with the exception of the mint in Potosí, Bolivia, where a major scandal was uncovered in 1648. It was discovered that from 1640 the Potosí assayer had been in collusion with a silver merchant issuing coins that were significantly debased. When the news of the debasement became public, the debased coinage was discounted as much as 50%. In order to restore public confidence in the coinage and keep the public from rejecting or discounting post-scandal coins, the Potosí mint, and other mints in the viceroyalty of Peru, changed the design of their coins. Thus the previously debased coins and the new issues of guaranteed quality could be distinguished the one from the other. The old Hapsburg shield on the debased coinage was replaced by the new "pillars" design [Figures 31 and 32]. Further, by an order of February 17, 1651, all old, depreciated Potosí cobs were to be returned to the mint and melted down to make full weight examples of the new pillar coinage (Freeman, p. 9).

Pre-1652 "Peruvians" were shunned or heavily discounted by the British colonists. Although most Spanish American cob coinage in the British colonies had been reduced in weight by clipping, filing or washing, the colonists could rely on the fineness of the coins and thus accepted them as sterling silver based on weight. However, the debased Peruvian cobs were considered to be below sterling fineness and needed to be assayed to determine their actual value so they could not be reliably traded even by weight! I do not know of any document from Massachusetts Bay during the late 1640's or early 1650's specifically referring to the Potosí debasement uncovered in 1648. However, as Phil Mossman has suggested (Mossman, p. 79), it seems possible the news of this scandal and the specter of debased coins may have acted as a catalyst prompting the Massachusetts legislature, now under the new English Commonwealth government, to take action against the daily inconveniences of counterfeit and clipped coinage that are mentioned by Hull and others as the reason for instituting the coinage act of 1652. In the same year that the Massachusetts Mint opened, 1652, the Potosí mint produced their first pillar coinage (See, Sumner, "Spanish Dollar," pp. 609-14 and Mossman, pp. 55-56).

Interestingly, Massachusetts Bay legislation distinguished three categories of eight reales: the Seville, pillar and Mexican varieties. A fourth variety, mentioned in legislation from several other British possessions such as the island of Montserrat and the colony of Connecticut, was the debased Potosí coins called "Peruvians," which were only accepted at a discount (Chalmers, p. 64 and Hoadly, vol. [4], August 1689 - May 1706, pp. 166-67 and 176-77). By specifically mentioning the Seville, pillar and Mexican varieties, the Massachusetts General Court was intentionally leaving the debased Potosí or Peruvian coinage out of their legislation. Of the cobs mentioned in the Massachusetts Bay legislation, the Mexican eight reales was the predominant variety found in Massachusetts Bay because of the widespread use of these coins in the West Indies. The Mexican "pieces of eight" like other varieties, had a Hapsburg shield on the obverse. However, the reverse of the Mexican design included a very distinctive cross with each extremity having a wedge shape followed by a round sphere. It was easily distinguished from cobs produced at any other mint [figure 33]. The "pillar" style referred to the reverse design of the eight reales coins produced in the post-debasement period at Potosí, Bolivia, as well as the post-1652 coins from Lima, Peru, and the smaller mints in Colombia at Santa Fe de Bogotá, La Plata and Cartagena (see Lasser on the Colombian mints). This style is now called the pillar and waves design showing the Pillars of Hercules with an abbreviation of the Spanish motto PLUS ULTRA (More beyond) as had appeared earlier on the first Spanish American coins made in Mexico under Charles I and his mother, the co-regent, Joanna. The obverse of the post-debasement coins was initially issued in 1652 with the lion and castle quadrants within a crowned shield but subsequent issues starting in 1653 transformed the shield into a cross of Jerusalem with a perpendicular bar extension on each extremity [figure 32]. The "Sevil" eight reales referred to mainland Spanish coins from the central mint in Seville. Since these cobs had to be transported from Spain they were probably less frequently encountered in Massachusetts Bay than the Mexican or pillar varieties. The "Sevil" coins displayed the crowned Hapsburg shield with the mintmark and denomination on the obverse while the reverse was divided into quadrants by a cross; in the upper left and lower right quadrants was a castle representing Castile and in the other two quadrants was a lion representing Leon. This design is often called the shield style [see figure 34 for a royal strike version]. The debased Potosí coins were the genesis of the "Peruvians." These pre-1652 cobs had a style that was similar to the "Sevil" variety but whereas the "Sevil" coins displayed an imperial crown, the Spanish American coins showed only a coronet [figure 31]. The "Peruvian" style of coin had been produced up to 1652 at Potosí and throughout the Viceroyalty of Peru, at mints at Santa Fe de Bogotá, Colombia and Lima, Peru. When the debasement scandal unfolded all mints in the Viceroyalty of Peru abandoned this design for the pillar style, thus all coins in the older style were identified as "Peruvians" no matter where they had been minted and were avoided or discounted by the British colonists.

❀❀❀❀❀❀❀❀❀❀❀

Chapter 16

The Eight Reales in England

The colonists residing in Massachusetts Bay in the 1650's were British subjects and, for the most part, had emigrated from England. Their traditions, laws and customs were modeled on those of England with modifications necessitated by colonial life which still depended on England and other British colonies for trade and supplies. The value and the role of the eight reales in England was central to how the Massachusetts colonists conceived, defined and valued this currency.

The sixteenth century

During the reign of Philip II of Spain (1556-1598) the eight reales, which were minted in both Spain and the Americas, became the preferred international currency. The coins were rather plentiful and were produced with a consistent weight and fineness. Furthermore, they had a higher silver content than other crown size coins such as locally produced German thalers and Dutch lion dollars or the nationally regulated French écu and British crown. Although eight reales were regularly used for international trade, the role and valuation of the eight reales in sixteenth century England is difficult to determine. This is partially due to the several Tudor debasements of the sterling standard so that British coinage frequently fluctuated in relation to the Spanish eight reales. The situation did not stabilize until 1601 at the end of the reign of Queen Elizabeth. By her order of July 29, 1601, the fineness of English coinage was set at .925 sterling silver with shillings authorized at 62 per troy pound of sterling silver, or 92.9 troy grains per shilling. This remained the British standard throughout the American colonial period; it was not revised until 1816.

In addition to the fluctuating value of English coinage during the sixteenth century, an even more significant impediment to understanding the role of the eight reales in England was the English prohibition of foreign coinage. Several laws had been passed prohibiting the importation of foreign coinage into England. During the Parliament of 1400 - 1401, early in the reign of Henry IV, it was noted that nobles of Flanders were quite common in England and traded at face value with English nobles even though the Flemish coins had a lower intrinsic value. To stop this damaging situation a law was passed (2 Henrici IV, cap. 6) stating, "...all money of gold and silver of the coins of Flanders, and of all other lands and countries beyond the sea, and also of Scotland, shall be voided out of the realm of England, or put to coin to the bullion of the same realm... ." Merchants were required to exchange foreign coins at the English stronghold of Calais in northern France because foreign coins brought into England were to be forfeited to the king (Ruding, vol. 1, pp. 249-50). This law was not repealed until the Parliament of 1623-1624 (21 Jacobi I, cap. 28, *Statutes,* vol. 4, part 2, p. 1239), although it is clear the regulation was antiquated and long out of date by that time. Indeed, such a regulation was impossible to enforce after the English lost Calais in battle in 1558 (on April 2, 1559, in the first of two treaties signed at Cateau-Cambrésis, the

British ceded their rights to Calais to the king of France in return for a payment thus terminating any British claim to the city). Even before the loss of Calais it is likely foreign coins, including some eight reales, found their way into the British Isles, but certainly following the loss of Calais several varieties of foreign coins circulated in England.

In 1560, a year after the loss of Calais, Queen Elizabeth attempted to regulate the value of foreign coins in England. Coinage regulation was reinforced by a proclamation issued on June 12, 1561, explaining that numerous foreign coins had been received by her subjects at rates above their intrinsic value. Therefore, no foreign coins except the French, Flemish and Burgundian crowns (to be valued as 6s) were to be current; all other foreign coins were to be exchanged at the London mint for English coins based on the intrinsic value of the foreign coins (Ruding, vol. 1, pp. 340-41). There are no Elizabethan regulations concerning the eight reales leading many numismatists to question if the coin had a prominent place in Elizabethan England. Challis has examined extant Exchequer records concerning bullion brought to the mint. From the few records he was able to uncover, he discovered only 7.36% of the bullion from the second half of 1567 was in Spanish coinage while in 1568 only 2.1% of the total bullion was from that source. However, the situation changed in late 1569, as from September of 1569 through February of 1570 Spanish coinage made up 81.4% of all bullion brought to the mint. Thus, it seems during Elizabeth's reign the eight reales grew in significance (Challis, *Tudor Coinage*, pp. 192-98). It is clear that by the later part of her reign this coin was considered to be a significant international monetary unit by the British. In a commission to the mint of January 11, 1601, it was stated that the "Company of Merchants of London Trading into the East Indies," commonly known as the East India Company, had several times requested to be allowed to transport Spanish silver coins to the Indies. Because this request had been denied, Queen Elizabeth authorized trade coins of eight, four, two and one testerns to be minted in London for circulation in the East Indies. The weight and fineness of these coins, known as *portcullis* money because of the gate depicted on the reverse, was based on the Spanish eight reales rather than on English coins (Ruding, vol. 1, p. 353).

The Proclamation of May 14, 1612

The role and value of the eight reales in Britain becomes clearer in the seventeenth century. On May 14, 1612, James I issued a proclamation with the objective of increasing the quantity of foreign silver and gold coinage brought to the London mint. Previously, the price the mint offered for foreign coins had been set rather low in order to increase mint profits. This policy was causing difficulties, since individuals preferred to sell their foreign silver and gold coins to merchants and goldsmiths, who offered higher prices than the mint. The king's proclamation was designed to increase the flow of bullion to the mint by setting new higher values at which the mint would purchase bullion or foreign coinage. Further, it commanded that anyone who either sold or purchased foreign coins or bullion above the rates issued in the proclamation would be fined double the value of the transaction and imprisoned. Individuals were free to sell or purchase bullion and foreign coins at the mint rate or at a lower rate but they could not legally offer to purchase coins or bullion above the mint rates. As to how the new rates were established the proclamation stated:

...the said rates are not precisely reduced to the fineness of the said pieces and bullion, yet the same were guided by the valuation of the merchants, which are best acquainted with the severall rates at which they are accepted abroad, where use sometimes prevaileth more than any exact computation. (Ruding, vol. 1, p. 368)

In the proclamation, a troy ounce of Spanish silver coins from Seville was rated at 60d (5s) as was an ounce of sterling plate, while an ounce of silver coins from Mexico was valued at 58d (4s10d). This rate implied Spanish silver was at sterling fineness, since an ounce of Seville silver and an ounce of sterling were of equal value. The mint purchased sterling plate at 60d (5s) per troy ounce, a price which provided them a nice profit since they coined 62d (5s2d) in money from each troy ounce of sterling. Their potential profit from Spanish and Mexican coins depended on the fineness of the specific coins. Spanish and Mexican silver were authorized at the same fineness, which was slightly higher than sterling, although we know from various assays of individual coins, they were often slightly over or slightly under sterling fineness. Assuming a fineness at the authorized rate, which equaled just about .931 fineness, Spanish silver would yield a profit for the mint that was a fraction over 2d per ounce while Mexican silver would yield a profit of just over 4d per ounce.

Interestingly, this proclamation treated Spanish silver and other foreign coins as commodities. It did not define what was considered to be a full weight eight reales, rather the value was given by the troy ounce instead of by the coin (or, as was said at the time, by weight rather than by tale). A troy ounce of silver equaled 480 grains. Thus, at the mint purchase price of 60d per ounce of Seville silver, the exchange rate for Spanish silver can be calculated at eight grains per 1d, while at 58d per troy ounce for Mexican silver the rate was 8.275862069 grains per 1d. If we assume a 420 grains (that is, a 17.5 pennyweight) eight reales as a full weight coin, a Seville eight reales would have a market value of 52.5d (4s 4.5d) and a Mexican eight reales would be 50.75d (4s 2.75d). As stated above, this did not reflect the intrinsic or assay value but rather was the rate adopted by the king as the highest allowable rate and also the rate at which the mint would purchase these coins.

In a proclamation of James I from May 13, 1613, we learn there were large quantities of lightweight clipped Spanish coins in circulation that were passing at the value of full weight coins, causing a loss to the receiver of such coins of up to a third in intrinsic value. The proclamation prohibited the passing of lightweight coins with offenders being fined or imprisoned. All lightweight Spanish coinage was to be taken to the Tower mint where the customers would receive payment based on bullion weight. The underweight coins would then be melted down to produce English silver (Ruding, vol. 1, p. 370).

The alteration debate of 1626

Some specific information on the value of eight reales coins in England is part of a debate that occurred in 1626 based on a proposal to Charles I initially put forward on April 25, 1625, by the former Warden of the mint in Scotland, John Gilbert. Gilbert proposed that English coinage be secretly reduced in weight so more coins could be minted from the same amount of silver and thereby increase the king's coffers. A mint indenture was authorized on August 14, 1626, to produce silver coins at 70s per troy pound. The mint purchased silver at

60s per troy pound and since 1601 had produced 62s in coin per troy pound, for a 2s profit. According to the new scheme profits would increase by 8s per troy pound, of which the king was to receive an additional 5s6d and the mint an additional 2s6d per pound of silver coined. As soon as the indenture was approved a debate ensued contesting the "alteration" of the coinage. Within a few weeks the king issued a proclamation on September 4, 1626, rescinding the August 14th indenture and returning to the weight standards that had been in force before the indenture was issued (Shaw, *Selected Tracts,* pp. 3-20).

During the final days of the debate, Sir Robert Cotton spoke before the Privy Council against the alteration. Fortunately, Cotton's speech and some related documents survive because they were published in 1651 in an anthology of Cotton's works edited by James Howell called the *Cottoni Posthuma.* Along with Cotton's speech the *Posthuma* contained supplementary material including "The Answer of the Committee appointed by your Lordships to the Propositions delivered by some Officers of the Mint, for inhancing his Majestie's monies of Gold and Silver, 2 September 1626." In this document the committee, which had been appointed by the Privy Council, stated the following concerning the eight reales: "But having examined it by the best Artists, we find it to be 11 ounces, 2d. weight fine, and in weight 17 penny weight, 12 grains,..." [2d. weight is an abbreviation for two pennyweight] (*Postuma,* p. 297, also in Shaw, *Selected Tracts,* p. 31). This phrase has been taken to refer to a mint assay (as in Sumner, "Coin Shilling," p. 248). The examination certainly refers to an assay in which the fineness and weight of the coin were measured, but there is no specific evidence as to who performed the assay. It may have been performed by a government agency such as the exchequer or possibly the assay was contracted to some London goldsmiths. Since the committee was investigating the veracity of statements made by the officers of the mint and the report was in opposition to their statements, it is quite likely the assay was not performed at the mint.

Unfortunately, the entire passage on the eight reales in the "Answer of the Committee" is rather brief and must be understood in context. One needs to read the preceding two paragraphs about the duties of the mintmasters and the situation with the rix dollar to understand the argument. The statement basically says the officers of the mint had "untruly" informed the Privy Council concerning the intrinsic value and the exchange rate of the rix dollar and the eight reales. The committee stated the mint officers had correctly affirmed the weight of a "Royal of Eight" was 17 dwt. 12 gr. (which equals 17.5 dwt. or 420 grains) but then the mint officers had incorrectly asserted the coin was only 11 ounces (that is, .91666) fine. The difference between the fineness reported in the assay performed at the request of the Committee of the Privy Council and the assay reported by the mint was a full two pennyweight. As mentioned above, early assays were not as precise as individuals would have wished and sometimes the results varied by as much as two pennyweight per troy pound. It was not until the more scientific assays of Sir Isaac Newton, especially in his major assay of 1702, that standards were set requiring a specific coin to be cut into pieces and assay results on the coin be replicated before issuing a statement on the silver content of a coin. Although this two pennyweight differential could have been a legitimate disparity, the Privy Council committee did not trust the veracity of the mint report.

The committee further charged that the mint had misrepresented the exchange rate, for the mint had stated a Royal of Eight passed in trade at 5s. As quoted above, the committee announced an assay "by the best Artists" showed the eight reales was indeed 420 grains in weight but that it was at sterling fineness of 11 oz. 2 dwt. (that is, .925). They then explained the eight reales,

> …doeth equal 4s. 4d. of our Sterling moneys, and passeth in London at that rate, and not otherwise, though holding more fine Silver by 12 grains and a half in every Royal of Eight, which is the charge of coynage, and a small overplus for the Gold-smiths gain. (Shaw, *Selected Tracts,* p. 31)

The additional 12.5 grains of silver that were above the 4s4d (52d) exchange rate would equal just a little over 1.6d. This is what the committee stated was the mint charge, that is, the difference between what the mint paid out for the item and the profit the mint would make when recoining the item. Adding the 1.6d to the 52d (4s4d) yields a value of 53.6d, which the committee stated was slightly low, since an eight reales of 420 grains, which they calculated as equivalent to sterling, would have an intrinsic value of 54.25d. The difference between the 53.6d and the full intrinsic value of 54.25d is .65d, which is the "small overplus" for the goldsmith. Essentially an individual could take eight reales to a goldsmith and exchange each full weight eight reales for 52d (4s4d) in English silver coinage. The goldsmith would then refine the silver to sterling bullion or plate and would gain 0.65d from each coin, or slightly more if the coin was heavier than 420 grains or had a fineness above .925 fine. The refined silver might then be taken to the mint where the goldsmith would be paid 52.65d for the sterling extracted from the eight reales. The mint would then use that sterling to produce 54.25d in coins for a profit of 1.6d.

The committee completed their discussion of the eight reales by questioning the exchange rate of 60d (5s) per eight reales stated by the officers of the mint to be the current rate. The committee assured the Privy Council this rate was incorrect and that "Merchants do all affirm" that the eight reales "passeth only at 4s. 4[d.] ob. of the Sterling moneys, and no higher ordinarily" [the d was inadvertently transcribed as ob, but it is found elsewhere in the same paragraph transcribed correctly when mentioning the rate] (Shaw, Selected Tracts, p. 31 and Sumner, "Coin Shilling," p. 248).

Thus, we have seen the eight reales became a significant coin in England from about 1570. According to the rates proclaimed by James I in 1612 a full weight Spanish eight reales would have the value of about 52d (4s4d) while a full weight Mexican eight reales would have a value of about 51d (4s3d). Unfortunately we do not know if the rate distinction between Spanish and Mexican eight reales was observed in daily trade. However, by the time of the alteration debate of 1626, during the reign of Charles I, it appears all varieties of full weight eight reales traded at 52d (4s4d).

Lightweight eight reales in the southwestern counties, 1644

A pamphlet printed in London in 1644 called *A Remedie Against The losse of the Subject by Farthing-Tokens,* stated that along the sea coast in the southwestern counties of Kent, Sussex and Hampshire numerous foreign coins were circulating above their intrinsic value including several varieties of German rix dollars and Spanish pieces of eight. The pieces of eight traded at 4s4d (52d), which the pamphlet stated was the correct value for full weight Seville coins, but these coins were lightweight. The author suspected they were overvalued by at least 4d (*Remedie*, p. 6). The pamphlet suggested these foreign coins be brought to the mint and melted into sterling coinage. It appears the circulation of large quantities of lightweight silver was limited to the southwestern coastal area where several individuals were engaged in smuggling operations with partners on the continent (Ruding, vol. 1, p. 403).

Rates for the eight reales during the Commonwealth

The market rate for a full weight Spanish eight reales remained unchanged at 4s4d (52d) through the end of the reign of Charles I and during the first few years of the Commonwealth. With the overthrow of the monarchy in 1649, the Commonwealth government tried to replace the system whereby special privileges and monopolies had been issued by the king to a few select nobles in return for favors or cash. Regarding trade and commerce the Commonwealth instituted policies that would give all merchants an opportunity to prosper and keep the population employed. On August 1, 1650, a commission was formed to advance trade and manufacture "...to the end that ye poore people of this Land may be set on work, and their Families preserved from beggary and Ruine, and that the Commonwealth might be enrighed thereby, and no occasion left either for Idleness or Poverty" (Firth, vol. 2, p. 403). Among the twelve charges to the commission was:

> *Seventhly,* They are duly to consider the value of the *English* Coyns, and the Par thereof, in relation to the intrinsic value which it bears in weight and fineness with the Coyns of other Nations : Also to consider the state of the Exchange, and of the gain or loss that comes to the Commonwealth by the Exchange now used by the Merchants. (Firth, vol. 2, p. 404)

Soon thereafter, on January 9, 1651, regulations on importation of bullion and foreign coins were relaxed. As mentioned above, importation of foreign coinage was made legal during the Parliament session of 1623-1624. By the 1623-1624 law, foreign coins were to be treated like bullion in that merchants were required to sell one-third of their shipment to the mint and pay a two percent duty on the reminder, although the remaining two-thirds could not be taken out of England. In 1630 Charles I had issued Lord Cottington a special license to import Spanish silver whereby he was required to sell one-third to the mint and was allowed to transport the remaining two-thirds as he wished (Ruding, vol. 1, p. 386). Subsequently, in 1632, due to the repeated requests of Thomas Mun, a director of the East India Company, that company was granted a license to export foreign silver (Ruding, vol. 1, p. 387 and Feavearyear, p. 95) but in other cases export was forbidden. On February 26, 1644, the Commonwealth reaffirmed the earlier regulations encouraging the importation of bullion (Firth, vol. 1, p. 391). However, the legislature recognized it would be difficult to encourage the importation of bullion while at the same time prohibiting its export, therefore additional concessions were offered under the new regulations of 1651. Merchants were still required to sell one-third of their shipment of bullion or foreign coins to the mint, but for the remaining two-thirds of the shipment they only needed to pay a one percent duty instead of the former two percent. Further, merchants were permitted to ship their remaining bullion or plate out of the country (Firth, vol. 2, p. 495). During that year the commission also fulfilled their seventh charge regarding the valuation of coins based on their intrinsic value. The British standard for the eight reales was defined as a 17.5 pennyweight (420 grains) coin at sterling fineness with a value of 54.25d. We find this rate in an exchange chart that is among the Commonwealth state papers, endorsed by the mint on November 18, 1651, listing the "realles of eight" at "4s6d1f" (54.25d) (Shaw, Selected Tracts, p. 86). This valuation, rounded to 4s6d (54d), held quite constant in England through the period of the operation of the Massachusetts silver mint and the entire colonial and Confederation era.

The Restoration

After the restoration of the monarchy under Charles II, the king realized English participation in international trade would suffer if he devalued foreign coinage to increase mint profits. Further, with the recall of all Commonwealth coinage and the need to replace earlier hammered royal coinage with milled coins displaying the new king's portrait, Charles had to induce his subjects to bring bullion to the mint. Thus, an act was passed for the encouragement of coinage that was to continue for five years from December 20, 1666, through December 20, 1671, but the central provisions of this law were regularly renewed for over 250 years up through 1925. By this law, individuals were to be given the full intrinsic value of any gold or silver coin, plate or bullion brought to the mint, without any deduction whatever. Accordingly, a full weight eight reales would yield about 54d depending on the fineness and the exact weight of the specific coin. To defray minting costs during this period, a tax of 10s per ton was levied on imported wine, vinegar, cider and beer. Further, there was to be a tax of 20s per ton on brandy and "Strong Waters" (Ruding, vol. 2, pp. 12-13; *Statutes,* vol. 5, pp. 598-600, 18-19 Caroli II, cap. 5 and Feavearyear, pp. 95-97). The specific value of a Spanish eight reales coin was not mentioned in this act, nor was the value of any foreign coin mentioned. These coins were treated as commodities with a value based on the quantity of sterling silver in the item, which would value a full 420 grains eight reales at 54d (4s6d). However, while London was recovering from the plague of 1665 and the fire of 1666, a proposal was put forward in 1667 by Fabian Phillips to debase English coinage. Phillips stated goldsmiths and bankers were acquiring rix dollars and pieces of eight for 51d (4s3d) each and then sending them to France where they received 58d (4s10d) for each coin or sending the coins to Ireland or Scotland where they traded at 60d (5s). This proposal was not adopted and the statements made by Phillips were never verified (Ruding, vol. 2, p. 13).

Eight reales in Ireland

In Ireland, foreign coinage was far more common than in England. Charles II sent a letter to the Lords Justice and Council for Ireland dated October 30, 1660, expressing concern at the quantity of base foreign coins in circulation there. He proposed they raise the value of the better quality coins and depress the value of the base coins, so as to keep the better quality items in the country and drive the base items out. Complying with the king's wish, a proclamation was issued on January 29, 1661, to become effective on February 2nd, listing the weights and rates of several foreign coins. In this proclamation the Mexico and Seville eight reales along with the rix and cross dollars were listed as full weight examples at 17 pennyweight (408 grains) with a value of 57d (4s9d), while a Peru eight reales along with a French Louis, also considered full weight at 17 pennyweight, were valued at 54d (4s6d). For each pennyweight deficiency there was to be a 3d deduction in value (Ruding, vol. 2, p. 3).

There were several difficulties with the execution and enforcement of this decree as was explained in another proclamation of June 6, 1683. At that time it was stated there were numerous problems with the weights used to balance and weigh the coinage. Apparently merchants used heavier weights when receiving money but used another set of lighter weights when making payments. Additionally, numerous Peru eight reales were imported into Ireland which frequently passed by the tale at the full value of 54d (4s6d) even though they were significantly underweight. But the document went on to explain that recently several merchants were only accepting these coins at 36d (3s) or 42d (3s6d), which was below their intrinsic value! The June 6th proclamation stated that the value of Mexican, Seville and pillar eight reales, as well as rix and cross dollars and the French Louis, were to be rated at 17 pennyweight and valued at 57d (4s9d), while the Peru eight reales was to be rated at 17 pennyweight with a value of 54d (4s6d), and all coins would sustain a 3d deduction for each pennyweight deficiency (Ruding, vol. 2, pp. 19-20). Thus, we see a crying-up of the value of the eight reales in Ireland in comparison to England. The English valued a 17.5 pennyweight (420 grains) eight reales at 54d (4s6d) while in Ireland a 17 pennyweight (408 grains) eight reales was valued at 57d (4s9d). Based on the English rate, a 408 grain coin would be valued at about 52d (that is, 52.45d, which would be rounded down to the nearest penny), thus the Irish 57d value represents about a 5d crying-up or about 9.25% above parity. At the time the legislated par of exchange for hard money was £105.56 Irish to £100.00 English, thus the rates represented a further crying-up or devaluation of Irish coinage. However, we discover the rates used in daily commerce varied from the proclamation values and there was a continuous struggle to keep the merchants honest (using correct weights) and to keep them from renegotiating the proclamation rates.

In 1689, after James II fled England, he occupied Ireland until William defeated his forces at the battle of the Boyne on July 1, 1690. A day after James triumphantly entered Dublin with the support of the population, he issued a proclamation on March 25, 1689, increasing the value of the coins then in circulation. The Mexico, Seville and pillar eight reales of 17 pennyweight were raised to 75d (6s3d) while the Peru eight reales of 17 pennyweight was valued at 57d (4s9d), with the same 3d deduction for each pennyweight deficiency (Ruding, vol. 2, p. 23). Also, the proclamation of James II was the only decree on Irish coinage valuations from the period to include English silver, with an English shilling given a value of 13d in Ireland. However the rates of James II did not last very long, if they were ever enforced at all. Undoubtedly, valuations were lower during the period of 1690 through 1696, for on May 29, 1696, under William III, a proclamation was issued raising the value of foreign coins in Ireland to keep them from being exported. At this time the Mexico, Seville and pillar eight reales of 17 pennyweight were raised to 64d (5s4d) while the Peru eight reales was valued at 58d (4s10d) (Li in his book *The Great Recoinage of 1696-9,* dated this proclamation to 1695 and assumed it related to values in England, pp. 32 and 58). The deficiency allowance was the same as in the past but here it was expressed to the half pennyweight as three halfpence for each half pennyweight wanting (Ruding, vol. 2, p. 39).

The recoinage of William III and the value of the eight reales in England

After many problems in England with older clipped coinage, William III asked Parliament to consider the situation. Over then next few years the older clipped hammered coinage was demonitized and replaced with new milled coins in what is now known as the "Great Recoinage of 1696-1699." The mint required large quantities of silver to accomplish this recoinage. Initially, a law was passed on January 21, 1696, to take clipped coinage out of circulation and send it to the mint for recoining. All clipped English coinage was to be accepted in payment of taxes at full face value through May 4th, and clipped coinage would be accepted at par by the Exchequer in payment of loans through June 24th. This brief window of opportunity brought £4,706,003 of clipped coins to the mint but large quantities remained in circulation (Feavearyear, pp. 136-37 and 139). Additionally, laws were crafted to encourage people to bring plate to the mint by offering a bonus above market value, but the extra inducement was not offered for foreign coins. It was ordered that for a six month period between May 4, 1696, but before November 4, 1696, "Wrought Plate or any vessells or other sort of Manufacture of silver" could be brought to the mint where the individual would obtain a troy ounce of lawful money (that is, 5s2d) for each ounce of sterling silver. Additionally, the individual would be given a receipt to be taken to the Exchequer for a supplemental "Reward" of 6d per troy ounce of sterling silver brought to the mint. This act was soon amended so no reward would be given unless the individual made an oath that the plate or other objects brought in had been manufactured on or before March 25, 1696. According to this statute, only wrought plate or manufactured products such as vessels were acceptable. The amendment was structured to prohibit individuals from melting any English (or foreign) coins to be turned into plate (7 & 8 Guilielmi III cap. 19 and amended in cap. 31, *Statutes* vol. 7, pp. 94-97 and 147).

On November 24, 1696, the House of Commons passed legislation ordering that after December 1, 1696, hammered English coinage would no longer be current except by weight at 62d (5s2d) per ounce. To encourage individuals to bring hammered English silver to the mint, an order was enacted that for the eight month period from after November 4, 1696, to before July 1, 1697, the mint would purchase all hammered English silver coinage brought to them at the rate of 64d (5s4d) per sterling ounce. This was a premium of 2d above the rate at which sterling coinage was produced (8 & 9 Guilielmi III cap. 2, *Statutes* vol. 7, pp. 162-64 and Ruding, vol. 2, pp. 48-49). In order to pay these premiums, a bill was passed in the House of Commons on February 24, 1697, levying a tax on paper, parchment and vellum for a period of two years from March 1, 1697. The tax was £20 per £100 value on paper manufactured in England and £25 per £100 value on imported paper, over and above the current duties. Importers were allowed a 10% discount for ready cash or were given the option of making the duty payment within a three month period if they gave security (8 & 9 Guilielmi III cap. 7, *Statutes* vol. 7, pp. 189-96).

As additional silver was needed, the Act of January 1696, encouraging silver plate to be brought to the mint, was extended and revised so that it was similar to the act concerning hammered coinage. On March 6, 1697, the House of Commons passed an act with a retroactive starting date that "Any wrought Plate of any sort or kind whatsoever" with the mark of the Hall of Goldsmiths in London (thus verifying its purity as sterling) could be brought to the mint between January 1, 1696/7, and November 4, 1697, where it would be purchased at 64d (5s4d) per troy ounce. If the silver did not have a goldsmith's mark, the individual could accept an offer made by the mint or request an assay. The earlier stipulation that had limited the statute to plate manufactured before March 25, 1696, was dropped. Since the mint was now accepting hammered English coins there was no need for stipulations meant to deter the melting of coinage. However, to prevent the newly minted milled English coins, which were issued at 62d per troy ounce, from being melted down into plate for the 2d per ounce profit, it was stipulated all wrought plate produced after March 25, 1697, was to be above the sterling standard (which was 11 oz. 2 dwt.) at 11 oz. 10 dwt. of fine silver per troy pound (8 & 9 Guilielmi III cap. 8, *Statutes* vol. 7, p. 196). It is quite likely several eight reales were melted by goldsmiths into sterling silver to be traded at the mint because this would represent the highest rate offered in England for the eight reales. At 64d (5s4d) per ounce or 1d per 7.5 grains, a full weight eight reales of 420 grains would be valued at 56d (4s8d), which was 2d above the standard rate of 54d (4s6d). Of course, this higher valuation was only available for a short period and only at the mint. It may not have affected the value of the eight reales in daily trade, other than inducing individuals to exchange their coins at the mint rather than spending them.

Newton's assays

Following the recoinage, Isaac Newton, the master of the mint, was asked to perform a major assay of foreign coinage so precise exchange rates could be determined. In Newton's assay of 1702 the pre-1642 Spanish eight reales, which he called "The Piastre of Spain or Sevil piece of 8 Reaus now raised to 10" was found to be 17.5 pennyweight but slightly under sterling fineness at .919 fine and was valued at 53.88d, which would have been rounded to 54d (Shaw, Selected Tracts, p. 140). In 1704 Newton assayed several varieties of eight reales and found all the examples to be at the full 17.5 pennyweight. He reported the weights and fineness but did not include values. William Sumner has reported these results and calculated the intrinsic value of each coin. The Seville and Mexican eight reales were slightly under sterling fineness at .921 which Sumner calculated at a value of 54.012d, the pillar coin was above sterling at .933 fine calculated by Sumner at 54.7387d while the Peru eight reales had the lowest fineness at about .905 fine for an intrinsic value of 53.06d (Sumner, "Spanish Dollar" pp. 614-15). These assays confirmed the 1651 valuation and insured that throughout the remainder of the American colonial period a full 17.5 pennyweight eight reales traded as currency in England at 54d (4s6d).

In conclusion, we see the eight reales usually traded at 52d (4s4d) during the early Stuart period. In 1651, under the Commonwealth, the eight reales was raised to its full intrinsic value of 54d (4s6d). With the exception of a brief period during the Great Recoinage, when eight reales could be sold to the mint for a premium of 56d (4s8d), the value of the coin remained at 54d (4s6d). In Ireland the eight reales traded at various rates with legislated rates averaging about a 10% crying-up from the English standard.

The exportation of silver and the use of the eight reales as a bullion substitute in late seventeenth and eighteenth century England

As mentioned above, Charles II authorized legislation that as of August 1, 1663, it became legal to export foreign coins as well as gold and silver bullion (Ruding, vol. 2, p. 11). From this point, foreign silver coins and especially the eight reales were treated as silver bullion and traded on the international market at fluctuating prices. Some indication of the quantity of eight reales and related foreign coins that found their way to England during the later part of the century can be gleaned from the following figures. A petition of several London goldsmiths was read in the house of Commons on April 9, 1690, stating that during the six month period from October 1, 1689, to March 31, 1690, a total of 286,120 troy ounces of silver bullion and 89,949 dollars in foreign coins had been exported from England. Also, John Houghton, the author of a weekly newspaper, *A Collection for Improvement of*

Husbandry and Trade, wrote that during the thirteen month period from March 19, 1690/1, through April 16, 1692, there were 169,953 ounces of silver and 84,756 foreign silver coins exported through the London customs office. Furthermore, in an anonymous booklet probably published in 1695, *The True Cause of the Present Scarcity of Milled Money,* stated that between May 24, 1689, and the date the essay was composed, a total of 2,315,615 ounces of bullion or melted silver had been exported to Holland along with 481,357 "Pieces of Eight and Dollars" (Li, p. 53). The most common silver coins, frequently called dollars, were the Spanish dollars or eight reales and the Dutch and German rix dollars or thalers. Although none of these figures are comprehensive, they all indicate a large number of eight reales and other foreign coins were imported into and then exported out of England to pay foreign debts.

Interestingly, the coins were always mentioned in relation to silver bullion. This is because the coins were used as bullion to pay debts and traded on the international market at bullion prices. These prices fluctuated daily and were always a point of negotiation. In general, prices declined when the supply of bullion increased with the arrival of treasure ships and prices rose as bullion was exported to the Orient. In December of 1693 an ounce of sterling was valued at 5s3d on the precious metals market, while in December of 1694 it was at 5s4d and rose to 6s5d by December of 1695 but was down to 5s2d by December of 1696 (Li, pp. 10-11). This fluctuation did not affect the face value of an eight reales in daily commerce, just as it did not affect the face value of an English shilling. It simply meant at times the bullion market value of the silver content of a coin would be worth slightly more or slightly less than the face value. A shilling would trade at 12d even though the commodity price of the silver in the coin fluctuated daily slightly above or below the face value of the coin. If the commodity price of silver dramatically increased it was more profitable to melt coins rather than to spend them at face value. In the case of the eight reales, a full weight coin was equal to 54d (4s6d) as currency, however, merchants often used these coins as a bullion surrogate. In these cases the coins were not melted down but rather they simply traded on the international market as if they were bullion. When used in this way the value of the eight reales fluctuated daily with the price of silver.

Chapter 17

The Valuation of the Eight Reales and the Price of Silver

in Massachusetts Bay

The Massachusetts Bay tax rate of 1640

The earliest valuation of silver in Massachusetts Bay is found in an order of the General Court from May 13, 1640, regarding the value at which specific items were to be accepted by the government when individuals presented these items as payment of their tax assessment. The record of the General Court stated:

> And it was ordered, that in payment silver plate should passe at 5s the ounce; good ould Indian corne, growing hear, being clean & marchantable, at 5s the bushell; summer wheate at 7s the bushell; rye at 6sh⁵ the bushell. (Shurtleff, vol. 1, p. 294)

Thus, anyone wishing to pay their tax with sterling dishes, bowls, cups or other forms of British plate would be offered 60d per troy ounce. This rate of 60d (5s) per troy ounce (480 grains) of sterling plate was the rate current in England, for the London mint purchased silver at 60d (5s) per troy ounce and then used it to mint 62d (5s2d) in silver coinage. At the rate of 60d (5s) per ounce, a Spanish American eight reales at the British standard of 17.5 pennyweight (420 grains), which the British considered to be of sterling fineness, would be valued at only 52.5d (4s 4.5d). Indeed, in 1640 an eight reales traded in London for 52d (4s4d). Since both Britain and Massachusetts Bay rated a troy ounce of sterling at 60d in 1640, it is quite likely an eight reales in Massachusetts Bay traded at 52d (4s4d) as it did in London.

The crying-up of silver

The relationship of parity in the value of silver between Massachusetts Bay and Britain soon changed. Indeed, it is quite likely the scarcity of silver coinage in Massachusetts Bay had caused some disparity between Massachusetts and Britain before 1640, even though sterling plate was rated at parity. As we have seen, in Britain a full 17.5 pennyweight (420 grains) Spanish American eight reales dollar traded at 52d (4s4d). However, in Massachusetts Bay the colonists regularly accepted a 17 pennyweight (408 grains) Spanish American eight reales as a full weight coin. This was also true in Ireland, where exchange rates survive from 1661, 1689 and 1695; all list a full weight Spanish eight reales at 17 pennyweight (Ruding, vol. 2, pp. 3, 23 and 39). Thus, even though the eight reales was rated at 52d in both Britain and the American colonies in 1640, it is possible the colonists maintained a lower standard if the half pennyweight differential, which is documented after 1650, was in effect earlier. This somewhat subtle distinction, indicating a possible divergence from parity, was soon made more apparent as the demand for silver coinage to conduct daily commerce became acute in Massachusetts Bay. Contemporaries stated there was a need to "cry-up" the value of silver (Mossman, pp. 46-47). During the General Court of June 14, 1642, Massachusetts Bay increased the value of the eight reales by 4d from 52d to 56d (4s8d) ["It was voted that ryalls of eight should passe at 4^{s}8^d a peece."], then three months later, during the General Court session of September 27th, the value was raised a further 4d to 60d (5s) (Shurtleff, vol. 2, pp. 20 and 23-24). When the Boston mint opened in 1652, a 17 pennyweight eight reales was trading at 60d (5s) in Massachusetts Bay, while in London a 17.5 pennyweight eight reales was trading at its full intrinsic value of 54d (4s6d).

The relative rates of Massachusetts and Spanish silver

The value of the Spanish American eight reales was central to the operation of the Massachusetts Mint. Essentially the function of the mint was to transform the crude and underweight Spanish American cob coinage, then in circulation, into a uniform coinage that could be accepted at face value. The text of the mint act specified precisely what items were to be accepted by the mint. In the version of the act passed by the House of Deputies on May 27, 1652, it stated:

> That all persons whatsoeuer haue libertie to bring in vnto the mint howse at Boston all Bullion plate or Spanish Coyne there to be melted & brought to the Allay of Sterling siluer…. (Crosby, p. 37)

Later in the document the same three items were mentioned again:

> …& It shalbe in the liberty of any person who brings into the mint howse any bullian plate or spanish Coyne as afforsaid to be present and se [see] the same melted & refined Allayed…. (Crosby, pp. 37-38)

These items were also mentioned in the June 20, 1652 document of the mint committee:

> …wee cannot but Judge it meete to Allow the said mint master, for Refyning and Coyning such bulljon, plate & mony, that shall be brought vnto them,…. (Crosby, p. 40)

Thus, according to a strict reading of the 1652 legislation, the mint was only required to accept and refine bullion, plate and Spanish coins, although the mint committee simply mentioned money rather than specifically stating Spanish coinage. Bullion refers to bars or ingots of silver of any fineness, while plate refers to dishes, bowls, cups, utensils and other household items made of silver, whether they were British items of sterling fineness or lower grade foreign silver. Spanish coins would primarily consist of Spanish American cob coinage rather than cobs from mainland Spain. These were the only items the mint was required to accept. From Hull's ledger, we cannot determine precisely what items were consigned to the mint since he usually just recorded the sterling weight, although he sometimes specifically stated the silver was as "sterling dollars," which meant Spanish American eight reales coins. He also mentioned some Spanish plate that was below sterling fineness and a consignment of 58 ounces of plate for which he made an allowance of two ounces to make it sterling. We also know there were also several critics of the mint who stated British coins had been melted at the Boston mint. Thus, there is evidence for the melting of cobs, plate and possibly some small amount of British silver coinage. However, if we examine the surviving records from the London mint, we discover as early as the Elizabethan era, in addition to all bullion and plate, coins from the French, Dutch and Spanish territories were received in large numbers. Of these various foreign coins the records indicate Spanish silver coinage predominanted (Challis, *Tudor Coinage,* pp. 192-94). It seems probable that the silver consigned to the Massachusetts Mint was predominantly Spanish American cobs and plate; this is certainly the impression from the Hull ledger. However, it is quite likely that, as in London, the Massachusetts Bay Mint accepted any silver individuals were willing to consign, including all "mony" (to quote the mint committee terminology), such as Dutch, French and German silver coins.

The mint act explicitly focused on crude Spanish cob coinage because that was the predominant circulating medium. In order to economically transform Spanish cobs into new Massachusetts silver coinage there needed to be some profit for both the mintmaster and the customer in the conversion process. When the mint opened in 1652, Massachusetts coinage was 22.5% overvalued in relation to British silver; since Spanish American silver was only overvalued by 11%, conversion to Massachusetts silver was advantageous. A mint customer would typically bring in a quantity of silver items to be melted down and refined to sterling. A hypothetical example of a consignment might contain 500 eight reales, 25 Dutch lion dollars and a silver goblet bearing the mark of a London goldsmith. The reales and the goblet would be accepted as sterling fineness and the customer would then be given a receipt for the total weight of these items. The non-sterling items, in this case the Dutch lion dollars at .750 fine, would be assayed if the fineness was unknown and a per ounce return would be calculated based on the reduction from the sterling standard; the weight of the non-sterling silver with the reduced return rate would be recorded on the customer's receipt. The total silver consigned to the mint would be used to make Massachusetts coinage and the customer would be given 74d in Massachusetts coinage per ounce of sterling consigned. Hull would retain the remainder of the coins as his commission and wastage allowance. In the following example, I wish to show the profit accrued from bringing eight reales to the mint so I am using an example based on a single coin, although, as discussed above, Hull may not have accepted such a small consignment. If a customer in 1652 happened to bring to the mint a Spanish American eight reales at the fully authorized weight of 423.9 grains, Hull would accept the coin as equivalent to sterling. Assuming this cob would be used to produce coinage at 72 grains of sterling per shilling with no wastage, the yield would be 70.65d, that is, 5s 10.65d in Massachusetts money. Allowing for the mint and wastage fees, totaling 18d per 20s coined (or .9d per shilling), the fees for this item would be 4.54875d. Thus, of the total 70.65d, the customer would receive 66d or 5s6d (mathematically the customer's portion was 66.10125d or 5s 6.10125d). Rather than pass the coin at the legislated rate of 60d (5s), even with the mint fees, the customer would realize a profit of 6d per full weight eight reales. Clearly, it was advantageous to bring full weight coins to the mint for conversion into Massachusetts shillings.

Sumner has explained the precise break even point was a Spanish American eight reales at 389.18 grains (Sumner, "Coin Shilling," p. 255). With the mint fees, the net return for the customer bringing a coin of this weight to the Boston mint would be 60d (5s) in Boston money, exactly the legislated value of a full weight eight reales. Any eight reales below this weight, that could be passed off as a full weight example at 60d (5s), would naturally be more valuable in its original state. However, because there were very few, if any, full weight

eight reales in Massachusetts Bay, it was common practice to trade these coins by weight rather than by the piece. Because the value of lightweight coins was determined by weight, bringing the coins to the mint was more advantageous than spending them. A clipped eight reales at say, 360 grains, would be valued at 51d in relation to a full 17 pennyweight (408 grains) coin at 60d (5s). However, if taken to the mint the same 360 grains coin would produce 60d in Massachusetts silver; subtracting the mint and wastage fees of 4.5d per five shillings, yields a return for the customer of 55.5d, which is 4.5d in profit. Basically, Spanish silver was overvalued by 11% while Massachusetts silver was overvalued by 22.5%, therefore even with the 7.5% mint and wastage fees an individual would gain 4% by converting Spanish silver to Massachusetts silver. Based on these exchange rates it was more profitable to bring all Spanish silver into the mint. To put this another way, a troy ounce of sterling silver converted into Massachusetts coinage was valued at 80d while a troy ounce of Spanish American silver (with a 17 pennyweight eight reales at 60d) was valued at 70.58d. This was a price differential of 9.42d per troy ounce, which favored conversion into Massachusetts coinage.

Theoretically, in addition to the price differential there would also be a small supplemental profit when converting Spanish cobs to Massachusetts sterling because Spanish silver had a higher silver content than Massachusetts silver. When Spanish cobs were deposited at the Massachusetts Mint a troy ounce (480 grains) of Spanish cob coinage at the authorized fineness of just about .931 fine would theoretically be refined down to .925 fine sterling by adding 3.11 grains of copper. If there was no wastage this would result in 483.11 grains of sterling, for a net gain of just over three grains of sterling (or slightly more than .5d in Massachusetts silver) per ounce.

However, there were several factors that would impact this additional profit. Most importantly was any fluctuation in fineness. Just as the weight of individual coins differed, so also, the fineness of the silver fluctuated. In the assays performed at the London mint under Isaac Newton during 1702 and 1704, five different eight reales were measured of which one was above the average Spanish fineness at .933 fine while the other four were actually slightly under the sterling standard, with examples at .905, .919 and two at .921 fine. Clearly, there would be no additional profit if the Newton examples had been brought to the Massachusetts Mint.

During the seventeenth century people did not perceive authorized fineness as a fixed number in the same way as we do in the twenty-first century. There was always some tolerance in coin weight built into coinage acts, but fineness was usually precisely defined. However, it would be more accurate for us to consider the authorized fineness as a "target" rather than a precise measure. Even in London, the government coin test, called the trial of the pyx, accepted a two pennyweight tolerance in fineness per troy pound (that is, a tolerance of 48 grains per every 5,760 grains). For sterling, which was defined as 11 ounces 2 pennyweight of fine silver per troy pound or .925 fine, the ideal was 5,328 grains of silver to 432 grains of copper per troy pound. With the two pennyweight (48 grains) per pound tolerance, sterling could be as low as 5,280 grains of silver per troy pound, which would calculate to a low of .9168 fine, on the other hand it could range as high as .9332 fine. Spanish silver was authorized at a fineness of .9305, which would calculate to 5,359.68 grains of silver and 400.32 grains of copper per troy pound. Using the British tolerance of two pennyweight per troy pound there would be an outside tolerance of 5,311.68 grains of silver per pound, which would calculate to .9222 fine. However, from the Newton assays we see the Spanish mints had a wider tolerance than the British, for three of the four Spanish examples were below .9222 fine. Indeed one example at .905 fine was below the low range for sterling, which was .9168 fine. Based on the technology of the times, contemporaries accepted small fluctuations in fineness as unavoidable. It was understood Spanish coinage had a higher authorized fineness than sterling but that the Spanish mints had a wider tolerance for error. Occasionally Spanish silver may have dipped below the low range for sterling, which was .9168 fine, but some examples would have a higher fineness than the sterling standard. On average, Spanish silver was within the same fineness range as the pyx tolerance for sterling, that is to say, between a high of .9332 fine and a low of .9168 fine. Thus, Spanish silver was considered to be the equivalent of sterling in fineness. It regularly traded as the equivalent of sterling in both Britain and America and Hull treated it as such.[1] From the evidence we have in the Newton assays, it seems there was no substantive fineness differential between sterling and Spanish cobs.

Further, even if there happened to be a consignment of Spanish silver that averaged at or above the authorized fineness of .9305 (or even .931 fine), it is quite unlikely there would be any advantage. The difference was so small it was almost impossible to reliably measure. There would only be 31.68 grains more of silver per troy pound (this is the difference between the sterling standard of 5,328 grains of silver per troy pound and the Spanish standard of 5,359.68 grains of silver per troy pound). This is a differential of about 1.32 pennyweight per troy pound, which is equivalent to 2.64 grains per troy ounce or .0132 grain per pennyweight. Even in London, the assays could not accurately measure such small differences. As mentioned previously, as late as 1696 the masters of the mint, Thomas Neale and Thomas Hall, wrote to the Lords of the Treasury that assays at the mint and assays at the Exchequer "…often differ, and sometimes as much as two pennyweights and better" [per troy pound] (Redington, p. 492, item 40). I suspect Hull did not even spend the time and effort to assay a melt of cobs. However, even if Hull did happen to assay a melt, it would not be economical to try to make such minor refining adjustments. This would require keeping the silver melted for a longer period and therefore more silver would vaporize, thus negating any benefit from reducing Spanish silver that was above sterling fineness. It appears when a customer brought Hull Spanish cobs that averaged slightly above sterling fineness Hull simply produced slightly finer coinage (see Mossman, p. 79 for an assay of Massachusetts silver at .926 fine).[2]

---

[1] During the alteration debate of 1626 the eight reales was stated to be of sterling fineness and in 1649 its value was officially set at 54.25d per 17.5 dwt. (420 grains), although it traded as 54d. At this time the London mint defined a penny as 7 grains, 14 mites, 20 droits, 2 perits and 12 blanks in sterling, which equalled 7.741926 grains of sterling. Using the official British rate of 54.25d per 17.5 dwt. eight reales, there are 7.7419354 grains of Spanish silver per penny, which is below sterling by only one one-hundred-thousandth of a grain.

[2] The citation in Mossman refers to George F. Chever, "Some Remarks on the Commerce of Salem from 1626 to 1740," *Historcial Collections of the Essex Insititute,* 1 (September 1859, number 4) pp. 118-43, where in a footnote on p. 125 Chever, citing the noted numismatist Matthew Stickney as his source, revealed the U.S. mint had assayed some Pine Tree shillings and determined their weight at 65 to 67 grains with a fineness of .926. It is possible the assayed samples had been clipped or filed and did not reflect their emission weight.

Spanish silver is rated above Massachusetts silver

For a period of twenty years after the opening of the mint in 1652, the value of Spanish American reales did not change in Massachusetts Bay, so it remained profitable to convert Spanish cobs into Massachusetts Bay coinage. However, during the 1660's several other British colonies followed the lead of Massachusetts and began crying-up the value of Spanish American silver to keep it from leaving their jurisdictions. Shortly before 1662 the value of an eight reales was increased from 54d (4s6d) to 56d (4s8d) in Barbados. In January of 1663, Bermuda raised the eight reales to 60d (5s) and a few years later on November 15, 1668, Barbados enacted the 60d (5s) rate. Then on September 29, 1670, Montserrat took an even bolder measure and rated the eight reales at 72d (6s) with Peru pieces at 60d (5s) and New England silver at face value. This law was copied and instituted in Antigua on August 14, 1672, and during that same year it was also enacted on the island of Nevis. During the first half of February of 1671, Jamaica was forced to compete with the other islands and raised the value of the eight reales to 60d (5s) (Chalmers, pp. 48, 153, 64 and 98). At these higher rates there was less economic incentive to take coinage out of the islands.

Faced with a diminishing supply of new silver in Massachusetts Bay, a proposal was put forward in the House of Deputies as early as June 2, 1669, to increase the value of a full 17 pennyweight eight reales from 60d (5s) to 72d (6s). In effect, this law would have increased the value of a troy ounce (20 pennyweight) of Spanish American silver from 70.58d (just above 5s10d) to 84.7d (just over 7s), which was higher than the 80d per ounce rate of Massachusetts silver. The proposal would have favored debtors over creditors and would have taken away all economic incentive for bringing Spanish cobs to the Massachusetts Mint. The legislation was defeated in the House of Magistrates and was not enacted (Crosby, pp. 105-6). Another undated proposal, attributed to 1671, was put forward by a Mr. Wharton, probably the Boston attorney Richard Wharton. He proposed raising the value of a Massachusetts shilling to 14d and raising the value of Spanish silver to 90d (7s6d) per troy ounce. This would value a 17 pennyweight eight reales at 76.5d, which, at 14d per shilling, would equal just a halfpenny less that five and a half shillings in Massachusetts coinage, or almost halfway between the current 5s value and the defeated 6s proposal. The advantage of the Wharton proposal was that it would rate Spanish cobs higher than their value in the West Indies thus drawing more silver to Massachusetts Bay. Additionally, by raising the value of Massachusetts silver the proposal kept Spanish cobs (at 90d per troy ounce) at a lower rate than Massachusetts silver (at about 93.3d per troy ounce). However, the proposal had several problems. It did not address the problem that increasing the value of the shilling would favor debtors and hurt creditors who had agreed to prices based on a 12d shilling. Also, the differential between Spanish and Massachusetts silver was so small that once mint fees were added there was no advantage in converting to Massachusetts silver. Again the proposal was rejected (Crosby, pp. 106-7).

As mentioned above, in 1670, Montserrat increased the value of the eight reales to 72d (6s) and soon thereafter other islands followed. Because the eight reales passed at only 60d (5s) in Massachusetts Bay, it was more profitable for individuals to export Spanish American cobs out of the Commonwealth rather than spending them or taking them to the mint to be transformed into Massachusetts coinage. From Hull's ledger, which survives for the period from October of 1671 through September of 1680, we discover only about £392 in coins were minted from October of 1671 through the end of 1672, and, of that amount all but £70 in coins was consigned by Hull from his inventory. The Massachusetts Bay economy was faced with both the exportation of Spanish cobs out of the Commonwealth and a drastic reduction in production at the Massachusetts Mint. In light of these developments, the House of Magistrates reassessed the situation and, in an attempt to keep Spanish American silver in the Commonwealth, concurred with the Deputies in passing a law on October 8, 1672, increasing the value of a full weight eight reales to 72d (6s).

The 1672 act regulating eight reales at 72d (6s) remained in effect for a decade. This law took away any profit from exporting Spanish cobs out of the Commonwealth thus halting the flow of Spanish silver out of Massachusetts, but at the same time it took away the economic incentive that had previously induced people to bring Spanish silver to the mint. Spanish silver was now rated at just over 84d (7s) per troy ounce while Massachusetts silver was only 80d (6s8d) per troy ounce thus, one actually lost money when converting Spanish silver to Massachusetts coinage! During this period several proposals were put forward to keep the mint in operation. In 1675 the mint fees were decreased and in 1677 Hull further reduced his fees on a personal, informal basis. In early 1680 several proposals were submitted to abolish the mint fees and debase Massachusetts coinage in an attempt to make it profitable once again to bring Spanish American silver to the mint. Hull understood the crying-up of the eight reales to 72d (6s) had greatly hurt his business and on June 6, 1680, he put forward a proposal to cry-up the value of an ounce of sterling silver in Massachusetts money from its current value of 80d per ounce to a new higher value of 96d per ounce while keeping Spanish silver at 84d per ounce. At the new rate Massachusetts silver would once again be more valuable than Spanish silver. Indeed, Hull suggested the customer would gain 7d to 7.5d when converting a full weight eight reales to Massachusetts shillings (Crosby, pp. 111-12). However, because of political problems with the Committee for Trade and Plantations and the London mint, the General Court understood they would not be allowed to further deviate from the British weight standard of 92.9 grains per shilling and thus Hull's proposal was rejected. Following this disappointment, Hull had no alternative except to further reduce his fees if he wished to attract silver into the mint, but nothing he did seemed to help. Indeed, even if Hull had been able to offer his services at no charge, it was still more profitable for individuals to spend or export Spanish cobs at 84d per ounce that it was to convert them into Massachusetts shillings at 80d per ounce.

With a 4d per ounce differential one might wonder why any Spanish silver would be consigned to the mint. Although there was a premium to be paid for converting cobs into Massachusetts silver, some Massachusetts coinage was still minted. Of course, a portion of this coinage was produced from bullion, plate or foreign silver coins other than cobs, such as lion and rix dollars, but some Spanish cobs continued to make their way into the mint. Sometimes the convenience of Massachusetts silver outweighed the cost because Boston merchants had a need for coins that could be readily exchanged at face value. Massachusetts silver allowed them to conduct transactions more quickly and efficiently. Also, coinage that could trade at face value rather than weight was better for the customer. There are several instances in the colonial period of merchants that did not have standard weights. Indeed, at Notre Dame we have a warrant from September 22, 1708, stating the Selectmen of the town of Bristol, Massachusetts, were summonsed to the next general session of the county court

"...for want of weights and measures (or rather for want of a standard in the town to try weights and measures)" (University of Notre Dame, Department of Special Collections, Colonial American Documents, Bristol, MA 1708). Further, some merchants were accused of intentionally using a heavier set of weights when accepting payment from a customer and then switching to a lighter set of weights when returning change or making payments to others! Such situations could result in even greater losses to the customer than would be incurred by converting one's silver at the mint. However, it is clear in most instances individuals preferred to put up with the inconveniences of using weights rather than lose money in the conversion process.

To further complicate the silver problem in Massachusetts Bay, at the same time production of Massachusetts coinage was on the decline, larger quantities of Massachusetts silver were being illegally exported out of the Commonwealth. Massachusetts coinage was intentionally lighter than British coinage. A Massachusetts shilling traded at a 25% differential from British coinage, thus a Massachusetts shilling was valued at 9d in British money. It was felt this low valuation would keep the coinage in Massachusetts Bay for one would sustain a 25% loss when using it outside of Massachusetts. However, with the crying-up of Spanish reales, Massachusetts coinage was no longer the lower valued medium. At 72d for a Spanish eight reales of 408 grains, a shilling in reales would be equal to 68 grains. At that time, a Massachusetts Bay shilling was legislated at 72 grains, thus based on the crying-up of Spanish silver, a Massachusetts shilling would be equivalent to 12.7d in Spanish silver. Therefore, one would gain up to a 0.7d advantage by exporting a Massachusetts Bay shilling over spending it in Massachusetts Bay for 12d. However in some areas such as Montserrat, Massachusetts silver was legislated at face value, which seemingly took away the advantage in exporting it out of Massachusetts. But, even in those areas, Massachusetts silver would have a more favorable rate in regard to returns or debts paid to Britain. Since the first years of the mint, Massachusetts silver was generally accepted at the exchange rate of 15d in Massachusetts silver for 12d in English sterling, while Spanish American cobs at 72d per eight reales of 408 grains, would require an equivalency of 16.2d in cobs to equal 12d in English sterling. Thus, one would save 1.2d per sterling shilling when paying British debts with Boston shillings. Because of the economic advantages from these higher returns in the West Indies, Massachusetts silver coins were being illegally exported in such quantities, the Commonwealth searchers could not keep smugglers at bay. The higher returns for eight reales resulted in less coinage production in Massachusetts Bay while at the same time more circulating Massachusetts coins were being illegally exported. An anonymous proposal to the General Court from May 19, 1680, stated: "little of late yeares (compared to what is laid up and carried away,) hath been coyned; and of that little, much dispersed into other Colony's" (Crosby, 109-11).

Spanish silver is reduced to parity with Massachusetts silver

To protect and promote the use of Massachusetts coinage within the Commonwealth, the General Court passed an act on May 24, 1682, reducing the value of the eight reales so that it would be at parity with Massachusetts silver. Since the colonials assumed both Massachusetts and Spanish coinage were at the sterling standard, the law stated they would trade Spanish silver by weight at the same rate authorized for Massachusetts silver coinage. Since Massachusetts silver was minted at a standard of 80d (6s8d) per troy ounce, Spanish silver was reduced from 84d (7s) per troy ounce to 80d per troy ounce; at the 80d per troy ounce standard, a full 17 pennyweight (408 grains) eight reales would be valued at 68d (5s8d).

The preamble to the act of May 24, 1682, is not quite clear. It stated that due to the export of Boston silver from the Commonwealth, the law was being enacted lowering the value of Spanish silver in order to keep "Money" from being exported. This explanation could be interpreted as meaning that by lowering the value of Spanish silver it would be more attractive to export Spanish rather than Massachusetts silver, thus reducing the drain of Massachusetts silver from the Commonwealth (but once again increasing the export of Spanish silver). It could also be interpreted as an attempt to take away the economic disadvantage of converting higher value Spanish silver into lower value Massachusetts silver and thereby increasing the production of Massachusetts silver. However, since the customer was required to pay the mint fees, the equalization of value would not be enough incentive to bring Spanish silver into the mint, as there would still be an economic disadvantage to the customer when bringing equal value Spanish silver to the mint for conversion into Boston silver.

The eight reales at 72d (6s)

Although the May 1682 legislation to reduce the value of Spanish silver was passed by the General Court, it is not known if this law was actually enforced in the marketplace. The law was clearly a source of contention and was soon overturned. Indeed, the final contract for the Massachusetts Mint expired on June 3, 1682, just nine days after the May 24th legislation was passed, but it had no effect on the minting operations since neither Hull nor Sanderson sought to renew the minting contract. Furthermore, on October 23, 1684, Charles II revoked the charter of Massachusetts Bay, invalidating all of the laws of the Commonwealth including the mint act of 1652 and the acts revaluing Spanish silver coinage. A new government was instituted under the royal governor Edmund Andros, who took office on December 20, 1686, as Governor of the Dominion of New England. Andros was given extensive authority including the right to regulate the value of foreign silver. Soon thereafter, on March 10, 1687, Andros enacted legislation valuing a full weight eight reales at 72d (6s).

On March 18, 1689, the citizens of Massachusetts rebelled against the oppressive Andros, imprisoning him and setting up a provisional government that continued in power until a new charter was granted to Massachusetts on October 7, 1691. The new government was constituted in May of 1692. Soon thereafter, in the fall session of the Assembly, on November 24, 1692, the eight reales was again legislated at 72d (6s) as part of an act against counterfeiting. However, because of concerns about the punishments handed out to counterfeiters, the Privy Council nullified the entire law on August 22, 1695. About a year after Massachusetts was notified of this event, the Assembly passed another act, on October 19, 1697, regulating the eight reales at 72d (6s). This act stated that full weight eight reales had long circulated at 72d (6s) each. The wording was:

> Whereas for many yeares past the money coyned in the late Massachusetts
> Colony hath passed currant at the rate or value it was stampt for, and good
> Sevil, pillar, or mexico pieces of Eight of full Seventeen penny weight, have
> also passed Currant at Six Shillings per piece... the Coynes before mentioned

shall stil be and continue currant money... at the respective values aforesaid, according as hath heretofore been accustomed. (Crosby, pp. 100-101 and *Acts and Resolves,* vol. 1, p. 296, Acts of 1697, chapter 16)

The eight reales in Massachusetts following the Proclamation of 1704

The 1697 act remained in place until the proclamation of Queen Anne in 1704 which set the value of the Spanish American eight reales at 72d (6s), but caused some concerns in Massachusetts. Crosby gives the essential documents relating to the proclamation through June of 1705 but overlooked a letter of July 1705 by Joseph Dudley that explains some of the problems the legislature had with the edict. The Governor of Massachusetts, Joseph Dudley, felt there would be some discrepancies to be resolved in that the colonists had regularly legislated a Spanish American eight reales at 17 pennyweight as a full weight coin, since this valued silver at 84d (7s) per troy ounce. However, in Britain the mint recognized a 17.5 pennyweight eight reales as a full weight example, which slightly decreased the value of silver to 80d (6s8d) per troy ounce. Dudley further discovered the legislature was unwilling to halt the circulation of lightweight silver. Although clipping was outlawed, there were no rules against passing clipped coins at a proportionally reduced rate. Indeed, most Spanish American silver coins in circulation in Massachusetts were underweight, clipped examples. In fact, the proliferation of clipped coinage had been given as the reason for the opening of the Massachusetts Mint in the act of May 26/27, 1652. Also, the Massachusetts act of October 8, 1672, had candidly stated concerning full weight Spanish American eight reales: "...inasmuch as few or no peeces of eight are of that weight" (Crosby, p. 80). Because of the shortage of hard currency within the colony it was important to be able to use all of the silver available including lightweight coins.

Additionally, a further complication arose. On June 30, 1705, the Massachusetts legislature voted to levy a tax on individuals and estates. Although not stated in the act there was a debate over the value at which Spanish American silver was to be credited when using silver to pay the tax. The legislature wanted silver to be valued at 96d (8s) per troy ounce, which equaled 72d (6s) per 15 pennyweight coin and would, therefore, value a 17 pennyweight Spanish American eight reales at 82d (6s10d) [or at the British standard of 17.5 pennyweight the Spanish American eight reales would be just over 84d (7s)]. This very favorable valuation, which exceeded the normal 72d (6s) rate, had been used in the past to encourage individuals to pay their tax with silver coinage in lieu of Massachusetts paper currency. These issues: the continued use of lightweight silver, increasing full weight coins from 17 to 17.5 pennyweight and the rate for Spanish American silver when accepted in payment of taxes, became stalling points in accepting the proclamation. On July 25, 1705, Dudley wrote to the Lords of Trade and Plantations:

> I have pursued the affair of the weight of money, in obedience to her Majesty's most gracious commands and that matter is thus: Seven Years since there was a Law of this Province allowed of by the late King, that all pieces of eight seventeen peny weight should pass for six shillings, and pretty well observed [this refers to the act of October 19, 1697]; So that I thought I had little to do only in obedience to Her Majesty's proclamation to add the half penny [that is, add the half pennyweight differential as Massachusetts at 17 pennyweight was below the British standard of 17.5

pennyweight for a full weight eight reales]; and accordingly, at the next immediate Session, the General Assembly agreed to the publication of Her Majesty's order, and their own affirmance of it in this Province unto the next General Assembly which sate in May last, when I expected and accordingly directed, in my Speech whereof a Copy is inclosed, That they would proceed to inforce Her Majesty's commands by adding just and severe penalties to any hereafter offering clipt money, or other light money by tale; but could not obtain so much as a Committee upon that affair till I would leave out the word Penalties, whereby I perceived plainly the representatives minds were altered, which they soon further declared in sending up their Vote to pay the tax of twenty two thousand pounds in silver at eight shillings the ounce, which is scarce fifteen peny weight for six shillings; and this they insisted upon for five weeks sitting, but I would not accept it and so refused their Votes peremptorily and have gotten the tax upon the old usage of seventeen penny weight, but nothing at all done to inforce the Proclamation, nor any penalty, and thereby the Country will be emboldened to use their late way of payment at fifteen penny, though I shall take care that the Court and officrs of receipt keep steady and allow no legal payment but of due weight. (*Acts and Resolves,* vol. 1, p. 579, Acts of 1705-1706, chapter 3, note)

The Lords of Trade and Plantations simply did not understand the problem of the lack of available full weight silver coinage. In their reply to Dudley they viewed the issue as a simple situation in which universal standards would promote prosperity and trade and would also curtail malefactors who clipped coins. In their letter of February 4, 1706, the Lords stated:

We observe what you write about the proceedings of the Assembly in relation to her Majesty's Proclamation for settling the rate of foreign coins in the Plantations, and have represented the same to her Majesty. You will do well to continue your endeavours to convince them of the necessity of complying with her Majesty's pleasure therein. Her Majesty's care in that matter is a great instance of her goodness, and her desire of the welfare of her subjects, which will evidently appear to them if they reflect that most contracts and bargains have their original from a demand of money, and must terminate in payment; That silver is the standard in proportion to its weight and fineness; That if adulterated coins be permitted to pass at the standard (above their intrinsic value) or be alterable at pleasure, it must have the same effect as a general allowance of false weights and measures, the consequence of which is deceit and confusion. You are further to represent to the Assembly that there lies a particular obligation on them to enforce a due obedience to her Majesty's commands herein, For that the regulation of the Rates at which Foreign Coins are to pass was calculated from a Law of their own ... You may likewise acquaint the Assembly that it is absolutely necessary to settle a true and uniform standard, in order to prevent clipping and coining and other deceits in Trade by crafty and designing men, by which means fair and honest dealings will be settled among yourselves and with your Neighbors, and Trade established upon a solid foundation, agreeable to equity and justice. The particular interest of some designing men ought not to over-ballance these considerations. (*Acts and Resolves,* vol. 1, pp. 579-80, Acts of 1705-1706, chapter 3, note)

Spanish silver priced as a commodity in eighteenth century colonial Massachusetts

Clipped eight reales cobs continued to circulate in Massachusetts at a prorated value based on a full 17 pennyweight example at 72d (6s). Also, Spanish American silver coinage was treated as silver bullion and traded as a commodity based on an agreed price per ounce of silver, usually, as we have seen, between 7s and 8s per troy ounce for the period through 1710 [which valued a full weight eight reales from 72d (6s) to 82d (6s10d)]. In later years the price of silver rose dramatically as the value of a Massachusetts shilling of account declined. The Massachusetts shilling was no longer based on sterling coinage but rather on paper currency. As more and more paper money was printed the value of paper currency declined, therefore, it took more paper money to equal a troy ounce of sterling. The rate continued to rise; in 1719 it took 144d (12s) in Massachusetts paper money to equal a troy ounce of sterling, which valued a 17 pennyweight eight reales at 122.4d (10s2.4d) while by 1729 it took a little over 240d (20s) in Massachusetts paper money to equal an ounce of sterling, putting a 17 pennyweight eight reales at 204d (17s). By 1739 it took slightly over 348d (29s) in paper to purchase an ounce of sterling sliver, giving the 17 pennyweight eight reales a value of 295.8d (24s7.8d). During the 1740's inflation was so dramatic that by 1749 it took 696d (58s) in Massachusetts paper money to equal a troy ounce of sterling silver, which valued a 17 pennyweight eight reales at 591.6d (49s3.6d) in Massachusetts money of account (McCusker, pp. 151-52).

The Massachusetts Mint was a business facing economic challenges. The survival of the mint depended on its margin of profitability which, in turn, was closely tied to the price of silver. The General Court insured the success of the enterprise by legislating that the intrinsic value of the silver in full weight Massachusetts coinage was to be 22.5% below the face value of the coins. As long as the price of silver did not increase the Massachusetts Mint would be profitable for both the mintmasters and the consignors. Indeed, Hull tried to make the operation as efficient and as profitable as possible. However, as the economies of the American and West Indian colonies expanded, larger quantities of silver were required to facilitate exchanges. As the demand for silver increased all forms of silver, including Spanish cob coinage, began to trade at a premium. Slowly the premium rose until, during the 1670's, it surpassed the 22.5% premium legislated for Massachusetts coinage. At that point the economic viability of the mint became questionable. Consignments were curtailed, production declined and mint fees were continually reduced in order to attract new consignments. Eventually the enterprise was no longer profitable and the mint portion of the shop business ceased. Following a period of political turmoil in the 1680's Massachusetts Bay hoped to reinstate the mint. However, the Royal Commissioners of the London Mint insisted the Commonwealth not be allowed to emit substandard underweight coins but rather be required to produce coinage at the British standards in both fineness and weight. The constant silver shortage in the colonies kept the price of silver high and made it impossible for the Commonwealth to profitably produce coinage at the standards required by the London mint. Without a sufficient supply of silver Massachusetts turned from minting coinage to printing paper currency.

Appendix I

Transcription and Commentary of the Shop Account
1671-1680

The personal ledger of John Hull is a folio size volume. If there had ever been any title or preliminary pages, they are now missing, along with the first 11 leaves of the text. The upper right corners of folios 12-14, containing the folio numbers, have not survived, but folios 15-171 are intact, with the original folio numbering in the hand of John Hull. The ledger ends abruptly on folio 171 verso, in the middle of some accounts, indicating that the original manuscript had more pages which are now lost. The ledger is deposited in The New England Historic Genealogical Society, Boston, Massachusetts, as MS Cb 110, volume 1.

Notes on the transcription - The headings: Year, Date, Text, £, s and d (for pounds, shillings and pence) which appear at the top of each page in my transcription are not contained in the Hull manuscript but have been added to make the information in each entry easier to understand. Brackets containing text in italic are editorial comments not found in the ledger. Reproductions of Hull's original handwritten account are illustrated in the figures. Figure 35 includes the full listing of accounts on folio 26 verso, while figures 36-41 reproduce enlarged details limited to the entries in the shop account.

Folio 26 verso

Account of the shop as debtor

Year	Date	Text	£	s	d
1671	October · 18	To 417oz. 1/2 sterling silver sent into ye shop to be minted } sterling [oz. ?] is £176	175	13	:
		To 111 ounces of plate — — —			
	24 October	To 208oz. sterling sent in to be minted which was [illegible] Trusdalls 64 · 3 · 0 ·	64	·3	:
	26 December	To 12 papers of files for account Coz. Allin —	·6	·6	:
	2 · 11	To plate & money 119, 136 ¼ } 255oz. ¼ —	:	:	:
1672	· 15 · 4	To money Lent —	·20	·8	:
	21 4	To money Lent —	·30	:	:
	29 4	To Put into Coyne 179oz. ½ —			
1673	August 25	To Put into ye mint house to be Coyned 265oz. sterling at 6s · 2d is £81 · 14 · 2			
	Sept	To Lent to the Country mony as Leager B folio 144	£ · 20	:	:
1674	Dec. 12	To Put into the mint house to Coyne 275oz. ½ sterling at 6 · 2d £84 · 19 · 0			
		4 Rings get in ye shop of mine 1 · 12 · 74			
1675	May · 8	To 369oz. ½ sterling silver dollars into ye mint house to be Coyned —			
	June 17	To 217oz. sterling silver dollars into ye mint House to be Coyned. 6 · 3 d · £67 · 16 · 3 —			
	July 17	To 12 Iron Potts & 3lb Small Wyre —	·5	:	·6
1676	June 14	To 496oz. ¾ sterling dollars to be Coyned //			

Contra Creditor

Folio 27 recto

Year	Date	Text	£	s	d
1671	November · 13	by mony received — £ · 170 · 13 · 0 }	175	13	:
		by given to Daniel Quinsey — 5 · 0 · 0 }			
	December 3	by mony for account Mr. Truesdall 64 · 3 · 0	· 64	· 3	:
		by mony I think for the files — 6 · 6 · 0	· · 6	· 6	:
	February · 6	by 119 ounces } sterling 255 received 136	: : :	:	:
1672	June 26	by mony received for Mʳ Danforth 13 · 17 & more for self - 6 · 3 · 0	· 20	:	:
	July 12	by mony received	· 30	· 8	:
	August 23	by mony received in viz the final produce of 179 ounces sterling ½			
1673	October · 25	by mony received in full of yᵉ 265 ounces	: : :	:	:
1674	June 30	by mony received	£ · 10	:	:
	December 31	by mony received	· 10	:	:
		by received the produce of £275 ounces ½			
1675	May · 22	by received out of the shop the produce of 369 ounces ½ sterling			
	July · 8	by received out of the shop the produce of 217 ounces			
	23	by mony received for Potts & wyre	· · 5	:	:
1676	July 12	by received of [for out of] shop produce of 496 ounces ¾ //			· 6

Shop Ledger - Commentary

section one: folios 26 verso - 27 recto, covering 1671-1676

In the discussion below, related debit and credit transactions are treated as a unit. A transcription of the related entries is followed by an explanation or commentary.

———————————————

[26 verso]

Account of the shop as debtor

[27 recto]

Contra Creditor

Comment: These are the titles of the two sides of the account. Clearly, Hull considered the coining operation to be part of his goldsmith business and listed items relating to both enterprises under his shop account. On the verso Hull used the title of "Account of the shop as debtor." This side of the account included a description and the price of items purchased for the shop as well as a dated listing of items and bullion deposited in the shop. The text portion of the ledger contains numerous notes on inventory and other items related to the shop, while the sums added in the far right represented debts to be paid from the shop income.

On the recto side of the account, for which the partial Latin title may be paraphrased as "On the other hand, the shop as creditor," Hull listed payments made to the shop. The text portion included numerous notes explaining the outcome of transactions recorded on the other side of the account. For example, on the debit side Hull included the date on which an item was deposited in the shop, while on the credit side he noted when the item had been returned to the owner. In the far right column of the credit side Hull listed sums paid into the shop but he did not list all income. Ideally Hull wanted the debit column on the verso and the credit column on the recto to balance. The credit column was not meant to show the shop's entire income, since all the income was not included in the far column. Rather, this column was to show that the transactions listed on the debit column had been paid or otherwise resolved. A zero balance between the verso with the debts of the shop and the recto with the shop income demonstrated all bills had been paid and all items left on deposit had been returned.

———————————————

[26 verso]

| 1671 October · 18 | To 417ᵒᶻ 1/2 sterling silver sent into yᵉ shop to be minted | } sterling [oz. ?] is £176 | 175 | 13 | ·· |
| | To 111 ounces of plate — — — — | | | | |

[27 recto]

| 1671 November · 13 by mony received — — — — — — — £ · 170 · 13 · 0 | | 175 | 13 | ·· |
| by given to Daniel Quinsey — — — — — — 5 · 0 · 0 } — | | | | |

Comment: The two entries under this date state 417.5 troy ounces of sterling silver and 111 troy ounces of plate (that is, household items as utensils, bowls or dishes) were sent to the shop to be minted into Massachusetts silver coins. English plate was regulated at sterling fineness and thus Hull did not always feel the need to state that plate was sterling. The two quantities came to a total of 528.5 troy ounces of sterling. On the credit side we see this consignment was completed on November 13th. Generally Hull calculated the quantity of silver coinage due to the customer based on the quantity of silver deposited at the mint. The return to the customer was 74d per troy ounce of sterling until June of 1675 when it was raised to 75d. However, in this entry Hull calculated the yield using the fully authorized rate of 80d (6s8d) per ounce. In no other case in the surviving records was this full rate used. This indicates Hull was producing the silver for himself or for the shop. Indeed, on the credit side Hull lists that £5 of the sum was given to Daniel Quincy. Daniel was the son of Edmund Quincy, who was the brother of Hull's wife. At the time Daniel was an apprentice at the shop [for further details see chapter 12].

At the full rate of 80d (6s8d) per ounce the total yield of this consignment equals £176 3s4d. Without calculating the fractional remaining half ounce, that is, using only 528 ounces, the total comes to £176, which is the total Hull calculated. In the far right column Hull subtracted 7s from the total to get £175 13s. In this example the wastage allowance at 1d per ounce is 44s for 528 ounces, so the 7s does not reflect the wastage allowance. Further, a half ounce of sterling equals 3s1d (37d) at the full 80d per ounce rate so the 7s cannot reflect a mistake of subtracting rather than adding a half ounce to the total. Exactly what the 7s deduction represents is unclear. On the credit side Hull stated £5 went to Quincy and £170 13s to the customer (in this case it appears Hull or the shop was the customer), thus accounting for the total yield.

[26 verso]

| 24 October | To 208ᵒᶻ sterling sent in to be minted which was *[illegible]* Trusdales   64 · 3 · 0 · | | 64 | · 3 | · · |

[27 recto]

| December 3 | by mony for account Mr. Truesdall   —   —   —   —   —   64 · 3 · 0 | | · 64 | · 3 | · · |

Comment: In 1652, Hull's fee had been approved at 5d per ounce with an additional 1d for wastage. Based on the legislated rate of 80d in coinage per troy ounce of sterling, once Hull's payment had been subtracted the customer would receive 74d (6s2d) in Massachusetts coinage per ounce of sterling deposited with the mint. In this example the customer's return on 208 troy ounces of sterling was £64 2s8d, which Hull rounded up by 4d to get £64 3s. If Hull produced coins at the precise legislated rate of 80d per ounce his total charge for this consignment would be £5 4s. However, the amount of coinage Hull retained as payment depended on the actual face value of the coins minted, this, in turn, varied based on the average weight of the coins produced and the actual amount of silver lost as waste. These figures are unknown for this production run. However, in later entries Hull did include the total number of coins minted from specified amounts of sterling. Based on these later examples we know Hull averaged 80.44d in Massachusetts coins per troy ounce of sterling. Using the 80.44d in coins per ounce of sterling as an average production rate, this consignment would produce a total return of £69 14s 3.52d which, after paying the customer £64 3s would give Hull a return of £5 11s 3.52d or just under 6.77% of the total mintage.

Mr. Trusdale (also, Truesdall and several other variants) is Richard Truesdall, one of the earlier settlers of Boston. According to J. Wingate Thornton, "The Gilbert Family," *New England Historical and Genealogical Register,* 4 (October, 1850) p. 342, "in 1672 Mary the widow and sole execitrix of Richard Truesdall, lately deceased, had her will drawn by Mr. John Hull." The Truesdalls had an account with Hull that is found on folios 28 verso - 29 recto of the ledger.

———————————————

[26 verso]

| 26December | To 12 papers of files for account Coz. Allin   —   —   —   —   — | | · · 6 | · 6 | · · |

[27 recto]

| | by mony I think for the files —   —   —   —   —   —   —   6 · 6 · 0 | | · · 6 | · 6 | · · |

Comment: This entry from December 26, 1671, refers to the delivery of twelve parcels of files for the shop, purchased for £6 6s. Here a file does not refer to a paper file but rather to a small abrasive metal tool used to smooth wood or metal. According to the Essex County probate records, the inventory of the possessions of Richard Mercer of Haverhill from April 14, 1671, listed a file at a value of 6d and the inventory of the possessions of Daniel Knight of Lynn from November 26, 1672, listed "4 old files, 18d" (*Essex County Probate Records*, vol. 2, pp. 245 and 305). These contemporary estimates price a used file in the range of 6d, down to 4.5d for an older file. Hull stated that he had acquired 12 papers of files. In this context "papers" refers to sheets of paper used as wrapping for small parcels (see, *The Oxford English Dictionary*, volume P, page 437 under paper, definition 6b). Possibly a paper or parcel of files contained a dozen files, that would give a total of 144 files for a per unit cost of 10.5d for a brand new file. We do not know the size of the files, but assuming the size was similar to the examples in the Essex probate records, a price of 10.5d seems reasonable considering a used file was valued at 6d. In an undated entry on the credit side of the account, that was obviously added sometime before the next entry, which dated to February 6, 1672, Hull recorded the payment for the files. He stated that he thought the bill had been paid using money. Occasionally in his ledger some payments were made using barter, beaver skins or other money substitutes. The files had been acquired from Hull's cousin Daniel Allin of London. Under the account with Allin, Hull wrote that on December 21, 1671, he had sold Jeremiah Dummer 2 papers of files for £1 1s and had acquired 12 papers of files for the shop at a cost of £6 6s (New England Historic Genealogical Society, MS Cb 110, vol. 1, ff. 30 verso - 31 recto).

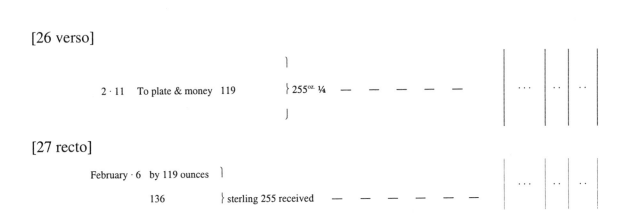

[26 verso]

2 · 11   To plate & money   119   } 255^{oz} ¼   —   —   —   —   —   . . .   .

[27 recto]

February · 6   by 119 ounces
136   } sterling 255 received   —   —   —   —   —   —   . . .   .

Comment: The date for this entry is January 2, 1672. The British did not begin the new year until March 25th, so January and February were considered to be the final two months of the previous year. Thus, on January 2, 1672, a consignment of 255.25 troy ounces of sterling was deposited at the shop. Hull stated this was "to plate and mony" which apparently meant part of the consignment went to coinage and part was used to make some household items such as bowls, dishes, cups or utensils. The consignment was ready for pick up on February 6, 1672. Hull did not calculate any return to the customer nor did he mention the quantity of coinage produced. Since Hull usually kept close track of the customer's return it is quite likely this coinage was for Hull, thus he kept the entire yield. If the entire sum had been minted, the total yield at 80.44d per ounce would be £85 11s 1f.

[26 verso]

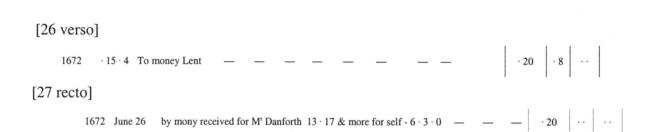

1672   · 15 · 4 To money Lent   —   —   —   —   —   —   — — | · 20 | · 8 | · · |

[27 recto]

1672 June 26   by mony received for Mᵣ Danforth 13 · 17 & more for self - 6 · 3 · 0   —   —   — | · 20 | · · | · · |

Comment: On June 15, 1672, the shop loaned out £20 8s, but the reason for the loan was unspecified. It appears £20 of this sum was paid back on June 26th, of which £13 17s was paid to Mr. Danforth and £6 3s went to Hull. The remaining 8s of the loan of £20 8s was carried to the following transaction, suggesting both loans were to the same individual. Mr. Danforth is probably John Danforth. Hull included an account for John and Mary Danforth in his ledger in 1677 on folios 138 verso - 139 recto.

The words Lent and Sent appear similar in Hull's handwriting. Both the L and the S have a loop at the top. They differ at the base of the vertical stroke. Note that the foot of the L goes directly to the right at a 90° angle, while the base of the S has a loop to the left of the vertical. For a comparison see the final entries under the Leonard Hoar account on folio 68 recto of the Hull ledger, where Hull uses the phrase "To Money Lent & Sent by John Hoar" in the fifth entry from the bottom and also uses the phrase in the last two entries.

[26 verso]

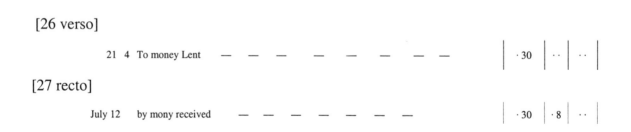

21 4 To money Lent   —   —   —   —   —   —   —   — | · 30 | · · | · · |

[27 recto]

July 12   by mony received   —   —   —   —   —   —   — | · 30 | · 8 | · · |

Comment: On June 21, 1672, the shop loaned out £30, again the reason for the loan was not specified. On the credit side we learn on July 12, 1672, a payment of £30 8s in money was received from the unspecified creditor.

[26 verso]

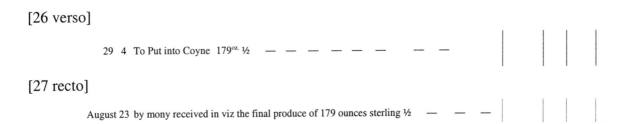

29 4 To Put into Coyne 179$^{oz.}$ ½   — — — — — —   — —

[27 recto]

August 23 by mony received in viz the final produce of 179 ounces sterling ½   —   —   —

Comment: On June 29, 1672, a shipment of 179.5 troy ounces of sterling silver was deposited at the mint to be coined into Massachusetts silver. In the credit column Hull stated the coins were ready for pick up on August 23, 1672. However, Hull did not calculate the return to the customer nor did he mention the quantity of coinage produced. Since Hull usually kept close track of the customer's return it is quite likely this coinage was for Hull thus he kept the entire yield. At 80.44d per troy ounce the silver would yield a total return of £60 3s3d.

[26 verso]

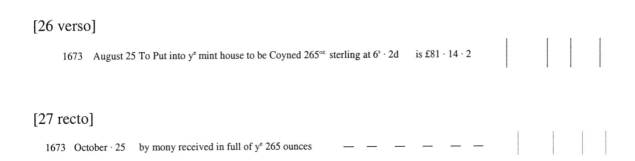

1673   August 25 To Put into y^e mint house to be Coyned 265$^{oz.}$ sterling at 6^s · 2d   is £81 · 14 · 2

[27 recto]

1673   October · 25   by mony received in full of y^e 265 ounces   — — — — — —

Comment: On August 25, 1673, a shipment of 265 ounces of sterling was deposited at the mint house to be coined. The consignment was ready to be picked up on October 25th. The customer's return at 74d (6s2d) per troy ounce was £81 14s2d, which was exactly what Hull calculated. Based on a total yield of 80.44d per troy ounce the consignment would produce £88 16s4.6d, leaving Hull with £7 2s2.6d.

[26 verso]

Sept   To Lent to the Country mony as Leager B folio 144   —   —   —   — | £ · 20 | ·· | ·· |

Comment: Only the month of the loan was recorded. This is one of the few entries lacking a specific day in the date area. Most likely this entry refers to 1673 as it follows an entry dated August 1673. The next entry is from December 17, 1674. This entry states that the shop loaned £20 to the Commonwealth of Massachusetts Bay. During this period individuals typically referred to the colony as their country. Hull explained the reason for this loan was listed in the previous ledger, called ledger B on folio 144 (the surviving ledger is ledger C). This does not represent an annual payment to the Commonwealth. The nature of the loan is unknown.

[27 recto]

1674   June 30   by mony received   —   —   —   —   —   —   —   —   —   — | £ · 10 | ·· | ·· |

Comment: On the credit side we learn on June 30, 1674, a payment of £10 in money from an unspecified source was received in the shop.

[26 verso]

1674   Dec. 12   To Put into the mint house to Coyne 275ᵒᶻ 1/2 sterling at 6 · 2ᵈ £84 · 19 · 0 | | | |

[27 recto]

by received the produce of £275 ounces ½ | | | |

Comment: The date could be December 12th or 17th, I have considered the second numeral a 2 as it has a small stroke to the right at the bottom of the number, similar to a 2, whereas Hull's 7 ends with a straight downward stroke. On December 12, 1674, a shipment of 275.5 ounces of sterling silver was brought to the mint house to be coined. On the credit side an undated annotation was added following the entry for December 31, 1674, signifying the consignment was completed. At 74d per ounce this yielded a return for the customer of £84 18s11d, which Hull rounded up by 1d to £84 19s. At a total return of 80.44d per troy ounce the consignment would produce £92 6s9.22d, which would leave Hull £7 7s9.22d.

[27 recto]

December 31   by mony received   — — — — — — — — — — | · 10 | ·· | ·· |

Comment: On the credit side we learn on December 31, 1674, a payment of £10 in money from an unspecified source was received in the shop.

[26 verso]

4 Rings get in yᵉ shop of mine   1 · 12 · 74

Comment: In this entry the date is added following the entry. Generally when writing dates numerically Hull gave the day followed by the month. Using this convention the date would be February 1st. The year is 1675, written in old style dating as 1674/5. The new year did not begin until March 25th so the previous year was used in dates between January 1 and March 24. The entry simply records the deposit of the rings into the silversmith shop on February 1, 1675, there is no mention of valuation or explanation why the rings were deposited. In a later entry, on folio 170 verso, Hull mentioned the rings were still in the shop in early 1679.

[26 verso]

1675   May · 8   To 369ᵒᶻ· 1/2 sterling silver dollars into yᵉ mint house to be Coyned

[27 recto]

1675   May · 22   by received out of the shop the produce of 369 ounces ½ sterling

Comment: On May 8, 1675, a total of 369.5 ounces of sterling dollars were deposited at the mint which was turned into coins and was ready for delivery on May 22nd. In Britain and the American colonies Spanish American eight reales were regularly assumed to be of sterling fineness, thus Hull's reference to sterling dollars refers to eight reales coins. This is the last ledger entry before the June agreement increasing the customer's return from 74d to 75d per ounce of sterling silver. In this entry the rate of return was not mentioned, nor was any payment specified in the credit column. Since there are no annotations relating to a customer's return it is possible this consignment was produced for Hull. At the rate of 80.44d per ounce the consignment would yield a total return of £123 16s11d.

[26 verso]

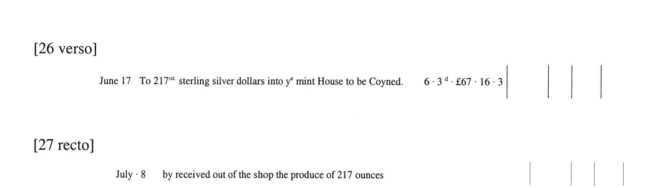

June 17   To 217$^{oz.}$ sterling silver dollars into y^e mint House to be Coyned.   6 · 3 ^{d} · £67 · 16 · 3

[27 recto]

July · 8   by received out of the shop the produce of 217 ounces

Comment: On June 17, 1675, a quantity of eight reales weighing 217 troy ounces was brought to the mint to be coined and was ready to be picked up on July 8th. This is the first example in the ledger using the reduced mint fees established in the third contract renewal of June 3, 1675, which increased the customer yield to 75d (6s3d) per ounce. At 75d per troy ounce this yielded a return for the customer of £67 16s3d, which is exactly what Hull calculated. Estimating a total yield of 80.44d per ounce, the consignment would produce £72 14s7.48d which would leave Hull a return of £4 18s4.48d.

[26 verso]

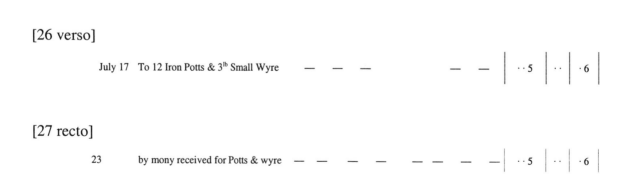

July 17   To 12 Iron Potts & 3^{lb} Small Wyre   —   —   —   —   — | · · 5 | · · | · 6

[27 recto]

23   by mony received for Potts & wyre   —   —   —   —   —   —   —   — | · · 5 | · · | · 6

Comment: On July 17, 1675, the shop purchased twelve iron pots and three pounds of "small" wire for £5 6d. I am not sure if "small" wire referred to several short lengths of wire or thin wire with a smaller than normal diameter. Iron pots were used in melting silver (see Chapter 11 for information on melting sterling at the mint). On the credit side of the account Hull recorded that payment was made six days later, on July 23, 1675. Hull stated "by mony received for Potts & wyre" meaning money he received out of the shop for payment of the goods, making it clear this was money taken out of the shop because the sum is included in the final column which listed the monies paid out and the value of the coinage returned to clients from the silver consigned to the mint. Thus, Hull sold the items to the shop.

[26 verso]

    1676   June 14   To 496^{oz} ¾ sterling dollars to be Coyned   //

[27 recto]

    1676 July 12   by received of of *[for out of]* shop produce of 496 ounces ¾   //

Comment: This is the final entry in the first section of the shop account, specifying that 496.75 troy ounces of sterling dollars, that is, Spanish American eight reales, were deposited in the mint on June 14, 1676, to be turned into Massachusetts silver coinage. On the credit side of the account we see the consignment was ready for pick up on July 12, 1676. Hull did not include any calculations with this entry, which leads me to suspect the consignment was for Hull. Obviously for personal consignments there was no need for Hull to calculate the customer's return and subtract it from the total to arrive at the mint fee and wastage. Using a production average of 80.44d per troy ounce of sterling this consignment would produce a total yield of £166 9s10.57d.

The double slash // was used by Hull to show the end of the final entry in the space allotted for an account. Hull continued the shop account on folios 133 verso through 134 recto.

❀❀❀❀❀❀❀❀❀❀❀

Account of the shopp as debtor

Folio 133 verso

Year	Date	Text	£	s	d
1677		To 21^{lb} of Quicksilver 5^s —	£ ·5	·5	..
	June 3·1676	To debit to y^e Country as by y^e Agreement for y^e mint one year —	·20	..	..
	3·1677	To debit to y^e Countrey for ditto a 2^d year —	·20	..	..
	20·2 to 27 of 2^d	To mony put in to y^e mint to Coyne 246 $^{oz.}$ / 393 / 417 / 191 / 328 ½ all sterling 1575·1/2 at 6·3^d per oz. is --- £ 492·6·10	..	..	..
		Spanish plate 186 / ditto 96 at 6^s per oz. --- 84·12·0			
	July·13	To sterling 125 $^{oz.}$ --- 125 at 6·3^d is --- 39·1·3			
	August 24	Paid to the shop the 24 ounces 3 pennyweight and 18 grains sterling which I formerly borrowed —			
1678	June·3·1678	To debit to the Countrey as per Agreement for one year —	·20	·5	..
		[cost of quicksilver and payments to Massachusetts Bay are totaled]	65	·5	..
	November·20	To sterling silver Put in to ye shop oz. 159·¾ } 1292·¼			
	January·20	To sterling silver Put in to the shop 1132·½			
	February·24	To mony Spanish sterling Put to Coyne —— ounces 400·			
	March·12	To Ballance Carried to folio 171 —	·9	18	..
			£ ·75	·3	..

Folio 134 recto

Contra Creditor

Year	Date	Text	£	s	d
1677					
	April · 4	by mony received — — — —	£ ·5	·5	··
		By several Parcels of mony received from May · 3ᵈ to August 29			
		By Coynage of which mony £ 671 · 12 at 12ᵈ per pound — £33 · 11 · 0			
	December 4	by borrowed 24 ounces 3 pennyweight · 18 grains · sterling			
		by 16 gold Rings for funerall of Mr Symonds at 10ˢ — — 8 · 0 · 0			
1678					
	January · 27	by mony received £300 ounces sterling — — — £100 · 12 · 0			
	30	by mony received 300 sterling — — — 100 · 12 · 0			
	Feb. 6	by mony received 300 sterling — — — 100 · 12 · 0			
	18	by mony received 392 ¼ sterling — — — 131 · 7 · 0			
		[the four above sums are joined with a bracket and then totaled] £ 433 · 3 · 0			
		by Coynage of £ 433 · at 12ᵈ per pound by agreement — 21 · 13 · 0			
		[the two mint fees and the price of the rings are totaled] £63 · 4 · 0	63	4	··
	March 12	by mony received 400 ounces sterling 133 · 18ˢ. Coynage at 12ᵈ — — — 6 · 14 · 0	6	14	··
			£ ·75	·3	··

//

Shop Ledger - Commentary

section two: folios 133 verso - 134 recto, covering 1677 - 1678

In the discussion below, related debit and credit transactions are treated as a unit. A transcription of the related entries is followed by an explanation or commentary.

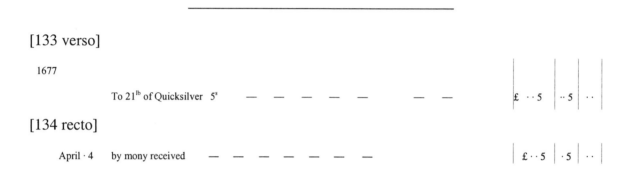

[133 verso]

1677

To 21^{lb} of Quicksilver 5^s — — — — —   — —   £ ·· 5 | ·· 5 | ··

[134 recto]

April · 4   by mony received   — — — — — — —   £ ·· 5 | · 5 | ··

Comment: This is the first entry under 1677, but it was not assigned to a month or day. Clearly, the agreement to purchase quicksilver was later than March 12th, the date of the previous entry, but must be before April 4th, which was the date associated with the payment. The text simply stated the shop purchased 21 pounds of quicksilver at 5s per pound. In the far right column Hull included the total cost of £5 5s which was added with the annual payments due to Massachusetts Bay to arrive at the total expense owed by the shop. On the recto Hull noted a payment of £5 5s in cash was received on April 4, 1677, without further comment. Most likely this entry relates to the quicksilver. Interestingly, Hull added the £5 5s received on April 4th in the far right column along with his mint fees to arrive at his total shop income. This does not follow Hull's standard payment practice. Usually a payment would have been listed with phrasing such as – 'by money received out of the shop for 21 pounds of quicksilver.' Instead, in this case, Hull simply recorded £5 5s as income. I suspect Hull personally purchased the quicksilver and then sold it to the shop. Then on the credit side of the account Hull simply added £5 5s to his income, showing he had taken that amount from the shop as payment for the quicksilver.

Quicksilver is another name for mercury, which was commonly extracted from cinnabar. Since the Middle Ages mercury has been used in the extraction of silver. A solution of mercury will attract any particles of silver that come into contact with it, forming a silver-mercury amalgam. The amalgam is then heated, vaporizing the mercury and leaving only the silver. This was the standard method for gilding objects in silver in colonial America. Quicksilver is also quite useful in cleaning tools and surfaces used in silversmithing as one is able to retrieve any remaining particles of silver.

[133 verso]

June 3 · 1676	To debit to yᵉ Country as by yᵉ Agreement for yᵉ mint one year	—	—	· 20	··	··
3 · 1677	To debit to yᵉ Countrey for ditto a 2ᵈ year	—	—	—	—	· 20	··	··

Comment: Following the quicksilver entry, which was completed by April 4, 1677, there were two entries for the annual payments due to Massachusetts Bay on June 3, 1676, and June 3, 1677. Since the entry that follows these two payments was dated April 20-27, 1677, we may assume the two payments were recorded sometime between April 4th and April 27th in 1677. These entries refer to the annual payment of £20 to Massachusetts Bay as stated in the seven year contract renewal of June 3, 1675. The agreement simply stated "the sajd minters are to pay in to the Treasurer of the Country, in mony, twenty pounds per Anno during abouesajd terme" (Crosby, p. 82). The "above said term" mentioned in the document was "this Seven yeare next to Come." Although the contract did not stipulate the reason for the payment, Hull refers to it as "for yᵉ mint." I believe Hull is referring to an annual payment for the right to hold the exclusive coining agreement with the Commonwealth, which is the subject of the agreement of June 3, 1675. It does not appear to be a fee paid for use of the shop or mint building.

[133 verso]

20 · 2 to 27 of 2ᵈ	To mony put in to yᵉ mint to Coyne	246 ᵒᶻ· 393 417 191 328 ½	} all sterling 1575 · 1/2 at 6 · 3ᵈ per oz. is – – – £ 492 · 6 · 10	···	··	··
	Spanish plate 186 ditto 96		} at 6ˢ per oz. — — 84 · 12 · 0			

Comment: In this entry Hull stated between 20 · 2, referring to the 20th of the second month, which was April, to the 27th of the second month, that is, April 20 to April 27, 1677, a number of shipments of silver were received to be turned into coinage. The five quantities of sterling were added together and the two quantities of Spanish plate were combined. The Spanish plate was valued at 6s per ounce, which is 3d less than the value of sterling silver. Thus, in this case, Spanish plate does not refer to eight reales coins because the coins were regularly considered to be of sterling fineness. I suspect Spanish plate referred to silver objects of a Spanish or Spanish American origin that were brought into the mint to be melted down. I do not know if these several shipments represented the holdings of a single customer or if they came from various sources, the brief time lapse between shipments appears to suggest a single source.

Hull calculated the customer's return based on the terms in his seven year contract with the Commonwealth signed on June 3, 1675, whereby the customer received 75d (6s3d) in coins per ounce of sterling deposited at the mint. In this case a total of 1575.5 troy ounces of sterling silver should yield a return to the customer of £492 6s10.5d, which Hull rounded down to £492 6s10d. This figure was included on the debit side of the ledger as the amount owed by the shop to the customer.

Unfortunately Hull did not include an entry on the credit side of the ledger so we do not know when the coins were ready for delivery. Furthermore, unlike later entries, Hull did not include the total number of coins produced, he only listed what was owed to the customer. Hull retained the remaining coinage as his fee and wastage, which he did not reveal. Based on later examples we know Hull averaged 80.44d in Massachusetts coins per troy ounce of sterling. Using the 80.44d in coins per ounce of sterling as an average production rate, the 1575.5 troy ounces of sterling would produce £528 1s1.22d, in coins, which could be rounded to £528 1s (10,561s), of which Hull would retain £35 14s2d for a return of just under 6.77%.

As to the Spanish plate, Hull offered the customer a return of 6s per troy ounce. This is 3d less than the return for sterling, reflecting the lower fineness of the Spanish silver. Again Hull simply calculated the return to the customer, which was £84 12s. Since Hull only listed the number of ounces of Spanish plate, we do not have the exact number of ounces of sterling. However, assuming Hull offered an equivalent value for the Spanish plate, we would expect that each troy ounce was deficient from the sterling standard by 3d, or, as 1d equaled 6 grains in Massachusetts sterling coins, a troy ounce of the Spanish plate would be 18 grains below sterling, so that a troy ounce of the Spanish plate would equal 462 grains of sterling. This would make the Spanish plate equivalent to 271.425 troy ounces of sterling (that is, 271 oz. 8 dwt. 12 gr. in sterling). Using the 80.44d in coins per ounce of sterling as an average production rate, the estimated 271.425 troy ounces of sterling would produce £90 19s5.426d, in coins, which could be rounded to £91 (1820s), of which Hull would retain £6 8s.

[133 verso]

July · 13   To sterling 125 ^{oz.} — —   125   at 6 · 3^d is   — —   39 · 1 · 3

Comment: On July 13, 1677, Hull received a shipment of 125 troy ounces of sterling to be turned into coinage. This is the final entry in the ledger where Hull calculated the customer's return based on the terms in his seven year contract with the Commonwealth signed on June 3, 1675, whereby the customer received 75d (6s3d) in coins per ounce of sterling deposited at the mint. In this case 125 troy ounces of sterling silver yielded a return to the customer of £39 1s3d, which Hull included on the debit side of the ledger as the amount owed by the shop to the customer.

Unfortunately Hull did not include an entry on the credit side of the ledger so we do not know when the coins were ready for delivery. Furthermore, unlike later entries, Hull did not include the total number of coins produced, rather he only listed what was owed to the customer. Hull retained the remaining coinage as his fee and wastage, but he did not reveal this amount. Based on an average return of 80.44d, the consignment would yield £41 17s11d (or just about 838s), of which Hull would retain £2 16s8d.

[134 recto]

By several Parcels of mony received from May · 3^d to August 29

By Coynage of which mony £ 671 · 12 at 12^d per pound — —   £33 · 11 · 0

Comment: Hull added an single undated entry on the credit side of his ledger for a series of shipments of silver that had been sent to the mint between May 3 and August 29, 1677, to be turned into Massachusetts coins. The date of the delivery of the coins is not specified but it was probably before December 4th, which is the date of the entry below it. These shipments were produced under a different fee schedule from the July 13, 1677 shipment and, therefore, the July 13th shipment is listed separately, even though that shipment was received during the inclusive dates of this shipment.

In this entry we see the first instance in which Hull took a smaller mint fee than he was due under his contract with Massachusetts Bay. Hull was allowed a mint fee of 4d per ounce plus a wastage allowance of 1d per ounce. However, Hull agreed to a fee of "12d per pound" of money struck (that is, pound as the value £1, not as a weight). Hull produced £671 12s in coins (13,432s) and therefore was entitled to £33 11s 7.2d but in his calculations Hull only asked for £33 10s. Formerly, Hull retained any extra coins that were produced from a consignment above the authorized 80d per troy ounce so that if Hull made the coins slightly underweight he would retain any extra coins produced. By this agreement, Hull's fee was directly based on the quantity of coins produced for the customer, thus any silver not wasted or any overages in production went to the customer. Of course, Hull would obtain a higher fee if more coins were produced, but by this agreement the customer made out significantly better than previously.

In this transaction Hull took £33 10s while the customer received £638 2s of the total £671 12s produced. Using Hull's average yield per ounce of sterling of 80.44d, we can speculate the quantity of silver minted was about 2005 troy ounces of sterling.

[134 recto]

December 4 by borrowed 24 ounces 3 pennyweight · 18 grains · sterling

[133 verso]

1678   August 24   Paid to the shop the 24 ounces 3 pennyweight and 18 grains sterling which I formerly borrowed

Comment: On December 4, 1677, Hull borrowed 24 oz. 3 dwt. 18 gr. in sterling silver from the shop inventory. At the legislated rate of Massachusetts silver, of 80d per ounce, this silver would be valued at £8 1s3d. Hull made a note of this loan on the credit side of the shop account, showing he owed the shop a credit to that amount. About eight-and-a-half months later, on August 24, 1678, Hull recorded that he replaced the sterling. This note was added to the verso or debit side, as were all deposits brought to the shop. This deposit was to cancel his loan listed on the credit side of the account.

[133 verso]

To debt to the Countrey as per Agreement for one year — — — —	· 20	··	··

Comment: This undated payment was recorded directly below an entry dated August 24, 1678, and is followed by an entry of November 20, 1678. Thus, this payment probably was made sometime between August 24th and November 20th, 1678. The entry refers to the annual payment of £20 to Massachusetts Bay as stated in the seven year contract renewal of June 3, 1675. The agreement simply stated "the sajd minters are to pay in to the Treasurer of the Country, in mony, twenty pounds per Anno during abouesajd terme" (Crosby, p. 82). The "above said term" mentioned in the document was "this Seven yeare next to Come." Although the contract did not stipulate the reason for the payment Hull refers to it as a "debt to the Countrey." I believe he is referring to an annual payment for the right to hold the exclusive coining agreement with the Commonwealth, which is the subject of the agreement of June 3, 1675. It does not appear to be a fee paid for use of the shop or mint building.

[133 verso]

[cost of quicksilver and payments to Massachusetts Bay are totaled]	65	· 5	··

Comment: Hull added the three £20 payments to Massachusetts Bay and the £5 5s cost of the quicksilver to arrive at a total of £65 5s the shop account owed to creditors.

[134 recto]

1678   by 16 gold Rings for funerall of Mr Symonds at 10ˢ — — —   8 · 0 · 0

Comment: On some unspecified date in late 1678 the shop was paid £8 for producing 16 gold rings at a cost of 10s each for distribution at the funeral of Mr. Symonds. Rings were commonly made for distribution to family members and dignitaries attending the funeral of a community leader. In his diary Judge Samuel Sewall mentioned he owned a cup full of funeral rings. Samuel Symonds was the Deputy Governor of Massachusetts Bay, whose death was recorded in Hull's diary as occurring on October 12, 1678 (Hull, *Public Diary*, p. 244).

[133 verso]

Nov · 20   To sterling silver Put in to yᵉ shop oz. 159 ·¾

                                                                    } 1292 · ¼

January · 20 To sterling silver Put in to the shop 1132 · ½

[134 recto]

January · 27 by mony received £300 ounces sterling — — —   £100 · 12 · 0

        30   by mony received 300 sterling — — — — —   100 · 12 · 0

Feb. 6   by mony received 300 sterling — — — — —   100 · 12 · 0

        18   by mony received 392 ¼ sterling — — — —   131 · 7 · 0

[the four above sums are joined with a bracket and then totaled]   £ 433 · 3 · 0

        by Coynage of £ 433 · at 12ᵈ per pound by agreement — — —   21 · 13 · 0

Comment: On November 20, 1678, a customer deposited 159.75 troy ounces of sterling silver at the mint to be turned into coins; then on January 20, 1679, an additional 1132.50 ounces of sterling was deposited for a total of 1292.25 troy ounces. It is not known if the two deposits were made by the same individual or if they represent two different customers, but Hull treated them as one grouping of production runs. These two deposits of sterling were divided into four production installments. Three of the installments were of equal weight, each containing 300 troy ounces of sterling and each of which produced £100 12s in coins which were delivered on January 27, 30 and February 6, 1679. Note that Hull mistakenly added a pound sign £ in the ounces area at the 300 ounces of January 27th. A final installment of 392.25 ounces of sterling, producing £131 7s in coins, was delivered on February 18 to complete the consignment. The turnaround time was quite fast on the larger January 20th consignment, since those coins were produced within one month from the date on which the silver was deposited in the shop.

Hull listed the full quantity of coinage produced so we can calculate the yield per ounce of sterling. Each of the first three shipments consisted of 300 troy ounces of sterling and produced £100 12s in Massachusetts silver coinage, which is an average of 80.48d per troy ounce. The final installment of 392.25 troy ounces of sterling produced £131 7s in Massachusetts silver coinage, which is an average of 80.367112d per troy ounce. Combining the four shipments together, 1292.25 troy ounces produced £433 3s in Massachusetts silver, which is an average of 80.445734d per troy ounce.

Hull continued to work at the 12d per £1 rate, which was a smaller mint fee than he was due under his contract with Massachusetts Bay. Hull produced £433 3s in coins, but we see in the final line he simply wrote £433 · without adding the final 3 for 3s [that is, £433 · 3]. At the full mintage of £433 3s, Hull was entitled to £21 13s1.8d which he rounded down to £21 13s. Based on the full allowance as stipulated in the 1675 agreement, Hull was allowed a mint fee of 4d per ounce plus a wastage allowance of 1d per ounce. Using this rate Hull would have had a mint fee of £21 10s9d and a wastage allowance of £5 7s8.25d for a total payment of £26 18s5.25d.

[134 recto]

[the two mint fees and the price of the rings are totaled]	£63 · 4 · 0	63	· 4	· ·

Comment: On the credit side of the account Hull added the income from the two mint fees and the payment for the rings made for Mr. Symonds's funeral to obtain a total of £63 4s, which he added to the far right column representing credits to the shop account.

[133 verso]

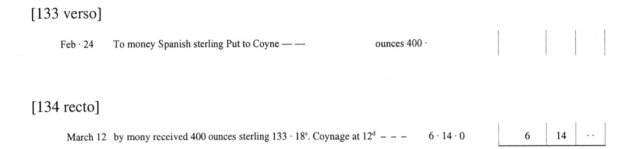

Feb · 24   To money Spanish sterling Put to Coyne — —   ounces 400 ·

[134 recto]

March 12   by mony received 400 ounces sterling 133 · 18ˢ. Coynage at 12ᵈ – – –   6 · 14 · 0   6   14   · ·

Comment: On February 24, 1679, a customer consigned 400 troy ounces of Spanish sterling, which probably consisted of Spanish American cob coinage since cobs were considered to be equal to sterling. In a little over two weeks the Spanish silver had been transformed into Massachusetts Bay coinage which was delivered on March 12th. Hull stated from the 400 troy ounces of sterling the mint produced £133 18s in Massachusetts coinage, an average of 80.34d per troy ounce.

Hull continued to work at the 12d per 20s rate, which was a smaller mint fee than he was due under his contract with Massachusetts Bay. The mint produced £133 18s in coins and therefore was entitled to £6 13s10.5d which Hull rounded up to £6 14s and the placed in the far right column as an additional credit to the shop. Based on the full allowance as stipulated in the 1675 agreement Hull was allowed a mint fee of 4d per ounce plus a wastage allowance of 1d per ounce. Using this rate Hull would have had a mint fee of £6 13s4d and a wastage allowance of £1 13s4d for a total payment of £8 6s8d.

[134 recto]

£ · 75 | · 3 | · ·

//

Comment: Hull added the March 12, 1678, mint fee to the running total of the shop income to arrive at £75 3s in credit for the shop. The double slash // was used by Hull to show the end of the final entry in the space allotted for an account.

[133 verso]

March · 12 To Ballance Carried to folio 171 — — — — — — —	··9	18	··
	£ · 75	· 3	··

Comment: After adding the March 12, 1678 entry on folio 134 recto Hull determined the shop account was carrying a credit balance of £75 3s. However, Hull did not forward the funds to the next space allocated to the account, which was on folio 171 recto. Rather, on folio 171 recto, between the entries of October 18 and November 21, 1679, Hull carried forward only £9 18s, which was the amount needed to balance the account. To reflect this Hull added the above entry to the credit side of the shop account on folio 133 verso. Hull wrote the total credits at the bottom of the column rlisting the shop debits. He then drew a line above the £75 3s to separate it from the debits and then wrote £9 18s above the line to show it was the amount carried over to folio 171 recto (see the comments on the related entry on 171 recto in section three of this appendix for the rationale in selecting this amount). Although the £9 18s seem to be aligned with the February 24, 1679 entry on the 400 ounces of Spanish sterling, it is actually below that entry and does not relate to it.

❀❀❀❀❀❀❀❀❀❀❀

Account of the shop as debtor

Folio 170 verso

Year	Date	Text	£	s	d
1679					
	April · 11 —	To 4 rings as fol. 27 left in ye shop 1 · 12 · 74 · long [illegible] ye tyme			
	May · 6 —	To 286 · ½ ounces of sterling			
	July · 21	To 131 · ½ of plate for which I paid Mr. Dummer — — — — £ 39 · 9 · 0			
		To 278 ounces sterling silver			
		To [*balance, crossed out*] due to the Countrey June 3 · 1679 for yearly rent of the mint as per Agreement June 3 · 1675 — — —	£ ·20	:	:
	November · 8	To 58 ounces of plate allowed 2 ounces to make it sterling — — —		:	:
	21	To put into yᵉ mint sterling silver to Coyne ounces 445 325 · 2 } 770 ½ ounces			
	August · 3	To put to the mint fine silver ounces 220 · 3 gets at · 6 · 6 £ [*i.e., per pound*]			
	4	538 · 3 547 · 1 [*totaled to*] 1306 · 3 £ 424 · 9 · 0			
	June 3 · 80	To due to the Country for yearly rent as per Agreement June 3 · 76	· 20	:	:
		[*the debits are added*]	£ · 40	:	:

//

Folio 171 recto

Contra Creditor

Year	Date	Text	£	s	d
1679	July · 16	by mony received out of yᵉ mint for Mr. Dummer plate — — £ 39 · 9 · 0			
	30	by 96 ounces sterling — £ 32 · 2 · 0 }			
		190 ½ sterling — 63 · 17 · 0 } £189 · 2 · 0 Coynage whereof	··9	·9	··
October 18		by 278 ounces sterling — 93 · 3 · 0 } at 12ᵈ per £ — — —	··9	18	··
		by Ballance brought from folio 134 — —			
November 21		by 56 ounces in mony made £ 18 · 14ˢ · by Coynadge —	···	18	·9
December 9		by 445 ounces in money made 149 · 5 Coynage at 12d —	··7	·9	·3
	26	by 325 ½ in money 109 · 6 Coynage at 12d —	··5	·9	·3
		[the mint fees and carry forward balance are totaled]	33	·4	3
1680	August 29	by 538 ounces ¾ at 6.6ᵈ — — — £ 175 · 2 · 0			
	September 4	by 220 ounces at 6.6ᵈ — 71 · 15 · 0			
	Sept. 10 & 27 10 & 2	547 · 1 at 6.6ᵈ — 177 · 12 · 0			
		[totaled to] £ 424 · 9 · 0			
		by money received out of the shop in June	··6	15	·9
		[the sums are totaled to]	£ · 40	··	[··]

//

Shop Ledger - Commentary

section three: folios 170 verso - 171 recto, covering 1679-1680

In the discussion below, related debit and credit transactions are treated as a unit. A transcription of the related entries is followed by an explanation or commentary.

[170 verso]

1679

To 4 rings as fol. 27 left in ye shop 1 · 12 · 74 · long [illegible] ye tyme

Comment: This entry on folio 170 verso, the debit side of the account, stated that four rings brought into the shop on February 1, 1675, were still on deposit in April of 1679. This deposit had been previously recorded in the ledger on folio 26 verso. Hull referred to the folio as folio 27, meaning the opening covering 26 verso through 27 recto.

[170 verso]

April · 11 — To 286 · ½ ounces of sterling

July · 21   To 278 ounces sterling silver

[171 recto]

	by 96 ounces sterling	—	£ 32 · 2 · 0
30	190 ½ sterling	— — —	63 · 17 · 0
Oct 18	by 278 ounces sterling	—	93 · 3 · 0

£189 · 2 · 0 Coynage whereof at 12^d per £ — —

·· 9 · 9 ··

Comment: On April 11, 1679, a customer deposited 286.5 troy ounces of sterling silver at the mint to be turned into coinage, a little over three months later, on July 21, 1679, an additional consignment of 278 troy ounces of sterling silver was brought to the mint. On the credit side of his ledger John Hull added the two consignments together as a single job totaling 564.5 troy ounces; it is possible these two shipments were from a single customer. We learn these two shipments of silver were turned into £189 2s in Massachusetts silver coinage in three installments. The first and smallest installment was undated but presumably occurred between the date of the previous entry, July 16, 1679, and the second installment, dated July 30th. These two installments equaled the 286.5 troy ounces of silver brought in on April 11th, thus the customer was required to wait about three and a half months, from April 11 until July 30th to have the silver turned into £95 19s in Massachusetts coins. It seems about the time the April 11 deposit was ready to be picked up, another almost equal shipment of sterling was deposied at the mint. This second shipment of 278 troy ounces was consigned on July 21st and was delivered on October 18th, which was a wait of just a few days less than three months for £93 3s in coinage.

Because Hull included the full quantity of coins produced, the yield per ounce of sterling can be determined. In the first installment the mint produced £32 2s in Massachusetts silver coinage from 96 troy ounces of sterling, which is an average of 80.25d per troy ounce. In the second installment the mint produced £63 17s in Massachusetts silver coinage from 190.5 troy ounces of sterling, which is an average of 80.44d per troy ounce. In the third installment the mint produced £93 3s in coinage from 278 troy ounces of sterling, which is an average of 80.417266d per troy ounce. For the entire consignment of three installments the mint averaged 80.3968d per troy ounce of sterling.

In this entry we also see Hull took a smaller mint fee than he was due under his contract with Massachusetts Bay. Hull was allowed a mint fee of 4d per ounce plus a wastage allowance of 1d per ounce which, for this consignment of 564.5 troy ounces of sterling would result in a mint fee of £9 8s2d and a wastage allowance of £2 7s 1/2d for a total payment of £11 15s 2.5d for this consignment of 564.5 ounces. However, Hull stated he had agreed to a fee of "12d per pound" of money struck (that is, pound as the value £, not as a weight). Hull produced £189 2s in coins and therefore was entitled to £9 9s 1.2d. Hull was allowed 0.6d per shilling but in his calculations he simply used the £189, yielding him a fee of 189s or £9 9s. Formerly Hull retained any extra coins that were produced from a consignment above the authorized 80d per troy ounce, so that if Hull made the coins slightly underweight he would retain any extra coins produced. By this agreement, Hull's fee was directly based on the quantity of coins produced for the customer, thus any silver not wasted or any overages in production went to the customer. Of course Hull would obtain a higher fee if more coins were produced but by this agreement the customer made out significantly better than previously.

[170 verso]

> May · 6 — To 131 · ½ of plate for which I paid Mr. Dummer — — —   — £ 39 · 9 · 0

[171 recto]

1679

> Jul· 16 by mony received out of yᵉ mint for Mr. Dummer plate — — £ 39 · 9 · 0

Comment: On May 6, 1679, Hull purchased 131.5 troy ounces of silver plate from his former apprentice Jeremiah Dummer at a cost of £39 9s. On July 16, 1679, Hull was reimbursed for this purchase since he recorded that he took £39 9s out of the mint account. It is not stated if the plate was used for coinage or for silversmithing but it may have been used for coinage as Hull specified he was reimbursed from the mint. However, Hull sometimes used the term shop when referring to the mint and he may have used the word mint when referring to the shop.

Hull had an active account with Dummer. The account is found on folios 44 verso through 45 recto of the ledger and lists several transactions between them. The extant portion of the account covers the period from July 3, 1672, through November 21, 1679, during which their dealings amounted to £204 9s8d. Some transactions refer to partnerships in which Hull paid one-third of the total (Dummer may have paid two-thirds or there may have been additional partners), but most entries simply record the dates on which an amount of money was agreed to be paid and the date on which it was actually paid, without further explanation of what was being purchased. A few entries mention payments in "Ryales" and "Pillar Pieces" which of course, refer to Spanish American cob coinage. The May purchase of plate is not mentioned in Hull's account with Dummer; it is only found in the shop account. There is no mention of the fineness of the plate; however, if it was sterling, this was a good deal for Hull. The purchase price equaled 72d per troy ounce, which was below the 80d market value of sterling minted into Massachusetts coinage.

[170 verso]

To [*balance, crossed out*] due to the Countrey June 3 · 1679 for yearly rent of the

mint as per Agreement June 3 · 1675   —   — —   — — —   £ · 20 ·· ··

Comment: This is the annual payment of £20 to Massachusetts Bay as stated in the seven year contract renewal of June 3, 1675. The agreement simply stated "the sajd minters are to pay in to the Treasurer of the Country, in mony, twenty pounds per Anno during abouesajd terme" (Crosby, p. 82). The "above said term" mentioned in the document was "this Seven yeare next to Come." Although the contract did not stipulate the reason for the payment Hull refers to it as the annual rent "of the mint." I believe he is referring to an annual rent or payment for the right to hold the exclusive coining agreement with the Commonwealth, which is the subject of the agreement of June 3, 1675. It does not appear to be a rental fee paid for use of the shop or mint building.

[171 recto]

by Balance brought from folio 134 — — — — — — — — — — | · · 9 | 18 | · · |

Comment: This undated entry was added sometime between the previous entry of October 18, 1679, and the following entry of November 21st. Hull simply stated he was bringing the balance forward from the previous space allocated to the shop account. The amount is found on folio 133 verso. Hull originally stated he was going to forward £75 3s as mentioned in his note at the bottom of folio 133 verso. This equaled the credits found on folio 134 verso. However, Hull must have used a portion of this money for some payment not listed in the shop account or he simply withdrew it from the shop account. Since the shop debits on folio 133 verso equaled £9 18s this was the only portion of £75 3s that Hull carried forward. It seems Hull took the remaining £65 4s out of the shop account.

[170 verso]

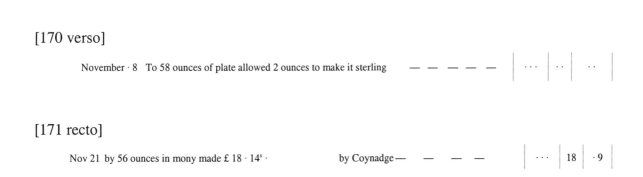

November · 8 To 58 ounces of plate allowed 2 ounces to make it sterling — — — — — | · · · | · · | · · |

[171 recto]

Nov 21 by 56 ounces in mony made £ 18 · 14ˢ ·   by Coynadge — — — — | · · · | 18 | · 9 |

Comment: On November 8, 1679, a customer deposited 58 ounces of plate which Hull determined to be below sterling fineness. Hull made an allowance of 2 troy ounces to bring the plate up to the fineness of sterling. If accurate, this would meant the plate was .893 fine. We know from an English statute passed on March 6, 1697, during the great recoinage that "Any wrought Plate of any sort or kind whatsoever" could be brought to the mint. If the silver did not have a goldsmith's mark, verifying it to be of sterling fineness, the individual could accept an offer made by the mint or request an assay (8&9 Guilielmi III cap. 8, *Statutes* vol. 7, p. 196). As Hull used the wording "allowed 2 ounces" rather than a statement such as "determined 2 ounces needed" or "by assay 2 ounces needed," it is possible Hull followed a similar procedure as was later used at the London mint and simply made an offer to accept the plate as equal to 56 troy ounces of sterling or he may have performed an assay and determinted the 58 oz. was .893 fine and simply used the word "allowed" rather loosely. The plate was deposited on November 8, 1679, and was delivered about two weeks later on November 21st. Hull stated he turned the plate into 56 troy ounces of sterling and produced £18 14s in Massachusetts silver coinage, at an average of 80.142857d per troy ounce.

Hull continued to work at the 12d per 20s rate which was a smaller mint fee than he was due under his contract with Massachusetts Bay. Hull was allowed a mint fee of 4d per ounce plus a wastage allowance of 1d per ounce which, for this consignment of 56 troy ounces of sterling, would result in a mint fee of 18s8d and a wastage allowance of 4s8d for a total of £1 3s 4d. However, Hull agreed to a fee of 12d per 20s. Hull produced £18 14s in coins and therefore was entitled to 18s 8.4d. Hull was allowed 0.6d per shilling but in his calculations he rounded up his fee to the nearest whole penny yielding him a fee of 18s9d.

[170 verso]

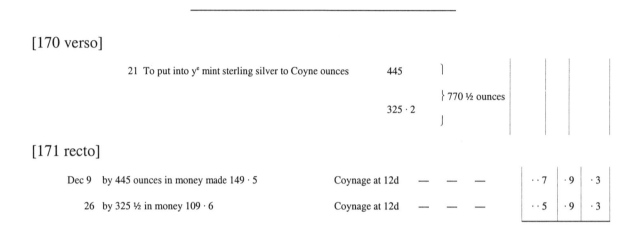

[171 recto]

Comment: On November 21, 1679, a customer deposited two quantities of sterling silver in the mint to be turned into coins; one lot contained 445 troy ounces and the other lot contained 325 1/2 troy ounces for a total of 770 1/2 troy ounces of sterling. In the consignment weight designation 325 · 2, the 2 following the middle dot is not a decimal. When designating sums of money Hull used the middle dot as a divider between pounds, shillings and pence as £32 · 2 · 0 for £32 2s or he used it as a place holder, hence £40 would be £ · 40 ·· ·· so the middle dot before the 40 would designate a place holder for the hundreds of pounds (that is, · 40). Also the middle dots represent the two place holders for shillings and the two place holders for pence. However, in this example of 325 · 2, Hull was designating weight rather than monetary units; when referring to weight Hull used the middle dot to represent quarters, thus the 2 represented 2/4th or 1/2 troy ounce. The plate was deposited on November 21, 1679, and was delivered in two installments, the first installment of 445 ounces was ready in about two-and–a-half weeks on December 9th while the second installment of 325.5 ounces was ready in just over an additional two weeks on December 26th.

Hull lists the full quantity of coinage made so we again can calculate the yield of coinage per troy ounce of sterling. Hull stated the 445 troy ounces of sterling produced £149 5s in Massachusetts silver coinage, which is an average of 80.494382d per troy ounce. The second installment of 325.5 troy ounces of sterling produced £109 6s in Massachusetts silver coinage, an average of 80.589861d per troy ounce. Combining the two shipments together 770.5 troy ounces of sterling produced £258 11s in Massachusetts silver or 80.53717d per troy ounce.

Hull continued to work at the 12d per 20s rate, which was a smaller mint fee than he was due under his contract with Massachusetts Bay. Hull was allowed a mint fee of 4d per ounce plus a wastage allowance of 1d per ounce. For the first installment of 445 troy ounces the full allowance would result in a mint fee of £7 8s4d and a wastage allowance of £1 17s1d for a total charge of £9 5s5d. However, Hull agreed to 12d per 20s. He minted £149 5s in coins and, therefore, was entitled to £7 9s3d, which is exactly what he took. For the second installment of 325.5 troy ounces the full allowance would result in a mint fee of £5 8s6d and a wastage allowance of £1 7s1.5d for a total charge of £6 15s7.5d. However, Hull agreed to a fee of 12d per 20s so for the £109 6s in coins produced, Hull was entitled to £5 9s3.6d which Hull rounded down to £5 9s3d. His total payment for the complete job came to £12 18s6d. Based on the full allowance Hull would have received a mint fee of £12 16s 10d and a wastage allowance of £3 4s 62.5d for a total payment of £16 1s 1/2d.

[171 recto]

| *[the mint fees and carry forward balance are totaled]* | 33 | · 4 | 3 |

Comment: On the credit side of the account Hull added up the mint fees received between October 18 and November 26, 1679, along with the £9 18s balance carried forward. The total was £33 4s3d.

[170 verso]

August · 3	To put to the mint fine silver ounces	220 · 3 gets at · 6 · 6 £ *[i.e., per pound]*					
4		538 · 3					
		547 · 1	£ 424 · 9 · 0				
	[totaled to]	1306 · 3					

[171 recto]

1680 Aug 29 by 538 ounces ¾ at 6.6^d — — — — — — — —	£ 175 · 2 · 0		
Sept 4 by 220 ounces at 6.6^d — — — — — — —	71 · 15 · 0		
Sept. 10 & 27 10 & 2 547 · 1 at 6.6^d — — — — — —	177 · 12 · 0		
[totaled to]	£ 424 · 9 · 0		

Comment: The August entry on folio 170 verso is not dated to a specific year. From the credit side of the account on folio 171 recto we discover this entry is dated 1680. This is one of the few instances where Hull neglected to include the change of the year in his entry. On August 3, 1680, a customer deposited 220.75 troy ounces of fine (that is, sterling) silver at the mint to be turned into coinage. As discussed above, in the entry for November 21, 1679, Hull used a middle dot in weight to represent quarters so, 220 · 3, represents 220 3/4th or 220.75 troy ounces. On August 4th two additional quantities of silver were deposited, one shipment was 538.75 troy ounces and the other was 547.25 troy ounces; in both instances Hull used the middle dot to designate fourths. Hull then added the total amount of fine silver deposited at the mint in this consignment as 1,306.75 troy ounces. On the credit side of his ledger we find the quantity of Massachusetts silver made from each of the three shipments and learn when the coins were ready for delivery. The first installment was the coinage made from 538.75 troy ounces of fine silver and was ready in about a month on August 29, 1680. The second installment, from the 220.75 ounces of silver, was ready six days later on September 4th. The date of the final installment of 547.25 ounces of silver is somewhat problematic. The date reads "Sept 10 & 27 10 & 2" in which the final 2 was originally another number overwritten as a 2 [see figure 41]. Further, a 7 appeared directly after the 2 but was overwritten as the 5 in the weight 547·1. It appears Hull first put the 10 directly under the 4 of the previous entry to designate the date as the 10th of the same month, that is September, and then added "& 27" but then he realized he would not be able to align the weights from the three installments as the 7 was directly over the hundreds place for the weight. It seems Hull then decided to align the three weights and wrote the 5 of 547·1 directly over the 7 of 27. To make up for obscuring the date he added "Sept. 10 & 27" in a more cursive script in the open left margin. Thus, it seems the third installment was delivered in two parts, or was ready on one day but not picked up until later. In any event is seems the entire consignment was completed and delivered by the end of September.

On folio 170 verso Hull wrote the total consignment "gets at · 6 · 6 £ [and then below and to the right] £ 424 · 9 · 0." This is confirmed on folio 171 recto where Hull included the yield. Here Hull gave the weight of each installment, then stated his fee "at 6.6d" and recorded the yield from the installment. Unlike the previous entries Hull did not calculate his mint fee from this yield, nor did he state "in money made" or some other phrase that would suggest the amount represented the entire yield. Rather it seems to me that Hull treated this entry somewhat differently from the previously entries. Like the entries from earlier years, it seems Hull did not record the total yield from the silver, rather he simply recorded that a specific number of ounces, at an agreed mint fee of 6.6d per 20s, would return a specific amount of money. I suspect this was not the total yield but rather was the quantity of money that was to be given to the customer.

If we interpret these quantities as the total yield, then it seems the individual coins were significantly overweight. Hull was authorized to produce 80d in coinage from each troy ounce but if we take the figures Hull gives for this total consignment, namely 1306.75 ounces of sterling to produce £424 9s, then Hull averaged only 77.955232d per troy ounce of sterling. Assuming the entire consignment was in shillings (8489s) the average weight per shilling would be 73.888561 grains without an allowance for wastage; assuming the maximum wastage, the average weight of a shilling drops to 72.964954 grains. Certainly, this would not be profitable and it does not correspond with the weights that can be calculated from Hull's other entries. It would indeed be uncharacteristic of Hull to be compromising his already reduced profits by producing overweight coins.

Alternatively, if we treat these amounts as the sums allotted to the customer, the average weight of the coins seems more reasonable in relation to Hull's other entries. However, before attempting to estimate the total yield and average weight of the coins from this consignment, we need to address the mint fee. In this entry we see Hull took an even smaller mint fee than in his previous agreements. Under his contract with Massachusetts Bay, Hull was allowed a mint fee of 4d per ounce plus a wastage allowance of 1d per ounce which, for this consignment of 1306.75 troy ounces of sterling, would result in a mint fee of £21 15s7d and a wastage allowance of £5 8s10.75d for a total of £27 4s 5.75d. However, Hull stated he had agreed to a reduced fee; this time it was not the fee he used in 1679 of "12d per pound" of money struck, but only slightly more than half of that fee, namely 6.6d per 20s of money (in this instance the dot is lower down and represents a decimal rather than a middle dot representing a fraction or a divider). Hull did not calculate his fee in this entry, he simply stated the fee rate. We must extrapolate the fee by calculating 6.6d per 20s in each of the three installments. For the first installment of £175 2s the fee would be £4 16s3.66d, rounded to £4 16s4d, while in the second installment of £71 15s the fee would calculate to £1 19s5.55d, rounded to £1 19s6d and for the third installment of £177 12s Hull's fee would be £4 17s8.16d, rounded to £4 17s8d, for a total of £11 13s6d. Adding this fee to the amount Hull lists as going to the customer, namely the £424 9s, we arrive at a total minting of £436 2s6d, which is rounded to £436 3s (8723s). Assuming this was the total mintage from the 1306.75 troy ounces of fine silver we arrive at an average yield of 80.1d in coinage per troy ounce (or an average of 71.9 grains per shilling), which is slightly higher that usual. This is in line with Hull's other consignments, thus in my estimation, adding the mint fee to the quantities given by Hull in this ledger entry produces a more reasonable interpretation of the information. Of course, it is possible Hull produced even more coins, possible as much as 80.44d per troy ounce, which would yield a total of 8760s (averaging 71.6 grains per shilling), and that he simply kept the additional 37s (£1 17s) in coinage, as had been done in earlier periods.

[170 verso]

June 3 · 80 To due to the Country for yearly rent as per Agreement June 3 · 76	· 20	· ·	· ·
[the debits are added]	£ · 40	· ·	· ·

//

Comment: This is the annual payment of £20 to Massachusetts Bay as stated in the seven year contract renewal of June 3, 1675. The agreement simply stated "the sajd minters are to pay in to the Treasurer of the Country, in mony, twenty pounds per Anno during abouesajd terme" (Crosby, p. 82). The above said term mention in the document was "this Seven yeare next to Come." Although the contract did not stipulate the reason for the payment, Hull refers to it as the annual rent for the mint. I believe he is referring to an annual rent or payment for the right to hold the exclusive coining agreement with the Commonwealth, which is the subject of the agreement of June 3, 1675. It does not appear to be a rental fee paid for use of the shop or mint building.

On the following line Hull added up the two annual payments in this listing for a total of £40 owed. The double slash // was used by Hull to show the end of the final entry in the space allotted for an account.

[171 recto]

by money received out of the shop in June	· · 6	15	· 9
[the sums are totaled to]	£ · 40	· ·	[· ·]

[//]

Comment: This is the final entry on the shop income side of the account. Hull needed to zero out the £40 shown on the debit side of the account before allocating the account some additional space in one of his two later ledgers. The total income listed on the credit side amounted to £33 4s3d while the total due the debit side of the ledger was £40. Apparently when the debits had been paid, in late September of 1680, he simply added the amount necessary to balance the account. He credited the shop account with £6 15s9d from money that had been received in June. Hull then added that amount as income to arrive at £40, which then made the two sides of the account equal. The bottom corner of the page is missing so the final two dots representing the pence in the total are missing and have been added in brackets. The double slash // was used by Hull to show the end of the final entry in the space allotted for an account.

Addenda to the Shop Account

There are some additional accounts in the Hull ledger which mention the shop. Two items are listed in the account with Mr. William Brenton. One is from June 3, 1672, "To Mrs. Sanford a silver whissle paid to the shop mony ··· / · 9 / · 4" [that is, 9s4d for a silver whistle to Mrs. John Sanford] and from May 27, 1673, "To [be] paid ye shop for mending a pott & 3 spoons and silver added 10 · 6" [that is, 10s6d] (ledger, folio 13 verso; illustrated in Jordan, "Mint," p. 2329). In the account with Sir Thomas Temple under May 3, 1673, "To lent Thomas in new money Twenty Pound Paid to ye shop a dram cup 8^s · 20 / · 8 / · ··" [that is, Temple owed Hull £20 8s for a loan of £20 in new or Massachusetts silver and for a silver dram cup from the shop that cost 8s. Apparently Hull paid the shop for the cup which may mean the item could have been made by Sanderson or an apprentice or it may simply be a reimbursment to the shop for the cost of the silver] (ledger, folio 37 verso). In the account with Joseph Eliot under the year 1674, we find "To two Gold Rings & bodkin £3 · 13" [that is, two gold rings and a thick blunt needle for £3 13s] (ledger, folio 85 verso]. And on January 28, 1678 [listed as 1677 because of the March new year] in the account with Leonard Hoar, "by mony out of the shopp for Plate 6 · 0 · 0" [That is a credit of £6 for silver plate delivered to the shop] (ledger, folio 74 recto). Undoubtedly a closer study of the complete ledger would reveal other entries.

The account of John Winchester and Dorman Morean of Muddy River (now Brookline)[1] include several payments for coal delivered to the shop. On February 28, 1674, [listed in the old style dating as 1673 since the new year began in March] is an entry: "By money of the shop for coals - for John Winchester ·· 1 / 10 /· ·" [that is, £1 10s]. Also, under November 17, 1674, "By money of the shop for 73 bushels 1/2 coal - for John Winchester ·· 1 / · 4 /· 6" [that is, 73.5 bushels for £1 4s6d]. And finally under December 3 [1674], "For charcoal to ye shop whose money for Dorman Morean ·· 2 / 17 / · 8" [that is, £2 17s8d] (New England Historic Genealogical Society, MS Cb 110, vol. 1, folio 40 recto; illustrated in Jordan, "Mint," pp. 2327-28).

Some additional comments on the charcoal entries are included below.

Massachusetts Bay did not have any coal mines, therefore coal, also called charcoal, was made from freshly cut lumber. Colliers would stack up to thirty cords of wood into piles shaped like domes that were 30 to 40 feet in diameter and about 10 to 14 feet high. Each pile was covered with dirt and leaves, then the collier began a controlled burn, or, more correctly, a controlled smolder. Over a period of about six days the wood was transformed into charcoal. Charcoal amounts differ based on the wood type. According to *Scribner's Lumber and Log Book*, every 100 parts of ash produces 25 parts charcoal, birch yields 24 parts charcoal, elm, oak and white pine each yield 23 parts, maple yields 22.8 parts, poplar yields 20 parts and willow 18 parts. It was also noted that a bushel of hardwood charcoal weighs 30 pounds while charcoal from softer wood, such as pine averages 29 pounds per bushel (quoted on http://www.allroutes.to/logging/history.htm as seen in December of 2001).

---

[1] Both Winchester and Morean are listed as residents of Muddy River in *1679 (Records of the Suffolk County Court 1671-1680*, part 2, p. 969).

Charcoal is an excellent fuel for melting and refining metal since it burns very hot. Unfortunately it also burns up quite fast and is therefore costly. Anthracite and other hard coals burn more slowly, but they must be extracted from mines deep in the earth and therefore were not available to the early settlers. Charcoal was the only option for coal in seventeenth century Massachusetts Bay. The Hammersmith Ironworks consumed 265 bushels of charcoal per ton of iron produced. They employed several laborers to chop wood for the colliers. The colliers, who actually made the charcoal, had a difficult job and were paid up to 5s per load. The colliers's remuneration was higher than the wages paid to the skilled ironworkers. This was a constant source of complaint because the ironworkers had far more strenuous jobs. Indeed a collier's pay was so good one ambitious collier even made more money than the ironmaster (Clarke, *Pioneer*, pp. 63-69).

A blacksmith only needed to heat metal, not melt it, and thus could rely on coals produced from a wood fire in an open hearth for sufficient heat. However, at the Hammersmith ironworks there was a continual 3,000° F fire in the furnace 24 hours a day requiring large quantities of charcoal. Similarly, at the Massachusetts Bay Mint there was a need to heat a furnace to high temperatures. The mint needed to achieve 2000° F for several hours in order to melt 25 troy pounds of silver. However, unlike Hammersmith, they only needed to perform melts sporadically, usually only when they had enough sterling to perform a full 25 troy pound melt. In the case of the mint, several bushels of charcoal would be consumed each time there was a need to fire up the furnace and perform a melt.

In Hull's ledger we find three purchases of coal for the shop in 1674; on February 28th Hull obtained £1 10s in coal, on November 17, 1674 he obtained 73.5 bushels for £1 4s6d and then on December 3rd he acquired an additional £2 17s8d of charcoal. Hull stated all this charcoal was for the shop, however we do not know if Winchester and Morean were his only suppliers. It is quite possible Hull acquired charcoal from other sources as well as Winchester and Morean. The mint would certainly have needed fuel in other years but no other coal deliveries are listed under the surviving portion of the Winchester and Morean account, which covers 1672-1681. Further, Winchester and Morean were not in the coal production business. They rented some land from Hull at Muddy River and occasionally delivered products as payment for their rent.

Of the three deliveries only one includes both a quantity and a value, the 73.5 bushels valued at £1 4s6d. Assuming each of the bushels weighed about 30 pounds, the total weight would be about 2,205 pounds or about one long ton at a cost of about 4d per bushel. We do not know if Hull consumed all of this coal in the two week period between November 17th and his next delivery on December 3rd. Possibly he was stockpiling coal for the winter. It is interesting to note that on December 12, 1674, a deposit of 275.5 troy ounces of sterling was recorded in Hull's ledger. Since no delivery date was given it is difficult to know when the consignment was melted and minted. It is impossible to estimate the shop's annual expense for fuel from these entries, although it does seem the cost was at least £5 12s2d per year and was in all probability much higher.

❉❉❉❉❉❉❉❉❉❉❉❉

Appendix II

A Chronological Listing of Documents and Events Relating to the Massachusetts Mint

August 22, 1642 - The culmination of several years of conflict between the Crown and the House of Commons occurred on January 4, 1642, when King Charles I unsuccessfully attempted to enter Parliament to arrest five members of the house and their ally Lord Edward Kimbolton, the Earl of Manchester. The king's disregard for parliamentary authority precipitated a strong anti-royalist reaction throughout the city. Six days later the king vacated London and started gathering allies throughout the countryside. On August 22nd Charles raised the Royal Standard at Nottingham and began issuing Commissions of Array to recruit soldiers into a Royalist army, inaugurating a long period of civil war.

January 27, 1649 - Following the capture of King Charles by the Parliamentary forces, the monarch was brought to London and put on trial. On this day, the Lord President of the Court, John Bradshaw, pronounced the verdict that "the said Charles Stuart, as a tyrant, traitor, murderer and public enemy to the good people this nation, shall be put to death by the severing of his head from his body" (Prall, p. 192). Two days later, on Monday, January 29th, when the king's death warrant was issued, only 59 of the 135 commissioners named to sit in judgment of the king actually signed the warrant. The execution took place on Tuesday, January 30, 1649, at 2:00 P.M.

May 19, 1649 - During the first half of 1649, Britain was transformed from a monarchy into a republic. On March 16th, Parliament abolished the monarchy and the House of Lords. Two months later, on May 19th, the nation was declared to be a Commonwealth governed by a Parliament consisting of a single chamber and an executive branch called the Council of the State with John Bradshaw as President and Oliver Cromwell as the First Chairman. On April 26, 1653, the Puritan military commander Cromwell dissolved the sitting Parliament, known as the Rump Parliament, and had a new Parliament installed consisting of his Puritan supporters. This new Parliament, known as the Little or Barebones Parliament, first assembled on July 4, 1653. On December 16, 1653, a new constitution was promulgated by the Parliament called, "The Instrument of Government." Article 33 of the document stated "That Oliver Cromwell, Captain General of the forces of England, Scotland and Ireland, shall be, and is hereby declared to be, Lord Protector of the Commonwealth of England, Scotland and Ireland and the dominions thereto belonging, for his life" (Prall, p. 260). With this action the government of the Commonwealth became known as the Protectorate. During the entire Commonwealth era (May 19, 1649 - March 16, 1660) , British colonies, and especially the Puritan Commonwealth of Massachusetts Bay, were freer to assert rights and liberties without fear of transgressing royal prerogatives or privileges.

[late 1651 or early 1652] - An order was issued by the Massachusetts Bay General Court to have silver coins, which were predominantly Spanish American cobs, stamped. The details of the legislation are unknown, possibly a counterstamp or mark was to be put on full weight examples, as was later proposed by the House of Deputies on June 2, 1669. The order has been lost and is only known indirectly, since it was mentioned in the preamble of an undated draft of the legislation to establish a mint. According to the preamble this order was recent but had never been put into practice because it was controversial and the General Court of Massachusetts Bay could not find anyone who would stamp the coins, thus it became void on the first of September. The wording was:

> ...fforasmuch as the new order about money is not well Resented [that is, not well received] by the people and full of difficultjes, and unlikely to take effect in regard no persons are found willing to try & stampe the same, ~~the sajd Order is Repealed.~~
>
> The Courte therefore Ordereth & enacteth that the printed order about
> Seauenth month
> mony shall be in force vntill the first of ~~July~~ next and no longer.

In revising this draft the final phrase in the preamble which stated "the sajd Order is Repealed" was deleted with a heavy black line, for the first point in the legislation explained the order was to be invalid on the first of the seventh month, which was September. The draft originally stated the order was to be in force until "the first of July next and no longer" but July was blotted out and "Seauenth month" was inserted [The seventh month was September because the British started the year in March.] (Crosby p. 34, also p. 31, footnote 1 for Resented as received).

[1652] - A committee of the Massachusetts Bay General Court produced an undated draft of an act to establish a mint in Boston, mentioned in the previous entry. The final form of the draft reflects the legislation passed by the General Court with only minor modifications regarding spelling and the use of punctuation, abbreviations and capitalization. From revisions and deletions made to this draft document, we can determine issues that were discussed and revised. For example, at the request of the House of Deputies the entire preamble, discussed above, was deleted from the draft. The deletion consisted of the first three lines of text, which were crossed out with an X.

The draft stated a mint would be established in Boston where plate, bullion and Spanish silver coinage would be melted to produce 12d, 6d and 3d silver coins at the British sterling standard (a fineness of .925) but the coins were to be lighter in weight than the British standard. The weight of a Massachusetts shilling was precisely defined at "three penny troj weight." This is exactly 72 grains, since a pennyweight in the troy scale equals 24 grains. Based on the English standard of 92.9 grains per shilling, Massachusetts silver was almost exactly 22.5% underweight. Massachusetts Bay minted silver at 80d (6s8d) per troy ounce of sterling silver while in England a troy ounce of silver was minted into 62d (5s2d) of coins.

The act stated that on the first of September, Massachusetts silver was to become legal tender along with English coinage. The two coinages were to be the only current money in the Commonwealth, unless the receiver consented to accept other coinage. However, in daily commerce foreign silver continued to be a significant part of the economy while English silver was rarely encountered. John Hull was named mintmaster. The design for the coinage was specified as being a flat, square planchet with NE stamped on one side and the denomination on the other side but this was revised to a round shape in the document discussed below dated to June 11th. In order to deter counterfeiting, the legislation also called for the coins to have a secret privy mark assigned by the Governor that was to be changed every three months. The mark was to be known only by the Governor and the sworn officers of the mint. It appears this provision was disregarded and that privy marks were never used. Also, a minting charge was established at 12d (1s) per 20s of coins produced; this charge had originally been 18d (1s6d), stated as "one shilling six-pence out of euery twenty shillings" but the six pence was blotted out at the request of the House of Deputies. However, the fees were increased on June 20 from 12d to 15d per 20s coined with a wastage allowance added, bringing the total back to 18d per 20s. It was also legislated that anyone bringing silver to the mint house could be present when the silver was refined to sterling. The customer would then be given a receipt for the weight of the sterling silver. On a prearranged future date the customer would return to exchange the receipt for the coins produced from that sterling, minus the minting charges.

Additionally, a committee was formed to expedite the implementation of the act. Members of the committee with their position in the General Court as of the elections of May 1652 follow: Richard Bellingham, one of the ten Assistants; William Hibbens (or Hibbins), another of the Assistants; Edward Rawson, Secretary to the General Court, and from the House of Deputies, Captain John Leveret and Lieutenant Thomas Clarke, who were the two elected Deputies representing Boston[1] (Crosby, pp. 34-35; Shurtleff, vol. 3, pp. 258-59 and vol. 4, pt. 1, pp. 76-77).

[1652] - When John Hull began keeping a diary he added several entries covering the period from his birth up to that time.[2] His entry for 1648 continued directly into 1652 without any mention of 1649-1651. Under the entry for 1648 he explained that he had been selected as a corporal under the command of Major Gibbons on about the 29th of May 1648. He continued with a reference to a promotion to the rank of sergeant in 1652 and then moved immediately into that year. The end of the entry for 1648 and the full entry for 1652 are as follows:

> ...After, when the town divided their one military company into four, I was chosen to be (and accepted) a sergeant, upon the 28th of the 4th month, 1652 [the fourth month was June].

---

[1] The General Court of the Commonwealth of Massachusetts consisted of the House of Magistrates and the House of Deputies. In 1652 the House of Magistrates included Governor John Endicot, Deputy Governor Thomas Dudley and ten Assistants who sat on the Governor's Council. The Assistants performed various official duties such as traveling to the counties where they served as judges for the quarterly sessions of the local courts. All the positions were elected annually. The House of Deputies was composed of representatives annually elected from each of the towns throughout the Commonwealth.

[2] Hull actually kept two diaries, one contained a listing of public events related to Massachusetts Bay, while the other contained entries detailing events relating to his family and private life. In both diaries the early sections were written at a single sitting using one type of ink indicating they were composed from memory years after the events, while subsequent entries were in different styles and different inks indicating they were added as the events occurred. Assuming the point at which one begins to find varying style entries represents the period when Hull started the diaries, the nineteenth century editor of the diaries, Samuel Jennison, suspected the *Public Diary* was begun about 1649 while the *Private Diary* was started later, around 1654 (see Hull, *Diaries,* introduction by Jennison on p. 116 and the appendix on the shorthand transcription by Edward Everett Hale dating Hull's marginal shorthand insertions to between April 8 and May 1, 1665, on pp. 279-80).

1652. Also upon the occasion of much counterfeit coin brought in the country, and much loss accruing in that respect (and that did occasion a stoppage of trade), the General Court ordered a mint to be set up, and to coin it, bringing it to the sterling standard for fineness, and for weight every shilling to be three pennyweight; i.e. 9d at 5s per ounce. And they made choice of me for that employment; and I chose my friend, Robert Sanderson, to be my partner, to which the Court consented.

Hull stated the shilling was to be sterling fineness, which was defined as 11 oz. 2 dwt. of silver per troy pound, or as we now express it, .925 fine and was to weigh three pennyweight (72 grains). Hull's final statement on the specifications of the coinage explains the Massachusetts shilling was to be equal in intrinsic value to 9d based on the pre-1601 British standard of 5s per troy ounce of sterling. At 60d (5s) per ounce (1 oz. = 480 grains), 1s would contain 96 grains of sterling silver so 72 grains of sterling would equal 9d. With the exception of a slight devaluation during 1578-1583, 5s per troy ounce was the British minting standard from 1560-1601; then on September 29, 1601, the shilling was reduced to 92.9 grains of sterling which equaled 62d (5s2d) in coins per ounce of sterling. It is quite likely Hull used the older standard since it did not involve the calculation of fractions. Even in his surviving accounts books, Hull would occasionally round up or down to the nearest whole number rather than take the time to calculate fractions; see the transcription and commentary of the shop entries in Hull's private ledger in Appendix I (Hull, *Private Diary*, pp. 145-46; Clarke, *Hull*, p. 57, and Crosby, pp. 31-32).

May 26, 1652 - The act to establish a mint in Boston was approved in the House of Magistrates of the Massachusetts Bay General Court. The legislation was essentially the same as the draft except the entire preamble found in the draft was deleted from the final act. To expedite the implementation of this legislation the act enjoined the mint committee:

> ...to Appoint the mint howse in some Convenjent place in Boston to Give John Hull master of the mint the oath suiteable to his place, and to Approove of all other officers and determine what else shall appeare to them as necessarily to be donne for the Carrying an end of the whole order. (Crosby, pp. 36-37, Shurtleff, vol. 4, pt. 1, pp. 84-85)

May 27, 1652 - The act to establish a mint in Boston was approved in the House of Deputies of the Massachusetts Bay General Court. The spelling and capitalization differed somewhat from the Magistrates's version but the wording was similar. The final phrase in the Deputies's version, "...& that all other Orders...repealed," also appeared in the draft version but was missing from the Magistrates's copy of the act (this section of the draft version is quoted in the accompanying studies in chapter one, p. 10 on "Contemporary References to the Mint House"). The passage in the Deputies's version enjoining the mint committee to expedite the act is given here for comparison with the quote in the previous entry:

> ...to appoynt the mint howse in some Convenient place in Boston to giue John Hull master of the mint the oath suteable to his place & to approue of all other Officers & determine what else shall appeare to them as Necessary

to be done for the Carying an End of the whole order, & that all other Orders concerning the Valuation or coyning of money past this court shalbe repealed. (Crosby, pp. 37-38, Shurtleff, vol. 3, pp. 261-62 and Clarke, *Hull,* pp. 58-59)

June 1, 1652 - There is no record of the specific day on which the 1652 spring session of the General Court finally adjourned, however the last recorded date in the session was Saturday June 1st. Following the close of the session the mint committee continued to carry out their assignment of expediting the mint act of May 26/27. The General Court was not able to officially vote approving the mint committee's actions until the fall session, which opened on October 19, 1652 (Crosby, p. 42).

June 10-11, 1652 - A mint committee document dated "Boston : 11: June. 1652" recorded the oath of office created for the deposition of the mintmasters and declared a revision to the shape of the coinage as described in the mint act passed by the General Court. The document stated, "Itt is Ordered that the Oath here vnder written shall be the oath that John Hull and Robt Saunderson shall take as aequall officers In the minting of mony &c." The oath then began as follows:

> Whereas yow : John Hull and Robert Saunderson are Appointed by the order of the Gennerall Courte bearing date the 10th of June 1652. to be officers for the massachusetts Jurisdiction in New England, for the melting, Refyning, and Coining of silver... .

The oath went on requiring the minters to swear that they would "faithfully and dilligently" produce coins of sterling fineness but at a weight reduction from the British standard (expressed in the document as a shilling at threepenny troy weight, which was 72 grains).

The second item in this document, on the change in the shape of the coinage, which is explained below, clearly indicates the General Court was no longer in session. Thus, the statement at the start of the oath that the General Court produced an order on June 10th appointing the mintmasters to their office is somewhat misleading since the General Court was no longer in session. Rather, it seems the statement in the oath should be interpreted as meaning that the May 26/27th act of the General Court had given the mint committee the power to administer the oath and to officially appoint individuals to the mint on behalf of the General Court. It would be more accurate to state the mint committee on behalf of the General Court produced the June 10th order. The specific date on which Hull actually took the oath of office is also problematic. The text states the order of appointment bears the date of June 10th but the mint committee document recording the deposition of the oath is dated June 11th. Possibly the committee sent out an order to Hull and to Sanderson on June 10th stating they could present themselves to be sworn into office and thus officially become appointed as officers of the Commonwealth. A marginal note beside the oath, added by Edward Rawson, the Secretary of the General Court and a member of the mint committee, stated, "Jo: Hull deposd accordingly ye Same day before ye Comittee. E. R S : Robt Saunderson deposed 19 6 mo 52." Thus, is seems Hull appeared before the committee to take the oath on either the tenth, which would have been the same day an order was issued, or, what seems more likely, that he came to swear his oath on the eleventh, which was the date on the committee document recording the event, while Sanderson waited until August 19th.

Below the oath a paragraph was added stating that although the act passed by the General Court called for the coinage to be "flatt and square" the committee determined the shape of the coins should be changed and the minters should produce coins "in A Round forme till the Gennerall Courte shall otherwise declare their minds." Crosby cites this document as Massachusetts Archives, Pec. vol. c, p. 40; it is reproduced in facsimile on the top half of the plate opposite page 41. The back side of this sheet of paper contains the mint committee's action of June 20, 1652 (Crosby, pp. 41 and 43, also facsimile opposite p. 41 and Clarke, *Hull,* pp. 59-60).

[June 1652] - An undated and incomplete draft of a mint committee action to erect a mint house and increase the minting fee, for which the final committee version also exists. The final version, which was signed by the committee members on June 20, 1652, has some revised wording but is substantially the same as the draft. This undated draft is signed, "John Hull mintmaster," also, in the hand of Edward Rawson, Secretary of the General Court, is "Robert Saunderson, his copartner." In the margin are the signatures of Simon Bradstreet and John Woodbridge. The Bradstreet and Woodbridge signatures had to have been added at a later date because Woodbridge was in England from 1647-1663. These two signatures may have been added in 1683 following the expiration of the final minting contract in June of 1682 (see the June 20th entry below for details of the content of the document and the entry under May 16, 1683, for the Bradstreet and Woodbridge signatures).

On the other side of this sheet of paper are four sketches of varying sizes of round coin designs [figure 30]. The first design is larger than the others and contains only a rim legend with the words "New England" followed by some indistinct letters that appear to be "Massachusetts in." The second design is somewhat smaller with only the rim legend "Massachusetts in." The next is the only sketch with a center design with the Roman numeral XII in a center circle and the legend "New England" with the date "165" (probably for 1652 in an outer ring). The final sketch simply contains the rim legend "New England" with what may be an initial "I" or a final flourish at about the 7:00 o'clock position. The sketches neither depict the initials NE as specified in the Act of May 26/27 nor is there any tree design as later specified in the General Court's October 19th revision of the coin design (Crosby, p. 39, with Hull signature from the recto and the four sketches from the verso included in the third quarter of the facsimile plate opposite page 41. Crosby cites this document as Massachusetts Archives, vol. c, p. 37).

June 20, 1652 - Action of the mint committee to erect a house for the melting, refining and coining of silver that was 16 feet square and 10 feet high. The action also approved the purchase of all the tools and implements needed for the mint at government expense. Additionally, the committee increased the fees due to the mint master to 15d for every 20s coined plus an allowance of 1d per ounce of silver for waste[3] (Crosby, p. 40, this document is the back of the sheet dated to June 11, 1652, containing the oath of office to be given to Hull and Sanderson, identified by Crosby as Massachusetts Archives, Pec. vol. c, p. 40).

---

[3] In the act of May 26/27 the fees had been set at 1s for every 20s coined

June 22, 1652 - Minutes of a mint committee meeting listing the steps and decisions taken to implement their action of June 20th. The minutes stated Isacke Cullimore had been selected to construct the mint house and that he was empowered to hire additional workers. The wording of the document was that a warrant had been issued to the Constables of Boston impressing Cullimore into service and that another warrant had been issued to Cullimore empowering him to impress other workmen carpenters into the service of the Commonwealth. Also, the committee announced a site had been selected for the mint stating, "That the said mint howse shall be sett upon the land of the said John Hull." Certainly there had been some negotiations with Hull concerning the location of the mint on his land rather than on publicly owned land, for along with the announcement of the selection of the site, the committee specified the provision that, if Hull should cease to be the mintmaster, Massachusetts Bay had the option of either purchasing the real estate from Hull or allowing Hull to purchase the structure based on a valuation made by "two Indifferent men" (Crosby, p. 42).[4]

August 19, 1652 - Edward Rawson, the Secretary of the General Court and a member of the mint committee, added a marginal note beside the oath of office given to the mintmasters (the oath was dated June 10, 1652, but was recorded on June 11th), stating Robert Sanderson deposed on August 19th. Presumably Sanderson, who had been living in Watertown, moved to Boston at this time in order to take up his position at the mint before the official opening on September 1st (Crosby, p. 41).

September 1, 1652 - According to the mint act of May 26/27, 1652, on September 1st a previous order about coinage was to become invalid. Also, on September 1st the coinage authorized by the May 26/27 mint act was to become valid and current. The legislation, as passed by the House of Magistrates on May 26th, began:

> Itt is ordered and by the Authoritje of this Court Enacted that the printed Order about mony shall be in force vntill the first of september next and no longer. And that from and after the first of september next the mony heerafter Appointed and expressed shallbe the Currant mony of this Commonwealth and no other vnlesse English (except the Receivers Consent therevnto:).... (Crosby, p. 36 and Shurtleff, vol. 4, pt. 1, p. 84)

October 19, 1652 - This is the opening date of the fall session of the General Court. Frequently legislation approved during a session was recorded under the opening date of that session. Under this date an order of the General Court was recorded, "ffor the prevention of washing or Clipping of all such peices of mony as shall be Coined within this Jurisdiction." The change in design on the coins passed in both houses. Each side of the coin was to have a rim inscription within a double ring and in the center a tree on one side and the date on the other. Specifications in the original act simply stated the coins would have NE on one side and the denomination on the other; there was no inscription, double ring, tree or date [Crosby, p. 44, gives both the version passed by the House of Magistrates and that passed by

---

[4] See the entry of October 4, 1667, below and the accompanying study on the Hull homestead and the location of the mint.

the House of Deputies; Shurtleff, vol. 3, p. 283 for the version by the Deputies and vol. 4, pt. 1, p. 104 for the version by the Magistrates]. Also, under this date the General Court recorded the funds that had been spent since the May session. The treasurer included the cost of the mint house along with prison costs without itemizing specific expenses as: "To several sums paid on the charge, - prisons and prisoners and keeper and executioner and mint house. All is £395. 12s. 2d" (Hull, *Diary,* appendix, p. 289 and Shurtleff, vol. 4, pt. 1, p. 104).

October 26, 1652 - The secretary of the Court recorded that the whole General Court voted to allow and approve the actions of the mint committee concerning the construction of a mint house at government expense as well as consenting to the increased minting fees. Although not specifically mentioned, the Court's consent also included the mint committee's decisions to acquire the necessary minting equipment at government expense and to allow for a waste allowance of 1d per troy ounce of silver. The Court further charged the committee to "...Continew in theire power till the next Election." Members of the General Court were elected in May to serve for a year; typically service consisted of participating in the spring and fall sessions of the legislature. In the election of May 1653, all the committee members were reelected to the General Court in the same positions except for Bellingham, who became Deputy Governor; also, we find Lieutenant Clarke was promoted to Captain. The promotion was probably due to the creation of three new military companies mentioned by Hull in his diary entry given above (Crosby, p. 41 and Shurtleff, vol. 4, pt. 1, p. 118 in the records of the session of the Magistrates, and for the 1653 election results, pp. 119-20).

October 28, 1652 - A dated note was added to the mint committee action of June 20, 1652, stating the whole General Court voted in favor of the establishment of a mint house and the increased mint fees as recommended in the June 20th action. A final line was added stating the mint committee was to stand until the next session of the General Court (Crosby, p. 40).

May 30, 1653 – Robert Sanderson was admitted as an inhabitant of Boston. It is likely the Sanderson family had moved from Watertown to Boston by this date. Possibly they were renting a home or residing on the Hull estate while they looked for a nearby property to purchase (Whitmore, *Boston Records*, p. 116).

December 3, 1653 – Robert Sanderson purchased a house and parcel of land from the widow Sarah Phippen for £40; the residence was two blocks east of the Hull estate (Suffolk Deeds, vol. 3, pp. 70-71).

May 12, 1654 - An order to prohibit the exportation of any Massachusetts Bay coins from the Commonwealth was passed by the House of Magistrates but voted down in the House of Deputies. The act stated the reason for minting coins was to assist the local economy and that the coinage was not meant to pay foreign debts. Because Massachusetts silver had a lower intrinsic value than British silver it was stated one would need to pay one-fourth more in Massachusetts money when purchasing foreign goods and the only way one could recover this difference was by extorting oppressively high prices for such goods in the local market and thereby ruin the economy.

> Whereas, the end of Coyning mony within this Commonwealth is for the
> more easy managing the traficque thereof within itself, & not Indended to
> make returns to other Countrjes, which cannot Advance any proffitt to such

as send it, but Rather a fowerth part Losse Vnlesse such persons doe oppresse & extort in the sale of theire goods to make vp the sajd losse ... and vtterly frustrate the end & vse of mony amongst vs.

This act would have required a searcher to be appointed in every port town with confiscated money being divided equally between the searcher and the Commonwealth. A revised order was passed in August (Crosby, pp. 104-5).

August 22, 1654 - An order of the General Court was approved by both houses limiting exportation of Massachusetts coinage out of the Commonwealth to twenty shillings per person and appointing nine searchers to stop smuggling. Confiscated coins were to be divided, one-third to the searcher and two-thirds to the Commonwealth. The searchers were: Peter Oliver and John Barrell for Boston, Jacob Greene for Charlestown, George Williams and Samuel Archer for Salem, Robert Lord for Ipswich, Henry Rice for Sudbury, Henry Sherborne for Piscataque [Portsmouth, New Hampshire] and Hercules Hawkins for the Isle of Shoals [off the coast of Rye, New Hampshire at the border with Maine] (Crosby, pp. 70-71 giving the version from the House of Magistrates; Shurtleff, vol. 3, pp. 353-54 for the Deputies's version and vol. 4, p. 1, pp. 197-98 for the Magistrates's version).

1654 - Edward Hull, the brother of John Hull, wrote a letter from London to Joseph Jenks, the master craftsman at the Hammersmith Iron Works in Saugus, Massachusetts. Apparently this letter was in reply to an earlier request from Jenks inquiring as to the availability of a die cutter. In his reply to Jenks, Edward Hull stated that he knew of a German die cutter who was willing to immigrate to Boston. It appears nothing came of this plan (Morison, p. 152).

1654 - John Mansfield of Charlestown petitioned the General Court to grant that he be allowed to be the "...Country searvantt for helping to quine & melt & fine silver with mr Hull & good man Saunders, in the country howse withe them." That is, he wanted to serve the country (Massachusetts Bay) by coining, melting and refining silver in the government mint house. Mansfield stated he had eleven-and-a-half years's experience as an apprentice in the trade. No action was recorded on the disposition of this petition nor was Mansfield mentioned in Hull's diaries, letters or ledger, probably indicating his request to work at the mint was not granted. See Chapter 13 for further details on Mansfield (Crosby, pp. 103-4 and Clarke, *Hull,* p. 31).

June 9, 1655 - General Robert Nenables, Vice Admiral William Penn and Captain Gregory Butler, who were the British Commissioners responsible for managing expeditions sent to America, presented a set of orders and regulations to Robert Wadeson, Captain William Crispin and Thomas Broughton, who were charged with traveling to Massachusetts Bay and acquiring £10,000 worth of provisions for the British army and fleet stationed at Jamaica. The fifth of the seven regulations stated:

> 5. You are to take notice that the intrinsic value of New England money is less in weight by one quarter than at London. As for example a shilling in New England is of the same weight as ninepence is at London. Which is mainly to be considered if you take up money. (Crosby, pp. 103-4 also *Manuscripts of the Duke of Portland,* vol. 2, p. 94 and Sumner, "Coin Shilling," p. 252)

September 17, 1658 – John Sanderson, the eldest son of Robert Sanderson and an apprentice at the Hull shop, died. Hull wrote in his his private diary, "My boy, John Sanderson, complained of his head aching, and took his bed. A strong feaver set on him; and, after seventeen days' sore sickness, he departed this life" (Hull, *Private Diary,* p. 148 and Kane, p. 879).

July 1, 1659 - Hull accepted two apprentices. He wrote in his diary:

> I received into my house Jeremie Dummer and Samuel Paddy, to serve me as apprentices eight years. The Lord make me faithful in discharge of this new trust committed to me, and let his blessing be to me and them!

Jeremiah Dummer, who engraved the plates for the first emission of Connecticut currency in 1709, became one of Boston's leading silversmiths while Samuel Paddy became a merchant in Jamaica. In 1681, Hull wrote in a letter to Paddy, who was then living in Jamaica,

> Had you abode here and followed your calling you might have been worth many hundred pounds of clear estate and you might have enjoyed many more helpes for your sole [soul]. Mr. Dummer lives in good fashion hath a wife and three children and a good estate, is a member of the church and like to be very useful in his generation. (Hull, *Private Diary,* p. 150 and footnote two; Clarke, *Hull,* pp. 132-33 for the quoted letter. Also see: Clarke and Foote, *Jeremiah Dummer: Colonial Craftsman* and Kane, Dummer on pp. 385-97 and Paddy on pp. 748-49)

Autumn 1659 - Production of the Lord Baltimore silver coinage commenced with 12d, 6d and 4d denominations at the Tower Mint in London; a pattern was produced for a copper 1d coin but it never went into production. The specific dates of production are unknown although it appears minting was underway by September or October. We do know that Richard Pight, the Clerk of Irons at the Tower of London, learned about the coinage and informed the authorities. An arrest warrant was issued for Cecil Calvert, Lord Baltimore on Tuesday October 4, 1659. Calvert appeared before the Privy Council on October 5th and seems to have been successful in defending his position because on October 12, 1659, he wrote a letter to the governing Council in Maryland stating he had procured the "Necessaries" for a coinage and recommended the Maryland colonial assembly pass a law authorizing his proposed coinage be accepted as legal tender. Because of the need to stop a rebellion in Maryland led by Josias Fendall during the period of March through November of 1660, the coinage legislation could not be addressed until April of 1661, when it was enacted. The coins were shipped to the colony and did circulate; on April 12, 1662, a law was passed requiring every household in Maryland to exchange sixty pounds of tobacco for ten shillings in Calvert's coins (For further details see: Crosby, pp. 123-32 and Hodder, "Cecil Calvert's Coinage").

March 16, 1660 - After several months of civil war in England the Commonwealth Parliament was dissolved.

May 8, 1660 - A proclamation was issued in England restoring the monarchy and elevating Charles II as King of England. On May 29th Charles entered London to assume his throne.

Hull mentions Charles's assumption of the throne in his public diary but misdated the event to May 31st (Hull, *Public Diary,* p. 195).

July 27, 1660 - A ship from England landed in Boston Harbor bringing two of Cromwell's confidants and judges, Major General William Goffe and Lieutenant General Edward Whaley, bearing the disheartening news of the restoration of the monarchy under Charles II. Both Goffe and Whaley had been among the 135 commissioners who sat in judgment against Charles I and were among the 59 commissioners who signed the king's death warrant. Apparently the generals had left London before Charles II assumed the throne but had learned of the event while their ship was still in the English Channel. The manner in which the generals learned the news could have resulted in their receiving less that exact information on the date and may be the reason for Hull's misdating of the event to the end of the month rather than the 29th. Goffe and Wahley resided in Cambridge for a few months. However, when it was learned they had not been included on the list of those pardoned for their actions, the Governor called a special session of the General Court on February 22, 1661, asking that the two be arrested, but the General Court did not agree. On February 26, 1661, Goffe and Wahley moved on to New Haven where they stayed with the Reverend John Davenport. They later left and moved from town to town until they settled in Hadley, Massachusetts (Hutchinson, *History,* edited by Mayo, vol. 1 pp. 183-85, Clarke, *Hull,* pp. 94-95 and Prince, *Mather Papers,* pp. 122-24).

October 16, 1660 - The Massachusetts Bay General Court formed a committee of Captain Daniel Gookin, Richard Russell, Anthony Stoddard and William Parks to obtain a more advantageous financial arrangement for the colony from the Boston mint. The tone of the document was rather stern stating that they hoped "...the Country may Reape some bennefitt after so long a forbearance" and if Hull and Sanderson did not consent it was declared "this Court Intends to agree with some other meete [meete = suitable] person to minte the money of this Country [that is, Massachusetts Bay]." The committee was to report their results at the following court to be held in May of 1661[5] (Crosby, p. 71; Shurtleff, vol. 4, pt. 1, p. 434 and p. 416 for the offices held following the elections of May 1660).

February 11, 1661 - Governor Endicot, by order of the General Court of Massachusetts Bay, sent a letter to Charles II stating they knelt before him as the restored king and asked that he protect the privileges and liberties conferred on them by a Patent from Charles I. The letter was entered into the record of the Colonial Papers on February 11th (Sainsbury, *Calendar 1661-1668,* pp. 8-10, item 26).

February 19, 1661 - Edward Godfrey, identified as "sometimes Governor of the Province of Maine" testified before the Council for Foreign Plantations (later known as the Committee of the Lords for Trade and Plantations). Godfrey stated that Massachusetts had "...usurped all the country into subjection ... in practice to be a free State" (Sainsbury, *Calendar 1661-1668,* pp. 12-13, item 33).

---

[5] Gookin was one of nine Assistants to Governor Endicott, Russell was also an Assistant and Treasurer for the Commonwealth, Stottard was one of the two Deputies from Boston while Parks was one of the two Deputies from Roxbury.

March 4 - 14, 1661 - Captain Thomas Breedon, Governor of Acadia and Nova Scotia, Edward Godfrey, Governor of Maine, along with John Gifford and Samuel Maverick among others, were ordered to testify before the Council of Foreign Plantations against Massachusetts Bay. On March 11th Breedon presented a book containing the laws of Massachusetts Bay which he suggested went far beyond the patent granted to the company and that Massachusetts found it difficult to "reconcile Monarchy and Independency." On March 14th Godfrey's testimony supported Breedon. At this time an undated petition was recorded which had been received from "divers persons who had been sufferers in New England on behalf of themselves and thousands there [i.e. in New England]" stating:

> Through the tyranny and oppression of those in power there, multitudes of the King's subjects have been most unjustly and grievously oppressed contrary to their own laws and the laws of England, imprisoned, fined, fettered, whipt, and further punished by cutting off of their ears, branding the face, their estates seized and themselves banished [from] the country.

Among the thirteen signatories were Gifford and Godfrey (Sainsbury, *Calendar 1661-1668,* pp. 15-19, items, 42, 45, 46, 49-53, quote from item 49 on pp. 16-17).

April 4, 1661 - At a meeting of the Council for Foreign Plantations a petition was read. The petition was addressed to the king from Ferdinando Gorges, the grandson of the Ferdinando Gorges who had been given a Patent to Maine, requesting the restoration of his lands (Sainsbury, *Calendar 1661-1668,* p. 22, item, 64).

April 8, 1661 - At a meeting of the Council for Foreign Plantations a letter was drafted to the provinces of New England informing them the Council had been appointed to manage the colonies and that they were to respond to charges made against them. It was also suggested that the colonies appoint agents to represent their positions to the Council when requested (Sainsbury, *Calendar 1661-1668,* pp. 22-23, item, 66).

April 29-30, 1661 - The Council for Foreign Plantations collected several petitions and reports against Massachusetts Bay. By this date, Robert Mason had petitioned for the restoration of his family Patent to New Hampshire. One particularly interesting item is an undated and unsigned letter thought to be by John Gifford as it accompanied a proposal signed by Gifford; both documents were endorsed by Sir Edward Nicholas, Secretary of State (June 1660 - October 1662). Gifford's signed proposal concerned various ore and mineral mines in Massachusetts and that topic was also mentioned in the unsigned letter. Gifford was appointed in 1650 as the third agent for the Company of Undertakers for the Iron Works in New England replacing Richard Leader. Gifford headed the operation of the Hammersmith Ironworks in Saugus, Massachusetts, until 1653 when he became involved in several lawsuits and ended up spending some time in jail. From October of 1658 through April of 1662, Gifford was in England bringing suits against just about everyone connected with the Ironworks enterprise. The summary of the unsigned letter, attributed to him, detailed several problems with the laws of Massachusetts Bay. This document contains the earliest reference accusing the Massachusetts Mint of illegal acts. The summary of the letter in the Calendar of Colonial Papers states:

...they have acted repugnant to the laws of England ; they have allowed the King's coin to be brought and melted down in Boston to be new coined there, by which means they gain threepence in every shilling, and lessen his Majesty's coin a full fourth. (Sainsbury, *Calendar 1661-1668,* pp. 24-26, item, 73-78 and 80, quote from item 78 on p. 26. For Gifford see, Hartley, pp. 139-64 and 215-43)

May 8, 1661 - In England the first royalist parliament of Charles II was seated.

May 22, 1661 - An entry under this date in the record of the General Court stated the decision of the Court relative to the findings of the mint committee were as follows:

> ...that this Committee should be reimpowered to treate with the mint masters, & to Receive the ten pounds above mentioned, & what else they Cann Gett by way of Recompence for the mint house for the time past... .

This clearly refers to the June 6, 1661, report that is discussed in the next entry. On several occasions the secretary of the General Court recorded the decisions of the Court session under the opening day of that session. In this case we have the dated document so we know exactly when the event occurred during the spring session of the General Court (Crosby, p. 72; Shurtleff, vol. 4, pt. 2, p. 12).

June 6, 1661 - The mint committee created by the General Court in October of 1660 submitted a report stating they felt that "the use of the mint & house required in justice some certaine part of the income received" to be paid to the government. The committee asked for a twentieth part, that is 5% of the profits. Hull and Sanderson would not agree to give the Commonwealth an annual percentage of the mint profits but offered £10 as a free gift, which the committee refused.[6] A note was added to the report stating the House of Deputies requested the mint committee "...be reimpowred to treate with the mintmaster, & to receive the ten pound above mentioned, & what else they cann gett by way of recompenc for the mint howse for the time past" (Crosby, p. 72).

June 7, 1661 - A note added to the June 6th report stated the House of Magistrates concurred with the decision of the House of Deputies (Crosby, p. 72).

June 10, 1661 - The General Court approved a declaration listing the liberties of the Commonwealth and explaining the Commonwealth's specific duties of allegiance to the king. Article eight of the liberties stated the Commonwealth held anything to be an infringement on their rights if it was prejudicial to the Commonwealth or contrary to their laws, so long as the item in contention was not contrary to English law (Shurtleff, vol. 4, p. 2, pp. 224-26; also in Hutchinson, *History,* edited by Mayo, vol. 1, pp. 439-40).

---

[6] Crosby, who stated he transcribed the document from the Archives, gives the name of one of the committee members as William Park, while the copy of the document as transcribed in the record of the General Court gives Parke, but in other instances, such as in the election results and in the October 16, 1660 text on the creation of the committee, the name is William Parks.

August 7, 1661 - At a special session of the General Court, after much debate on the specific wording of the document, the Court issued a proclamation stating Charles II had been:

> ... lawfully proclaymed and crouned accordingly, wee therefore doe [do], as in duty wee are bound, oune [own] & acknouledge him to be our soveraigne lord & king, and doe therefore hereby proclaime & declare his said majesty Charles the Second, to be laufull King of Great Brittaine, France & Ireland, & all other territories & dominions thereunto belonging. (Shurtleff, vol. 4, pt. 2, p. 31)

Also, a letter addressed to the king containing this message was dispatched to London (Shurtleff, vol. 4, pt. 2, pp. 30-33; Hart, vol. 1, p. 472; Hutchinson, *History,* edited by Mayo, vol. 1, pp. 187-88).

August 8, 1661 - In Boston, Charles II was publicly proclaimed king over the colony of Massachusetts Bay by Edward Rawson, secretary of the General Court. As part of the official ceremonies soldiers paraded in the central square and cannons were fired from both the city battlements and the ships in the harbor. Also, as Hull so pointedly stated, "All the chief officers feasted that night at the charge of the country" [the country being the Commonwealth] (Hull, *Public Diary,* pp. 203-4 entry for 8th of the 6th, and Clarke, *Hull,* p. 96).

November 9, 1661 - The complaints against Massachusetts Bay made during the first months of the year continued with testimonies of mistreatment of Quakers. On September 9th the king sent a letter to Governor Endicott requesting all imprisoned Quakers be sent to England. On November 9th Edward Rawson, Secretary of the Massachusetts General Court, sent a letter to William Morice, one of the two British Secretaries of State,[7] characterizing the Quakers as disturbers of the peace and requesting the king's favor and protection of the liberties and privileges that Massachusetts Bay had enjoyed for the past thirty years (Sainsbury, *Calendar 1661-1668,* pp. 30-32, 55-56, 61; items, 88-90, 168 and 192).

December 24, 1661 - Simon Bradstreet and John Norton were selected by a group of magistrates, deputies and church elders on December 24th to be sent to the court of King Charles in London as advocates for the Commonwealth's interests and liberties. Bradstreet was one of the Governor's nine Assistants and was one of two Commissioners for the Commonwealth to the United Colonies of New England, while Norton was the Minister of the First Church of Christ in Boston[8] (Hutchinson, *History,* edited by Mayo, vol. 1, p. 188; Hull, *Public Diary,* p. 204 and Clarke, *Hull,* p. 99).

December 31, 1661 - At a special session of the General Court the selections of Bradstreet

---

[7] Sir William Morice served as Secretary of State June 30, 1660 - September 1668.

[8] The printed edition of Hull's diary, as well as the edition of the records of the Essex County Court and many entries in the Calendar of State Papers, Colonial Series, edited by Sainsbury, use the name Broadstreet whereas several contemporary sources and modern usage are consistent as Bradstreet.

and Norton as the agents for Massachusetts Bay were confirmed. Also, it was ordered that a letter be drafted to the congregation of the First Church of Christ in Boston imploring them to allow their minister a leave of absence (Shurtleff, vol. 4, pt. 2, pp. 37-40).

January 11, 1662 - The First Church of Boston consented that their minister the Reverend John Norton should undertake the voyage to England on behalf of the Commonwealth (Hull, *Public Diary,* p. 205).

February 1, 1662 - Hull included several details in his diary concerning preparations and events relative to the departure of the delegation. He stated a committee chosen by the General Court spent several days at the end of January:

> ...preparing, propounding, and concluding the going of the said messengers, during which time the weather hindered the ships sailing. Feb. 1. The said committee went home. The same day or night, Mr. Norton was taken sick, full of pain... Feb.5 ... The ship was stopped for five days to see whether Mr. Norton might, in that time, be fit to expose his body to the seas,... . (Hull, *Public Diary,* p. 205)

February 10, 1662 - Hull stated, "Mr. Norton, Mr. Broadstreet, Mr. Davis, and myself, went on shipboard" in Boston. The next morning they set sail for England. Mr. Davis was Captain William Davis who had been mentioned in Hull's public diary under 1652 as one of two commissioners (the other being John Leveret) sent to Manhattan to negotiate with the Dutch and whose death was later recorded by Hull in 1676. In the December 31, 1661 special session of the General Court, Captain William Davis had been selected to be part of a four person committee allowed to make agreements to procure money for the Commonwealth with the authorization of the General Court (Hull, *Private Diary,* p. 153 and *Public Diary,* p. 205, on Davis see Hull's *Public Diary,* pp. 174 and 242; also Clarke, *Hull,* p. 97, and Shurtleff, vol. 4, pt. 2, pp. 39-40).

February 27, 1662 - Thomas Hutchinson in his *History of the Colony and Province of Massachusetts Bay* (first published in 1764), reported the French ambassador to England sent a letter from London dated February 27, 1662, mentioning the arrival of two deputies from New England who were defending the position that Acadia should not be returned to France. Hutchinson suspected these individuals were Thomas Temple and Colonel Crowne since Cromwell had granted them part of Acadia and Nova Scotia. This is confirmed by the minutes of the Privy Council for February 26, 1662, which state Temple had arrived in London "on Thursday last." Thus Temple, who was Baronet of Nova Scotia[9] and an ardent supporter of Massachusetts Bay, was in London before Norton and Bradstreet arrived (Hutchinson, *History,* edited by Mayo, vol. 1, p. 191 and Sainsbury, *Calendar 1661-1668,* p. 77, item 240).

---

[9] Temple was Baronet of Nova Scotia and Governor of Acadia. These lands were later ceded to the French by the Treaty of Breda in July 1667, but were not turned over until 1670, at which time Temple took up residence in Boston.

March 24, 1662 - Hull and the Massachusetts Bay delegation arrived in London. In his public diary Hull mentioned Norton and Bradstreet's meetings with the Lord Chancellor began a few days after the group arrived. Hull also mentioned the results of these meetings reporting:

> ...they had fair promises of a full grant to their whole desire in the country's [Massachusetts Bay] behalf. But their writing, which they drew in order thereunto, at last unsigned; and another letter, wherein was sundry things for the country to attend which seemed somewhat inconsistent with our patent and former privileges... .

These insights into the proceedings led Clarke to speculate that John Hull may have been an advisor to the committee. Furthermore, the numerous details Hull included in his public diary on the committee selection and preparations as well as his concerns about Norton's illness just prior to their departure, as listed above, additionally support the theory that Hull had some personal involvement in this enterprise. Clarke notes a reference from a letter by a W. W. to the Reverend John Davenport of New Haven dated March 15, 1662, stating "Mr. Bradstreete & Mr. Norton (with Capt. Davies & Mr. Hull the Goldsmith, are gon with them as there attendance) went from Boston the 10th of February in the new ship built there, & are sent as that Collonies Agents to the King" (Hull, *Private Diary,* p. 153 and *Public Diary,* pp. 205-6, also Clarke, *Hull,* p. 97 and Hutchinson, *History,* edited by Mayo, vol. 1, pp. 188-91. For the W.W. letter see, Prince, *Mather Papers,* pp. 169-70 and p. 126 for the key to the shorthand).

[sometime during the 1662 negotiations] - An interesting episode from the 1662 negotiations was related in a later document. In 1684, a committee of the Massachusetts Bay General Court was appointed to produce a response to King Charles II concerning the right of the Commonwealth to retain its charter. In a draft of a report by the committee dated October 30, 1684, outlining a proposed response to the king there is a passage about the mint which included the following detail:

> For in 1662, when our first agents were in England, some of our money was showed by Sir Thomas Temple at the Council-Table, and no dislike thereof manifested by any of those right honourable persons: much less a forbidding of it.

Later retellings of this event embellished the Temple presentation to include the story of Temple telling the king that the Massachusetts coins displayed the royal oak at Whiteladies, where Charles had hidden on September 6, 1650, to escape capture following his defeat at Worcester on September 3rd by Cromwell's forces. Unfortunately, the month and day of Temple's presentation were not recorded in this 1684 document. In fact, the entire passage on the mint was struck from the final version of the official 1684 response. Although Temple arrived in London about a month before Norton and Bradstreet, the 1684 document stated this specific presentation by Temple took place after the Massachusetts Bay delegation was in London. It is interesting to note Temple was a friend of Hull, who was named as one of four executors in Temple's will. Possibly Hull, who may have been an advisor to the delegation, was in London when this event occurred (Crosby, pp. 75-76; the appendix to Hull's *Diary,* p. 282 and Hutchinson, *History,* edited by Mayo, vol. 1, p. 191).

late April, 1662 - In his private diary Hull stated:

> After about one month's stay there [in London], went down into the country, visited my own kindred and town, and went as far as Hull to see my cousin Hoar. Returned safe to London, despatched my business there, and through the good hand of God, arrived again at my own home the 3rd of September, and found all in health.

How long Hull spent visiting relatives is not mentioned nor do we know when he returned to London. In order to arrive in Boston by September 3rd, Hull must have left London by about mid-July. Hull's hometown was Market Harborough. His cousin Leonard Hoar (or Hoare), was a former Massachusetts Bay resident and Harvard graduate of 1650 who had returned to England where he obtained a doctorate in science and medicine from Cambridge University in January 1671, and then returned to Massachusetts Bay at the request of the Third Church in Boston. He arrived on July 8, 1672, to discover Charles Chauncy, President of Harvard had died on February 19th; within a month Hoar was elected by the Board of Overseers as Harvard's new president. However, after three years in office he was forced to resign and died soon thereafter (Hull, *Private Diary,* pp. 153 and on Hoar, the *Public Diary,* pp. 232-33, 235, 236, 238 and 241 as well as Clarke, *Hull,* pp. 156-58).

May 7, 1662 - An order of the General Court to begin minting twopence coins is in the Record of the General Court under this date, which was the date of the commencement of the Court session. Frequently all acts of a session were recorded under one date. In this case the original draft of the order exists and is precisely dated as May 16, 1662 (Crosby, pp. 73-74; Shurtleff, vol. 4, pt. 2, pp. 51-52).

May 16, 1662 - The General Court passed an order for the minting of twopence coins. During their initial year of production, the mint was to produce fifty pounds in twopence for every hundred pounds coined, thereafter twenty pounds of twopence were to be produced for every hundred pounds. The order was to remain in force for seven years. It is not clear if the order refers to troy pounds of sterling consigned to the mint or the value of the finished coins in Massachusetts monetary units of account. I suspect the document relates to production issues and probably refers to troy pounds (Crosby gives the draft of this order on p. 73 with a facsimile of the document, cited by Crosby as Massachusetts Archives, Volume C, p. 86, reproduced on the lower fourth of the plate opposite page 41. The final order, as found in the Record of the General Court, is in Crosby on pp. 73-74 and in Shurtleff, vol. 4, pt. 2, pp. 51-52).

June 28, 1662 - King Charles II sent a letter to the Massachusetts Bay delegation of Norton and Bradstreet confirming the Commonwealth's patent and charter and "...all the privileges and liberties granted unto them in and by the same," along with an offer to renew the charter whenever the Commonwealth desired it. The letter also pardoned subjects for treasonous acts committed during the interregnum but required the Commonwealth's laws to be reviewed and anything against the king's authority or government should be annulled and repealed. He also required an oath of allegiance to the king be administered and that freedom and liberty should be allowed to any individuals wishing to follow the practices of the Church of England. This letter was unfavorably received by the Puritan settlers of Massachusetts Bay. The settlers understood their rights to govern and create laws for the colony were being questioned; further they had little toleration for the Church of England or any other non-

Puritan sect. The citizens of Massachusetts Bay generally considered the mission to have been a failure (Hutchinson, *History,* edited by Mayo, vol. 1, pp. 187-88; the full letter is in *Hutchinson Papers*, vol. 2, pp. 100-4; Sainsbury, *Calendar 1661-1668,* pp. 93-94, items 314-15; Crosby, p. 86, quotes a faulty transcription of a document by Edward Randolph from May 28, 1682, that dates this letter to February. See the entry under May 28, 1682, below; all other sources, including the transcription of the letter, give June as the month).

mid-July - Hull, Norton and Bradstreet must have left London by this time in order to complete the five to seven week crossing back to Massachusetts by the start of September.

September 3, 1662 - John Hull arrived back in Boston on the ship, *Society*, from his trip to England. John Norton and Simon Bradstreet also returned from London on this voyage (Hull, *Private Diary,* pp. 152 and 153 also, *Public Diary,* p. 206, and Clarke, *Hull,* p. 97).

April 23, 1664 - King Charles II appointed Colonel Richard Nichols, George Cartwright, Sir Robert Carr and Samuel Maverick as Royal Commissioners with full power to examine and determine all complaints and appeals concerning the liberties and privileges granted to the New England colonies in various charters (Shurtleff, vol. 4, pt. 2, p. 157; Hutchinson, *History,* edited by Mayo, vol. 1, pp. 443-44 and Sainsbury, *Calendar 1661-1668,* pp. 199-204, items 708-27, item 709 states a copy of the commission was misdated to April 25th).

July 23, 1664 - The English naval gun ships, *The Guinea* and *The Elias*, arrived in Boston Harbor with Nichols and Cartwright. Three days earlier two other gun ships, that had lost their way in a storm, *The Martin* and *The William and Jane,*[10] had arrived in Portsmouth, New Hampshire (Pascataway), with Carr and Maverick. In Boston, Nichols and Cartwright asked Governor Bellingham to summons his Council. The Council met on July 26th and was presented with the king's letter of April 25th explaining the power given to the royal commissioners. The first task of the commissioners was to subdue New Netherland for Britain; they were not able to return and address the situation in Massachusetts Bay until the spring of 1665 (Shurtleff, vol. 4, pt. 2, pp. 157-83; Clarke, *Hull,* p. 135-36, Hart, vol. 1, p. 485; Hull, *Public Diary,* p. 212 and Sainsbury, *Calendar 1661-1668,* p. 221-22, items 774-75).

1665 to 1668 - Maine was temporarily restored to the heirs of Sir Ferdinando Gorges. In 1622 Ferdinando Gorges (1566-1647) and John Mason had received grants from the Council of New England (the successor to the Plymouth Company) for the territory between the Merrimac and Kennebec rivers; Gorges obtained the area now called Maine, while Mason acquired the region now called New Hampshire. In 1639 Gorges was granted a charter as the lord proprietor of Maine. During the English Commonwealth the territory of Maine was gradually annexed to Massachusetts during 1652-1658. In 1652 Kittery and Agamenticus (York) were annexed, in 1654 Wells, Saco and Kennebunkport followed and in 1658 Casco Bay (Portland) and the surrounding areas of Black Point, Spurwink and Blue Point were

---

[10] Hart, vol. 1, p. 485, says one of the ships was the *William and Mary* but as this event predated the reign of William and Mary it seems more likely the ship was the *William and Jane* mentioned in a different context in Hull's *Public Diary,* p. 201. There was also a ship named the *William and John* (*Records of Suffolk County Court: 1671-1680*, part 2, pp. 858-59).

added. Maine was called the county of Yorkshire in Massachusetts Bay. In 1664 Parliament decided in favor of a claim brought by Gorges's grandson against Massachusetts and acted on Mason's claim making New Hampshire an independent royal colony (Merrimac remained with Massachusetts). Three years after assenting to Parliament's decision, Massachusetts reasserted their claim to Maine, finally purchasing the Gorges claim in 1677 for £1,250. Massachusetts was proprietor of Maine until the new Massachusetts Bay charter of 1691 made Maine an integral part of the colony (For details on Maine see, Palfrey, vol. 1, p. 403 and Sainsbury, *Calendar 1661-1668,* pp. 214, 301, 306 and 608, items 748-51, 1001, 1010 and 1835 and for New Hampshire, pp. 310-15, items 1020-21 and 1024).

May 1, 1665 - Colonel Richard Nichols arrived back in Massachusetts Bay from New York; the other commissioners had returned a few months earlier from courts and inquests they had been conducting with various Indian tribes and other New England settlements (Hull, *Public Diary,* p. 216).

May 8, 1665 - The king's commissioners sent a letter to the General Court requesting a copy of the Commonwealth's laws to see if any were "Contrary & derogatory to the king's authority & Government" (Shurtleff, vol. 4, pt. 2, p. 194; Crosby, p. 77).

May 18, 1665 - Expecting bad news from the royal commissioners, the General Court passed an order they hoped would placate the king. They stated:

> This Court, accounting it theire duty, according to their poore ability, to acknowledge their humble thanks to his majesty for his many & continued gracious expressions of his tender care & fatherly respect to his colony, doe order that in the best commodity that may be procured in this his colony... [be acquired for the king's navy to the value of £500].

However, due to a shortage of funds the order was never carried out (Shurtleff, vol. 4, pt. 2, p. 150 and Crosby, p. 77).

May 24, 1665 - The king's commissioners send a letter to the General Court requesting twenty six articles be repealed or amended in the Commonwealth's laws. The Massachusetts laws had been published as a book arranged topically rather than chronologically, so that the various regulations on a specific subject were listed together under a main subject heading, with the various headings arranged alphabetically. The laws regarding the mint and coinage were listed under the subject heading "Money." In the printed edition of the laws, published in 1660 at Cambridge, Massachusetts, the section on Money was found on pages 61-62. The king's commissioners referred to this printed edition of the laws in their comments. Article Twenty-two of their letter requested the repeal of the coining act stating,

> That, page 61, title Money, the law That a mint house, etc, be repealed; for coyning is a royall prerogative, for the usurping of which ye act of indemnity is only a salvo. (Shurtleff, vol. 4, pt. 2, pp. 211-13 with the quote on p. 213; Crosby, p. 77, Toppan, "Right to Coin," p. 220 and Cushing, *Laws,* vol. 1, pp. 131-32 which reproduces pp. 61-62 of the 1660 edition of the laws)

August 7, 1665 - Some ships arrived in Boston from England under the command of Captain Pierce, which were to return to England with masts for the king's navy.[11] Apparently a letter arrived on the ships, for on that same day the Royal Commissioner Samuel Maverick presented a document (called a *Significavit*)[12] to the General Court from Secretary of State, William Morice, in London explaining the king ordered a committee of four or five representatives to answer on behalf of the Commonwealth; the group was to include Governor Richard Bellingham and Major William Hawthorne. Hull noted in his diary the document had not been specifically addressed to any person or group (it was not superscribed) and that it lacked an official seal (Hull, *Public Diary,* p. 222).

September 11, 1666 - The General Court ordered two very large masts be procured by the Deputy Governor, Francis Willoughby, and shipped to England for presentation to Sir William Warren and navy commissioner Captain John Taylor as gifts for the king's navy "…as a testimony of loyalty & affection" (Shurtleff, vol. 4, pt. 2, p. 318 and Crosby, p. 77).

September 12, 1666 - An entry in the diary of John Hull explained the General Court considered what to do in response to the writ of *Significavit.* Hull stated it was decided to send a letter and a gift of two very large masts for the king's navy, but that the Commonwealth would not send any representatives (Hull, *Public Diary,* pp. 222-23 and Crosby, p. 77).

October 10, 1666 - The General Court ordered the two masts obtained in September be sent to England. Additionally, "a shipps loading more" was to be contracted as a present to the king for the following year (Shurtleff, vol. 4, pt. 2, pp. 327-28 and Crosby, p. 77).

December 24, 1666 – Joseph Sanderson, who was Robert Sanderson's second son, died at the age of 24. Joseph had apprenticed at the Hull shop. An inventory of his possessions at the time of his death verifies he was active as a silversmith. However, Joseph did not own essential but expensive equipment such as a forge or an anvil, indicating he was working in the Hull shop as a journeyman at the time of his death (Kane, pp. 24 and 879-80).

May 15, 1667 - The General Court appointed another committee to obtain some annual allowance for the Commonwealth from the profits of the mint "…in consideration of the charge the country hath binn at in erecting a mint house, & for the use of it for so many yeares, without any considerable sattisfaction." The committee members were: Thomas Danforth, an Assistant to Governor Bellingham and first Commissioner for the Commonwealth in the United Colonies, Major General John Leveret, also an Assistant and Commissioner in reserve, Captain George Corvin (or Corwin), one of two Deputies from Salem, Anthony Stoddard, one of two Deputies from Boston and William Parks, one of two Deputies from Roxbury (Shurtleff, vol. 4, pt. 2, pp. 330 and 333; Crosby, p. 78).

---

[11] The Royal Navy regularly purchased masts at a cost of £95 to £115 each (Clarke, *Hull,* p. 45 and Carlton).

[12] A *Significavit* was a writ usually issued by the Chancery in ecclesiastical cases for the arrest of excommunicated persons and heretics.

July 1, 1667 - The date of the conclusion of the apprenticeships of Jeremiah Dummer and Samuel Paddy. Hull had stated in his diary that he had taken the two as apprentices on July 1, 1659, for a period of eight years (Hull, *Private Diary,* p. 150).

October 4, 1667 - The committee of the General Court finalized an agreement with Hull and Sanderson stating the minters would pay £40 into the treasury within six months "In Consideration of the Countrys disbursments in the said aediffices, & for Interest the Generall Court hath therein." Presumably this payment was to reimburse the government for construction costs and appears to have been made to acquire the rights to the government's interest in the mint buildings. Moreover, Hull and Sanderson agreed to pay £10 annually to the Commonwealth for the next seven years (Shurtleff, vol. 4, pt. 2, p. 347 and Crosby, p. 78).

October 9, 1667 - The fall session of the General Court was convened on October 9th and the October 4th agreement was officially recorded in the Massachusetts Bay Court Record by the secretary of the General Court. In a codicil to the document, the Court thanked the committee for their efforts and requested the agreement be entered into the Court record (Shurtleff, vol. 4, pt. 2, p. 347 and Crosby, p. 78).

May 1668 - A diary entry by Hull mentions "The General Court sent a shipload of masts as a present to the king's majesty" (Hull, *Public Diary,* p. 227 and Crosby, p. 77).

May 19, 1669 - The General Court passed a second order to prevent the exportation of more than twenty shillings in Massachusetts silver per person from leaving the Commonwealth, similar to the order of August 22, 1654, but increasing the number of searchers from nine to ten and redistributing them as follows: Captain James Oliver and Thomas Brattle for Boston, Captain John Allen for Charlestown, Edmond Batter[13] for Salem, Elias Stileman for Piscattaqua (Portsmouth, New Hampshire), Samuel Ward for Marblehead, Ensign Fisher for Dedham, Moses Paine for Braintree, William Kerley for Marlboro and Lawrence Bliss for Springfield. Their powers were broadened and described more forcefully, the searchers were:

> ...impowred & required to search for & seize all moneyes of the Coyne of this Jurisdiction that shall bee found or discovered in any ship ... [or] in any person's pocket, cloake, bag, Portmantle, or any other thing belonging to them... [The searchers were further empowered to]... breake open any chest, Trunck, Box, Cabbin, Cask, Truss, or any other suspected place or thing where they or any of them conceive money may be Concealld & seize the same; and also they or either of them are empowered to require such assistants from any Constables or others as to them may seeme Expedient, who are to aid them, upon the penalty of fforty shillings fine for every neglect. (Shurtleff, vol. 4, pt. 2, pp. 420-21 and Crosby, p. 79)

June 2, 1669 - A proposal was debated to increase the value of Spanish eight reales to six shillings and smaller denominations proportionally. Also, an individual was to be appointed

---

[13] The 1669 edition of the new laws and 1672 edition of the complete laws of Massachusetts lists Batter's first name as Edward. See Cushing, *Laws,* vol. 1, p. 218 and vol. 2, p. 344.

to put a stamp or mark on each coin that was full weight and of sterling fineness. Underweight or debased coins would not be marked and no one would be enjoined to accept the unmarked coins as lawful payment. The legislation did not define a full weight coin but in Massachusetts Bay a 17 pennyweight (408 grains) eight reales was considered a full weight example. This legislation passed in the House of Deputies but was defeated in the House of Magistrates (Crosby, pp. 105-6).

November 16, 1669 - John Hull departed Boston for London on business "to settle all former accounts with my uncle, and all persons with whom I had dealings." He arrived at the house of his uncle, Thomas Parriss, on January 5, 1670, and stayed until June 8th. Parriss served as Hull's agent in London, acquiring merchandise for Hull to sell in Boston (Hull, *Private Diary,* pp. 159-60).

August 3, 1670 - Hull landed back in Boston (Hull, *Private Diary,* pp. 159-60).

[1671] - An undated proposal by Richard Wharton was assigned to 1671 by Joseph B. Felt, who organized the Massachusetts Archives financial papers in the early nineteenth century. This proposal suggested increasing the value of a Boston shilling to 14d, a sixpence to 7d, a threepence to 4d and twopence to 3d and also increasing the value of Spanish American eight reales "dollars" to 90d (7s6d) per ounce. This would value a 17 pennyweight eight reales at 76.5d, which at 14d per shilling, would equal 5s6.5d in Massachusetts coinage. Spanish gold pistoles were also rated in this proposal as well as penalties against clipping with provisions to have swore officers of the Commonwealth weigh and assay coins upon request. The proposal was not adopted (Crosby, pp. 106-7).

October 18, 1671 - September 27, 1680 - Ledger entries concerning production at the mint survive from this period in John Hull's unpublished ledger C, which is preserved in the New England Historic Genealogical Society in Boston, Massachusetts, designated as Manuscript Cb 110. A transcription of the text of the mint account and a commentary on each transaction is presented in Appendix I.

May 15, 1672 - The General Court denied a petition by Joseph Jenks that would have allowed him to coin money. Jenks had been the master craftsman at the Hammersmith iron foundry in Saugus, Massachusetts, from the start of operations in 1648 until the foundry closed ca. 1670 (Shurtleff, vol. 4, pt. 2, p. 528 and Crosby, p. 79).

October 8, 1672 - The General Court realized,

> ...peeces of eight are more value to carry out of the country then they will yield to mint into our coyne, by reason whereof peeces of eight which might else come to coyning are carried out of the country.

To curtail this exportation of Spanish silver, the General Court increased the value of a full weight eight reales to six shillings (or 33.33% above the value of the silver content of a full weight eight reales based on the English standard). Further, as the law observed, "inasmuch as few or no peeces of eight are of that weight" all Spanish silver, whatever the weight, was to be stamped by Hull and Sanderson with the letters NE and the true weight of the coin. This 33.33% crying-up made Spanish coins more valuable than Massachusetts silver, which had a face value that was only 22.5% above the silver content value based on the English standard. There is no evidence the weighing and stamping of Spanish silver ever took place [see figure 34] (Shurtleff, vol. 4, pt. 2, p. 533-34; Crosby, p. 80 and the appendix to Hull's *Diary,* p. 296).

November 1673 - Hull entered in his diary, "November, I accept Samuel Clark, son of Jonas Clark, as an apprentice for eight years" (Hull, *Private Diary,* p. 162, this entry follows a December entry but does not necessarily mean it refers to November of the following year, 1674, see footnote 1 on p. 149 of the printed edition of the diary explaining entries were not always added on the day of the event. On Clark, or Clarke, see Kane, pp. 286-87).

1674 - John du Plisse was convicted in Boston of passing pewter counterfeit coins, possibly counterfeit Massachusetts silver (Scott, *Counterfeiting in Colonial America,* pp. 16-17 and Glasser, p. 12).

September 1, 1674 - Joseph Blandchard and George Grimes were charged with coining base money and held over on £20 bail to appear at the next county court in Cambridge, Massachusetts. There are no further records on this case (Scott, *Counterfeiting in Colonial America,* p. 17).

March 12, 1675 - The Committee for Trade and Foreign Plantations was instituted. This group consisted of appointed members from the Privy Council who were to meet weekly and report back to the Council. It replaced an earlier committee organized during the restoration of Charles II in 1660. The earlier group, known as the Council for Plantations, or, the Council for Foreign Plantations, changed its name to the Council for Trade and Plantations in November of 1672 (Sainsbury, *Calendar 1675-1676,* pp. 182-83, items 460-61, on the name change in 1672 see Sainsbury, *Calendar 1669-1674,* pp. 432 and 438, items 961 and 974).

May 1675 - The Calendar of State Papers records the contents of a notebook by the British Secretary of State, Sir Joseph Williamson,[14] covering the years 1674-1677 that contained comments on various British colonies, but focused on Newfoundland. Under the date of May 1675, the notebook included several questions and observations on Massachusetts Bay including information on the Massachusetts Mint taken from the petition filed by the Council for Plantations on April 30, 1661, and attributed to John Gifford. Williamson stated, "They melt down all English money brought in there into their own coin, making every shilling 15d to avoid the carrying it out" (Sainsbury, *Calendar 1675-1676,* pp. 154-63, item 405 with the quote on p. 156).

May 12, 1675 - At a session of the General Court convened on May 12th it was recorded that the former agreement with the mint masters had expired, therefore a committee of any three magistrates was authorized to make a new agreement for coining money,

---

[14] Sir Joseph Williamson was a member of the Privy Council and Secretary of State June 1674 - February 10, 1679.

...with such persons as they shall thinke meet [meet = suitable], and to make such an Agreement with them for the Coyning of the mony of this Jurisdiction as may be most encouraging to all persons who have bullion to bring in the same mint.

The magistrates included the Governor, Deputy Governor and the eleven Assistants (Shurtleff, vol. 5, pp. 29-30 and Crosby, p. 81).

June 3, 1675 - Hull and Sanderson signed a seven year renewal of their mint contract. They agreed to lower mint fees from 15d per 20s to 12d per 20s minted (20s equaled three troy ounces thus reducing the fee from 5d per troy ounce to 4d per troy ounce) but they retained the wastage fee of 1d per troy ounce of silver. The agreement also required the minters to pay an annual fee to the treasury of £20 (up from £10); in return Hull and Sanderson were allowed to, "Continue to mint what Silver bullion shall Come in for this Seven yeares next to Come, if either of them live so long,... ." The General Cout mint committee members signing the agreement were Governor John Leveret and two of his Assistants, Simon Bradstreet and Edward Tyng (Crosby, pp. 81-82).

June 17, 1675 - On this date Hull recorded the first coin order in his private ledger at the new rate which lowered Hull's total fees to 5d per troy ounce and increased the customer's yield from 74d per troy ounce of sterling to 75d per troy ounce. The order was for 217 troy ounces of silver that was turned into coinage and then delivered to the customer on July 8th (New England Historic Genealogical Society, Boston Massachusetts, Personal Ledger of John Hull, Manuscript Cb 110, vol. 1, ff. 36v-27r).

June 20, 1675 - February 12, 1677 - King Philip's War. An assault at the colonial settlement in Swansea on June 20th soon escalated into a full scale war with the Narraganset, Nipmuck and Wampanoag tribes allied against the colonists and their Mohegan allies. Captain Thomas Savage led an expedition from Boston to attack the Mount Hope (Bristol, Rhode Island) headquarters of the Indian leader of the Wampanoags, Sachem Metacom (sometimes Metacomet or Pometacom), known as King Philip. Over the next year several major battles took place until Philip was finally killed at Mount Hope on August 11, 1676 (in his public diary on p. 242 John Hull gives the date as August 12th). Following the death of Philip there were no more major battles, but several skirmishes took place until the signing of a treaty on February 12, 1677. At the outbreak of the war the General Court appointed a "Committee for the war" of which John Hull was a member and treasurer (Hart, vol. 1, pp. 542-54 and Clarke, Hull, pp. 165-77).

July 9, 1675 - A special session of the General Court was convened to levy taxes and impress materials needed for a military expedition against the Indians. Also, the agreement between Hull and Sanderson and the committee of the General Court dated June 3rd was approved by the General Court and entered into the Massachusetts Court Record (Shurtleff, vol. 5, pp. 43-44 and Crosby, p. 81).

December 2, 1675 - The minutes of the committee meeting of the Lords of Trade and Plantations state a report entitled, "A narrative of the settlement of the Corporation of Massachusetts Bay and Capt. Wyborne's account of things in 1673," was submitted to the Lords on December 1st by Robert Mason and read at the committee meeting of December

2nd. Captain John Wyborne had spent three months in Boston in 1673 while his ship, the H.M.S. *Garland*, was being supplied and refitted. In his narrative on Massachusetts Bay Captain Wyborne complained of several irregularities, arbitrary laws and resistance to the king's commissioners. Concerning money he stated:

> ...as soon as any English money is brought there, it is melted down into their coin, making of each shilling fifteen-pence to keep it from being carried out again. (Sainsbury, *Calendar 1675-1676,* item 721 on pp. 306-8 with the quote on p. 306)

March 10, 1676 - The date of the composition of a letter at Whitehall Palace in Westminster in the name of King Charles II to the government and magistrates of Massachusetts Bay requesting them to send agents to London within six months of receipt of the letter to argue the case for Massachusetts against the claims of Robert Mason (for New Hampshire) and Ferdinando Gorges (for Maine).[15] The letter also requested that the bearer of the letter, Edward Randolph, be admitted into the Massachusetts Bay Council so he could report to the king on their proceedings (Toppan, *Randolph,* vol. 2, pp. 192-94 and Sainsbury, *Calendar 1675-1676,* p. 358, item 838).

March 20, 1676 - Edward Randolph received instructions from the king to deliver the royal letter to Massachusetts Bay. Also appended were supplementary instructions from the Lords of the Committee for Trade and Plantations detailing twelve areas of inquiry on which Randolph was to bring back intelligence; these areas of inquiry concerned the government and laws of the colony, the population, religion, military strength, economic resources, imports and exports, boundaries, taxes, relationships with other colonies and related information. Included was an abstract of information on Massachusetts which Randolph was to verify; there was neither mention of coinage in this abstract, nor was it directly targeted as an area of inquiry (Toppan, *Randolph,* vol. 2, pp. 196-201 and Sainsbury, *Calendar 1675-1676,* pp. 360-63, items 844-49).

June 10, 1676 - Edward Randolph arrived in Massachusetts Bay on the ship, *Welcome,* as a royal informer. During his stay Randolph made trips to Portsmouth, New Hampshire, and New Plymouth (Toppan, *Randolph,* vol. 1, Memoir, pp. 52-58 and texts in vol. 2, pp. 194 and 201-2, also Hall, *Randolph,* pp. 20-21 and Sainsbury, *Calendar 1675-1676,* pp. 402-3, item 945).

June 17, 1676 - Within a week of landing in Boston, Randolph wrote a long letter to the British Secretary of State, Sir Henry Coventry,[16] including much information on Massachusetts Bay but with no reference to minting (Sainsbury, *Calendar 1675-1676,* pp. 406-9, item 953).

---

[15] The heirs of Mason and Gorges had pressed for their claims at the time of the Restoration, but Charles II did not address this issue until after his war with Holland had been concluded by the Treaty of Westminster on February 9, 1674. Unfortunately just as the king was ready to address the situation, Massachusetts Bay was unable to respond due to the economic strains caused by the Indian war against "King Philip."

[16] Henry Coventry was Secretary of State July 8, 1672 - April 1680.

July 30, 1676 - Edward Randolph departed from Boston for London, arriving in Dover on September 10th (Toppan, *Randolph,* vol. 1, Memoir, pp. 52-58 and texts in vol. 2, pp. 194 and 201-2, also Hall, *Randolph,* pp. 20-21 and Sainsbury, *Calendar 1675-1676,* pp. 402-3, item 945).

September 20, 1676 - Soon after returning to London, Randolph sent a report to the king on September 20th detailing his meetings with numerous New England government officials in Massachusetts and New Hampshire. He explained the Governor of Massachusetts Bay,

> ...freely declared to me that the lawes made by your Majestie and your parliament obligeth them in nothing but what consists with the interest of that colony, that the legislative power is and abides in them solely to act and make lawes by virtue of a charter from your Majesties royall father.

Randolph went on to state he met several colonists who complained "...of the arbitrary government and oppression of their magistrates and doe hope your Majestie will be pleased to free them from this bondage by establishing your own royall authority among them..." (Toppan, *Randolph,* vol. 2, pp. 216-25 with quotes from pp. 219 and 223, also in *Hutchinson Papers,* vol. 2, pp. 240-51 with the quotes from p. 243 and 247 and Sainsbury, *Calendar 1675-1676,* pp. 455-66, item 1037).

October 12, 1676 - Randolph sent a lengthy report to the members of the Committee for Trade and Plantations detailing much information and presenting several criticisms of the government in Massachusetts Bay. The report was read at the meeting of November 16, 1676. Randolph answered each of the twelve areas of inquiry the committee had requested him to investigate. Part of his answer to their first inquiry, "Where the Legislative and Executive Powers of the Government of New England are seated," was a discussion of the structure of the government which included the following comments concerning Massachusetts coinage:

> And as a marke of soveraignty they coin mony stamped with the inscription Mattachusets and a tree in the center, on the one side, and New England, with the year 1652 and the value of the piece, on the reverse. Their money is of the standard of England for finenesse, the shillings weigh three pennyweight troy, in value of English money ninepence farthing, and the smaller coins proportionable. These are the current monies of the colony and not to be transported thence, except twenty shillings for necessary expenses, on penalty of confiscation of the whole visible estate of the transporters.
>
> All the money is stamped with these figures, 1652, that year being the era of the commonwealth, wherein they erected themselves into a free state, enlarged their dominions, subjected adjacent colonies under their obedience, and summoned deputies to sit in the generall court, which year is still commemorated on their coin.

Interestingly, at this point in time, Randolph did not include the coinage comments under his answer to the second point of inquiry which was "What Laws and ordinances, are now in force there, derogatory or contradictory to those of England, and what Oath is prescribed by the Government." To this question Randolph included ten points but nothing on coinage (*Hutchinson Papers,* vol. 2, pp. 210-41 with the quote on pp. 213-14; also in Toppan, *Randolph,* vol. 2, pp. 225-59 with the quote on p. 229; Toppan, "Right to Coin," p. 221 and Sainsbury, *Calendar 1675-1676,* pp. 463-68, item 1067. Crosby, pp. 75-76, gives an incomplete quote which he attributes to a publication of 1769, undoubtedly Crosby is referring to the *Hutchinson Papers,* which is an anthology of documents on Massachusetts history first published in 1769 by Thomas Hutchinson).

October 31, 1676 - William Stoughton and Peter Bulkley had been selected as agents to represent Massachusetts at the king's court and on this day set sail for London (Hull, *Public Diary,* p. 242).

November 17, 1676 - Randolph sent a letter to King Charles II giving general information on the state of affairs in Massachusetts Bay and explaining it seemed Massachusetts would not send over any agents since they felt they had not disobeyed any royal command (Toppan, *Randolph,* vol. 2, pp. 259-61 and Sainsbury, *Calendar 1675-1676,* pp. 494-95, item 1138).

December 13, 1676 - An undated letter from the Massachusetts Bay Governor John Leveret and the General Court was presented in London by the Massachusetts agents and read in the King's Council on this day. The letter apologized for not sending agents earlier. They stated the colony had been in the middle of a war against several Indian tribes and all their resources had been expended on defense, therefore, they had not been able to address the king's request. However, now that the main enemy, the Indian Sachem known as King Philip, was dead, they were assigning William Stoughton and Peter Bulkley to be their agents defending the Massachusetts claims to New Hampshire and Maine (Toppan, *Randolph,* vol. 2, pp. 262-65 and Sainsbury, *Calendar 1675-1676,* p. 513, item 1186).

May 6, 1677 - Edward Randolph forwarded a brief memorandum to the Committee on Foreign Affairs entitled, "Representation of ye Affaires of New England," or sometime referred to as, "The present State of the affaires of New England." This document listed eight accusations against Massachusetts Bay as follows: (1) they were usurpers without a royal charter, (2) they did not take an oath of allegiance to the king, (3) they protected Goffe and Whaley, who had participated in the murder of Charles I, (4) "They Coyne money with their owne Impress," (5) they had murdered some English Quakers because of their religious beliefs, (6) they opposed the king's commissioners in the settlement of New Hampshire and Maine, (7) they imposed an oath of fidelity to Massachusetts Bay on all inhabitants and finally, (8) they violated the acts of trade and navigation robbing the king of his custom duties. This document was forwarded to the Lords of Trade and Plantations for discussion at their meeting on June 7th, which led to further investigations (Hall, *Randolph,* pp. 33-36 and Toppan, *Randolph,* vol. 2, pp. 265-68 as well as Toppan, "Right to Coin," p. 221 and Sainsbury, *Calendar 1677-1680,* pp. 79-80, items 218-20. Also, under the date 1680 this list is found in *Hutchinson Papers,* vol. 2, pp. 264-65 and Toppan, *Randolph,* vol. 3, pp. 78-79).

June 2, 1677 – This is the date on proposal of a committee of the General Court produced in consultation with John Hull[17] to induce individuals to bring bullion to the mint and stop the exportation of coinage. Two options were proposed; one was to raise the value of the current coin or make the shilling nine to twelve grains lighter, while the other option was to abolish minting fees by financing the mint out of the treasury of the Commonwealth. The legislators stated the cost of a free mint was unknown but that it would certainly be a substantial burden or as they put it, "...we find the Charge uncertain but great." Further, they candidly stated both options were "attended with Difficulty." They felt if the General Court would double the duties on imported wine, brandy and rum, the funds could be used to partially pay the cost of the mint. The proposal died in committee and never came up for a vote (Crosby, p. 108 and appendix to Hull's *Diary,* p. 299, also Shurtleff, vol. 5, pp. 131-33 for election results).

June 7, 1677 - The minutes of the meeting of the Committee of the Lords of Trade and Plantations requested the cases of Mason and Gorges against Massachusetts Bay be expedited. Additionally, Randolph's memorandum to the Committee on Foreign Affairs was forwarded and read at this meeting. In discussing the memorandum the Lords decided they should seek legal opinions before acting. On June 8th an order of the king in Council stated the Lords of Trade and Plantations were to seek the opinions of such judges as they saw fit. Also, on the 8th, the Lords of Trade and Plantations issued a report stating the Massachusetts agents were to be notified that they would be required to answer the observations of Randolph as well as defend against the claims of Mason and Gorges (Toppan, *Randolph,* vol. 2, pp. 268-72 and Sainsbury, *Calendar 1677-1680,* pp. 102-3, items 289-90 and 294 for the events of June 7-12 and pp. 79-80, item 218 on the document of May 6th).

June 12, 1677 - The minutes of the meeting of the Committee of the Lords of Trade and Plantations stated the committee discussed the eight point memorandum by Edward Randolph. Under the heading, "Concerning Misdemeanours of the Bostonians, etc." the Lords responded stating Randolph's first and second points were to be referred to the judges and the King's Council, the committee would inquire into the third point and examine the Massachusetts charter on the fourth and fifth points, while the sixth, seventh and eighth points were to be "looked upon as matters of State." The fourth point, on the coinage of money, was mentioned in the same sentence in which they responded to the fifth point on the execution of some English Quakers in 1659. The committee stated,

> The Fourth Head concerning Coining of Money And The Fifth that they have put His Majesties Subjects to death for Religion are to be referred, and examination to bee made whether, by their Charter, or by the right of making Laws they are enabled soe to doe. (Toppan, *Randolph,* vol. 2, pp. 271-72; Toppan, "Right to Coin," p. 221 and Sainsbury, *Calendar 1677-1680,* pp. 103-4, item 294)

---

[17] There were three committee members, their names and positions as of the elections of May 23, 1677, follow: from the eleven members of the House of Magistrates, Joseph Dudley, the second commissioner for the United Colonies; and from the thirty-one members of the House of Deputies, Richard Waldron, representative from Dedham and Daniel Fisher (or Ffisher) representative from Dover (now in New Hampshire). John Hull was not a member of either house but he had been elected Treasurer of the General Court.

July 19, 1677 - The Lords of Trade and Plantations conducted hearings on the charges made by Randolph. Randolph was brought in to testify. Then, William Stoughton and Peter Bulkley, who had traveled to London as agents of the Commonwealth to defend the Massachusetts Bay claims to New Hampshire against the claim of Robert Mason and to Maine against the claim of Ferdinando Gorges, were brought in and ordered to defend the Commonwealth against Randolph's charges. According to a report of the meeting made by the Lords of Trade and forwarded to the king by the Lord of the Privy Seal, the agents answered that they had not been authorized to speak on behalf of Massachusetts except in the land claim disputes. However, they consented to reply "as private men, and His Majesties subjects, as far as they were acquainted with the occurrence and transactions of ye Government under which they had lived." Concerning coining the minutes report:

> That Upon the Article where they are charged to have coyned money, they confess it, and say they were necessitated to it, about the yeare 1652, for the support of their Trade, and have not, hitherto, discontinued it, as being never excepted against, or disallowed by His Majesty And doe therefore submit this matter to His Majectie and beg pardon if they have offended. (Toppan, *Randolph,* vol. 2, pp. 274-77 with quote on 276, Toppan, "Right to Coin," p. 221 and Sainsbury, *Calendar 1677-1680,* pp. 122-23, items 350-51)

July 20, 1677 - An order of the king in Council was issued that the Lords of Trade and Plantations were to meet every Thursday until the business with the Massachusetts agents was resolved. The order contained a summary of the reply made by the Massachusetts agents to Randolph's charges. The agents did not respond to Randolph's first point (that the Massachusetts colonists were usurpers without a royal charter) so Stoughton and Bulkley's reply to the coining charge was summarized as point three (even though it was the fourth point in Randolph's memorandum) as follows:

> (3). The coining of money : About 1652 the necessity of the country calling for it in support of commerce, they began to coin silver money to pass current in their own colony and not to be exported, which money they have continued to coin, no prohibition having been received from the King, for which they implore the King's pardon, and beg that the privilege being of prejudice to none yet extremely useful to the colony may be continued under what impress the King pleases. (Sainsbury, *Calendar 1677-1680,* pp. 124-26, item 354 with the quote on p. 125)

July 27, 1677 - The Massachusetts Bay agents were again called to a meeting of the Committee of the Lords of Trade and Plantations. According to the committee minutes the agents were told the decision of the committee on several points. The committee asked for a commission to look into the boundary disputes, they insisted the Navigation Act be "religiously observed," and explained that some Massachusetts Bay laws would need to be revised while any future laws should be sent to the Privy Council for review. Concerning the mint the minutes stated:

> That Whereas they had transgressed, in presuming to Coyne Money, which is an Act of Sovereignty, and to which they were by noe Grant sufficiently

authorized, That tho' His Majesty may, upon due application, grant them a Charter containing such a Power; yet they must sollicit His Majesties Pardon for the offence that is past. (Toppan, *Randolph,* vol. 2, pp. 277-80 with the quote on p. 278 and Toppan, "Right to Coin," p. 222)

The committee assured Stoughton and Bulkley that "His Majestie will not destroy their Charter, but rather by a Supplemental one to bee given them, set all things right that are now amiss" (Toppan, *Randolph,* vol. 2, pp. 277-80 with the quote on pp. 279-80 and and Sainsbury, *Calendar 1677-1680,* pp. 135-36, item 371).

August 2, 1677 - Stoughton and Bulkley were again brought before the committee of the Lords of Trade and Plantations where they were further lectured on the errors of the Massachusetts government and told what they must do. In regard to the mint the Lords were rather lenient stating that the agents would need to discuss the matter with the Attorney General about soliciting the king's pardon for past offenses of coining money without authority. Also, the Attorney General was to attend to the action:

> That an Additional Charter bee prepared containing a Power from His Majestie to Coyn Money, and to make all forreigne coins current in that Country. (Toppan, *Randolph,* vol. 2, pp. 281-84 with the quote on p. 283 and Toppan, "Right to Coin," p. 222)

The news of the pronouncements of the Lords of Trade and Plantations was gratefully received in Massachusetts since the charter had not been abolished and the Commonwealth hoped they would be granted a minting license (Hall, *Randolph,* pp. 37-39; Palfrey, vol. 2, pp. 212-13 and Sainsbury, *Calendar 1677-1680,* pp. 140-42, items 380-81).

August 1677 - By personal agreement with his customers Hull discounted his mint fees to 12d per £1 of coins minted. The last order in Hull's personal ledger at the full authorized fee of 4d per troy ounce and 1d for wastage per ounce (totaling 5d per ounce) was an order consigned to the mint on July 13, 1677, but with no completion or delivery date recorded. The first order listed at the rate of 12d per £1 of coins minted was an order consigned to the mint on May 3, 1677, but not completed for delivery until August 29, 1677 (New England Historic Genealogical Society, Boston Massachusetts, Personal Ledger of John Hull, Manuscript Cb 110, vol. 1, ff. 133v-134r).

October 10, 1677 - The decisions of the fall session of the Massachusetts General Court were recorded under this date. A proclamation was issued that a day of Thanksgiving would be observed on November 15th. The preamble to the proclamation stated the reasons for the observance were because God had spared them from an outbreak of an infectious disease and because God had been on their side in the London proceedings,

> ...frustrating the hopes of our Malicious Adversaries and graciously considering us in the midst of our fears, giving us favour in the eyes of our Soveraign Lord and King, and his most horourable Council as Letters received from Agents do fully inform us... .(Cushing, *Laws,* vol. 3, p. 519. This preamble is found in the printed version of the law but it was not included in the record of the General Court, see Shurtleff, vol. 5, p. 156; the

preamble is summarized in Sainsbury, *Calendar 1677-1680,* p. 164, item 429)

Also, an order in the record of the General Court under this date stated the treasurer would provide the king with ten barrels of Cranberries, two hogsheads of their best samp[18] and three thousand codfish (Shurtleff, vol. 5, p. 156 and Crosby, p. 82).

Additionally, two other laws were instituted. The General Court resolved that "...the acts of Trade and Navigation be exactly and punctually observed by this his Majesties Colony" (Cushing, *Laws,* vol. 3, p. 517; Shurtleff, vol. 5, p. 155 and listed in Sainsbury, *Calendar 1677-1680,* pp. 172, item 460 as having been passed on October 26th). But in partial defiance of another suggestion from the Lords of Trade and Plantations the General Court revived the oath of fidelity formerly required of inhabitants of the Commonwealth "requiring all persons as well inhabitants as strangers (that have not taken it) to take an Oath of Fidelity to the Country" [the country refers to Massachusetts Bay]. (Cushing, *Laws,* vol. 3, pp. 516-17 and Shurtleff, vol. 5, p. 154-55).

October 22, 1677 - The General Court sent a letter to their agents in London, Stoughton and Bulkley, stating they were optimistic about the future and would forward an additional £1,000 to them so they could continue their work. The letter encouraged them to defend the Massachusetts patents to New Hampshire and Maine. The Court also stated, "As for the coynage, or any other additionall priviledge offered, (not prejudiciall to our charter,) wee would not slight, but humbly accept." They also encouraged the agents to protect the shipping and fishing rights of the Commonwealth. The letter concluded that they hoped the men of Portsmouth would be able to send the king a ship load of masts if the king would send a ship to pick them up and from Boston; the General Court would send the king some codfish, samp and cranberries (Shurtleff, vol. 5, pp. 163-64; Crosby, p. 82 and Hall, *Randolph,* pp. 39-40).

October 24, 1677 - Governor Leveret, with the consent of the General Court, sent a letter to the British Secretary of State, Sir Joseph Williamson. A summary of the letter recorded in the State Papers of the Public Record Office in London explained the letter thanked the secretary for his "...most friendly and christian rediness to promote the equity and righteousness of their cause..." in the face of false representations made against them (Sainsbury, *Calendar 1677-1680,* p. 171, item 456).

December 16, 1677 - Stoughton and Bulkley forwarded a petition to the king requesting that the New Hampshire towns of Dover, Portsmouth, Exeter and Hampton remain under the jurisdiction of Massachusetts. This letter gave further details on the agents's assessment of the question concerning the mint. The summary of the petition stated the agents explained that they had:

> ...received a signification of the King's promise of pardon to the Massachusetts Government, and particularly of the offence of coining money without the King's authority, with His majesty's license for setting

---

[18] Samp is coarsely ground Indian corn made into a porridge.

up a Mint within said Colony for coining gold and silver with such impress as His Majesty shall think fit to pass current in said colony only... [the agents then went on to] implore His Majesty to add the grant of these four towns, with the land and royalties, and the liberty of coining money. (Sainsbury, *Calendar 1677-1680,* pp. 211-12, item 587 with the quote on p. 211)

December 22, 1677 - Hull as Treasurer of Massachusetts Bay sent a letter to the Commonwealth's agents in London that the ship *Blessing* had been loaded with 1,860 codfish (of which 700 were between two and three feet long and the rest under two feet), ten barrels of cranberries and three barrels of samp (Hull, *Diary,* pp. 129-31, this document is quoted in a memoir of Hull that precedes the actual diaries, also see Crosby, pp. 82-83).

January 23, 1678 - The December 16, 1677 petition of Stoughton and Bulkley, along with a counter petition by the claimants Mason and Gorges, were forwarded from the King's Council to the Lords of Trade and Plantations with a request they they send a report on the matter back to the Council (Sainsbury, *Calendar 1677-1680,* p. 211, item 456).

March 21, 1678 - Robert Mason (claimant to a patent for New Hampshire and cousin to Edward Randolph) sent a letter to the Secretary of State, Sir Joseph Williamson. However, since the Secretary was absent, no action was taken. On March 22nd a notice of the letter was recorded in the Journal of the Committee of the Lords of Trade and Plantations (Sainsbury, *Calendar 1677-1680,* p. 224, item 627).

March 25, 1678 - Robert Mason explained to the Committee of the Lords of Trade and Plantations that he had learned the two Massachusetts agents, Stoughton and Bulkley had made an agreement to purchase the Gorges claim to the Province of Maine. He further stated the agents had made overtures to him concerning the purchase of his claim to New Hampshire. Upon hearing this, the committee once again looked into the charges made by Edward Randolph and the counter arguments made by the Massachusetts agents (Sainsbury, *Calendar 1677-1680,* pp. 224-26, items 629-32).

March 28, 1678 - Stoughton and Bulkley attended a meeting of the Lords of Trade and Plantations where they stated they had obtained a copy of Randolph's extensive report against Massachusetts Bay (of October 12, 1676) and hoped to publicly discredit it by reopening the inquiry. Robert Mason appeared before the committee stating he had given the report to the representatives from Massachusetts Bay because he had been duped into believing a servant to the Lord of the Privy Seal had previously given them a copy (Hall, *Randolph,* p. 42; Toppan, *Randolph,* vol. 2, pp. 286-87; Palfrey, vol. 2, p. 216 and Sainsbury, *Calendar 1677-1680,* pp. 229-30, item 640).

April 8, 1678 - Edward Randolph attended a meeting of the Lords of Trade and Plantations explaining his October 1676 report had been confidential and that the Massachusetts agents could only have obtained it surreptitiously. Moreover, Randolph explained the October 1677 session of the Massachusetts General Court had only addressed the Lords's request that the colony adhere to the Navigation Acts but the General Court had been silent on other areas of concern and that they had reimposed the oath of fidelity. The minutes of the meeting also state that he reported, "Nor had they even suspended their Coining of money (which they confess to bee a crime) until His Majesties Pleasure bee knowne." Following the testimony of Mason and Randolph, the Committee on Trade and Plantations inquired of the Massachusetts agents if these events were correct. Once it was determined these events had occurred the committee changed their attitude and took a stern stance against Massachusetts Bay, sending an inquiry to the Attorney General asking whether the Massachusetts charter could be nullified (Hall, *Randolph,* pp. 41-44; Toppan, *Randolph,* vol. 2, pp. 289-98 with the quote on coining money from p. 295 and Sainsbury, *Calendar 1677-1680,* pp. 233-36, item 653).

April 18, 1678 - A petition and a report by Edward Randolph against Massachusetts Bay were read and discussed in a meeting of the Lords of Trade and Plantations. The petition was put forward on behalf of some of the king's "loyal subjects" living in Boston, who were being asked to take an oath of fidelity to Massachusetts Bay. Randolph stated since the Massachusetts agents had obtained his private report it was feared they would share the information with the Massachusetts government and thereby "laying a scene of ruin to those persons whose names are expressed" in the document (Sainsbury, *Calendar 1677-1680,* pp. 240-42, items 666-68).

April 27, 1678 - On April 26th the Privy Council read and discussed a report summarizing the April 18th meeting of the Lords of Trade and Plantations. The next day, on the 27th, a letter was sent from the king to the Massachusetts General Court ordering an oath of allegiance to the king be administered to all subjects in the colony; a copy of the oath to be used was enclosed (Cushing, *Laws,* vol. 3, p. 536; Toppan, *Randolph,* vol. 3, pp. 1-2 and Sainsbury, *Calendar 1677-1680,* pp. 247-48 and 250, items 685-86 and 691).

May 6, 1678 - On behalf of Massachusetts Bay, the Boston merchant, John Usher, had traveled to London and on this day paid £1,250 for the Gorges patent to Maine. The Treasurer of Massachusetts Bay, John Hull, personally extended his own credit, guaranteeing loans, in order to obtain the needed funds (Palfrey, vol. 2, p. 217 and Clarke, *Hull,* p. 180).

May 16, 1678 - At a meeting of the Lords of Trade and Plantations attended by Stoughton and Bulkley, the opinion of the Attorney General was read, stating the offenses of Massachusetts Bay were sufficient to void their charter. This was the start of the process that would lead to the issuing of the writ *Quo warranto* against Massachusetts. Also, on this day, the committee, with the consent of the king, directed that a commission be issued to Edward Randolph to make him Collector of Customs in New England (Hall, *Randolph,* pp. 44-45; Toppan, *Randolph,* vol. 3, pp. 2-6 and Sainsbury, *Calendar 1677-1680,* pp. 253-54, items 703-6).

June 13, 1678 - Over the vehement protests of the Massachusetts agents, William Stoughton and Peter Bulkley, on this day, the British Customs Commissioner, at the request of the Committee for Trade and Plantations and with the recommendation of the king, issued Edward Randolph a commission as the first royally appointed Collector, Surveyor and Searcher of Customs for New England. However, Randolph did not leave London until September of 1679. He first sailed to New York to meet Governor Andros, arriving in New York on December 7, 1679 (Hall, *Randolph,* pp. 45-46 and 52-53).

October 2, 1678 - The letter of October 10, 1678 (below) was entered in the Record of the General Court under this date (Crosby, p. 83). Also, the new laws and orders of the fall session of the General Court were recorded under this date. The first item was a new law requiring all British subjects aged sixteen or over to take an oath of allegiance to Charles II. Copies of the oath, which had been enclosed in the king's letter of April 27th, were printed and sent to each magistrate, justice of the peace and constable in the Commonwealth (Shurtleff, vol. 5, p. 192-94).

October 7, 1678 - The letter of October 10, 1678 is also entered in the Records of the General Court under this date (Shurtleff, vol. 5, pp. 201-3 and Crosby p. 83).

October 10, 1678 - On this date a letter was sent by the General Court to the Commonwealth's agents in London, William Stoughton and Peter Bulkley. The letter included an explanation that the mint was needed to keep up the colony's prosperity and that this prosperity increased the king's customs that they paid annually. The General Court also stated they would change the "Impresse" on their coins (that is, the images and legends) if the king wished (Shurtleff, vol. 5, pp. 201-3, Crosby, p. 83 and Toppan, "Right to Coin," p. 222).

October 15, 1678 - A letter was sent from Governor Leveret of Massachusetts to British Secretary of State Williamson stating that the Massachusetts Governor, Council and General Court had taken an oath of allegiance to the king (Sainsbury, *Calendar 1677-1680*, pp. 307-8, item 840).

December 6, 1678 - The October 15th letter of Governor Leveret was read at the December 6th meeting of the Committee of the Lords of Trade and Plantations in the presence of the two Massachusetts agents. Also, at this meeting a proposal for the establishment of a mint in Jamaica was forwarded to the Warden and officers of the Mint for comment (Sainsbury, *Calendar 1677-1680*, pp. 307-8, item 840).

February 5, 1679 - In a follow-up to the letter of October 15th Massachusetts Governor Leveret communicated to the British Secretary of State Sir Joseph Williamson that the oath of allegiance to the king had been administered throughout Massachusetts (Sainsbury, *Calendar 1677-1680*, p. 322, item 878).

February 7, 1679 - This is the date of a reply to the Lords of Trade and Plantations from Henry Slingesby, Master of the Mint, regarding the Earl of Carlisle's request to establish a mint in Jamaica. Slingesby endorsed the establishment of a mint if the coins adhered to the British weight and fineness. Also, the Earl would be required to "...raise three or four thousand pounds in Jamaica itself, for the expense of buildings and engines, and a thousand pounds at least annually for repairs and for salaries... ." However, in his oral presentation before the Lords of Trade and Plantations on February 8th, Slingesby mentioned the "dangerous consequence" of the proposed mint. The danger was that the mint would not adhere to the British standards. Rather than elaborate on this point Slingesby simply referred the Lords to a previous discussion in a mint report of November 14, 1662, concerning the establishment of a mint in Ireland (Sainsbury, *Calendar 1677-1680*, p. 326, items 883 and 884).

February 21, 1679 - Having received a favorable report from the Lords of Trade and Plantations, the king in Privy Council ordered that the Earl of Carlisle would be allowed to erect a mint as long as he complied with the requirements as stated in the report from Henry Slingesby, Master of the Mint (Sainsbury, *Calendar 1677-1680,* pp. 331-32, items 901 and 903).

May 20, 1679 - It is recorded in the Colonial Entry Book of the State Papers that a letter was to be written allowing the Massachusetts agents, William Stoughton and Peter Bulkley, to return home, but two other agents with broad authority were to be sent to London within six months. The letter also stated that after the two departing agents arrived back home in Massachusetts they were expected to intercede on behalf of the king in the several matters that had been discussed during their stay in London (Toppan, *Randolph,* vol. 3, pp. 44-45 and Sainsbury, *Calendar 1677-1680,* pp. 361-62 on p. 362, item 996).

June 20, 1679 - The Earl of Carlisle wrote to the Lords of Trade and Plantations that he would not be able to conform to the requirements as stated in the report from Henry Slingesby, Master of the Mint. The Earl stated:

> If we should make our coin of the same weight and fineness as the coin of England, we should never keep any money in the Island [i.e. Jamaica], which is our principal difficulty. In New England they raise money one-fourth, a ninepence goes for twelvepence, which fills them full of money; yet though the current money here be raised above its value they carry off this Island all our ready money to other plantations, to the great incommoding of the inhabitants in their trade with one another.

The letter was received by the Lords on August 26th and read at the committee meeting of October 9, 1679 (Sainsbury, *Calendar 1677-1680,* pp. 378-79, item 1030 with the quote on p. 379).

August 8, 1679 - Peter Loephilin was accused of making rash speeches in Boston and was arrested a few days later on August 12th. While searching his chest the authorities discovered silver clippings, a crucible, a melting ladle and a strong pair of shears. On September 2, 1679, Loephilin was convicted of clipping coins and sentenced as follows: he was to be confined in the pillory for two hours and was to have both ears cut off. Additionally, he was to pay a surety of £500 and also pay all the fees associated with his case. This incident may have renewed the debate concerning the value of Spanish American eight reales for a new proposal on that topic was put forward at the end of October (Hull, *Diary,* appendix, p. 300 and Scott, *Counterfeiting in Colonial America,* pp. 15-16).

October 31, 1679 - A proposal was debated to value all Spanish eight reales at six shillings. The act of October 8, 1672, which was then in force, was based on weight so only full weight eight reales were valued at six shillings. This proposal was to value all eight reales, regardless of weight, at six shillings. In colonial times this was called accepting coins by the piece or by tally (or as they said by "tale") rather than by weight. The proposal passed in the House of Deputies but was defeated in the House of Magistrates (Crosby, p. 108 and appendix to Hull's *Diary,* p. 300).

December 25, 1679 - William Stoughton and Peter Bulkley arrived back in Boston (Clarke, *Hull,* p. 182 and Hull, *Public Diary,* p. 246).

January 1680 - Edward Randolph took up his position in Boston as Collector of Customs for New England (Hall, *Randolph,* p. 54).

January 4, 1680 - Randolph wrote the first of several letters to the Lords of Trade and Plantations giving information on the colony. In the surviving abstract of this first letter, recorded in the Colonial series of the State Papers under the date of February 25, 1680 (vol. 44, no. 31), it states Randolph mentioned "That the Government of Boston continue still to collect customs & Coine money" (Toppan, *Randolph,* vol. 3, pp. 56-61 on p. 57; Toppan, "Right to Coin," p. 222 and Sainsbury, *Calendar 1677-1680,* pp. 487-90, item 1305, see p. 488).

February 4, 1680 - The General Court reported that Stoughton and Bulkley had returned to Massachusetts. The two agents were thanked for their long and faithful service and the Treasurer was ordered to pay each agent £150 "...as a small retribution for such their service, & an expression of our good affection to them" (Shurtleff, vol. 5, p. 263).

May 19, 1680 - An anonymous proposal recommending the abolition of mint fees was forwarded to the General Court. The document is in the handwriting of Isaac Addington, the secretary of the General Court. The proposal stated customers consigning silver to the mint would typically loose 6.25% or more in value when converting their silver into Massachusetts shillings. At the current rates it was cheaper for individuals to export their foreign coins and bullion or sell them to an exporter, rather than bring them to the mint. Because of this situation "little of late yeares (compared to what is laid up and carried away,) hath been coyned; and of that little, much dispersed into other Colony's." Thus the author called for a "free mint." This proposal contained the earliest surviving reference to the Boston shilling as a pine tree shilling. The sentence explained that both Spanish silver and Massachusetts Pine Tree coinage were readily accepted in trade, therefore an individual did not gain anything by having a Spanish cross dollar converted to pine tree shillings. The proposal stated, "the impress adds nothing to the intrinsick value, a spanish Cross in all other places being as well esteemd as a New England pine." The proposal was not adopted.

A related undated draft in the same hand, encouraged the importation of plate, bullion and Spanish coins and the submission of those items to the mint. It also requested that the mint be made free but that the mintmaster be paid annually by the Commonwealth treasurer based on the current coinage rates. The proposal was not adopted.

Another undated draft proposal in the handwriting of John Saffin (who became speaker of the house in 1686) stated Massachusetts silver was becoming scarce throughout the Commonwealth and so he requested abolishing all mint fees and paying the mintmaster annually out of the Commonwealth treasury based on the current coinage allowance. He believed this would encourage individuals to bring foreign coins and bullion into the mint. All these proposals were brought before the General Court but none were adopted. [The Mexican piece of eight included a unique cross in which each of the four ends concluded with a wedge shape followed by a round sphere. In 1653, the Potosí, Lima, Bogotá, La Plata and Cartagena mints started using the distinctive cross of Jerusalem with a perpendicular bar extension on each extremity. Mainland Spanish varieties had a simple Greek cross with no design at the extremities, consisting of a thin line dividing the four quadrants of the Castile and Leon shield [see figures 32-34]. Thus, the contemporary term "Spanish Cross" would refer to a New World eight reales and not to the Cross dollar from the Spanish Netherlands. (Crosby, pp. 109-11 and appendix to Hull's *Diary,* pp. 300-301).

May 27, 1680 - John Burrell and William Shore of New Jersey were convicted in New York City "for Coyning of ffalse Boston money" and for transporting the counterfeit money into New York and trying to pass it off. Burrell confessed to the offenses and was ordered to pay restitution while Shore was sentenced to be punished with thirty lashes. It has been questioned as to whether the two were actually counterfeiting coins or if they were just passing counterfeits produced by others (Scott, *Counterfeiting in Colonial New York,* p. 2).

June 6, 1680 - An anonymous proposal, in the handwriting of John Hull, was forwarded to the General Court to make the shilling twelve grains lighter and other denominations proportional. The rationale given was that if underweight foreign coins were passed at full value without attention to their weight or fineness the Commonwealth would be the looser and only those "strangers" who brought underweight coins into Massachusetts would make a profit. Hull explained lighter coins would be less likely to be exported from the Commonwealth. Also, it would encourage more silver to be brought to the mint because individuals with full weight pieces of eight would gain an additional 7d to 7.5d over the current rate of return. Details in the proposal include: using a different date for the lighter coins to make them easily distinguished from the heavier coins and an explanation how the lighter coins were to be used and valued in relation to the heavier coins that were currently being produced. The coins were to continue to be of sterling fineness and coinage and wastage fees would remain as they currently were in the seven year renewal signed on June 3, 1675. The proposal was not adopted (Crosby, pp. 111-12 and appendix to Hull's *Diary,* pp. 301-2).

August 3, 1680 - Hull further reduced his mint fees by personal agreement with his customers from 12d per £1 of coins minted to 6.6d per £1 of coins minted. The first order at the rate of 6.6d per £1 was an order consigned to the mint on August 3, 1680, and completed on September 27, 1680 (New England Historic Genealogical Society, Boston, Massachusetts, Personal Ledger of John Hull, Manuscript Cb 110, vol. 1, ff. 170v-171r).

September 30, 1680 - King Charles II sent a letter to the Governor and Council of Massachusetts Bay requiring them to give allegiance to the king and respect his commands. Appended was a version of Edward Randolph's memorandum of May 6, 1677, retitled, "Representation of the Bostoneers, 1680," which enumerated eight allegations against Massachusetts Bay including "They coyne money of their owne impress" (*Hutchinson Papers*, vol. 2, pp. 261-65 with Randolph's *Representation* on pp. 264-65).

February 25 - March 16, 1681 - Several drafts were formulated concerning the instructions to be given to the Commonwealth's London agents. These instructions contained information on the necessity of the mint. The final version, produced almost a year later, is listed below under the date February 15, 1682 (Crosby p. 84).

April 6, 1681 - A petition from Edward Randolph to the king was read in the King's Council. Two days later, on April 8th, the petition was sent to the Committee for Trade and Plantations for examination. This petition was entered into the record of the Committee for Trade and Plantations on the 9th. It requested that a writ of *Quo warranto* be issued against Massachusetts for several continued violations. Among the offenses was,

> And they do also continue to Coine money which their Agents in their Petition to your Magestie acknowledged a great crime & misdemeanor & craved your Majesties Pardon to the Government for soe doing;

For this offence, plus several others, Randolph accused Massachusetts of High Treason (Toppan, *Randolph,* vol. 3, pp. 89-92 and Toppan, "Right to Coin," p. 222. Also, Fortescue, *Calendar 1681-1685,* pp. 26-27, item 68, where Francis Gwyn, who recorded the minutes of the meeting mistakenly gave the year as 1680).

April 16, 1681 - Randolph sent a letter to Leoline Jenkins, the British Secretary of State,[19] on proceeding with the *Quo warranto*. Appended was a brief list, "Part of the Articles of High Misdemeanors objected against ye Government of Boston in New England." The first of the five numbered articles stated "they have erected a publick Mint & Coine money" (Toppan, *Randolph,* vol. 3, pp. 96-97 and summary in Fortescue, *Calendar 1681-1685,* pp. 31-32, items 83-84).

August 9, 1681 - Lord Thomas Culpepper testified before the Lords of Trade and Plantations. Culpepper had been governor of Virginia and had visited Boston from August 24 through about October 15, 1680, during his return voyage to London. Culpepper stated Edward Randolph's writings had been sent to him and that he could confirm most of Randolph's statements. Concerning the coinage he stated:

> As to the mint at Boston I think that, especially as it is managed, it is extremely prejudicial to all the King's subjects in what place soever, that deal with them. They call the piece that they coin a shilling, and it is current in all payments great and small, as, without special contract (in which no one can lose [sic] less than ten per cent.), equal with the English shilling; and this though it is not so fine in itself and weighs but three pennyweight against the English four. It is impossible to prevent the loss by bills of exchange, for they value their bills as they please and exact six per cent. coinage of all silver brought in their mint, to say nothing of loss of time. If therefore it be no longer connived at, it is absolutely necessary that the English shilling be made current there by law or proclamation at sixteenpence, and so proportionally, the coinage made more moderate and speedy. (Fortescue, pp. 99-100)

See Chapters Six and Ten for further details (Crosby, p. 86; Fortescue, *Calendar 1681-1685,* pp. 99-100, item 200; Mayo, *Hutchinson,* vol. 1, p. 280 and Hull, *Public Diary,* p. 247).

---

[19] Leoline Jenkins, 1623-1685, was a member of the Privy Council and Secretary of State April 26, 1680 - April 4, 1684.

October 21, 1681 - A letter from the king to the General Court listed several complaints against the Commonwealth including the fact "That you presume to continue your mint, without regard to the penalties thereby incurred." The king also commanded the General Court that "fit persons be sent over, without delay, to answer these complaints, with powers to submit to such regulations of government as his Majesty should think fit... ." A second royal letter was also sent proclaiming Randolph to be the Collector of Customs and expressing the need for Massachusetts to send agents to London without delay (Crosby, p. 86; Mayo, *Hutchinson,* vol. 1, pp. 281-82 and for a summary of a draft of the letter sent to the Lords of Trade and Plantations see Fortescue, *Calendar 1681-1685,* pp. 129-30, item 266. For the Randolph commission, Toppan, *Randolph,* vol. 3, pp. 110-13 and Fortescue, *Calendar 1681-1685,* pp. 128-29, items 264-65).

November, 1681 - The date of the conclusion of the apprenticeship of Samuel Clarke. Hull had stated in his diary that he had taken Clarke as his apprentice in November of 1673 for a period of eight years (Hull, *Private Diary,* p. 162).

February 15, 1682 - During a special February session of the General Court the king's letters of October 21st were read. It was decided the Court would expedite the process of selecting agents to be sent to London. On February 15th the General Court composed instructions for their London agents that included information concerning the necessity of the mint. The instructions stated,

> You shall informe his majestie that we tooke up stamping of silver meerley upon necessitie, to prevent cheats by false peeces of eight, which were brought hither in the time of the late confusions, and wee have been well informed that his majestie had knowledge thereof, yet did not manifest nay dissatisfaction thereat until of very late; and if that be a trespasse upon his majesties royal prerogative, of which wee are ignorant, wee humbly beg his majesties pardon and gratious allowance therein, it being so exceeding necessary for our civil commerce, & no way, as wee humbly conceive, detrimentall to his royal majestie.

The "time of the late confusions" is a reference to the period from the outbreak of civil war in 1642 through the demise of the English Commonwealth in 1660 (Shurtleff, vol. 5, pp. 333-34, 346-49 with the quote on p. 347; Crosby, p. 83 and Toppan, "Right to Coin," p. 223. The letter of instructions is dated February 15th, but it was included in the record of the General Court under the date of March 17, 1682).

March 20, 1682 - The General Court voted for two members of the Court to be offered the position as agents to represent the interests of the Commonwealth of Massachusetts Bay in London. William Stoughton came in first with 21 votes and Joseph Dudley was second with 18 votes. However, the record stated Mr. Stoughton persisted in manifesting "greate dissatisfaction" in accepting the position. Therefore, on March 23rd another election was held where Captain John Richards was selected as the second London agent for the Commonwealth (Shurtleff, vol. 5, p. 346 also Crosby, p. 83 and Mayo, *Hutchinson,* vol. 1, p. 282).

March 23, 1682 - Immediately following the announcement of the selection of John Richards as a replacement for Stoughton, the instructions for the agents, which carried the date of February 15, 1682, were entered into the Record of the General Court. See the February 15th entry above.

May 24, 1682 - The General Court legislated Spanish silver to "…pass amongst us as currant Money of New England, according to their weight in the present New England Coyne." This meant Spanish silver was to be put on par with Massachusetts silver, minted at 80d (6s8d) per troy ounce of sterling. This was a reduction over the previously legislated value of Spanish American coin, found in the act of October 8, 1672, where full weight eight reales had been legislated at 72d (6s), equaling 84.7d (just over 7s) per troy ounce. The 1682 law meant a 17 pennyweight Spanish American eight reales was to be reduced in value from 72d (6s) to 68d (5s8d). It is generally thought this was enacted in a last minute effort to bring more silver into the mint, because the mint contract was to expire in about a month. Since the increased valuation of Spanish silver had been legislated in October of 1672 there was no economic incentive for individuals to bring Spanish silver into the mint and have it converted into Massachusetts silver. The petitions of May 9 and June 6, 1680, explained little silver was being brought into the Massachusetts Mint so coinage production and concurrently minting profits were dramatically declining. However, the General Court would not support any of the suggestions in the petitions so nothing was done to save the mint until this act, which passed just before the mint contract expired.

However, the actual wording of the law does not fully explain the situation. The law, as it was promulgated and displayed to the public as a single sheet broadside, survives reproduced in Cushing. The version of this act, as found in draft legislation and as recorded by the General Court (found in Shurtleff and Crosby) has some minor wording differences from the broadside. The preamble of this legislation is not quite clear. It stated that due to the export of Boston silver from the Commonwealth this law was being enacted, lowering the value of Spanish silver, in order to keep "Money," that is, Massachusetts silver, from being exported. The explanation of how they were going to keep Massachusetts silver in the Commonwealth could be interpreted as meaning that by lowering the value of Spanish silver it would be more attractive to export Spanish rather than Massachusetts silver, thus reducing the drain of Massachusetts silver (but increasing the export of Spanish silver). It could also be interpreted as an attempt to take away the economic disadvantage of converting higher value Spanish silver into lower value Massachusetts silver. However, since the customer was required to pay the minting fees, the equalization of value would not be enough incentive to bring Spanish silver into the mint, as there would still be an economic disadvantage to the customer when bringing equal value Spanish silver to the mint for conversion into Boston silver.

Although the May 1682 legislation to reduce the value of Spanish silver was passed by the General Court, it is not known if this law was actually enforced in the marketplace. This law was certainly a point of contention for there were several later laws reestablishing the 6s valuation of the eight reales. Following the dissolution of the Massachusetts Bay charter, the royal governor Edmund Andros overturned the law on March 10, 1687, returning to the 6s valuation. After the fall of Andros, the 6s value of the Spanish American eight reales was included in an anti-counterfeiting law of November 24, 1692, but because of disagreements on the penalties for counterfeiting, the law was disallowed by the Privy Council on August 22, 1695. The 6s valuation was again reinstated in the Act of October 19, 1697, and continued to be the legal rate in Queen Anne's proclamation of June 18, 1704 (Cushing, *Laws,* vol. 3, p. 577; Shurtleff, vol. 5, p. 351 and Crosby, pp. 84-85 also see below under March 10, 1687 and October 19, 1697).

May 28, 1682 - Edward Randolph composed "Articles of high Misdemeanor, exhibited against the General Court sitting 15th February, 1681" [that is, February 1682, as the new year began in March] elaborating on seven articles. In article six, which explained Massachusetts had neglected to repeal all laws contrary to the laws of England as required by the king's letter of June 28, 1662, Randolph specifically stated,

> ...by perticuler direction from the Right Honorable the Lords of the Committee of trade and plantations to their late Agents in 1678 by which meanes coining money (acknowledged in their Agents petition to his Majestie A great crime & misdemeanor, who then craved his Majesties pardon to the government for the same) is continued to this day. (Toppan, *Randolph,* vol. 3, pp. 130-32 and in *Hutchinson Papers,* vol. 2, pp. 266-68; with a summary in Fortescue, *Calendar 1681-1685,* pp. 238-39, item 526 also see Crosby, pp. 85-86 [Crosby, following Hutchinson, misdates the king's letter to February 28, 1662]; also see Hall, *Randolph,* p. 73)

May 31, 1682 - Governor Bradstreet wrote to the British Secretary of State Leoline Jenkins that the Massachusetts Bay agents Joseph Dudley and John Richards, would depart from Boston for London on the next ship (Fortescue, *Calendar 1681-1685,* p. 240, item 529 and Mayo, *Hutchinson,* vol. 1, p. 283).

June 3, 1682 - This is the official expiration date of the final Commonwealth mint contract with Hull and Sanderson, that is, seven years after the agreement had been signed on June 3, 1675. It is unknown exactly when the mint finally closed. A year later, in June of 1683, Edward Randolph, while in London, stated to the Lords of Trade that "They persist in coining money" which indicates the mint may have still been in operation. Randolph had departed Boston on April 2, 1683. It is unknown if he had the latest news on the disposition of the mint at the time of his departure or if he simply included this statement in his presentation because it was part of his standard arguments against the Commonwealth.

On October 1, 1683, John Hull died. We know the mint building was on Hull's property (this is the structure Hull called "ye shop" as suggested in Chapter One of the accompanying study). Sanderson continued working in the shop until May of 1687, when he sold his portion of the silversmith business to Samuel Sewall. Although silversmith work continued at the shop until 1687, we do not know if any minting was performed at the shop after the expiration of the seven year mint contract on June 3, 1682. As discussed below in the entry for May 16, 1683, two undated signatures added to the draft of the action to construct the mint house may relate to the closing of the establishment. It is likely the mint officially closed sometime between May of 1683 and May of 1685, possibly minting ceased when Hull's estate was divided in March of 1684 as any mint equipment owned by Hull may have been liquidated at that time.

A letter of November 22, 1684, from the Chamber Council in London to the Commissioners of the Treasury inquired as to whether the Commissioners of Customs should "...continue or set aside the further exercise of such a mint." Frequently this has been interpreted as referring to the possible reestablishment of the mint, implying that by the end of 1684 the mint was no longer in operation. The first reference specifically mentioning the close of the mint is in a letter from Edward Randolph from Boston dated May 29, 1686, where Randolph stated, "...since they have Ceased coining their money is every day shipd off for England." The first actual use of the word "reestablishment" in relation to the Boston mint is found in a letter from the Commissioners of the London Mint dated July 15, 1686. Although the topic of reestablishing the mint was discussed for several years, it never came to fruition.

August 20, 1682 - The Massachusetts agents Dudley and Richards arrived in London but without the authority to revise the charter (Palfrey, vol. 2, p. 249).

August 24, 1682 - Dudley and Richards appeared before the Lords of Trade and Plantations presenting the committee with a petition from the Governor and Company of Massachusetts Bay to the king (Fortescue, *Calendar 1681-1685,* pp. 277-78, items 660 and 662).

October 11, 1682 - The date of the opening of the fall General Court. The legislation of October 12th, as amended on October 16th, was added to the Record of the General Court under this date (Shurtleff, vol. 5, p. 373).

October 12, 1682 - The House of Magistrates issued an explanation of the May 24th law stating more precisely that the eight reales would be paid and received at "Six Shillings and Eight Pence the ounce, troy weight." This clarification meant Spanish coins would still be valued by weight and not by the piece (or as the colonials said, "by tale") and that the standard measure was 80d per troy ounce, which was the standard by which Massachusetts silver was authorized. The House of Deputies concurred. The draft of this action survives with the date of October 11, which was the opening of the fall session of the General Court. Also, like most legislation this action is recorded under the date of the opening of the session, however the legislation survives and is dated October 12th (Crosby, pp. 84-85, including the act of October 12th and a draft of this action dated October 11th and Shurtleff, vol. 5, p. 373, where it is recorded under October 11th).

October 16, 1682 - The act of May 24th was further amended in the House of Deputies so that smaller denomination Spanish silver coins would also circulate at a proportional rate on par with Massachusetts silver. The House of Magistrates approved the amendment on the same day (Crosby p. 85; Cushing, *Laws,* vol. 3, p. 580 and Shurtleff, vol. 5, p. 373, where it is recorded under October 11th).

March 30, 1683 - The Lords of Trade and Plantations had requested the General Court give Dudley and Richards authority to revise the charter. However on this day the General Court sent their agents instructions requesting them not to make any concessions concerning the charter and refusing to give them the authority to amend it. Furthermore, the instructions stated "If they proceed to a quo warranto, yow may, if it can be safely donn, humbly desire to be excused from answering it, as having no power committed to yow so to doe" (Shurtleff, vol. 5, pp. 391-92 and Hall, *Randolph,* p. 78).

April 2, 1683 - Edward Randolph set sail from Boston to London (Hall, *Randolph,* p. 78).

May 16, 1683 - In the elections for the General Court of Massachusetts Bay, Simon Bradstreet was elected Governor and John Woodbridge was elected as one of the Assistants. Woodbridge had left Massachusetts for England in 1647 where he remained until 1663, finally returning on the ship, *Society,* under the command of Charles Clark, which landed in Boston on July 27, 1663. Although Bradstreet was active as Governor or an Assistant most of his life, Woodbridge only held the office of Assistant from 1637 through 1641, and then again from May 16, 1683 through May of 1685. Woodbridge was present at the special General Court of May 6, 1685, but he was not reelected in the May 27th elections. This has significance for the history of the mint in that the signatures of Bradstreet and Woodbridge are found in the margin of the draft of an action written in June of 1652 by the mint committee. This action was to erect a mint house, purchase the necessary equipment for the operation of the mint and renegotiate the minting fees. Interestingly, this draft document was signed by John Hull ("John Hull mintmaster"). Sanderson was not present but Edward Rawson, who was the Secretary of the General Court and a member of the mint committee, added "Robert Saunderson, his copartner" (see above under June 1652). Possibly the mintmasters' signatures were added to this draft to signify an agreement between the minters and the Commonwealth. Whereas the Hull and Sanderson signatures were contemporary with the creation of the document, the Bradstreet and Woodbridge signatures certainly date to after 1663. It seems quite likely they were added sometime between May 16, 1683, and May 6, 1685, when both men were leading elected officials of the Commonwealth. Possibly the signatures were added to signify the dissolution of the mint. If so, this event probably occurred soon after the settlement dividing Hull's estate was approved by the Suffolk County Court on March 13, 1684 (Hull, *Public Diary,* p. 209 and Shurtleff, vol. 1, pp. 191, 194, 227, 287-88, 336 and vol. 5, pp. 407, 436-37, 472 and 475).

June 4, 1683 - The Committee of the Lords of Trade and Plantations received a document from Edward Randolph titled, "Articles against the government and Company of Massachusetts bay in New England," in which he brought seventeen charges against the Commonwealth. The Massachusetts Mint was listed as his first article, about which he wrote, "They have erected a Publick mint in Boston and Coine money with their Own Impresse" (Toppan, *Randolph,* vol. 3, pp. 229-30; Toppan, "Right to Coin," p. 223 and Fortescue, *Calendar 1681-1685,* pp. 440-41, item 1101).

June 12, 1683 - In the presence of Massachusetts agents Dudley and Richards, Edward Randolph appeared before the Lords of Trade and Plantations explaining the Massachusetts agents had not been given the authority to modify the charter. He also presented the Lords with a document, "Articles against the Massachusetts," in which he brought twelve charges against the Commonwealth. The Massachusetts Mint was listed as article twelve, stating "That they Coin Money" (Toppan, *Randolph,* vol. 3, pp. 229-30 and Fortescue, *Calendar 1681-1685,* pp. 445-46, items 1120-21).

June 13, 1683 - The day after Randolph's testimony, the Lords ordered the Attorney General to prepare a writ of *Quo warranto*[20] and that Randolph assist in preparing the document. On the same day an undated petition from Randolph to the king was recorded in which Randolph asked that a writ of *Quo warranto* be brought against Massachusetts. Randolph sent additional petitions to the king against Massachusetts, one was concerned with customs irregularities (June 13) while another was against the levying of taxes in Massachusetts to defray the expenses of their agents in London (June 28). Randolph continued to send additional letters to the king and other officials outlining the offenses of Massachusetts. This letter writing campaign finally ended in mid-July, when Randolph prepared to return to Massachusetts (Hall, *Randolph,* p. 79; Toppan, *Randolph,* vol. 3, pp. 237-44 and Fortescue, *Calendar 1681-1685,* pp. 447, 451-53 items 1124, 1135 and 1147).

June 27, 1683 - The King's Bench issued a writ of *Quo warranto* against the Governor and Company of Massachusetts Bay requiring them to defend the charter. The writ named thirty individuals including Governor Simon Bradstreet, Deputy Governor Thomas Danforth and the Assistants as well as several other government officials. The writ listed Massachusetts officials as of the election of May 24, 1682, using the same order of names as is found in the General Court records. Since John Hull was one of the elected Assistants that year, he was named in the writ (Shurtleff, vol. 5, pp. 350, for the 1682 election results and pp. 421-22 for the text; Hart, vol. 1, p. 565 and Hutchinson, *History,* edited by Mayo, pp. 284-87).

July 20, 1683 - The *Quo warranto* was officially signed by the King's Council in Whitehall. Also, by an order of Council, Edward Randolph was selected to carry and announce the writ *Quo warranto* in Boston. On July 26th Randolph began looking for a gunship to transport him to Boston so he could arrive with authority. While Randolph was still seeking transportation, Dudley and Richards left London to bring the news of the writ to Boston. By August 3rd Randolph had narrowed the choice down to the ship *Rose* or the *Richard.* Randolph was given permission to leave on August 17th and departed a few days later on the ship *Rose* under the command of the young New England adventurer, Captain William Phips (Hall, *Randolph,* pp. 79-81, Toppan, *Randolph,* vol. 3, pp. 245-55; Baker and Reid, *The New England Knight,* pp. 32-36 and Fortescue, *Calendar 1681-1685,* pp. 454 and 456, items 1152 and 1159-60).

August 24, 1683 - The Minutes of the Provincial Council in Philadelphia indicate that warrants were to be issued for the arrest of Charles Pickering and Samuel Buckley for counterfeiting "Spanish Bitts and Boston money." They were accused by Robert Fenton (or Felton) who said he had made the dies for the operation. Newman has suggested the operation was limited to Spanish bitts and probably did not produce Massachusetts silver. Indeed the trial documents only refer to Spanish silver, namely, bitts and pieces of eight (Scott, *Counterfeiting in Colonial Pennsylvania,* pp. 1-6 and Newman's comments in, *The Colonial Newsletter* vol. 17, Oct. 1978, serial no. 53, p. 666).

September 21, 1683 - Sir Thomas Lynch, Governor of Jamaica, addressed the Jamaica Assembly in successfully defeating a proposal to raise the value of a piece of eight from 4s6d to 6s (Fortescue, *Calendar 1681-1685,* p. 502, item 1262).

---

[20] This is a legal action inquiring into the validity of a franchise or a liberty asking "By what authority" one exercises the liberty in question.

October 1, 1683 - John Hull died (Clarke, *Hull*, p. 186; Kane, p. 569 says September 30th).

October 4, 1683 - Governor Edward Cranfield of New Hampshire proposed an order, with the support of his Council, for raising the value of foreign silver. However, the Assembly would not pass the measure into law. This episode was mentioned in a letter the Governor wrote to Leoline Jenkins on October 19th (Fortescue, *Calendar 1681-1685,* pp. 521-22, item 1316, see attachment 1).

October 22, 1683 - Joseph Dudley and John Richards arrived back in Boston bringing news of the *Quo warranto* writ (Toppan, *Randolph,* vol. 3, p. 273 and Mayo, *Hutchinson,* vol. 1, p. 286).

October 26, 1683 - Edward Randolph landed in Boston from London with the writ *Quo warranto* and a letter from King Charles II stating that if the colony made full submission to royal authority, the king would let them retain a modified charter. The documents were delivered to the governor on the morning of October 27th (Toppan, *Randolph,* vol. 3, p. 275 and Hutchinson, *History,* edited by Mayo, vol. 1, pp. 286-88).

November 7, 1683 - A special session of the General Court was convened at which time the writ and the letter from the king were entered into the court record. Over the next months, the General Court debated a response. The majority of the House of Magistrates was ready to capitulate to the king but the House of Deputies (the lower house) refused to consent. The stalemate continued through the remainder of the year. On November 21, 1683, the Deputies even voted down a proposal that would have allowed the Magistrates to send a letter to London permitting their agent (Robert Humfreys, a British barrister) to present himself before the King's Bench and explain the situation so the Commonwealth would not default. On December 7, 1683, the Magistrates sent a letter to the British Secretary of State, Leoline Jenkins, explaining their deadlock with the House of Deputies (Shurtleff, vol. 5, pp. 420-25, Toppan, *Randolph,* vol. 3, pp. 275-78, 295-96; Hutchinson, *History,* edited by Mayo, vol. 1, pp. 286-88 and Fortescue, *Calendar 1681-1685,* p. 563, item 1445 as well as Randolph's account on pp. 599-600, item 1566 and another letter from the Massachusetts Governor and Magistrates received in London on March 22, 1684, on p. 610, item 1603).

November 7, 1683 - At the special session of the General Court, Judith Hull and Samuel Sewall presented a petition from the estate of John Hull requesting the government pay accounts owed to John Hull. Apparently as early as 1673 Hull had personally paid several government expenses; further credit was extended to the Commonwealth throughout his term as treasurer during King Philip's War and continuing to 1680. He even extended his personal credit in London to the Commonwealth agents, Stoughton and Bulkley, and personally countersigned loans to finance the purchase of the Gorges patent to Maine. The petitioners sought £1,700 that Massachusetts owed to Hull for the period from May 1678 through October 1680. A committee was constituted to investigate the petition, consisting of: William Stoughton, Joseph Dudley, Elisha Hutchinson, Richard Sprague and William Johnson (Shurtleff, vol. 5, pp. 427-28 and Clarke, *Hull,* pp. 170-77, 180-82, 185 and 192).

November 27, 1683 - The committee of the General Court assigned to investigate the Hull family petition concluded the Commonwealth owed Hull £545 3s 10.5p. Apparently Hull had borrowed £400 at interest from John Phillips of Charlestown, in order to pay Commonwealth debts so the committee ordered Phillips be paid with interest and that the petitioners be paid £50 to settle their account in full. Even though Hull's account books showed the Commonwealth owed him £1,700, the petitioners accepted this settlement as final (Shurtleff, vol. 5, pp. 428-29 and Clarke, *Hull,* pp. 191-92).

December 5, 1683 - At another special session of the General Court the Hull petition and its resolution were entered into the record with the statement, "The Court approoves of this returne of ye committee" (Shurtleff, vol. 5, pp. 427-29).

December 1683 - Edward Randolph left Boston for London arriving in February of 1684. He made a formal report to the king on February 29th concerning the reception of the writ (Toppan, *Randolph,* vol. 3, pp. 275-79; Hall, *Randolph,* p. 82 and Fortescue, *Calendar 1681-1685,* pp. 599-600, item 1566).

February 23, 1684 - In New York, the Governor's Council ordered a proclamation be published against counterfeit coins as the Governor had information "...of som false Coyne in Boston, Spanish moneys not weighty, & Counterfeited by som of ye neighboring Colonies." This does not necessarily refer to counterfeit Massachusetts silver but rather probably refers to lightweight and counterfeit Spanish American cobs in Boston (Scott, *Counterfeiting in Colonial New York,* p. 3).

March 10, 1684 - Edward Rawson, Secretary of the General Court, drew up an agreement concerning the claims for government funds put forward on behalf of the estate of John Hull. The agreement stated payments were being ordered as specified by the General Court on November 27, 1683, and that they would fully and absolutely release the Governor and the Company of Massachusetts Bay from any further claim by Judith Hull, Samuel Sewall or his wife Hannah. This document was recorded into the book of records of the General Court on March 16, 1684 (Shurtleff, vol. 5, pp. 433-34).

March 12, 1684 - John Hull had died without having drawn up a will. Therefore, on this day a proposal for the division and settlement of his estate was submitted to the Suffolk County Court by the executors of his estate (who probably were Daniel Quincy, John Alcock and Eliakim Mather since they acted as witnesses) in agreement with Hull's wife, Judith, and their daughter, Hannah, and Hannah's husband, Samuel Sewall. The proposal left to Judith Hull the "...mansion house ... and all tenements, shop, out-houseing and buildings whatsoever on any parts of said land standing." Judith was also granted half of all the household goods and one-third part of "...all trading stock, goods wares merchandizes, monys, debts and whatsoever else is belonging to the personal estate." The remaining two-thirds of his personal estate (and some additional holdings) went to his daughter Hannah and her husband Samuel Sewall. It is not mentioned if any minting equipment was involved or whether the equipment remained with Sanderson (or if Hull's minting or silversmithing equipment may have been sold or given to someone else, such as one of Hull's past apprentices). The agreement was approved by the court on the 13th and recorded on the 14th (Hull, *Diary,* addenda, copy of the agreement from the Suffolk County Register of Deeds, pp. 257-62).

April 16, 1684 - A writ of *Scire facias*[21] was issued by the Chancery of Charles II in Westminster detailing the charges against Massachusetts Bay, including the establishment of the mint. Following standard practice the writ was addressed to the Sheriff, in this case, as in the earlier *Quo warranto* writ, the *Scire facias* was incorrectly addressed to the Sheriff of Middlesex County, Boston, (it should have been Suffolk County) who was given six weeks to locate and bring the addressees named in the writ before the court. This writ was against the Company of Massachusetts Bay rather than specific individuals (Hutchinson, *History,* edited by Mayo, vol. 1, p. 288 and Toppan, *Randolph,* Memoir in vol. 1, pp. 227-28).

May 13, 1684 - In London, Attorney General Robert Sawyer issued an opinion on the writ *Quo warranto* in response to objections by the sheriff of Middlesex County in Massachusetts. Sawyer agreed with the sheriff that the *Quo warranto* writ had been incorrectly addressed, for Boston was the county seat for Suffolk county, whereas the seat of Middlesex County was Cambridge, on the other side of the Back Bay. The writ had been addressed to the wrong sheriff! Also, and more importantly, Sawyer agreed the writ had been delivered too late, after the period for returning the summons was past. Sawyer suggested dropping the matter and instead concentrating on the writ of *Scire facias* against the Company of Massachusetts Bay to repeal their patent (Toppan, *Randolph,* Memoir in vol. 1, pp. 227-28 and text in vol. 3, pp. 297-99, Toppan, "Right to Coin," p. 223 where the text is misdated to 1683; Hall, *Randolph,* p. 83 and Fortescue, *Calendar 1681-1685,* pp. 631-32, item 1677).

June 2, 1684 - A second writ of *Scire facias* was issued by the Chancery of Charles II in Westminster again detailing the charges against the Commonwealth including the establishment of the mint. Once again the writ was incorrectly addressed to the sheriff of Middlesex County. On June 12th, Robert Humfreys, a London lawyer who was acting as the agent for Massachusetts Bay, requested a continuance until Michaelmas (September 29th) so the Commonwealth could respond. The request was denied and on June 18, 1684, judgment was entered against the Commonwealth (Hutchinson, *History,* edited by Mayo, vol. 1, pp. 288-89; Fortescue, *Calendar 1681-1685,* pp. 652 and 655, items 1742 and 1755; also Crosby, pp. 112-13).

July 2, 1684 - Edward Rawson, Secretary of the General Court of Massachusetts Bay, received a copy of the judgment against the Commonwealth for not appearing in Westminster to answer the writ of *Scire facias.* However, a copy of the writ did not reach Boston until September, long after the period for their appearance at Westminster had passed. Soon after the writ reached Boston, a special session of the General Court was called and a committee was formed to draft a reply to the king (Hutchinson, *History,* edited by Mayo, vol. 1, pp. 288-89).

---

[21] The writ of *Scire facias* was a legal action issued by the chancery requiring the sheriff to present specific individuals or corporations before the court where they would be required "To show cause" why some action should not be taken against them or why their letters patent or charter should not be revoked. One significant difference from the earlier writ was that the earlier writ of *Quo warranto* had been issued by the King's Bench and judgments from that court were subject to appeal whereas Chancery judgments were not subject to appeal.

July 16, 1684 - A letter from Edward Randolph was read at the committee meeting of the Lords of Trade and Plantations. The committee minutes stated that Randolph explained Joseph Dudley and other royalists who had been magistrates in Massachusetts Bay for many years and supported the king "were with great contempt and scorn left out of that number because they voted for submission." That is, long standing members of the General Court, who wished to concede to the king were voted out of office. Randolph further stated the Governor had been busy repairing the fortifications and that "the Acts of Trade and Navigation are now rendered insignificant" and that against the orders of the king, Massachusetts continued to collect taxes (Fortescue, *Calendar 1681-1685,* p. 669, item 1808).

October 15, 1684 - In a special session of the General Court a letter was drafted to be sent to King Charles stating they had only been informed by private letter of the writ of *Scire facias* and had no legal notice of it within the six weeks limit for a response. On that same day they composed a second letter which was sent to their agent in London, Robert Humfreys, stating:

> That now a scire facias should come from the Chancery, directed to the sheriffs of Middlesex, & to be returned within six weekes, & procedure against us upon their returne of two nihills, cannot but amaze us [two 'nihills' (or more correctly nihils) is a Latin legal reference to two 'no shows'] .

The Massachusetts General Court was amazed because both the first and the second writ had been addressed to the wrong sheriff; furthermore, the Chancery required them to respond to the second writ within six weeks although it took longer than six weeks for the writ to reach them (Shurtleff, vol. 5, pp. 456-59 and Fortescue, *Calendar 1681-1685,* p. 706, item 1902).

September 27, 1684 - A report from the Commissioners of the Mint (John Buckworth, Charles Duncombe and James Hoare) to the Lords of the Treasury was forwarded to the Committee of the Lords of Trade and Plantations stating that no advantage could be gained by an act proposed for the West Indian island of Nevis to raise the value of a piece of eight from 4s6d to 6s. On the same day the Commissioners of Customs forwarded their opinion to the Committee concurring with the mint report (Fortescue, *Calendar 1681-1685,* pp. 691-92, items 1874-76).

October 23, 1684 - King Charles II abolished the Charter of Massachusetts Bay.

October 30, 1684 - In a draft report dated October 30, 1684, from the committee of the General Court, there is a passage about the origin and history of the mint. The passage stated:

> And as for the minting and stamping pieces of Silver to pass amongst ourselves for xiid, vid, iiid, we were necessitated thereunto, having no staple Commodity in our Country to pay debts or buy necessaries, but Fish & Corn; which was so cumbersom & troublesom as could not be born.

The passage did not mention the 1662 Oak Tree twopence because the statement was describing the situation in 1652. The draft then explained many individuals had resorted to using personal promissory notes (IOU's):

...for some years Paper-Bills passed for payment of Debts; which were very subject to be lost, rent or counterfeited...

These were followed by "...a considerable quantity of light base Spanish Money... ." The committee went on to explain many individuals encountered problems from the continual clipping and counterfeiting of the Spanish American silver cob coinage which destabilized the local economy. This situation:

> ...put us upon the project of melting it down, & stamping such pieces as aforesaid to pass in payment of Debts amonst our selves. Nor did we know it to be against any Law of England, or against His Majesties Will or pleasure, till of late; but rather that there was a tacit allowance & approbation of it. For in 1662, when our first Agents were in England, some of our Money was showed by Sir Thomas Temple at the Council-Table, and no dislike thereof manifested by any of those right honourable persons: much less a forbidding of it... .

The entire mint passage was struck from the final version of the committee report read before the General Court, as was a passage directly responding to the writ *Scire facias*. The final letter sent to the king was dated January 28, 1685 (Crosby, p. 76, the appendix to Hull's *Diary,* p. 282 and Toppan, "Right to Coin," p. 224).

November 22, 1684 - On this day, William Blathwayt[22] sent a letter in the name of the Chamber Council in London to Henry Guy, Secretary of the Treasury.[23] The letter stated the Lords of the Committee for Trade and Foreign Plantations had asked the Commissioners of Customs to draft instructions relating to trade and navigation for the newly appointed governor of Massachusetts Bay, Colonel Kirk. In formulating these instructions the Commissioners of Customs had a question, namely:

> Their Lordships having likewise taken notice that a mint has hitherto been kept up and imployed at Boston in New England, for the Coyning of money different in value and alloy from that of England, and it being now in his majesty's power to continue or set aside the further exercise of such a mint... .

To that end, the letter continued with a request that the Lord Commissioners of the Treasury receive the opinion of the Commissioners of the Mint on this matter and inform the King's Council of their opinion so instructions could be given to Colonel Kirk [Kirk was never installed as governor] (Crosby, pp. 86-87 and Fortescue, *Calendar 1681-1685,* p. 732, item 1956).

---

[22] William Blathwayt (1649?-1717) purchased the position of Secretary at War, a position synonymous with a clerkship of a committee of the Council. On October 22, 1686, Blathwayt became the Clerk of the Privy Council.

[23] Henry Guy (1631-1710) was Secretary of the Treasury from March 1679 through Christmas 1688. He then moved to other posts including Commissioner of Custom before returning as Secretary of the Treasury from 1692 through 1695.

January 15, 1685 - The Commissioners of the Treasury passed the Chamber Council letter to the Commissioners of the London Mint. On this day the Commissioners of the Mint (Philip Loyd, Thomas Neale, Charles Duncombe and James Hoare) sent a report to the Commissioners of the Treasury concerning the Boston mint. The report stated they had examined 12d, 6d and 3d pieces of Massachusetts silver and found them to be of sterling alloy but discovered them to be lighter by about 21 grains per shilling, which they estimated at nearly 2 pence and 3 farthings per shilling or about 22.5% below the value of British silver coins. The committee recommended, if the king:

> …shal think fitt to settle a Mint in NE, for making of Coyns of silver, of 12 pences, 6d, & 3d, that they be made in weight & fineness answerable to his Majestys Silver Coyns of England , & not otherwise [the document is dated 1684 as the new year did not start until March]. (Crosby, pp. 87-89 and appendix to Hull's *Diary,* pp. 302-4)

January 28, 1685 - At a special session of the General Court a letter was sent to the king which did not go into many specifics but did state:

> …upon the scire facias late brought against us in the Chancerie, of which wee never had any legall notice for our appearance and making answer; neither was it possible in the time allotted, that we could. Had wee had oppertunity, it would have binn easy to demonstrate our innocency ... allow us sincerely to proffess, that not one of the articles therein objected were ever intended, much less continnewed, to be done in derrogation of your most royall prerogative, or to the oppression of your subjects. (Shurtleff, vol. 5, pp. 466-67)

February 6, 1685 - Sometime between 11:00 AM and noon King Charles II died at Whitehall Palace. On the same day his Roman Catholic brother James II was proclaimed king; James ascended to the throne on February 16th (Fortescue, *Calendar 1681-1685,* p. 769, item 2069 and Fortescue, *Calendar 1685-1688,* p. 1, items 1 and 3).

April 20, 1685 - James II was publicly proclaimed king in Boston. The festivities included a large parade and a salute in the form of a volley of shots from about fifty pieces of ordinance at Noddle's Island in Boston Harbor (Shurtleff, vol. 5, pp. 473-74 and Fortescue, *Calendar 1685-1688,* pp. 31-32, items 137-38).

July 24, 1685 - The General Court sent a letter to King James II humbly imploring him for pardon and requesting that he not vacate the charter because they saw such an action as "tending to the ruin of this your majesties budding plantation" (Shurtleff, vol. 5, pp. 495-96).

October 10, 1685 - In London, at the suggestion of Edward Randolph, a royal commission was granted to Joseph Dudley on this date allowing him temporary authority over the Massachusetts Bay government as President of his Majesties Provincial Council and Vice Admiral of the seas in the colony of Massachusetts. Dudley was a long standing and well respected inhabitant of Massachusetts Bay who was pro-royalist and had regularly been elected as one of the Assistants (or Councilors) to the governor from 1676-1683 and in 1685. Randolph felt Dudley was more moderate than most of the Puritans and more amenable to royal control over the province (Fortescue, *Calendar 1685-1688,* see the letters of Randolph read at the Committee meetings of the Lords of Trade and Plantations on August 18 and September 2, 1685, on pp. 77 and 87-88, items 319 and 350).

May 14, 1686 - The ship H.M.S. *Rose* landed in Boston with a copy of the king's commission to Dudley to create a new government and a copy of the judgment against Massachusetts Bay (Fortescue, *Calendar 1685-1688,* p. 188, item 674).

May 17, 1686 - Joseph Dudley and his Councilors presented the General Court with his commission for a new government (Cushing, *Laws,* vol. 3, pp. 629-31 and Hart, vol. 1, pp. 572-73 and 608).

May 20, 1686 - The General Court responded to Dudley's commission stating they saw some problems since there were no specifics on the administration of justice and there were abridgments of liberties. The General Court stated they could not give their assent to the document but they would remain loyal subjects and "humbly make our Addresses unto God, and in due time to our Gracious Prince for our Relief" (Cushing, *Laws,* vol. 3, p. 621).

May 25, 1686 - A proclamation was issued disbanding the General Court and constituting the new provincial government. The royal commission was publicly read before the General Court; then Dudley and his Council took their oath of office and Dudley made a speech explaining that there would be little change in the daily administration of the government. The General Court was disbanded but the charter of Massachusetts Bay was still active; this was an intermediate period between a true Commonwealth and the subjugation of Massachusetts as a royal colony (Cushing, *Laws,* vol. 3, pp. 623 and 631-32; Hart, vol. 1, pp. 572-73 and 608; also Fortescue, *Calendar 1685-1688,* pp. 200-1, item 702).

May 29, 1686 - In a letter from Boston, Edward Randolph told William Blathwayt it was very difficult to find any silver and that it was necessary to either reestablish the mint or have silver shipped from England. Since the mint ceased operation silver coinage had been exported but the supply was not replenished. This is the first quote specifically stating the mint has closed. Randolph stated:

> ...and now I feare The Treasurey of this Country is departed with the old Magistrates. There is a necessity either to have the mint here regulated or to have money from England for since they have Ceased coining their money is every day shipd off for England or other countryes so that tis a hard matter to gett 100lb in silver. (Goodrick, *Randolph,* vol. 6, pp. 171-74 with the quote on p. 172)

July 2, 1686 - The Council of Virginia sent a letter to the king requesting he allow the Assembly to pass an act raising the value of the piece of eight and the French crown to 5s each. The letter was received in London on September 5th [also see the entry for April 30, 1687] (Fortescue, *Calendar 1685-1688,* p. 210, item 746).

July 15, 1686 - The date of a letter from the Commissioners of the Mint (Philip Loyd, Thomas Neale, Charles Duncombe and James Hoare) to the Lord High Treasurer, Lawrence

Hyde, Earl of Rochester[24] concerning the topic, "a Mint to be reestablisht in New England." Crosby has pointed out the title of this letter implied the Massachusetts Mint was not in operation at that time. The letter stated a copy of the mint commissioner's report of January 15, 1685, was appended. The letter discussed that a patent issued to Thomas Vyner to mint small silver coins in Ireland had been revoked after the Treasurer and the Mint Commissioners reported to the Council on the inferior quality of the coinage. Moreover, they explained a colonial mint application had been denied to Lord Carlisle, the governor of Jamaica, in 1678, because of the fear that coins would be produced below the British standard for weight and fineness. [Actually the "denial" was in the form of a restriction requiring Lord Carlisle to adhere to the British standards. It was pronounced in February of 1679 but it is listed here as 1678 since the new year did not begin until March.] (Crosby, excerpt on p. 90; appendix to Hull's *Diary,* with the full text on pp. 304-5 and Fortescue, *Calendar 1685-1688,* p. 266, item 944, document 2).

September 23, 1686 - At the request of the Lord Treasurer, Lawrence Hyde, two reports on the reestablishment of the Boston mint, along with some supplementary papers, were sent from Henry Guy, Secretary of the Treasury, to William Blathway (Blathwayt) for the use of the Committee for Trade and Plantations. One report, written by the agents for Massachusetts, explained in six paragraphs why the mint should be reestablished. The arguments focused on the objections made by the Commissioners of the Mint that Massachusetts silver was not equal to the British standard. The six arguments were as follows: (1) the value of money depended on the value of goods; (2) the value and weight of English silver coin had fluctuated several times since it was established by William the Conqueror; (3) the only returns brought to Massachusetts Bay were commodities and Spanish silver eight reales of varying weight, and therefore varying values, which necessitated the erection of a mint where silver coins of a uniform quality could be produced as a standard for payments; (4) that the New England standard has been in place for many years and altering it would enrich landlords and creditors at the expense of tenants and debtors; (5) without a mint Spanish silver would be the predominant coin and the inconveniences related to underweight coinage, which was the problem the mint wished to stop by closing the mint, would persist; and finally (6) Massachusetts did not ask for Letters Patent to be granted for the creation of a private mint as was requested by Thomas Vyner (or Viner) in Ireland in 1662, rather, the Massachusetts Mint would be under the control of and for the profit of the king.

The second report, written by the Commissioners of the Mint,[25] refuted each point made in the first report. They stated (1) the first point was incorrect in that the value of goods was dependent on the quantity of money and not the other way around; (2) whenever the English standard was changed all mints conformed to the change; (3) the point concerning commodities and Spanish silver was deemed irrelevant as commodities and Spanish silver were used in England but they did not affect the English minting standards; (4) concerning the fourth point the Commissioners thought future transactions should be at the English

---

[24] Lawrence Hyde (1641-1711) was the First Lord of the Treasury and a member of the Privy Council from November 19, 1679, through January 4, 1687.

[25] The Commissioners of the mint were: Philip Loyd, Thomas Neale, Charles Duncombe and James Hoare.

standard but all past debts should be discharged at the former rate of Massachusetts silver which they calculated at a 25% differential of 15s in British coinage per £1 in Massachusetts coinage; (5) to the fifth point the Commissioners stated Spanish silver should be treated as a commodity and not as a standard coin; and finally (6) if the king wished to establish a mint in New England, the Commissioners of the Mint would offer rules and instructions for its establishment.

Also appended were the reports of January 15, 1685, and July 15, 1686, as well as the Massachusetts Mint act of 1652 and subsequent regulations against exporting Massachusetts silver [A month after this letter, on October 22, 1686, Blathwayt became the Clerk of the Privy Council] (Crosby, pp. 91-94 and Fortescue, *Calendar 1685-1688,* pp. 266-68, item 944 as appendices to the king's order of October 27, 1686, as follows: the pro mint report is document 5 and the report against the mint is document 7, the supplementary documents included the January 1685 report as document 3, the July 1686 report as document 2 and the 1652 mint act with related Massachusetts regulations as document 4, documents 1 and 6 were simply cover letters).

October 13, 1686 - A report from the Lords of the Committee for Trade and Foreign Plantations concerning the mint in New England was sent to the king stating they did not feel the reestablishment of the mint was in the interest of the king. The Lords felt trade would prosper if the new governor, Sir Edmund Andros, had the right to regulate Spanish pieces of eight and other foreign coins (Crosby, p. 94 and Fortescue, *Calendar 1685-1688,* pp. 256-57, items 905 and 909).

October 27, 1686 - An Order of Council was issued by King James II at Whitehall Palace in Westminster against the reestablishment of the Boston mint but giving the governor the right to regulate eight reales and other foreign coins. Appended to this order were copies of all the documents forwarded from the mint on September 23rd (Crosby, pp. 94-95 and Fortescue, *Calendar 1685-1688,* pp. 266-68, items 944-45, the individual documents appended to this order are identified in the entry for September 23, 1686).

October 31, 1686 - A letter from the king was sent to Edmund Andros, the royal governor designate of Massachusetts, giving him the power to regulate pieces of eight and other foreign coin (Crosby, p. 95).

December 20, 1686 - Edmund Andros landed in Boston from England to rule as the governor of "The Dominion of New England." He was to oversee the abolition of the Commonwealth's charter by dismantling the government and laws of Massachusetts Bay (Palfrey, vol. 2, pp. 319-20 and Hutchinson, *History,* edited by Mayo, p. 300, give the year as 1686; however, in Hart, vol. 1, p. 583 the year is given as 1687).

March 10, 1687 - Andros regulated the value of foreign silver and gold coins, overturning the law of May 24, 1682, and reestablishing the value of a full weight Spanish American eight reales at 6s (in 1682 it had been legislated at 5s6d). The minutes of his Council records stated,

> That all peices of Eight of Civill [that is, Seville] Pillar and mexico of 17ᵈ
> 1/2 weight shall payment at six shillings a peice, and that the present New

England money do pass for value as formerly, the half peices of Eight quarters Royalls and half Royalls do pass pro rata (as meant Coyn and Value) Spanish pistolls at 4 penny 6 grains at 22d N.E. Money. (Toppan, "Right to Coin," p. 224, there is no text between "shall" and "payment" in the minutes, more appropriately the minutes should have included something like, "shall be accepted as payment at... .")

The reference to "17d 1/2 weight" refers to 17.5 pennyweight. Most colonial legislation recognized a 17 pennyweight coin as a full weight example but the Royal Mint used 17.5 pennyweight (In addition to Toppan also see, Fortescue, *Calendar 1685-1688,* pp. 340-41, items 1172 and 1183).

April 30, 1687 - The Commissioners of Customs sent a letter to the Lords of the Treasury against the July 2, 1686 request from Virginia that they be allowed to raise the rates of foreign coinage. The Commissioners felt coins should circulate at their intrinsic value, otherwise the valuations would hinder trade and defraud creditors. The report was received by the Lords of Trade and Plantations on May 3rd and read in committee on May 18th where they concurred with the commissioners findings (Fortescue, *Calendar 1685-1688,* pp. 362 and 370, items 1127 and 1259).

May 11, 1687 – In Hull's extant ledger C on folio 85 verso the account with Joseph Eliot showed a balance due on July 7, 1680, of £23 8s8d which was carried forward to ledger E on folio 11. Apparently as late as 1687 the debt had not been completely paid. In May of 1687 Sewall added a note to the account in the surviving ledger C as follows: "Note – May 11, 1687. I paid mr. Saunderson 36s 6d & so ye whole shop – Debt for ye Gold, is mine. S.S." This note implies in May of 1687 Sewall paid Sanderson for the outstanding balances owed to the shop and thereby became the party to whom the shop debts were owed. Thus it seems in 1687, when Sanderson was 79 or 80, he retired and sold the remaining shop account assets to Sewall, who supervised the Hull estate for his mother-in-law, Judith Hull.

April 7, 1688 - Increase Mather departed Massachusetts for England. Edward Randolph had been looking for him since March 30th to serve him with an arrest warrant. Mather reached London on May 25th where he hoped to intercede on behalf of the colonists of Massachusetts Bay against the arbitrary rule of Andros (Toppan, *Randolph,* vol. 2, Memoir, p. 64).

June 26, 1688 - Richard Holt requested the use of Skinner Hall to produce tin American Plantations tokens valued at 1/24th of a Spanish American real (a farthing) for distribution in the British colonies of North America. Examples of the coin were sent to the Commissioners of the Treasurer on July 27, 1688, and then on August 13th the samples were sent on to the Royal Mint for comment. No further records on the coins are extant. Holt's tin coin was produced but most likely it was never distributed in the colonies.

1688 - The tract, "New England Vindicated," defended the Boston mint since it had used the correct silver fineness and had been established during the Commonwealth when there was no king. The tract also mentioned the coinage of Lord Baltimore and coinage by the East India Company as examples of other coins produced for colonial use (Crosby, p. 113).

November 5, 1688 - William of Orange landed in England at Torbay to make good his claim to the throne. He quickly gained widespread support including the endorsements of Lords Grafton and Churchill, the Duke of Marlborough. Faced with William's impending entry into the city, on the 11th of December the Catholic King James II fled London. The next day a provisional government was established. Soon thereafter James was captured and brought back to London, which William had taken on December 19th. On December 22nd, James escaped. A month later, on January 22, 1689, Parliament was summoned to assemble. On January 28, 1689, the House of Commons declared "the popish prince" James to have abdicated the throne. The House of Lords preferred the word vacated to abdicated. An agreement was reached in a conference of both houses and the crown was offered to Mary with William as regent. This offer was refused by William so Parliament offered the crown to both of them jointly. The Protestants William III and Mary were then declared King and Queen of England. In March of 1689 James established himself in the Catholic city of Dublin. He remained there until William defeated his forces at the Battle of the Boyne on July 1, 1690, when James fled to France.

April 4, 1689 - John Winslow landed in Boston bringing news of the abdication of the hated papist James II and the success of William of Orange (Hart, vol. 1, p. 600).

April 18, 1689 - Some frontier troops who had mutinied against Andros arrived in Boston. Realizing the mutineers faced imminent arrest, the citizens of Boston rioted. News spread that Governor Andros was planning to depart on the frigate H.M.S. *Rose* so at about 10:00 o'clock in the morning the ship was seized and the commander, Captain John George, was taken prisoner. A government consisting of Simon Bradstreet (who had been the last elected governor in the Commonwealth before Dudley assumed power in May of 1686) and other former Massachusetts Bay legislators set up headquarters in the Town Hall between 11:00 AM and noon where a declaration supporting William of Orange was promulgated. Edward Randolph, Justice Benjamin Bullivant and other Andros supporters were captured and placed in jail. The soldiers joined the revolt so that by the afternoon a total of about five thousand men in arms laid siege to the fort where Andros was seeking refuge. Two officers and twelve soldiers defended the fort. Andros capitulated and was taken away under armed escort. The next day the fort was taken. On Saturday, April 20th, "The Council for the Safety of the People and the Conservation of the Peace" was constituted at the initiation of the Boston ministers with Bradstreet as President and charged to create a new provisional government (Hart, vol. 1, pp. 600-3; Moody, pp. 45-57 and 85, also Fortescue, *Calendar 1689-1692,* pp. 33, 59-62, 66-68, 92-95, items 96, 180-82, 196 and 261).

May 22-24, 1689 - A convention of representatives from the several towns and villages of Massachusetts was held in Boston. In a resolution of May 24th the convention unanimously voted to reinstate the elected officers from the General Court of 1686 and that the government be constituted under the charter of Massachusetts Bay abiding by the laws as they were on May 12, 1686 (Cushing, *Laws,* vol. 3, pp. 643, 645 and 647 and Moody, pp. 392-95).

June 5-6, 1689 - A reconstituted General Court met with a newly elected lower house. The full group convened on Wednesday June 5th under the auspices of "The Council for the Safety of the People and Conservation of the Peace." On June 6th Governor Simon

Bradstreet, Deputy Governor Thomas Danforth and a council consisting of those who had been elected in 1686 under the old charter took their oaths and assumed their former offices. The official name of the body became, "The Convention of the Governour and Council, and Representatives of the Massachusetts Colony." This remained the official name of the government until a new charter was granted to Massachusetts on October 7, 1691, although the body was frequently referred to as the General Court (Hart, vol. 2, pp. 3-4 and Moody, pp. 86-92).

August 12, 1689 - King William III sent a letter from Whitehall to the Governor, Council and Convention of Representatives of the Colony of Massachusetts giving the group the authority to continue their administration until further instructions were received. The letter did not reach Boston until December 3rd. No further instructions were sent until the new charter was issued in October of 1691 (Moody, pp. 175-76 and Fortescue, *Calendar 1689-1692,* p. 119, item 332).

December 3, 1689 - A Convention of the Governor, Council and Representatives, otherwise known as a special session of the General Court, was convened "by Order of the Governour and Council upon the Arrival of a Ship from London." The ship carried three letters from the king which were read on the opening day of the convention. One letter, dated July 13, 1689, requested that Andros and the other prisoners be sent to England. The most important letter, dated August 12, 1689, signified the king's approval of their actions and acceptance of their administration, while the third letter, from August 15th, instructed Massachusetts to restore the sails and some other items taken from the frigate *Rose.* [On April 22nd the Council for the Safety of the People had ordered the sails of the *Rose* be brought ashore to prevent any supporters of Andros from escaping.] The king's letter of August 12th was gratefully received and was printed by Richard Pierce for distribution (Moody, pp. 56 and 174-77).

January 24, 1690 - The General Court issued instructions for their London agents to follow in negotiating the rights and privileges to be included in a new royal charter for Massachusetts Bay. The leader of the group, Increase Mather, minister of the Second Church in Boston, had arrived in England back on May 25, 1688, to plead with James II and stayed on to petition William III for a new charter. In late 1689 with the prospects of negotiations for a new charter imminent, Massachusetts Bay appointed Elisha Cooke and Thomas Oakes as additional agents to assist Mather; also, Henry Ashurst, a wealthy London non-conformist was appointed as an agent. Among the instructions issued by the General Court in the document of January 24, 1690, which Cooke and Oakes brought to London, was, "...to Solicite, That the Liberty of Coynage may be allowed us" (Crosby, p. 96; Hart, vol. 2, pp. 4-7; Moody, pp. 197-99 and Fortescue, *Calendar 1689-1692,* p. 212, item 739).

February 10, 1690 - Two ships departed Boston for London. One ship, under the command of Richard Martin sailed directly for England carrying Cooke and Oakes to assist Mather in negotiations for a new charter. The other ship, *The Mehitabell,* under Captain Gilbert Bant, took the hated Andros and the royal informer, Edward Randolph, along with Joseph Dudley (who had been under house arrest) and five other Andros supporters back to England [the five were John Palmer, John West, James Graham, George Farewell and James Sherlock. On June 7, 1689, Justice Benjamin Bullivant, who had been jailed on April 18th, was freed in Boston upon payment of a £3,000 bond]. The *Mehitabell* anchored off Nantasket for five days before setting out for England on February 15th. Captain Bant arrived in London by mid-April and petitioned the king for payment for the passage of the prisoners. On April 14th charges were drawn up against the eight defendants and read on the 16th, on the 24th the eight formally denied the charges (Hall, *Randolph,* p. 129; Moody, pp. 93 and 203-4; Goodrick, *Randolph,* vol. 6, pp. 334-35 and vol. 7, pp. 342-44; Fortescue, *Calendar 1689-1692,* pp. 246 and 251-52, items 827-28 and 844-45).

March 1690 - William Grimes of Billerica was accused of making two Massachusetts shillings out of pewter or lead. It appears his indictment was lost and he was never convicted (Scott, *Counterfeiting in Colonial America,* pp. 17-18).

April 23, 1690 - As part of an ongoing struggle against the French, known as "King William's War," Sir William Phips departed from Boston on board the gunship *Six Friends* to lead a militia contingent and four other ships waiting at Nantasket. The expedition attacked and defeated the French settlement at Port Royal, Acadia (now called Annapolis Royal, Nova Scotia) and then spent several days looting and plundering. Phips returned to Boston victorious on May 30, 1690, with a considerable wealth in plunder (Baker and Reid, *The New England Knight,* pp. 87-95).

Mid-August 1690 - Sir William Phips set sail, at the head of an armada of 34 vessels and 2,300 troops, departing Boston to attack the French fort of Quebec, commanded by Louis de Baude, Comte de Frontenac. Due to inclement weather, the fleet did not arrive at Quebec until October 6th. Continued bad weather, smallpox, poor planning and a strong defense by the French necessitated a retreat within a week. Phips's second in command, John Walley, bore the blame because he had led the 1,200 ground troops and was unable to advance on the town (partly due to the fact that the artillery had been unloaded on the wrong side of the St. Charles river!). The failure of this campaign necessitated the paper currency emission of December 10, 1690, since the expected victory and anticipated booty planned to be used to pay for the expedition did not materialize (Baker and Reid, *The New England Knight,* pp. 96-107).

December 10, 1690 - The General Court authorized an emission of £7,000 in paper currency to pay for military expenses related to an unsuccessful attempt to take Quebec in the fall of that year. This was the first public paper currency issued in the western world (Cushing, *Laws,* vol. 3, p. 667, for a facsimile edition of the original act and Moody, pp. 290-91).

soon after January 7, 1691 - Sir William Phips departed Boston for London, arriving on March 4, 1691. Phips went to London to defend his military record, encourage further expeditions against the French in Canada, promote his own career and fortune as well as to assist his good friend Increase Mather and the Massachusetts agents in negotiations relating to a new Massachusetts charter. By mid-April Phips had exonerated himself from blame for the failed Quebec expedition and was becoming influential in the formulation of the new charter (Baker and Reid, *The New England Knight,* pp. 108-32).

February 3, 1691 - The General Court was convened by special order of the Governor (Moody, p. 295).

February 6, 1691 - The General Court authorized an additional emission of paper currency beyond the £7,000 limit that had been authorized in December of 1690. The notes of this new second emission were issued under the date of February 3rd, which was the date of the opening of that special session of the General Court [since the new year did not begin until March 25th, the year printed on the notes was February 3, 1690, which in new style is February 3, 1691] (Moody, pp. 296-97).

May 21, 1691 - Following the spring elections held on May 20th, the General Court convened on the 21st for the spring session (Moody, pp. 307-9).

May 26, 1691 - The General Court passed legislation limiting the size of both currency emissions to an aggregate total of £40,000. In effect, this limited the February 3rd emission to £33,000. As often was the case, this order was recorded under the opening date of the court and thus is frequently dated to May 21st (Moody, pp. 311-12).

August 10, 1691 - Based on an interpretation of various letters and diaries, it seems on August 10th William Phips and Massachusetts's London-born agent, Henry Ashurst, made an agreement with Henry Finch, the Earl of Nottingham, conceding to support more stringent royal controls over the colony as proposed by the Lords of Trade and approved by the Privy Council and the king, contrary to the wishes of Increase Mather and the other Massachusetts agents. On August 20th Phips and the Massachusetts agents were summonsed to attend a meeting of the Lords of Trade where the Earl of Nottingham reported that concerning the proposal for the Massachusetts charter, "Sir William Phips had been with him to lett him know that the New England agents did acquiesce therein." This led to the acceptance of the British plan and brought Phips into favor with the Lords of Trade. From that point Phips was designated as a principal participant and speaker for several proposals brought forward on behalf of Massachusetts (Baker and Reid, *The New England Knight,* pp. 119-22 and Fortescue, *Calendar 1689-1692,* p. 525, item 1706).

October 7, 1691 - King William III signed a new charter for Massachusetts Bay. Under the old charter all governmental officers were elected annually. The reconstituted government under the new charter consisted of a governor, lieutenant governor and a secretary appointed by the king with a treasurer who was annually elected by the General Court. The Assembly consisted of two houses, a Council of 28 members selected annually by the General Court and a House of Representatives annually elected by freeholders in town meetings. The General Court consisted of the governor and the Assembly. All bills needed to pass both houses and had to have the approval of the governor. The governor with the consent of the Council made judicial appointments; however the salary of the governor and judges was under the control of the House. The king's disallowance of any act had to be signified within three years (Hart. vol. 2, pp. 10-12; Moody, pp. 599-620 and Fortescue, *Calendar 1689-1692,* p. 550, item 1806).

October 16, 1691 - Martin Williams, a bricklayer from Salem was convicted of having counterfeited and passed off five eight reales in Salem during April. His punishment was to stand in the pillory for one hour per day for three days and to pay all fees associated with his trial (Scott, *Counterfeiting in Colonial America,* p. 17).

November 27, 1691 - The Privy Council confirmed the appointment of William Phips as the first royal governor of Massachusetts under the new charter. News of the appointment reached Boston on January 24, 1692 (Baker and Reid, *The New England Knight,* pp. 126-32 and Fortescue, *Calendar 1689-1692,* p. 572, item 1917).

January 19, 1692 - A letter was sent from the Royal Mint Commissioners Ben Overton, Thomas Neale and James Hoar to the Lords Commissioners of the Treasury concerning a proposal put forward by William Phips and the Massachusetts delegation for the minting of silver coinage in Massachusetts. The letter was written in reply to an inquiry sent to them on January 12, 1692 by Lord Treasurer Henry Guy:

> ...touching the Proposalls, and Reasons offered to their Majesties by Sir William Phipps, etc., for obtaining their Majesties Royall favour to be granted to the Genrall Court in the Province of the Massachusetts Bay in New England to Privelige them with Liberty of Coyning for the Benefitt of their Majesties Subjects in that Territory.

In their reply the Royal Mint Commissioners stated:

> wee Conceive it very probable, That most of the Monies which have been coined in New England from the year 1652 (when they had the priveledge of Coining,) may still remain there. Soe that it is scarce credible (as they suggest) that shoppkeepers and those that are buyers should labour under such difficulties for want of Small Monies for Change, Since the coyned monies of New England are the shilling, Sixpence, three Pence, and two Pence, Besides Small Spanish Coins.

They also expressed the opinion that if the colony needed smaller denomination coins "They may be Supplyed with Pence, Halfe Pence, and farthings of Tinn, from England, to their Majesties Advantage." Further, they refuted the statements of the colonists that other "English Plantations" had been granted the privilege of coinage, explaining the application to mint coins by the Governor of Jamaica was not granted and that the East India Company coinage was restricted to circulation in India. They then concluded that if the Province of Massachusetts Bay was granted the privilege of coining money it should be required to conform to the British weight and fineness for silver coins. This is the last surviving record concerning the reestablishment of the Massachusetts Mint [The document is dated 1691 as the English new year did not start until March] (text in Crosby, pp. 96-97 and summary in Redington, p. 214).

May 14, 1692 - Sir William Phips arrived back in Boston on the ship, *Nonsuch.* Ceremonies for the arrival of the new governor were reserved because the ship arrived in port on a Saturday evening and the Puritans strictly enforced "blue laws" regarding the observance of Sunday, which started at sunset on Saturday. On Monday, the government of Massachusetts Bay was constituted under Phips according to the new Royal Charter of 1691. Writs were issued for elections to the House of Representatives (Baker and Reid, *The New England Knight,* pp. 130-32 and Hart, vol. 2, p. 15).

1692 - The Salem witchcraft trials were conducted with Hull's son-in-law, Samuel Sewall, as one of the judges. The first arrest occurred on February 28, 1692, and the final eight executions took place on September 22nd (Hart, vol. 2, pp. 38-47).

November 24, 1692 - The Massachusetts General Court passed an act against counterfeiting in two sections. Section one stated Massachusetts silver would pass current at face value while a full weight Spanish American eight reales, that is, a piece of eight at 17 pennyweight, would pass at 6s each. (On May 24, 1682, the Spanish American eight reales had been legislated at 5s6d but that was overturned by Andros on March 10, 1687. Based on the wording of the Act of October 19, 1697, it seems the coin frequently traded at 6s in daily commerce.) Section two of the November 24, 1692 Act set the penalty for counterfeiting at forfeiting double the value of the money counterfeited, as well as spending time standing in the pillory and having one ear cut off (Crosby, pp. 99-100, *Acts and Resolves,* vol. 1, pp. 70-71, Acts of 1692-1693, chapter 31).

October 7, 1693 - Robert Sanderson died.

August 22, 1695 - The entire November 24, 1692 act against counterfeiting (both sections) was disallowed by the Privy Council since it was thought the crime of counterfeiting should be punished as it was in England. The section revaluing the Spanish American eight reales to 6s was also included in the repeal (Crosby, p. 100 and *Acts and Resolves,* vol. 1, pp. 70-71, Acts of 1692-1693, chapter 31).

May 30, 1696 - The Lieutenant Governor of Massachusetts[26] and the Council ordered a committee of both houses to be formed to investigate proposals to stop the exportation of money from the colony. The committee members were Samuel Sewall, John Foster and Eliakim Hutchinson from the Council with Nathan Byfield, Nehemiah Jewet, Nathaniel Oliver and John Eyre from the House (Crosby, pp. 98-99).

June 2, 1696 - The committee requested its charge be expanded to include counterfeiting and revaluing silver as well as the exportation of coins. On the verso of the paper containing the order of May 30, 1696, is a proposal put forward by Samuel Sewall on behalf of the committee that, "In addition to the Act against Counterfeiting, Clipping, Rounding, Filing, or impairing of Coyne," they wished to propose that "the Coyne of the late Massachusetts Colony" along with Spanish silver pass current at seven shillings per troy ounce [this equaled six shillings per eight reales which was 33.33% above parity with Britain; because the face value of Massachusetts silver was only 22.5% above the British standard, the proposal would increase the face value of Massachusetts silver by a little over 11%]. The proposal also requested a "Suitable Clause to be drawn up, to prevent the Exportation of Money" (Crosby, p. 99).

---

[26] Phips left office on November 17, 1694. Lieutenant Governor William Stoughton served as acting governor until Richard Coote, the Earl of Bellomont, took office as governor on May 26, 1699. Coote left office on July 17, 1700, and Lieutenant Governor Stoughton again took over as acting governor until his death on July 7, 1701. At that time the Council acted as governor until Joseph Dudley took the office of governor on June 11, 1702. Dudley continued in that post until 1715 (*Massachusetts Royal Commissions*, p. xxxiv).

October 19, 1697 - An act for ascertaining the value of coins current in the province was passed by the Council, once again placing the value of the eight reales at six shillings but retaining Massachusetts silver at face value. [The 6s valuation for a full weight eight reales had been proposed as early as June 2, 1669, and was first enacted in legislation of October 8, 1672. The valuation had been officially lowered to 5s6d by the Act of May 24, 1682, and then raised back to 6s by Andros on March 10, 1687. The 6s rate was also part of the anti-counterfeiting legislation that was passed on November 24, 1692, but the Privy Council had invalidated that act on August 22, 1695. Massachusetts silver continued to circulate at face value throughout this period. Although the eight reales had been legislated at different rates over the years it seems, based on the wording in the preamble to the 1697 act, that full weight eight reales had passed at the 6s rate in general commerce for several years.] The act stated:

> Whereas for many yeares past the money coyned in the late Massachusetts Colony hath passed currant at the rate or value it was stampt for, and good Sevil, pillar, or mexico pieces of Eight of full Seventeen penny weight, have also passed Currant at Six Shillings per piece... the Coynes before mentioned shall stil be and continue currant money... at the respective values aforesaid, according as hath heretofore been accustomed.

The act was read in the House of Representatives on October 19th and was passed by that body on the same day. The law was published on October 21st (Crosby, pp. 100-101 and *Acts and Resolves,* vol. 1, p. 296, Acts of 1697, chapter 16).

December 22, 1697 - An act prohibiting the exportation of money from the colony was passed. This act limited the amount of coins a person could take out of the colony to £5 and required the master of each vessel to swear an oath that, to the best of his knowledge, there was no smuggling on his ship. This act was of limited duration, remaining in force only until the end of the May 1700 session of the General Assembly (which began on May 29, 1700, and continued until at least July 13th, when the last acts passed in the session were recorded). The law had three readings in the House, was voted and sent up for concurrence on the 21st and was passed by the Council and published on the 22nd. This act was unfavorably received in England because there was no clause allowing coinage or bullion to be imported into England. The British Solicitor General, Hawles, wrote against this act on August 9, 1700. A letter from the Council of Trade and Plantations to the Lord Justices, on October 9, 1700, stated the act was temporary and already had the desired result so nothing further needed to be done. However, in a letter of October 30, 1700, to Massachusetts Bay Governor Richard Coote, the Council stated that the act should not be revived (Crosby, pp. 101-2 and *Acts and Resolves,* vol. 1, pp. 306-7 and comments on the English reaction on p. 308, Acts of 1697, chapter 24).

February 21, 1701 - An act against the making or passing of base or counterfeit money was brought before the Council. According to the act some individuals had recently begun emitting brass and tin coins that were being passed at the rate of one penny [there was no penny denomination in Britain only the farthing and the halfpenny]. The preamble stated:

> Whereas some persons, for private gain, have of late presumed to Stamp and
> Emit peices of brass and Tin at the rate of a penny each, not regarding what
> loss they thereby bring on others, which, if not timely remedyed, may prove
> greatly detrimental to his Majesties Subjects, and embolden others to be so
> hardy as to attempt the doing of the like,... .

The punishments for stamping, emitting or passing counterfeit coins included a fine not exceeding £50 and up to six months imprisonment per offence as well as paying triple the value of all counterfeit pieces passed. It was further ordered that anyone who had issued such pieces with their mark on the items would be required, for a period of three months following the publication of the act, to pay any person lawful currency in exchange for these items according to the rate at which the coins passed. Since the law mentioned that issuers had included their mark [that is, their initials or other identifying mark] on the coins, it seems these items probably represented privately produced merchant tokens rather than the products of surreptitious counterfeiting operations. The act was passed by the Council and sent to the House of Representatives for a first reading (Crosby, pp. 114-15 and *Acts and Resolves,* vol. 1, p. 445, Acts of 1700-1701, chapter 17).

February 28, 1701 - The act against making or passing base or counterfeit money was read a second time in the House of Representatives.

March 3, 1701 - A report of a Committee of the General Court on financial matters recommended the following four measures: (1) They wished to value the Spanish gold pistole at twenty four shillings. (2) They suggested that eight reales weighing "more or less than seventeen peny wait do pass at seaven Shillings per ounce Troy waight, in all payments of ten pounds & upward" (i.e. lightweight eight reales would pass at six shillings in large transactions, this is often referred to in colonial documents as by "tale" or by piece or tally rather than by weight). (3) They also suggested a copper coin (possibly a penny) be issued with the simple statement, "That Provinc penc be made of Copper & pass Curant for change of Mony." Finally they suggested (4) incorporating a bank of credit to emit paper currency (Crosby, pp. 116-17).

March 6, 1701 - The report on financial matters was read in the Council and sent down to the House of Representatives (Crosby, pp. 116-17).

March 8, 1701 - The report on financial matters was read a first time in the House of Representatives (Crosby, pp. 116-17).

March 12, 1701 - The report on financial matters was read for a second and third time in the House of Representatives and put to a vote. The first and third paragraphs (on the valuation of gold and the minting of coppers) passed, while the second and fourth paragraphs (on eight reales and the bank) were rejected. The act was then sent up to the Council for a vote (Crosby pp. 116-17).

March 12, 1701 - The act against making or passing base or counterfeit money was read a third time in the House of Representatives, after which it was put to a vote, passed and was adopted. The act was published on March 14th (Crosby, p. 115 and *Acts and Resolves,* vol. 1, p. 445, Acts of 1700-1701, chapter 17).

March 13, 1701 - The Council rejected the suggestions in the report on financial matters. The act was not adopted (Crosby, pp. 116-17).

May 21, 1701 - In London, Samuel Davis submitted a proposal to Lords Commissioners of the Treasury for the production of small change coins with different mottoes and devices for the various colonies in the West Indies and the continent of North America. In all, he proposed four series: one series for Barbados, another for Jamaica, a different series for the Leeward Islands and a single series for all the colonies on the continent! These were to be, "halfe pence and pence of Copper or a Mixed metall, and of halfe ye value the English Small Money is made." On the same day the proposal was submitted to the Commissioners of the Mint for comment. Their reply is listed below under July 9th (Crosby, p. 140-41).

July 9, 1701 - The Commissioners of the Royal Mint (Sir Isaac Newton, Sir John Stanley and Sir Charles Ellis) replied to the Commissioners of the Treasury concerning the proposal of Samuel Davis. They did not support the proposal stating that although "the Plantations in America are in great Want of Small Money," the face value of the coins should be as close as possible to the sum of the intrinsic value of the metal plus the minting costs. Further, they stated that small change should be made of copper similar in quality to the copper used in Britain so as to discourage counterfeiting. The mint correctly realized the use of more malleable metals such as tin, lead or brass encouraged counterfeiting. They had recently experienced this problem having introduced tin small change coinage in 1684 but within a decade were forced to reinstate copper farthings in 1693 and halfpence in 1694 because of extensive counterfeiting. The mint reply further explained if an agreement was to be contracted with Davis, a specific quantity of coinage to be minted needed to be stated and the markings on the coins should be easily distinguished from the British coppers to prevent them from circulating in England. Since there was no further action on the Davis proposal, it seems the proposal was tabled (Crosby, p. 141).

July 7, 1702 - The London mintmaster, Isaac Newton, along with his associates, John Stanley, warden of the mint, and Charles Ellis, mint comptroller, submitted their report to Sidney Godolphin, Lord High Treasurer of England, concerning their extensive assay of 44 foreign silver and 12 foreign gold coins, detailing the intrinsic value of each coin in relation to the intrinsic value of British coinage. Several assays were performed at the mint (for example in 1696, 1704 and 1717) as well as numerous additional assays of individual coins, but the 1702 assay was the most comprehensive and the results of this assay were used as the basis for the coinage valuations issued in Queen Anne's Proclamation of 1704. (Mossman, chapters 1-2 for extensive coverage; also the report is edited in William A Shaw, *Select Tracts and Documents Illustrative of English Monetary History 1626-1730,* London: Wilsons and Milne, 1896, rpt., New York: August M. Kelley Publications, 1967, pp. 136-49; also see the web page "The 1702 Assay," in the Notre Dame Colonial Currency site at: http://www.coins.nd.edu/ColCurrency/CurrencyIntros/Intro1702Assay.html)

November 21, 1702 - The General Court authorized an emission of £6,000 in indented bills of credit. This constitutes the third Massachusetts emission. The notes were completely redesigned from those in the two previous emissions and printed from three new plates engraved by John Coney. These plates were modified and continued to be used for several subsequent emissions through 1711. On July 27, 1703, the size of the emission was increased by £5,492 to a total of £11,492. [Newman, *Early Paper,* 3rd ed., p. 182, confuses the acts, as he refers to Acts of October 15, 1702, and March 27, 1703, as authorizing a total of £10,000 for this emission. Actually October 15, 1702, was the opening date of the fall session, with the only currency act of that session being dated November 21st. Also, the March 27, 1703 Act was against counterfeiting and clipping, it did not address the size of the 1702 currency emission.] (See: *Acts and Resolves,* vol. 1, p. 503-4, Acts of 1702, chapter 8 and the note on p. 508; also for the increase to the emission see pp. 520-25, Acts of 1703-1704, chapter 3, especially the top of p. 521).

March 17, 1703 - A proposal from William Chalkhill, formerly a coiner at the Tower Mint in London but then residing in Boston, was sent from the House of Representatives to the Council for reading. The proposal stated that Chalkhill was willing to go to England to purchase £10,000 in copper money at a price agreed upon by the General Court (Crosby, p. 225).

March 19, 1703 - A committee was formed to investigate Chalkhill's proposal. The members were: John Walley, Penn Townsend and Andrew Belcher of the Council and Nehemiah Jewett, Samuel Checkley and Samuel Phips of the House of Representatives (Crosby, pp. 225-26).

March 26, 1703 - The committee produced a favorable report suggesting an agreement be finalized but limited to £5,000 for coins "in Pence." The report was read in the Council on this day (Crosby, p. 226).

March 27, 1703 - The report was sent down to the House of Representatives where it was resolved the report be accepted and that a committee of John Walley, Andrew Belcher, Samuel Legg and Samuel Checkley be empowered to draw up articles of agreement with Mr. Chalkhill. The resolve of the House was sent up to the Council where it was put up for concurrence but was voted down; however, the Council added the proposal could be "refer'd to Consideration at the next Court, if then offered." There are no further records that this topic was ever brought before the General Court again (Crosby, p. 226).

March 27, 1703 - An act was passed against either counterfeiting or impairing, diminishing or debasing any of the money established to be current in Massachusetts Bay by washing, clipping, rounding, filing or scaling. Offenders would be punished by being "set in the pillory by the space of one whole hour, and have one of his ears nailed thereto" as well as being whipped with up to forty lashes and paying a fine. Additionally, anyone "duely convicted of buying or receiving any clippings, scalings or filing of money" was to be fined £20. The act was passed on the 27th and published on the 29th (*Acts and Resolves,* vol. 1, p. 514, Acts of 1702-1703, chapter 2).

March 24, 1704 - An act was passed to emit an additional £10,000 in bills of credit to be received into the treasury for payment of debts. The act was passed on the 24th and published on the 29th. There were several additional emissions within the next twelve months authorized by the resolves as follows: £5,000 on June 30, 1704; £7,000 on August 17, 1704; £ 12,000 on November 18, 1704; and £8,000 on February 27, 1705 (*Acts and Resolves,* vol. 1, p. 540-41, Acts of 1703-1704, chapter 16 and notes on p. 542 concerning a bill of November 13, 1703, and a resolve of December 2, 1703, concerning this emission; also pp. 561-62 for the emissions of June 20, 1704 through February 27, 1705).

June 18, 1704 - Queen Anne issued a proclamation setting the standard value for foreign silver coins in all British colonies at 33.33% above par with England, so the eight reales would be valued at six shillings in all colonies. Generally, this meant foreign silver would trade in the colonies at a rate of 33.33% above the valuation established in the Assay of 1702 (Crosby, pp. 117-18).

November 28, 1704 - Governor Joseph Dudley delivered Queen Anne's proclamation to the Massachusetts Council (Crosby, p. 119).

March 3, 1705 - The Council passed a resolution ordering Queen Anne's proclamation be issued. The resolution further stated only coinage of full weight would pass "by Tale" (that is, by the piece) according to the rates stated in the proclamation and the laws of the province. The resolution was sent down to the House of Representatives where an amendment was added that lightweight money was to be pro-rated at 7s per troy ounce; this was to remain in effect until further provisions could be made at the next assembly. The resolution was sent back up to the Council and was voted into law on the same day (Crosby, pp. 119-20).

June 1, 1705 - The Council appointed five of its members and the secretary of the General Court to serve on a joint committee[27] for, "annexing of Penaltys on such as shall offer money by tale, under Due weight, and further for the reforming of the money." The proposal was sent down to the House for concurrence, where it was given a first reading (Crosby, p. 121).

June 5, 1705 - The Council's proposal for a joint committee was given a second reading in the House of Representatives (Crosby, p. 121).

June 7, 1705 - The House passed the Council's proposal with an amendment adding ten members of the House to the joint committee.[28] This amendment was agreed to in the Council (Crosby, p. 121).

June 8, 1705 - The joint committee issued their report stating Queen Anne's proclamation of 1704 was to "...be revived and continued without Limitation" and that, "...some skilful person be appointed to calculate a Table of the due proportions of Coines and Silver of Sterling alloy by the Ounce Troy to the weight of a peny, and that Copy's thereof be printed." They also stated "some other skilful person" should make brass weights in the troy scale for the various denominations and that the weights carry an official government seal (Crosby, pp. 121-22).

---

[27] Members of the committee were: Elisha Hutchinson, William Browne, Samuel Sewall, Eliakim Hutchinson, Samuel Legg and the secretary of the court, Isaac Addington.

[28] House members added to the committee were: Samuel Checkley, Captain Stephen French, Major Samuel Brown, Nathaniel Knolton, Major James Converse, Captain Thomas Oliver, Samuel Clapp, Ephram Pierce, Samuel Knowles and Captain Preserved Clapp.

June 9, 1705 - The report of the joint committee was read in the Council (Crosby, p. 122).

June 11, 1705 - The report of the joint committee was given a second reading and accepted by the Council with the amendment that the use of paper currency (that is, bills of public credit) emitted by Massachusetts Bay were also acceptable for payment of debts. This was sent down for concurrence by the House but no further action is recorded (Crosby, p. 122).

April 5, 1715 - A letter to the General Court from their agent, Jeremiah Dummer, in London mentions that some people in Britain having heard of:

> ...the Exigency which the Countrey was reduc't to for want of money, or some other medium of trade, have started a project for the coining base money here, (that is to Say, one third copper, and the rest silver) to pass in New England, which they pretend will answer all the necessities of trade, tho' in truth it will answer nothing but their own private gain,... .

Dummer stated he spoke to several individuals in the ministry who assured him nothing would come of the project. Jeremiah Dummer (1681 - May 19, 1739) was the son of the silversmith Jeremiah Dummer (September 14, 1645 - May 24, 1718). The elder Dummer had been apprenticed to John Hull and engraved the plates for the first Connecticut Currency in 1709 (Crosby 141-42; Clarke and Foote, *Jeremiah Dummer: Colonial Craftsman,* pp. 14, 23 and 40).

August 20, 1722 - This is the date of the death of John Coney, one of Boston's leading silversmiths and the engraver of the three plates used for the November 21, 1702 paper currency emission and several subsequent emissions. On September 3, 1722, his widow Mary Coney, and the executors of the Coney estate (Samuel Gerrish, Jonathan Williams and William Tyler) signed an obligation stating that £2,000 was to be paid to the probate court, apparently for Coney's outstanding debts. The obligation required that a "true and perfect Inventory" of all Coney's assets be produced by December 3rd of that year and that the estate be settled by September 3, 1723. An itemized inventory listing all of Coney's tools, properties and other assets with a valuation assigned for each entry was created and signed by Jonathan Williams, Jonathan Jackson and Andrew Tyler on October 15, 1722. The third item on the second page of the inventory was "An Engine for Coining with all Utensils belonging thereto" valued at "£10 10s" (mistranscribed by Clarke in his Hull biography on p. 133 as £10-0-0). Although there is no evidence as to the origin of this coining engine, it is sometimes thought the machine may have passed down from Hull to his apprentice Jeremiah Dummer and then to Coney, for Coney was related by marriage to Dummer. Coney's first and second wives died ca. 1679 and on April 17, 1694, respectively. On November 8, 1694, Coney married his third wife, the former Mary Atwater, with whom he had six children. Mary's sister Hannah Atwater had married Dummer in 1672. Thus, it is possible this machine represented some of the equipment used in the Massachusetts silver mint.

The disposition of the coining engine, or as we would call it, the coining press, is unknown. The entire estimated valuation of Coney's estate was £3,714-2s-11.5d, of which

£1,198-2s-11.5d represented the value of all his possessions along with cash received on outstanding accounts from clients, while the remaining £2,516 represented the value of his real estate. Apparently after the inventory was tallied, an additional £70 3s in cash came in from monies owed to Coney. Also, deeds were discovered for two additional parcels of land of 500 acres each, one in Connecticut and the other in Providence, Rhode Island. Precisely which items were sold to satisfy the £2,000 obligation is not known. Apparently the executors began selling off the estate soon after the inventory was completed, since an advertisement in the *Boston Gazette* for November 5-12, 1722, stated, "This evening the remaining part of the Tools of the late Mr. Coney are to be sold. About 5 a Clock." The notice implies that by early November all of Coney's tools had been sold.

It seems the Coney inventory was not filed with the probate court until around the December due date since the probate judge, Samuel Sewall, added a dated note to the inventory on January 7, 1723 [the document used 1722, as the new year did not begin until March] stating Mary Coney and Samuel Gerrish had presented the inventory to him and had sworn it was a complete account of John Coney's estate. No further documents exist. It seems the inventory had proven to the court that the estate would be able to pay the £2,000 requested by the probate court. It also seems that the executors were able to liquidate the estate within the one year period authorized by the court (Clarke, *Coney,* pp. 12-13, with four pages of unnumbered plates reproducing the obligation and full inventory of the estate included between these two pages).

❀❀❀❀❀❀❀❀❀❀

List of Figures

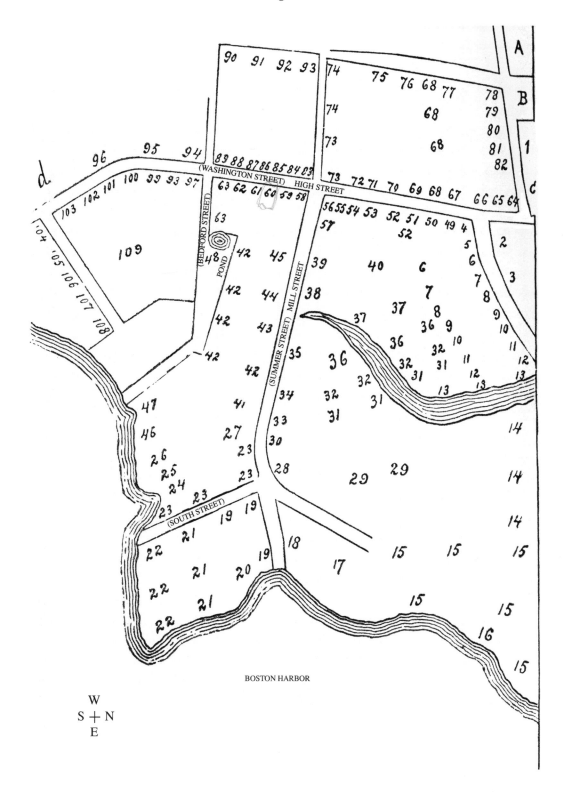

Figure 1 - Detail of the homestead lots listed in *the Book of Possessions* in what now is the center of the Boston shopping district. Whitmore designated this portion of the town as section F. The homestead of Robert Hull is lot 60. From Whitmore, 1881, p. 74 with the addition of period street names and modern street names in parenthesis.

Figure 2 - A silversmith at a wind oven. In the foreground on the floor is a crucible with a cover (5) and the iron brace (7) used to stabilize the crucible. Leaning against the oven is a pair of tongs (6) used to place the crucible into and take it out of the oven. To the right an assistant prepares compounds used in gold and silversmithing. From Lazarus Ercker, *Treatise on Ores and Assaying*, translated by Pettus in *Fleta Minor*, 1683, detail from sculpture 25 on p. 200.

Figure 3 - An example of an outdoor foundry furnace from Agricola's 1556 treatise *De re metallica* as published by Hoover, p. 482.

Figure 4 - A large London goldsmith shop from ca. 1675. In the foreground is a forge with a variety of tools. Two men work the forge (5 and 9) while three others shape bowls and pots with sledgehammers (11). Finishing work and engraving is performed at the back of the room (16 and 17). In the center of the room a large assay oven is in operation (13 and 15) while to the right an individual weighs the assays (14). Frontispiece from the 1677 work, *A Touch-stone for Silver and Gold Wares. Or, A Manual for Goldsmiths,* by William Badcock.

Figure 5 - A silversmith in front of an assay oven. To the right of the oven is a tray with lead buttons to be assayed. Below, hanging on a hook, is a face protector with a slot in the center through which the fire can be viewed. From Lazarus Ercker, *Treatise on Ores and Assaying*, translated by Pettus in *Fleta Minor*, 1683, detail from sculpture 19 on p. 153.

Figures 6 and 7 - Cupel preparation. In figure 6, above, one individual is washing ash in a large vat of water while another is forming cupels. Figure 7, below, shows the cupels. In the lower right are ash balls that are placed in metal collars and then shaped with pestles to form various size cupels.' As seen in figure 6, the pestle is hit with a wooden block to form the ash into the shape of the collar with an indent or bowl at the top. In figure 7 the second item from the left in row two, designated as number 5, represents a stack of small cupels ready to be baked in an oven. The stacked cupels are not to scale with the other items in this illustration. From Lazarus Ercker, *Treatise on Ores and Assaying*, translated by Pettus in *Fleta Minor*, 1683, details from sculpture 5 on p. 24.

Figure 8 - The muffle. On the floor to the right of the oven is a complete muffle showing the protective dome and the passageway (listed as A and C, with the slots in the dome listed as B). Parts of a muffle and various assay-related tools are in the foreground on the floor. In the center, in the open oven, one can see a muffle in use. Wood and coals are dumped directly on top of the muffle dome so it cannot be seen, however the muffle passageway is visible. It prevents the coals from obstructing the view of the cupel that is inside the muffle. When the oven door is closed the arched opening in the door will line up with the muffle passageway giving the assayer a direct view of the assay. From Agricola's 1556 treatise *De re metallica* as published by Hoover, p. 489.

Figures 9 and 10. Two varieties of NE shillings, representing two obverse and two reverse punches. Figure 9, Stack's, *Hain Collection*, lot 1, a Noe II-A at 71.7 grains. Figure 10, Stack's, *Hain Collection*, lot 3, a Noe III-C at 69.8 grains. Images are 4x. The NE sixpence and threepence are not illustrated. Images are 4x.

Comments about these two coins follow the proposed steps of manufacture as described in the text, namely: rolling strips of stock, cutting the stock into small squares, punching the squares and finally cutting the coins to a round shape.

There are several small marks on the planchets, most notably, the four raised dots at 3:00 o'clock (or 270° counterclockwise) on the obverse of the Noe II-A representing imperfections in the wrought iron rollers that were used to flatten and smooth the strips of stock. The flattened stock was cut into small squares and then punched. Mike Hodder has noted the impressions show faint outlines of doubling, especially evident in the XI of the XII on the Noe III-C. This indicates the punch was struck with a hammer or mallet more than once when impressing the coin. Each subsequent strike would deepen and usually cover the earlier impression. Blows that were slightly off center resulted in the doubling. The outline of the entire punch is visible on the Noe II-A, especially on the reverse, demonstrating how the punch face was a somewhat square area with incised numerals. When the blank stock was struck, the plain field on the surface of the punch pushed the planchet metal down and smoothed it, while the incised areas accepted the planchet metal and created raised numerals or letters. The square of stock was flipped over with a coin turn and the process was repeated for the other side.

Obverse punch III was cracked. The crack is represented on the coin as a raised line of metal from the middle of the bottom of the E running through the ending flourish of the N to the corner of the punch mark. Mike Hodder has explained there are more Noe III-C shillings than any other NE variety, leading him to suspect the Noe III obverse and C reverse punches saw more use than the other punches.

The Noe II-A appears to be round but is slightly oval in shape while the III-C is clearly elongated at the 6:00 o'clock (or 180°) position of the obverse. This elongated or oblong example suggests these coins were hand cut with shears from small squares of stock after the squares had been impressed. The oblong appearance of Noe III-C is due to the high position of the XII. It seems the obverse and reverse punches were impressed on a small square of silver. The coin was being cut out in a round shape when the cutter noticed the XII had been struck a little too high on the square planchet. In order to preserve the denomination, the coin had to be cut in a more oblong shape. Usually the denomination was lower down on the planchet allowing the entire reverse punch outline to remain uncut while retaining a fairly round shape to the coin.

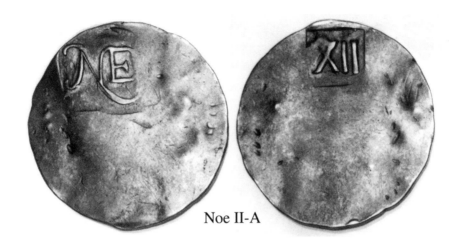

Figure 9 - Courtesy of Stack's Rare Coins

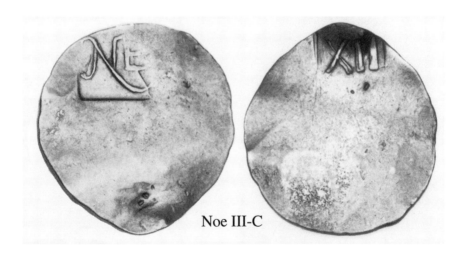

Figure 10 - Courtesy of Stack's Rare Coins

Figure 11 - A pair of rocker dies dated 1598 (M D IIC) for a German thaler. Note the curved engraved surfaces and the protruding shank at the back that was used to secure the die into the central shaft of the press. Used with permission from Denis R. Cooper, *The Art and Craft of Coinmaking*, figure 73a.

Figure 12 - Three smaller table mounted rocker presses from the Cesky Krumlov Collection in the Czech Republic. All three presses show a square opening in the lower shaft for the insertion of the rocker die. The presses on either end have teeth over the entire circumference of the gears and thus allow for an unlimited reciprocating motion of the rocker dies. The center press has wheel gears that only contained teeth over half of the circumference (note the back side of the top gear), thus limiting the movement of the dies. Used with permission from Denis R. Cooper, *The Art and Craft of Coinmaking*, figure 56.

Figure 13 - A large floor mounted rocker press from the Cesky Krumlov Collection in the Czech Republic. This illustration shows the press with rocker dies in place. Used with permission from Denis R. Cooper, *The Art and Craft of Coinmaking*, figure 56.

Figures 14 and 15. Two Willow Tree shillings representing two obverse and one reverse dies. Figure 14, Stack's, *Hain Collection*, lot 4, a Noe 1-A at 67.9 grains. Figure 15, Stack's, *Hain Collection*, lot 5, a Noe 2-A at 69.7 grains. Images are 4x. The Willow Tree sixpence and threepence are not illustrated. Images are 4x.

Because of the numerous errors in the few surviving coins from the Willow Tree series an illustrated plate of selected examples by variety is not sufficient for serious study. A plate, or series of plates, illustrating all known Willow Tree specimens is needed as the defects in each coin are usually unique to that specimen. For example, Noe illustrates an example of a Willow Tree shilling with an A reverse in which the date is properly impressed with no doubling (Noe, *NE and Willow*, plate III, figure 2 and plate VIII). The two A reverse examples shown here both have pronounced double dating, but the doubling differs on each specimen. The Noe 1-A displays two 6's and two 2's (166522), while the very rare Noe 2-A shows two 1's and two 2's (116522). In each case the double 2's are in different positions. Further, the legend above the numeral 2 in the 1-A example is DOOM, while the 2-A specimen contains the correct DOM. If we had six specimens of the A reverse to examine, we would discover each coin would have unique errors.

The two examples illustrated here indicate the errors were not in the die. Rather, the examples display errors related to impressing the images on each individual specimen. Further, the dramatic nature of these errors, such as the erratic alignment of bead segments and the presence of fully double letters and numbers, suggests the rockers were not sufficiently secure in the press. Possibly, the tolerance of the die shank was not accurate so that there was not a tight fit when it was inserted into the opening in the shaft of the press. It is also possible the pins fastening the die shank to the press did not fully stabilize the die. Any instability would be accentuated as soon as the press was operated and the dies began rotating back and forth on the shaft. That the errors appear more dramatic on the reverse or date side suggests the reverse die was in the upper position. The upper die would be more prone to slippage or "give" as the weight of the die worked to destabilize it, unlike the lower die where the weight of the die worked with gravity to make it more secure into the press.

Noe 1-A

Figure 14 - Courtesy of Stack's Rare Coins

Noe 2-A

Figure 15 - Courtesy of Stack's Rare Coins

Figures 16 and 17. Two Oak Tree shillings representing two obverse and two reverse dies. Figure 16, Stack's, *Hain Collection*, lot 19, a Noe 4 at 74.6 grains. Figure 17, Stack's, *Hain Collection*, lot 51, a Noe 14 at 72.5 grains. Images are 4x.

The Oak Tree series does not exhibit the doubling and related impression problems found in many Willow Tree specimens. I attribute these improvement to increased familiarity with, and expertise in, managing the reciprocating action of the rocker press. Also, it seems the mint learned to work within close tolerances and was able to more securely fasten the dies to the shafts of the press. The mint produced more acceptable coinage as they gained more control over the minting process.

Figure 16, the Noe 4 Oak Tree shilling, was selected as the center dot is prominently displayed on both the obverse and reverse. This dot is also found on the Willow tree coins but because of wear it is usually more difficult to locate (the center dot is visible on the obverse of figure 14 and is present but less obvious on the obverse of figure 15). The dot represents a small hole in the center of each die that appears as a raised dot on the coin. The hole was made by the sharp point of a compass as it was used to circumscribe two circular borders for the placement of the beads. These rings defined the area for the center images and the rim inscription. Sometimes the dot was obscured on the die; it may have been etched off when designing the obverse tree or it may have been overpunched with the date or denomination on the reverse. Center dots are visible on several varieties of Willow, Oak and Pine Tree coinages.

Figure 17, a Noe 14 Oak Tree shilling, is known as the Spiney Tree variety. This is an example of a die that was recut several times. The obverse die is the same as was used on Noe varieties 10-13. Each time it was reused the worn die was recut. By the time of the final recutting, on Noe 14, the tree trunk and primary branches were rather thick, giving the smaller outer branches the appearance of thorns or spines. This is also one of several varieties that includes a backward N on the obverse legend IN. Backward lettering, especially the N, was a common mistake as the engraving had to be done in reverse, since it represented a mirror image of the coin. Sometimes the engraver lapsed and incised a non-reverse letter; this resulted in a reverse letter on the coins made from that die.

Noe 4

Figure 16 - Courtesy of Stack's Rare Coins

Noe 14

Figure 17 - Courtesy of Stack's Rare Coins

Noe 20

Figure 18 - Courtesy of Stack's Rare Coins

Noe 21

Figure 19 - Courtesy of Stack's Rare Coins

Figures 18 and 19. Two Oak Tree sixpence representing one obverse and one reverse die. Figure 18, above, Stack's, *Hain Collection*, lot 57, a Noe 20 at 33.7 grains. Figure 19, below, Stack's, *Hain Collection*, lot 58, a Noe 21 at 35.3 grains. An Oak Tree threepence. Figure 20, next page, above, Stack's, *Hain Collection*, lot 64, a Noe 24 at 17.3 grains. An Oak Tree twopence. Figure 21, next page below, Stack's, *Hain Collection*, lot 75, Noe 29 at 10.9 grains. Images are 4x.

Figure 18, a Noe 20 Oak Tree sixpence, represents the first use of this set of dies. On the obverse the first S in MASATHVSETS was weak in the die and is faint on all examples. This specimen has a crack or void at that location. Also, as was frequently the case with smaller denomination coins, a slight misalignment of the rockers resulted in impressed coins that did not accurately align. As is explained both in the text and below in the discussion of the Pine Tree small denomination coinages, the result is that the top part of the obverse legend is frequently missing from these coins. Further, as to this specimen, Mike Hodder has noticed there is a Oak Tree shilling undertype. This example is from a strip of sterling that was impressed as shillings and then reused for sixpence. The strip may have been recycled intentionally as an overrun or because of some defect, on the other hand it may have been inadvertently sent through the press a second time, mistaken as an unused strip

Noe 24

Figure 20 - Courtesy of Stack's Rare Coins

Noe 29

Figure 21 - Courtesy of Stack's Rare Coins

The obverse die of Noe 20 was recut twice. The first recutting was for Noe 21 as seen in figure 19. The faint S was recut, but the recutting was improperly executed. Rather than cut the letter as a mirror image, the letter was simply cut as it would normally be seen. This resulted in a backward S on the coins. When the recut rockers were replaced in the press the obverse and reverse were accurately aligned, thus none of the obverse was lost when the coins were clipped out of the strip. Hodder states at some point during the use of the Noe 21 dies the two rocker dies clashed, disfiguring the backward S and affecting the adjacent MA. The backward S and the weakened letters were corrected in the second recutting, for Noe 22. The reverse die of Noe 20-22 was also used with another Pine Tree sixpence obverse to create the Pine Tree sixpence Noe 32.

Figure 20, the threepence, represents the work of a novice engraver, most probably an apprentice. Not only is the tree rather crude but there is also a backward S (the first S in MASATHVSETS). Figure 21, the twopence, represents an early example of this single die pairing. There are many variety numbers for this die pair (Noe 29-34) based on recutting and wear. Both of these smaller denominations show obverses that are slightly off center. As mentioned in the text, with the rocker press, minor discrepancies in alignment were more noticeable on smaller sized coins.

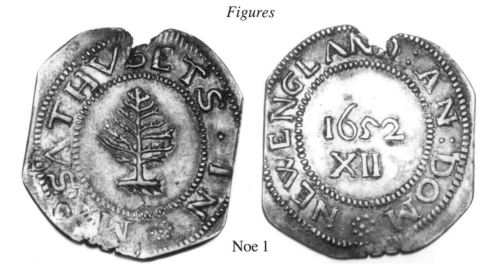

Noe 1

Figure 22 - Courtesy of Stack's Rare Coins

Noe 1

Figure 23 - Courtesy of Stack's Rare Coins

Figures 22 through 25. "Large Planchet" Pine Tree shillings, representing two obverse and two reverse dies. Figure 22, above, Stack's, *Hain Collection*, lot 89, a Noe 1 at 73.6 grains. Figure 23, below, Stack's, *Hain Collection*, lot 93, a Noe 1 at 72.1 grains. Figure 24, , next page, above, Stack's, *Hain Collection*, lot 94, a Noe 2 at 69.9 grains. Figure 25, next page, below, Stack's, *Hain Collection*, lot 99, a Noe 3 at 72.73 grains. Images are 4x.

The "large planchet" Pine Tree varieties were produced on a rocker press from strips of stock rather than from planchets. In this series the images engraved on the dies were made somewhat larger in diameter than the Oak Tree shilling engravings. The coins from these dies are about 3mm. broader and somewhat thinner than the Oak Tree shillings. Broader and thinner surfaces are easier to align and impress with rocker dies than smaller and thicker surfaces. Figure 22, a Noe 1 at 73.6 grains, is above the statutory weight. The straight cut marks on the sides were certainly made at the mint when the specimen was cut out of the strip. Portions of unstruck planchet can be seen at the top of the obverse and bottom of the reverse. In this case the cutter did not want to damage the inscription when clipping out the coin. If the dramatic straight clips had been illegal post-emission lightening of the coin, the

Noe 2

Figure 24 - Courtesy of Stack's Rare Coins

Noe 3

Figure 25 - Courtesy of Stack's Rare Coins

clipper would surely have shaved off the excess areas, making the legend "tight" but giving the coin a rounder and less clipped appearance. Figure 23, another Noe 1, at 72.1 grains, is also heavy and has a similar clipping history at the mint. In this case the unstruck excess sterling is in the same position on both sides and could have been removed without any damage to the impressed area. Again, any post-emission clipping would certainly have removed this "extra" sterling. Clearly both examples represent trimming performed at the mint and demonstrate that the coins were certainly cut out of strips after being impressed.

In figure 24, a Pine Tree Noe 2, the surface area for the impression on the dies was quite broad. In fact, in this variety, the dies were too large. The letters in the legend of the coins from this die were usually trimmed quite close to keep the coins within the weight limit. The obverse includes a backward N in IN. Figure 25, a Pine Tree Noe 3, actually represents the same rocker dies. As Mike Hodder noted, the center image was the first area to wear down on rocker dies. The central tree of Noe 2 wore out and the die was recut with a completely new tree, therefore Noe reclassified the dies as a Noe 3. The obverse legend, including the backward N, as well as the reverse are the same as are found in Noe 2. These coins provide further evidence that the Massachusetts Bay Mint used a rocker press.

Figure 26 - Courtesy of Stack's Rare Coins

Figure 27 - Courtesy of Stack's Rare Coins

Figures 26 and 27. Small Planchet Pine Tree shillings, representing two obverse dies and one reverse die. Figure 26, Stack's, *Hain Collection*, lot 133, a Noe 16 at 72.7 grains. Figure 27, Stack's, *Hain Collection*, lot 140, a Noe 17 at 71.9 grains. Images are 4x.

These two coins reflect the screw press technology of the 1670's. The planchets are smaller, thicker and rounder, representing the use of a planchet cutter. The pre-cut planchets were fed into a screw press. Unlike rocker press dies, the obverse and reverse cylinder dies of the screw press automatically lined up. Rarely are small planchet shillings off center; and when they are out of alignment the variation is very slight as in this example of a Noe 17. Also, screw press dies held up much better than the rocker dies. In this case the reverse die was used in Noe varieties 16-22 without any recutting required. The extensive use of the reverse dies, such as this one, led Mike Hodder to suggest the obverse dies, which wore out faster, were the hammer dies, while the reverse die was the stationary anvil die.

Noe 33   Noe 34

Figure 28 - Courtesy of Stack's Rare Coins   Figure 29 - Courtesy of Stack's Rare Coins

Figures 28 and 29. A Pine Tree sixpence. Figure 28, on the left, Stack's, *Hain Collection*, lot 166, a Noe 33 at 34.3. A Pine Tree threepence. Figure 29, on the right, Stack's, *Hain Collection*, lot 170, a Noe 34 at 18.4 grains. Images are 4x.

These are typical examples of Pine Tree small denomination coinage. The coins display all the characteristics of rocker press technology. They were impressed on a strip and were then cut out. When the coins were cut the reverse impressions were facing up. This was because the reverse displayed the denomination. Since the dies rarely aligned this meant the image on the side facing down, that is the obverse, suffered from being clipped down.

Figure 30 - Four sketches for the design of Massachusetts silver found on the reverse of a sheet of paper containing the minutes of a mint committee meeting from June of 1652. From Crosby, the four sketches are found in the third quarter of the facsimile plate opposite p. 41. Crosby cites this document as Massachusetts Archives, vol. c, p. 37.

Figure 31 - A crude pre-1652 cob eight reales from the Potosí mint during the reign of Philip IV (1625-1665). The coin was emitted from the mint with deep fissures or cracks. Coins in this condition regularly circulated in Boston. This example weighs 418.0 grains, from the Robert H. Gore, Jr. Numismatic Collection, Department of Special Collections, University of Notre Dame Libraries. Used with permission. Image is 1.5x.

Figure 32 - A pillar cob eight reales from the Potosí mint with the revised design, dated 1653, by Assayer E, Antonio de Erugeta. From the wreck of the *Jesus María del la Limpia Concepción* (the *La Capitana*), which sunk on October 27, 1654. This example weighs 414.8 grains, from the Robert H. Gore, Jr. Numismatic Collection, Department of Special Collections, University of Notre Dame Libraries. Used with permission. Image is 1.5x.

Figure 33 - A well worn Mexican cob eight reales from the reign of Philip IV (1625-1665), issued by Assayer P, who was active 1634-1665. On the reverse is the counterstamp 7L at 7:00 o'clock. The differences in the reverse crosses on the Mexican and Potosí coinage is apparent, even on this highly circulated specimen. This example weighs 365.9 grains, from the Robert H. Gore, Jr. Numismatic Collection, Department of Special Collections, University of Notre Dame Libraries. Used with Permission. Image is 1.5x.

Figure 34 - A "royal strike" Spanish eight reales from the regal mint at Segovia, dated 1617. Except for the mintmark, these coins have the same design as the more common cobs produced in Seville. This specimen contains an NE counterstamp on the reverse. On October 8, 1672, the Massachusetts Bay General Court approved legislation that Hull and Sanderson would counterstamp Spanish silver coins with their true weight and the initials NE. The order never went into effect. However, at some later date, probably in the nineteenth century, someone counterstamped a few dated Spanish silver intending to pass them as authentic counterstamped coins. They neglected to include the weight, which was the primary reason for the legislation. For another example see Mossman, (p. 85, figure 15). This example is used with permission from the collection of William Snyder. Image is 1.5x.

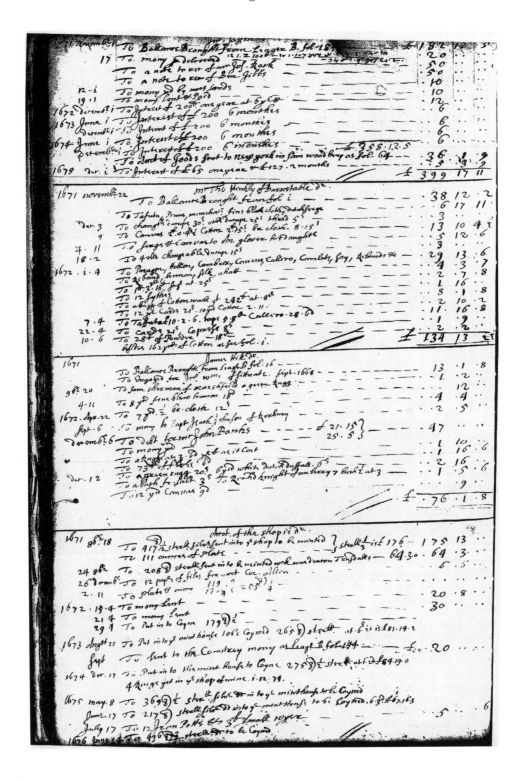

Figure 35 - The Hull ledger showing the entire page for folio 26 verso. This is the left side of a double opening and shows the debit side of the specific accounts, the right side of the opening shows the credit side of the same accounts. The bottom account is the first part of the shop account. Account books of John Hull (MS Cb 110), vol. 1. The R. Stanton Avery Special Collections Dept., New England Historic Genealogical Society. Used with permission.

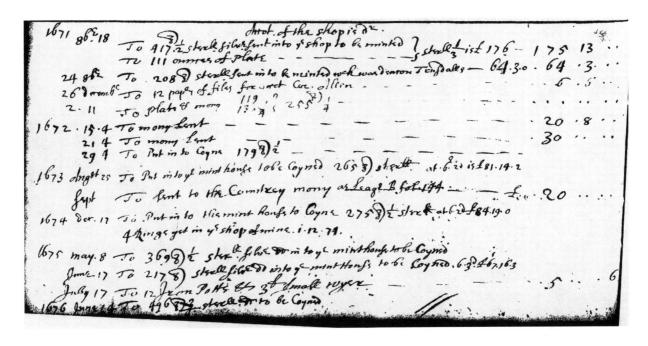

Figure 36 - The Hull ledger, detail showing the debit side of the Shop Account on folio 26 verso. Account books of John Hull (MS Cb 110), vol.1. The R. Stanton Avery Special Collections Dept., New England Historic Genealogical Society. Used with permission.

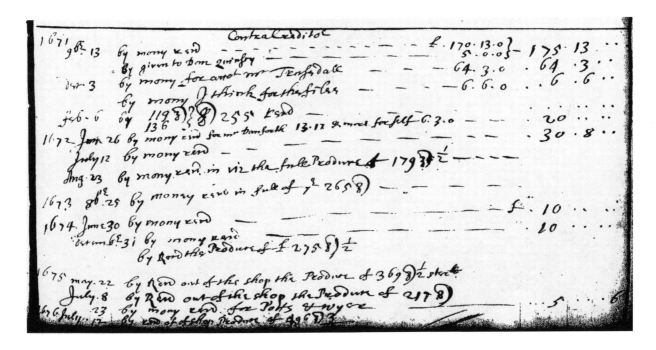

Figure 37 - The Hull ledger, detail showing the credit side of the Shop Account on folio 27 recto. Account books of John Hull (MS Cb 110), vol. 1. The R. Stanton Avery Special Collections Dept., New England Historic Genealogical Society. Used with permission.

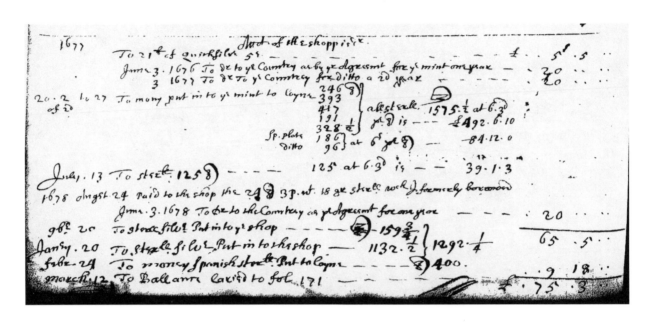

Figure 38 - The Hull ledger, detail showing the debit side of the Shop Account on folio 133 verso. Account books of John Hull (MS Cb 110), vol. 1. The R. Stanton Avery Special Collections Dept., New England Historic Genealogical Society. Used with permission.

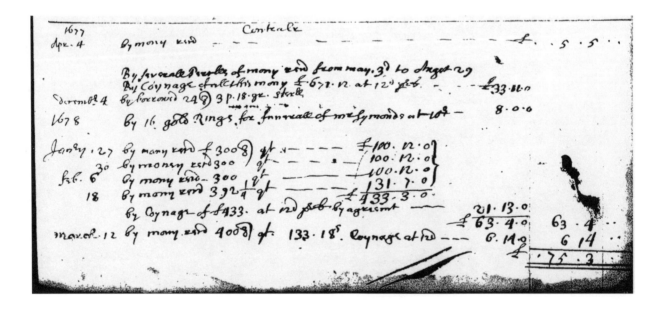

Figure 39 - The Hull ledger, detail showing the credit side of the Shop Account on folio 134 recto. Account books of John Hull (MS Cb 110), vol. 1. The R. Stanton Avery Special Collections Dept., New England Historic Genealogical Society. Used with permission.

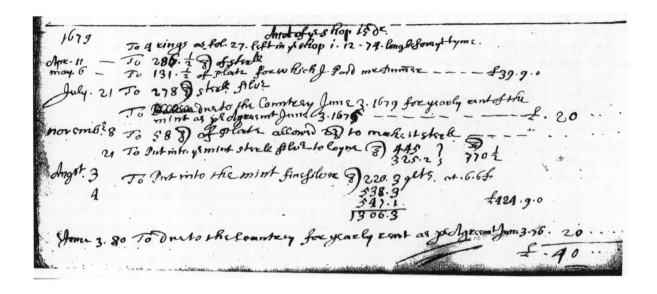

Figure 40 - The Hull ledger, detail showing the debit side of the Shop Account on folio 170 verso. Account books of John Hull (MS Cb 110), vol.1. The R. Stanton Avery Special Collections Dept., New England Historic Genealogical Society. Used with permission.

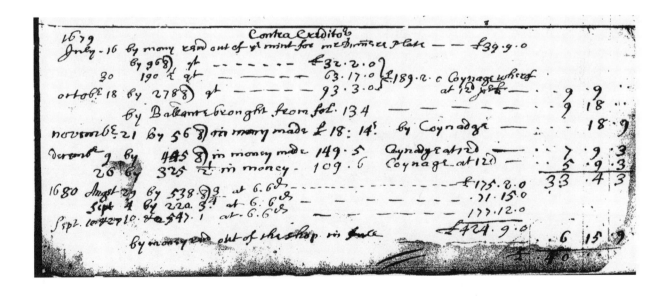

Figure 41 - The Hull ledger, detail showing the credit side of the Shop Account on folio 171 recto. Account books of John Hull (MS Cb 110), vol.1. The R. Stanton Avery Special Collections Dept., New England Historic Genealogical Society. Used with permission.

Julian Calendar
1671

JANUARY.

Su.	Mo.	Tu.	We.	Th.	Fr.	Sa.
1	2	3	4	5	6	7
8	9	10	11	12	13	14
15	16	17	18	19	20	21
22	23	24	25	26	27	28
29	30	31	*	*	*	*
*	*	*	*	*	*	*

JULY.

Su.	Mo.	Tu.	We.	Th.	Fr.	Sa.
*	*	*	*	*	*	1
2	3	4	5	6	7	8
9	10	11	12	13	14	15
16	17	18	19	20	21	22
23	24	25	26	27	28	29
30	31	*	*	*	*	*

FEBRUARY.

Su.	Mo.	Tu.	We.	Th.	Fr.	Sa.
*	*	*	1	2	3	4
5	6	7	8	9	10	11
12	13	14	15	16	17	18
19	20	21	22	23	24	25
26	27	28	*	*	*	*

AUGUST.

Su.	Mo.	Tu.	We.	Th.	Fr.	Sa.
*	*	1	2	3	4	5
6	7	8	9	10	11	12
13	14	15	16	17	18	19
20	21	22	23	24	25	26
27	28	29	30	31	*	*

MARCH.

Su.	Mo.	Tu.	We.	Th.	Fr.	Sa.
*	*	*	1	2	3	4
5	6	7	8	9	10	11
12	13	14	15	16	17	18
19	20	21	22	23	24	25
26	27	28	29	30	31	*

SEPTEMBER.

Su.	Mo.	Tu.	We.	Th.	Fr.	Sa.
*	*	*	*	*	1	2
3	4	5	6	7	8	9
10	11	12	13	14	15	16
17	18	19	20	21	22	23
24	25	26	27	28	29	30

APRIL.

Su.	Mo.	Tu.	We.	Th.	Fr.	Sa.
*	*	*	*	*	*	1
2	3	4	5	6	7	8
9	10	11	12	13	14	15
16	17	18	19	20	21	22
23	24	25	26	27	28	29
30	*	*	*	*	*	*

OCTOBER.

Su.	Mo.	Tu.	We.	Th.	Fr.	Sa.
1	2	3	4	5	6	7
8	9	10	11	12	13	14
15	16	17	18	19	20	21
22	23	24	25	26	27	28
29	30	31	*	*	*	*
*	*	*	*	*	*	*

MAY.

Su.	Mo.	Tu.	We.	Th.	Fr.	Sa.
*	1	2	3	4	5	6
7	8	9	10	11	12	13
14	15	16	17	18	19	20
21	22	23	24	25	26	27
28	29	30	31	*	*	*

NOVEMBER.

Su.	Mo.	Tu.	We.	Th.	Fr.	Sa.
*	*	*	1	2	3	4
5	6	7	8	9	10	11
12	13	14	15	16	17	18
19	20	21	22	23	24	25
26	27	28	29	30	*	*

JUNE.

Su.	Mo.	Tu.	We.	Th.	Fr.	Sa.
*	*	*	*	1	2	3
4	5	6	7	8	9	10
11	12	13	14	15	16	17
18	19	20	21	22	23	24
25	26	27	28	29	30	*
*	*	*	*	*	*	*

DECEMBER.

Su.	Mo.	Tu.	We.	Th.	Fr.	Sa.
*	*	*	*	*	1	2
3	4	5	6	7	8	9
10	11	12	13	14	15	16
17	18	19	20	21	22	23
24	25	26	27	28	29	30
31	*	*	*	*	*	*

Figure 42 - The British Julian calendar for 1670/1

Julian Calendar
1672

JANUARY.

Su.	Mo.	Tu.	We.	Th.	Fr.	Sa.
*	1	2	3	4	5	6
7	8	9	10	11	12	13
14	15	16	17	18	19	20
21	22	23	24	25	26	27
28	29	30	31	*	*	*

FEBRUARY.

Su.	Mo.	Tu.	We.	Th.	Fr.	Sa.
*	*	*	*	1	2	3
4	5	6	7	8	9	10
11	12	13	14	15	16	17
18	19	20	21	22	23	24
25	26	27	28	29	*	*

MARCH.

Su.	Mo.	Tu.	We.	Th.	Fr.	Sa.
*	*	*	*	*	1	2
3	4	5	6	7	8	9
10	11	12	13	14	15	16
17	18	19	20	21	22	23
24	25	26	27	28	29	30
31	*	*	*	*	*	*

APRIL.

Su.	Mo.	Tu.	We.	Th.	Fr.	Sa.
*	1	2	3	4	5	6
7	8	9	10	11	12	13
14	15	16	17	18	19	20
21	22	23	24	25	26	27
28	29	30	*	*	*	*

MAY.

Su.	Mo.	Tu.	We.	Th.	Fr.	Sa.
*	*	*	1	2	3	4
5	6	7	8	9	10	11
12	13	14	15	16	17	18
19	20	21	22	23	24	25
26	27	28	29	30	31	*

JUNE.

Su.	Mo.	Tu.	We.	Th.	Fr.	Sa.
*	*	*	*	*	*	1
2	3	4	5	6	7	8
9	10	11	12	13	14	15
16	17	18	19	20	21	22
23	24	25	26	27	28	29
30	*	*	*	*	*	*

JULY.

Su.	Mo.	Tu.	We.	Th.	Fr.	Sa.
*	1	2	3	4	5	6
7	8	9	10	11	12	13
14	15	16	17	18	19	20
21	22	23	24	25	26	27
28	29	30	31	*	*	*

AUGUST.

Su.	Mo.	Tu.	We.	Th.	Fr.	Sa.
*	*	*	*	1	2	3
4	5	6	7	8	9	10
11	12	13	14	15	16	17
18	19	20	21	22	23	24
25	26	27	28	29	30	31

SEPTEMBER.

Su.	Mo.	Tu.	We.	Th.	Fr.	Sa.
1	2	3	4	5	6	7
8	9	10	11	12	13	14
15	16	17	18	19	20	21
22	23	24	25	26	27	28
29	30	*	*	*	*	*
*	*	*	*	*	*	*

OCTOBER.

Su.	Mo.	Tu.	We.	Th.	Fr.	Sa.
*	*	1	2	3	4	5
6	7	8	9	10	11	12
13	14	15	16	17	18	19
20	21	22	23	24	25	26
27	28	29	30	31	*	*

NOVEMBER.

Su.	Mo.	Tu.	We.	Th.	Fr.	Sa.
*	*	*	*	*	1	2
3	4	5	6	7	8	9
10	11	12	13	14	15	16
17	18	19	20	21	22	23
24	25	26	27	28	29	30

DECEMBER.

Su.	Mo.	Tu.	We.	Th.	Fr.	Sa.
1	2	3	4	5	6	7
8	9	10	11	12	13	14
15	16	17	18	19	20	21
22	23	24	25	26	27	28
29	30	31	*	*	*	*
*	*	*	*	*	*	*

Figure 43 - The British Julian calendar for 1671/2.

Julian Calendar
1673

JANUARY.

Su.	Mo.	Tu.	We.	Th.	Fr.	Sa.
*	*	*	1	2	3	4
5	6	7	8	9	10	11
12	13	14	15	16	17	18
19	20	21	22	23	24	25
26	27	28	29	30	31	*

FEBRUARY.

Su.	Mo.	Tu.	We.	Th.	Fr.	Sa.
*	*	*	*	*	*	1
2	3	4	5	6	7	8
9	10	11	12	13	14	15
16	17	18	19	20	21	22
23	24	25	26	27	28	*
*	*	*	*	*	*	*

MARCH.

Su.	Mo.	Tu.	We.	Th.	Fr.	Sa.
*	*	*	*	*	*	1
2	3	4	5	6	7	8
9	10	11	12	13	14	15
16	17	18	19	20	21	22
23	24	25	26	27	28	29
30	31	*	*	*	*	*

APRIL.

Su.	Mo.	Tu.	We.	Th.	Fr.	Sa.
*	*	1	2	3	4	5
6	7	8	9	10	11	12
13	14	15	16	17	18	19
20	21	22	23	24	25	26
27	28	29	30	*	*	*

MAY.

Su.	Mo.	Tu.	We.	Th.	Fr.	Sa.
*	*	*	*	1	2	3
4	5	6	7	8	9	10
11	12	13	14	15	16	17
18	19	20	21	22	23	24
25	26	27	28	29	30	31
*	*	*	*	*	*	*

JUNE.

Su.	Mo.	Tu.	We.	Th.	Fr.	Sa.
1	2	3	4	5	6	7
8	9	10	11	12	13	14
15	16	17	18	19	20	21
22	23	24	25	26	27	28
29	30	*	*	*	*	*

JULY.

Su.	Mo.	Tu.	We.	Th.	Fr.	Sa.
*	*	1	2	3	4	5
6	7	8	9	10	11	12
13	14	15	16	17	18	19
20	21	22	23	24	25	26
27	28	29	30	31	*	*

AUGUST.

Su.	Mo.	Tu.	We.	Th.	Fr.	Sa.
*	*	*	*	*	1	2
3	4	5	6	7	8	9
10	11	12	13	14	15	16
17	18	19	20	21	22	23
24	25	26	27	28	29	30
31	*	*	*	*	*	*

SEPTEMBER.

Su.	Mo.	Tu.	We.	Th.	Fr.	Sa.
*	1	2	3	4	5	6
7	8	9	10	11	12	13
14	15	16	17	18	19	20
21	22	23	24	25	26	27
28	29	30	*	*	*	*
*	*	*	*	*	*	*

OCTOBER.

Su.	Mo.	Tu.	We.	Th.	Fr.	Sa.
*	*	*	1	2	3	4
5	6	7	8	9	10	11
12	13	14	15	16	17	18
19	20	21	22	23	24	25
26	27	28	29	30	31	*

NOVEMBER.

Su.	Mo.	Tu.	We.	Th.	Fr.	Sa.
*	*	*	*	*	*	1
2	3	4	5	6	7	8
9	10	11	12	13	14	15
16	17	18	19	20	21	22
23	24	25	26	27	28	29
30	*	*	*	*	*	*

DECEMBER.

Su.	Mo.	Tu.	We.	Th.	Fr.	Sa.
*	1	2	3	4	5	6
7	8	9	10	11	12	13
14	15	16	17	18	19	20
21	22	23	24	25	26	27
28	29	30	31	*	*	*

Figure 44 - The British Julian calendar for 1672/3.

Julian Calendar
1674

JANUARY.

Su.	Mo.	Tu.	We.	Th.	Fr.	Sa.
*	*	*	*	1	2	3
4	5	6	7	8	9	10
11	12	13	14	15	16	17
18	19	20	21	22	23	24
25	26	27	28	29	30	31

FEBRUARY.

1	2	3	4	5	6	7
8	9	10	11	12	13	14
15	16	17	18	19	20	21
22	23	24	25	26	27	28
*	*	*	*	*	*	*
*	*	*	*	*	*	*

MARCH.

1	2	3	4	5	6	7
8	9	10	11	12	13	14
15	16	17	18	19	20	21
22	23	24	25	26	27	28
29	30	31	*	*	*	*

APRIL.

*	*	*	1	2	3	4
5	6	7	8	9	10	11
12	13	14	15	16	17	18
19	20	21	22	23	24	25
26	27	28	29	30	*	*

MAY.

*	*	*	*	*	1	2
3	4	5	6	7	8	9
10	11	12	13	14	15	16
17	18	19	20	21	22	23
24	25	26	27	28	29	30
31	*	*	*	*	*	*

JUNE.

*	1	2	3	4	5	6
7	8	9	10	11	12	13
14	15	16	17	18	19	20
21	22	23	24	25	26	27
28	29	30	*	*	*	*

JULY.

Su.	Mo.	Tu.	We.	Th.	Fr.	Sa.
*	*	*	1	2	3	4
5	6	7	8	9	10	11
12	13	14	15	16	17	18
19	20	21	22	23	24	25
26	27	28	29	30	31	*

AUGUST.

*	*	*	*	*	*	1
2	3	4	5	6	7	8
9	10	11	12	13	14	15
16	17	18	19	20	21	22
23	24	25	26	27	28	29
30	31	*	*	*	*	*

SEPTEMBER.

*	*	1	2	3	4	5
6	7	8	9	10	11	12
13	14	15	16	17	18	19
20	21	22	23	24	25	26
27	28	29	30	*	*	*

OCTOBER.

*	*	*	*	1	2	3
4	5	6	7	8	9	10
11	12	13	14	15	16	17
18	19	20	21	22	23	24
25	26	27	28	29	30	31

NOVEMBER.

1	2	3	4	5	6	7
8	9	10	11	12	13	14
15	16	17	18	19	20	21
22	23	24	25	26	27	28
29	30	*	*	*	*	*
*	*	*	*	*	*	*

DECEMBER.

*	*	1	2	3	4	5
6	7	8	9	10	11	12
13	14	15	16	17	18	19
20	21	22	23	24	25	26
27	28	29	30	31	*	*

Figure 45 - The British Julian calendar for 1673/4.

Julian Calendar
1675

JANUARY.								JULY.						
Su.	Mo.	Tu.	We.	Th.	Fr.	Sa.		Su.	Mo.	Tu.	We.	Th.	Fr.	Sa.
*	*	*	*	*	1	2		*	*	*	*	1	2	3
3	4	5	6	7	8	9		4	5	6	7	8	9	10
10	11	12	13	14	15	16		11	12	13	14	15	16	17
17	18	19	20	21	22	23		18	19	20	21	22	23	24
24	25	26	27	28	29	30		25	26	27	28	29	30	31
31	*	*	*	*	*	*		*	*	*	*	*	*	*

FEBRUARY.								AUGUST.						
*	1	2	3	4	5	6		1	2	3	4	5	6	7
7	8	9	10	11	12	13		8	9	10	11	12	13	14
14	15	16	17	18	19	20		15	16	17	18	19	20	21
21	22	23	24	25	26	27		22	23	24	25	26	27	28
28	*	*	*	*	*	*		29	30	31	*	*	*	*

MARCH.								SEPTEMBER.						
*	1	2	3	4	5	6		*	*	*	1	2	3	4
7	8	9	10	11	12	13		5	6	7	8	9	10	11
14	15	16	17	18	19	20		12	13	14	15	16	17	18
21	22	23	24	25	26	27		19	20	21	22	23	24	25
28	29	30	31	*	*	*		26	27	28	29	30	*	*

APRIL.								OCTOBER.						
*	*	*	*	1	2	3		*	*	*	*	*	1	2
4	5	6	7	8	9	10		3	4	5	6	7	8	9
11	12	13	14	15	16	17		10	11	12	13	14	15	16
18	19	20	21	22	23	24		17	18	19	20	21	22	23
25	26	27	28	29	30	*		24	25	26	27	28	29	30
*	*	*	*	*	*	*		31	*	*	*	*	*	*

MAY.								NOVEMBER.						
*	*	*	*	*	*	1		*	1	2	3	4	5	6
2	3	4	5	6	7	8		7	8	9	10	11	12	13
9	10	11	12	13	14	15		14	15	16	17	18	19	20
16	17	18	19	20	21	22		21	22	23	24	25	26	27
23	24	25	26	27	28	29		28	29	30	*	*	*	*
30	31	*	*	*	*	*		*	*	*	*	*	*	*

JUNE.								DECEMBER.						
*	*	1	2	3	4	5		*	*	*	1	2	3	4
6	7	8	9	10	11	12		5	6	7	8	9	10	11
13	14	15	16	17	18	19		12	13	14	15	16	17	18
20	21	22	23	24	25	26		19	20	21	22	23	24	25
27	28	29	30	*	*	*		26	27	28	29	30	31	*

Figure 46 - The British Julian calendar for 1674/5.

Julian Calendar
1676

JANUARY.

Su.	Mo.	Tu.	We.	Th.	Fr.	Sa.
*	*	*	*	*	*	1
2	3	4	5	6	7	8
9	10	11	12	13	14	15
16	17	18	19	20	21	22
23	24	25	26	27	28	29
30	31	*	*	*	*	*

FEBRUARY.

Su.	Mo.	Tu.	We.	Th.	Fr.	Sa.
*	*	1	2	3	4	5
6	7	8	9	10	11	12
13	14	15	16	17	18	19
20	21	22	23	24	25	26
27	28	29	*	*	*	*

MARCH.

Su.	Mo.	Tu.	We.	Th.	Fr.	Sa.
*	*	*	1	2	3	4
5	6	7	8	9	10	11
12	13	14	15	16	17	18
19	20	21	22	23	24	25
26	27	28	29	30	31	*
*	*	*	*	*	*	*

APRIL.

Su.	Mo.	Tu.	We.	Th.	Fr.	Sa.
*	*	*	*	*	*	1
2	3	4	5	6	7	8
9	10	11	12	13	14	15
16	17	18	19	20	21	22
23	24	25	26	27	28	29
30	*	*	*	*	*	*

MAY.

Su.	Mo.	Tu.	We.	Th.	Fr.	Sa.
*	1	2	3	4	5	6
7	8	9	10	11	12	13
14	15	16	17	18	19	20
21	22	23	24	25	26	27
28	29	30	31	*	*	*

JUNE.

Su.	Mo.	Tu.	We.	Th.	Fr.	Sa.
*	*	*	*	1	2	3
4	5	6	7	8	9	10
11	12	13	14	15	16	17
18	19	20	21	22	23	24
25	26	27	28	29	30	*
*	*	*	*	*	*	*

JULY.

Su.	Mo.	Tu.	We.	Th.	Fr.	Sa.
*	*	*	*	*	*	1
2	3	4	5	6	7	8
9	10	11	12	13	14	15
16	17	18	19	20	21	22
23	24	25	26	27	28	29
30	31	*	*	*	*	*

AUGUST.

Su.	Mo.	Tu.	We.	Th.	Fr.	Sa.
*	*	1	2	3	4	5
6	7	8	9	10	11	12
14	14	15	16	17	18	19
20	21	22	23	24	25	26
27	28	29	30	31	*	*

SEPTEMBER.

Su.	Mo.	Tu.	We.	Th.	Fr.	Sa.
*	*	*	*	*	1	2
3	4	5	6	7	8	9
10	11	12	13	14	15	16
17	18	19	20	21	22	23
24	25	26	27	28	29	30
*	*	*	*	*	*	*

OCTOBER.

Su.	Mo.	Tu.	We.	Th.	Fr.	Sa.
1	2	3	4	5	6	7
8	9	10	11	12	13	14
15	16	17	18	19	20	21
22	23	24	25	26	27	28
29	30	31	*	*	*	*
*	*	*	*	*	*	*

NOVEMBER.

Su.	Mo.	Tu.	We.	Th.	Fr.	Sa.
*	*	*	1	2	3	4
5	6	7	8	9	10	11
12	13	14	15	16	17	18
19	20	21	22	23	24	25
26	27	28	29	30	*	*

DECEMBER.

Su.	Mo.	Tu.	We.	Th.	Fr.	Sa.
*	*	*	*	*	1	2
3	4	5	6	7	8	9
10	11	12	13	14	15	16
17	18	19	20	21	22	23
24	25	26	27	28	29	30
31	*	*	*	*	*	*

Figure 47 - The British Julian calendar for 1675/6.

Julian Calendar
1677

JANUARY.

Su.	Mo.	Tu.	We.	Th.	Fr.	Sa.
*	1	2	3	4	5	6
7	8	9	10	11	12	13
14	15	16	17	18	19	20
21	22	23	24	25	26	27
28	29	30	31	*	*	*

FEBRUARY.

Su.	Mo.	Tu.	We.	Th.	Fr.	Sa.
*	*	*	*	1	2	3
4	5	6	7	8	9	10
11	12	13	14	15	16	17
18	19	20	21	22	23	24
25	26	27	28	*	*	*

MARCH.

Su.	Mo.	Tu.	We.	Th.	Fr.	Sa.
*	*	*	*	1	2	3
4	5	6	7	8	9	10
11	12	13	14	15	16	17
18	19	20	21	22	23	24
25	26	27	28	29	30	31
*	*	*	*	*	*	*

APRIL.

Su.	Mo.	Tu.	We.	Th.	Fr.	Sa.
1	2	3	4	5	6	7
8	9	10	11	12	13	14
15	16	17	18	19	20	21
22	23	24	25	26	27	28
29	30	*	*	*	*	*

MAY.

Su.	Mo.	Tu.	We.	Th.	Fr.	Sa.
*	*	1	2	3	4	5
6	7	8	9	10	11	12
13	14	15	16	17	18	19
20	21	22	23	24	25	26
27	28	29	30	31	*	*

JUNE.

Su.	Mo.	Tu.	We.	Th.	Fr.	Sa.
*	*	*	*	*	1	2
3	4	5	6	7	8	9
10	11	12	13	14	15	16
17	18	19	20	21	22	23
24	25	26	27	28	29	30
*	*	*	*	*	*	*

JULY.

Su.	Mo.	Tu.	We.	Th.	Fr.	Sa.
1	2	3	4	5	6	7
8	9	10	11	12	13	14
15	16	17	18	19	20	21
22	23	24	25	26	27	28
29	30	31	*	*	*	*

AUGUST.

Su.	Mo.	Tu.	We.	Th.	Fr.	Sa.
*	*	*	1	2	3	4
5	6	7	8	9	10	11
12	13	14	15	16	17	18
19	20	21	22	23	24	25
26	27	28	29	30	31	*

SEPTEMBER.

Su.	Mo.	Tu.	We.	Th.	Fr.	Sa.
*	*	*	*	*	*	1
2	3	4	5	6	7	8
9	10	11	12	13	14	15
16	17	18	19	20	21	22
23	24	25	26	27	28	29
30	*	*	*	*	*	*

OCTOBER.

Su.	Mo.	Tu.	We.	Th.	Fr.	Sa.
*	1	2	3	4	5	6
7	8	9	10	11	12	13
14	15	16	17	18	19	20
21	22	23	24	25	26	27
28	29	30	31	*	*	*

NOVEMBER.

Su.	Mo.	Tu.	We.	Th.	Fr.	Sa.
*	*	*	*	1	2	3
4	5	6	7	8	9	10
11	12	13	14	15	16	17
18	19	20	21	22	23	24
25	26	27	28	29	30	*

DECEMBER.

Su.	Mo.	Tu.	We.	Th.	Fr.	Sa.
*	*	*	*	*	*	1
2	3	4	5	6	7	8
9	10	11	12	13	14	15
16	17	18	19	20	21	22
23	24	25	26	27	28	29
30	31	*	*	*	*	*

Figure 48 - The British Julian calendar for 1676/7.

Julian Calendar
1678

JANUARY.

Su.	Mo.	Tu.	We.	Th.	Fr.	Sa.
*	*	1	2	3	4	5
6	7	8	9	10	11	12
13	14	15	16	17	18	19
20	21	22	23	24	25	26
27	28	29	30	31	*	*

FEBRUARY.

Su.	Mo.	Tu.	We.	Th.	Fr.	Sa.
*	*	*	*	*	1	2
3	4	5	6	7	8	9
10	11	12	13	14	15	16
17	18	19	20	21	22	23
24	25	26	27	28	*	*

MARCH.

Su.	Mo.	Tu.	We.	Th.	Fr.	Sa.
*	*	*	*	*	1	2
3	4	5	6	7	8	9
10	11	12	13	14	15	16
17	18	19	20	21	22	23
24	25	26	27	28	29	30
31	*	*	*	*	*	*

APRIL.

Su.	Mo.	Tu.	We.	Th.	Fr.	Sa.
*	1	2	3	4	5	6
7	8	9	10	11	12	13
14	15	16	17	18	19	20
21	22	23	24	25	26	27
28	29	30	*	*	*	*

MAY.

Su.	Mo.	Tu.	We.	Th.	Fr.	Sa.
*	*	*	1	2	3	4
5	6	7	8	9	10	11
12	13	14	15	16	17	18
19	20	21	22	23	24	25
26	27	28	29	30	31	*

JUNE.

Su.	Mo.	Tu.	We.	Th.	Fr.	Sa.
*	*	*	*	*	*	1
2	3	4	5	6	7	8
9	10	11	12	13	14	15
16	17	18	19	20	21	22
23	24	25	26	27	28	29
30	*	*	*	*	*	*

JULY.

Su.	Mo.	Tu.	We.	Th.	Fr.	Sa.
*	1	2	3	4	5	6
7	8	9	10	11	12	13
14	15	16	17	18	19	20
21	22	23	24	25	26	27
28	29	30	31	*	*	*

AUGUST.

Su.	Mo.	Tu.	We.	Th.	Fr.	Sa.
*	*	*	*	1	2	3
4	5	6	7	8	9	10
11	12	13	14	15	16	17
18	19	20	21	22	23	24
25	26	27	28	29	30	31

SEPTEMBER.

Su.	Mo.	Tu.	We.	Th.	Fr.	Sa.
1	2	3	4	5	6	7
8	9	10	11	12	13	14
15	16	17	18	19	20	21
22	23	24	25	26	27	28
29	30	*	*	*	*	*
*	*	*	*	*	*	*

OCTOBER.

Su.	Mo.	Tu.	We.	Th.	Fr.	Sa.
*	*	1	2	3	4	5
6	7	8	9	10	11	12
13	14	15	16	17	18	19
20	21	22	23	24	25	26
27	28	29	30	31	*	*

NOVEMBER.

Su.	Mo.	Tu.	We.	Th.	Fr.	Sa.
*	*	*	*	*	1	2
3	4	5	6	7	8	9
10	11	12	13	14	15	16
17	18	19	20	21	22	23
24	25	26	27	28	29	30

DECEMBER.

Su.	Mo.	Tu.	We.	Th.	Fr.	Sa.
1	2	3	4	5	6	7
8	9	10	11	12	13	14
15	16	17	18	19	20	21
22	23	24	25	26	27	28
29	30	31	*	*	*	*
*	*	*	*	*	*	*

Figure 49 - The British Julian calendar for 1677/8.

Julian Calendar
1679

JANUARY

Su.	Mo.	Tu.	We.	Th.	Fr.	Sa.
*	*	*	1	2	3	4
5	6	7	8	9	10	11
12	13	14	15	16	17	18
19	20	21	22	23	24	25
26	27	28	29	30	31	*

FEBRUARY.

Su.	Mo.	Tu.	We.	Th.	Fr.	Sa.
*	*	*	*	*	*	1
2	3	4	5	6	7	8
9	10	11	12	13	14	15
16	17	18	19	20	21	22
23	24	25	26	27	28	*
*	*	*	*	*	*	*

MARCH.

Su.	Mo.	Tu.	We.	Th.	Fr.	Sa.
*	*	*	*	*	*	1
2	3	4	5	6	7	8
9	10	11	12	13	14	15
16	17	18	19	20	21	22
23	24	25	26	27	28	29
30	31	*	*	*	*	*

APRIL.

Su.	Mo.	Tu.	We.	Th.	Fr.	Sa.
*	*	1	2	3	4	5
6	7	8	9	10	11	12
13	14	15	16	17	18	19
20	21	22	23	24	25	26
27	28	29	30	*	*	*

MAY.

Su.	Mo.	Tu.	We.	Th.	Fr.	Sa.
*	*	*	*	1	2	3
4	5	6	7	8	9	10
11	12	13	14	15	16	17
18	19	20	21	22	23	24
25	26	27	28	29	30	31
*	*	*	*	*	*	*

JUNE.

Su.	Mo.	Tu.	We.	Th.	Fr.	Sa.
1	2	3	4	5	6	7
8	9	10	11	12	13	14
15	16	17	18	19	20	21
22	23	24	25	26	27	28
29	30	*	*	*	*	*

JULY.

Su.	Mo.	Tu.	We.	Th.	Fr.	Sa.
*	*	1	2	3	4	5
6	7	8	9	10	11	12
13	14	15	16	17	18	19
20	21	22	23	24	25	26
27	28	29	30	31	*	*

AUGUST.

Su.	Mo.	Tu.	We.	Th.	Fr.	Sa.
*	*	*	*	*	1	2
3	4	5	6	7	8	9
10	11	12	13	14	15	16
17	18	19	20	21	22	23
24	25	26	27	28	29	30
31	*	*	*	*	*	*

SEPTEMBER.

Su.	Mo.	Tu.	We.	Th.	Fr.	Sa.
*	1	2	3	4	5	6
7	8	9	10	11	12	13
14	15	16	17	18	19	20
21	22	23	24	25	26	27
28	29	30	*	*	*	*
*	*	*	*	*	*	*

OCTOBER.

Su.	Mo.	Tu.	We.	Th.	Fr.	Sa.
*	*	*	1	2	3	4
5	6	7	8	9	10	11
12	13	14	15	16	17	18
19	20	21	22	23	24	25
26	27	28	29	30	31	*

NOVEMBER.

Su.	Mo.	Tu.	We.	Th.	Fr.	Sa.
*	*	*	*	*	*	1
2	3	4	5	6	7	8
9	10	11	12	13	14	15
16	17	18	19	20	21	22
23	24	25	26	27	28	29
30	*	*	*	*	*	*

DECEMBER.

Su.	Mo.	Tu.	We.	Th.	Fr.	Sa.
*	1	2	3	4	5	6
7	8	9	10	11	12	13
14	15	16	17	18	19	20
21	22	23	24	25	26	27
28	29	30	31	*	*	*

Figure 50 - The British Julian calendar for 1678/9.

Julian Calendar
1680

JANUARY.

Su.	Mo.	Tu.	We.	Th.	Fr.	Sa.
*	*	*	*	1	2	3
4	5	6	7	8	9	10
11	12	13	14	15	16	17
18	19	20	21	22	23	24
25	26	27	28	29	30	31
*	*	*	*	*	*	*

FEBRUARY.

Su.	Mo.	Tu.	We.	Th.	Fr.	Sa.
1	2	3	4	5	6	7
8	9	10	11	12	13	14
15	16	17	18	19	20	21
22	23	24	25	26	27	28
29	*	*	*	*	*	*

MARCH.

Su.	Mo.	Tu.	We.	Th.	Fr.	Sa.
*	1	2	3	4	5	6
7	8	9	10	11	12	13
14	15	16	17	18	19	20
21	22	23	24	25	26	27
28	29	30	31	*	*	*

APRIL.

Su.	Mo.	Tu.	We.	Th.	Fr.	Sa.
*	*	*	*	1	2	3
4	5	6	7	8	9	10
11	12	13	14	15	16	17
18	19	20	21	22	23	24
25	26	27	28	29	30	*
*	*	*	*	*	*	*

MAY.

Su.	Mo.	Tu.	We.	Th.	Fr.	Sa.
*	*	*	*	*	*	1
2	3	4	5	6	7	8
9	10	11	12	13	14	15
16	17	18	19	20	21	22
23	24	25	26	27	28	29
30	31	*	*	*	*	*

JUNE.

Su.	Mo.	Tu.	We.	Th.	Fr.	Sa.
*	*	1	2	3	4	5
6	7	8	9	10	11	12
13	14	15	16	17	18	19
20	21	22	23	24	25	26
27	28	29	30	*	*	*

JULY.

Su.	Mo.	Tu.	We.	Th.	Fr.	Sa.
*	*	*	*	1	2	3
4	5	6	7	8	9	10
11	12	13	14	15	16	17
18	19	20	21	22	23	24
25	26	27	28	29	30	31
*	*	*	*	*	*	*

AUGUST.

Su.	Mo.	Tu.	We.	Th.	Fr.	Sa.
1	2	3	4	5	6	7
8	9	10	11	12	13	14
15	16	17	18	19	20	21
22	23	24	25	26	27	28
29	30	31	*	*	*	*

SEPTEMBER.

Su.	Mo.	Tu.	We.	Th.	Fr.	Sa.
*	*	*	1	2	3	4
5	6	7	8	9	10	11
12	13	14	15	16	17	18
19	20	21	22	23	24	25
26	27	28	29	30	*	*

OCTOBER.

Su.	Mo.	Tu.	We.	Th.	Fr.	Sa.
*	*	*	*	*	1	2
3	4	5	6	7	8	9
10	11	12	13	14	15	16
17	18	19	20	21	22	23
24	25	26	27	28	29	30
31	*	*	*	*	*	*

NOVEMBER.

Su.	Mo.	Tu.	We.	Th.	Fr.	Sa.
*	1	2	3	4	5	6
7	8	9	10	11	12	13
14	15	16	17	18	19	20
21	22	23	24	25	26	27
28	29	30	*	*	*	*
*	*	*	*	*	*	*

DECEMBER.

Su.	Mo.	Tu.	We.	Th.	Fr.	Sa.
*	*	*	1	2	3	4
5	6	7	8	9	10	11
12	13	14	15	16	17	18
19	20	21	22	23	24	25
26	27	28	29	30	31	*

Figure 51 - The British Julian calendar for 1679/80.

Postscript on a Newly Discovered NE/Willow Overstrike

Two weeks before this book was to be sent to the printer I received word of a newly discovered Willow Tree shilling. On May 20, 2002, Gary Trudgen sent me an e-mail copy of a news release from Stack's Rare Coins that will be used for a brief illustrated article by Michael Hodder in the forthcoming issue of *The Colonial Newsletter* (it will be volume 42, no. 2, August, 2002, serial number 120). The Stack's press release described the coin as holed but "one of the most sharply struck Willow Tree Shillings known, with complete legends, full tree, and a complete date and denomination." The coin weight is listed at 71.8 grains with a diameter of 27.7 mm vertical by 26.3 mm horizontal and a reverse die axis of 180° (that is, a coin turn).

Mike Hodder has identified the Willow Tree obverse as a Noe 3 die and the reverse as a hitherto unknown die that he designated as Noe F, making the shilling a Willow Tree Noe 3-F. However, what makes this coin even more remarkable is that it was struck over an NE shilling. The NE undertype has a Noe I obverse punch while the reverse numerals are from a hitherto unknown punch that Mike Hodder has designated as reverse E, making the shilling an NE Noe I-E.[1]

The coin weight, at 71.8 grains, is rather substantial considering the item is holed. The eleven NE shillings from the 1991 American Numismatic Society COAC exhibition had an average weight of 70.54 grains (ranging from 72.3 to 67.7 grains) and the three Hain examples averaged 71.2 grains (ranging from 72.1 to 69.8 grains), while the average weight for the Willow Tree shillings in those two samplings was even lower (the heaviest was 71.7 grains) and none of those coins were holed! Apparently the overstruck shilling did not suffer metal loss when it was holed. The hole was not drilled, which would have resulted in a smooth rim around the hole but with some metal loss, rather, it was partially punched through on each side. For this reason metal was not lost but was simply pushed outward mushrooming around the hole creating a ridge or lip at the edge of the hole on each side.

Another unusual and interesting feature of the newly discovered shilling is that it is the only know example where one variety of Massachusetts silver was reused to strike a different variety. Since the NE shilling is the undertype on the newly discovered coin, we now have conclusive numismatic proof that NE coins were made prior to the Willow Tree series. This substantiates the legislative evidence of May 26/27, 1652, that stated the coins would have NE on one side and the denomination on the other; while the revision to the legislation made during the General Court session of October 1652 stated the design would be changed to include an inscription, double ring, tree and date. However, as mentioned above on page 85 in footnote 3, Mike Hodder has suggested some NE Noe III-D shillings

---

[1] Noe used Roman numerals for designating obverse punches used on the NE shillings, but he used Arabic numerals in his listing of Willow Tree obverse dies. In both series he used upper case letters for the reverse. Within the Oak and Pine Tree series Noe did not classify dies, rather, he used an Arabic numeral to designate each variety combination consisting of a specific obverse with a specific reverse.

may have been produced at a later period in the history of the mint as souvenir items, thus one may not conclude all NE shillings predate the Willow Tree series.

The discovery coin is also interesting in relation to production procedures at the mint. As mentioned both in Chapter Seven and in the explanations to several of the figures of Massachusetts silver illustrated in this book, a variety of details on Massachusetts silver coins lead us to assume the Willow, Oak and Pine Tree series, with the exception of the small planchet Pine Tree shillings, were impressed at the mint by feeding strips of sterling silver into a rocker press. Aside from the NE/Willow overstrike, the only other documented restamping of Massachusetts silver coins at the mint are Oak Tree sixpence that have an Oak Tree shilling undertype (see Bowers and Ruddy, *The Garrett Collection, Part III*, p. 17, lots 1208 and 1209 for two examples of Oak Tree sixpence, a Noe 15 and a Noe 20, as well as Hodder, *Hain*, p. 62, lot 57, for another example of a Noe 20 sixpence which is illustrated as figure 18 in this book on p. 300). From these examples it seems that occasionally (at least once during the production of the Noe 15 and at least one other time, if not more, during the production of the Noe 20 sixpence) a strip of sterling was impressed using the shilling dies and then, before the coins could be cut out, the strip was sent through the sixpence dies and reimpressed. Possibly this was done intentionally due to some defect in the shillings or because the mint had produced more shillings than they had planned for that consignment; on the other hand the strips may have been inadvertently sent through the press a second time, having been mislaid and then mistaken for unused stock.

The newly discovered Willow Tree shilling is the only example of a Massachusetts coin that went through two completely different methods of production, namely the hammer and punch method used for the NE series and the rocker press that was used for the Willow Tree coinage. In general we can determine how this specimen was produced. It was first punched as an NE coin and later put through a coin press equipped with Willow Tree dies. However, there are various possible explanations as to why this coin was produced. By investigating these theories we may gain a more precise understanding of the steps used in these two production methods.

One theory is that the NE shilling may have been in circulation and was used in a pinch, as a substitute for stock, to confirm die alignment. Hull or Sanderson may simply have taken this fairly plain NE shilling out of their pocket and then carefully placed it on the dies. The crank on the press was then operated which rocked the dies together and impressed the coin as a test, to determine if the affixed Willow Tree rocker dies were aligned properly. Based on standard minting practices this seems rather unusual, for one would assume that an alignment procedure would usually be performed with a strip of silver. Perhaps when the dies had been affixed to the press and were ready for their final alignment test the silver consigned to the mint was being melted and cast into strips so that no strips were available, therefore the NE coin was used.

Another theory is that some unemitted NE shillings were intentionally sent through the press to reface them with the newer Willow Tree design. It has been hypothesized the discovery coin could represent one of the last shillings produced in the NE series. But rather than emitting these last NE coins, the mint impressed them on the newly acquired rocker press as one of the first Willow Tree production runs. However, this hypothesis requires one to assume an NE Noe I obverse punch was in use at the end of the NE series and that the Noe Willow Tree shilling obverse die 3 was the initial die in that series. The NE Noe III obverse punch is the sharpest and most skillfully produced of the three known obverse NE punches and therefore is generally considered to have been produced after obverse punches I and II. This is supported by the observation that obverse punch Noe III is also thought to have been used for some NE coins that were produced late in the history of the mint on round planchets made in a planchet cutter. Regarding the other two obverse NE punches, it is generally considered that Noe II lasted longer than Noe I (Hodder, *Hain*, pp. 26-28). From this it is usually deduced that Noe I is the earliest punch, followed by Noe II and then Noe III. Although it would seem obverse punch Noe III had the longest life, the ordering of these punches is based on reasonable assumptions and not on hard evidence. Similarly, due to the few Willow Tree shillings that are extant, we cannot conclusively prove an emission sequence for the Willow Tree dies. However, as discussed in Chapter Seven above, Willow Tree shilling obverse die Noe 3 is generally considered to be the final obverse die in the series. Thus, accepting the hypothesis that a Noe I NE obverse could be at the end of the NE series while a Noe 3 Willow Tree obverse may be at the start of that series, requires some rethinking of the generally accepted emission sequence for these dies.

It has also been suggested a strip of older NE shillings from a previous consignment was uncovered during the Willow Tree era and simply sent through the press. This assumes that the earlier NE series were punched out on a strip and then cut from the strip, as was done with the later rocker press coins. This is certainly a possibility. However it is also possible that the strips were cut into blank squares that were then punched, as that would allow for easier alignment of the obverse and reverse punches. There simply is not enough evidence to make a definitive conclusion on this point.

On the obverse of the discovery coin the NE undertype is very well aligned with the Willow Tree overtype. In the photographs the full N of NE is visible, it is located at the cross above the tree. On the reverse the full X of XII is visible as is the bottom half of the II. The top half of the first I and a portion of the top half of the second I were destroyed by the hole. If the NE or the XII had been somewhat off center we could say part of the Willow Tree coin did not use the same metal as the NE coin. This would mean the NE shilling had to have been punched on a strip that was then reused. The photographs indicate the NE undertype could have been a completed coin that was reused, however it is also possible the coin was on a strip of metal that was simply well aligned in the Willow Tree dies.

These preliminary comments on the newly discovered overstruck NE shilling have been added to stimulate further discussion. Additional study on this newly discovered specimen and other, as yet to be discovered coins, may assist in uncovering new details as to how early Massachusetts silver coinage was produced.

I would like to thank Mike Hodder, Phil Mossman and Gary Trudgen for sharing their preliminary thoughts on this new find with me via e-mail. The above theories and comments were extracted from this discussion and do not necessarily represent the final opinion of any participant. Further, I am grateful to Stack's Rare Coins for allowing me to illustrate this coin and to Mike Hodder for providing me with photographs within one day of my request.

Courtesy of Stack's Rare Coins

Photo credit – Gina Fuentes, The New York Historical Society

Figure B - Obverse. A Willow Tree shilling Noe 3 with an NE obverse Noe I undertype. In the NE from the Noe I obverse undertype the N is visible near the cross above the willow tree. The top of the first stroke of the N touches the inner beads, the left arm of the cross touches the second stroke of the N and the right arm extends into the final stroke.

Courtesy of Stack's Rare Coins

Photo credit – Gina Fuentes, The New York Historical Society

Figure C - Reverse. A newly identified Willow Tree shilling reverse designated as Noe F. The top of the 5 in the date 1652 was not impressed due to the sunken field around the XII in the NE undertype. The undertype also represents a newly identified reverse called NE Noe E. In the XII most of the X can be seen to the left of the hole. The top half of the first I and a portion of the top half of the second I were destroyed by the hole.

Bibliography of Works Cited

The Acts and Resolves, Public and Private, of the Province of Massachusetts Bay: to which are Prefixed the Charters of the Province. With Historical and Explanatory Notes, and an Appendix., edited by, John H. Clifford, Ellis Ames and Abner C. Goodell, Volume 1, Boston: Wright & Potter, printers to the State, 1869.

Agricola, Georgius. *De re metallica,* originally published in 1556, translated by Herbert Clark Hoover and Lou Henry Hoover, first published in *The Mining Magazine*, London, 1912. Reprint, Dover: New York, 1950.

Anderson, Robert Charles. *The Great Migration Begins: Immigrants to New England 1620-1633,* three volumes, New England Historic Genealogical Society: Boston, 1995.

Baker, Emerson W. and John G. Reid. *The New England Knight: Sir William Phips, 1651-1695,* Toronto: University of Toronto Press, 1998.

Butts, Allison. and Charles D. Coxe. *Silver: Economics, Metallurgy, and Use,* Princeton: D. Van Nostrand, 1967.

Calbetó de Grau, Gabriel. *Compendio de las piezas de ocho reales,* two volumes, San Juan: Ediciones Juan Ponce de Léon, 1970.

Carlotto, Tony. *The Copper Coins of Vermont and those Bearing the Vermont Name,* Chelsea, MI: The Colonial Coin Collectors Club, 1993.

Carlson, Stephen P. *Joseph Jenks: Colonial Toolmaker and Inventor,* Eastern National Park and Monument Association, 1985. This informative 37 page pamphlet is sold at the Saugus Iron Works restoration site. It was first published in 1973 then revised in 1975 and 1978. The site is part of the National Park Service.

Carlton, William. "Masts for the King's Navy," *New England Quarterly,* 13 (March, 1939), pp. 4-18.

Challis, Christopher Edgar. *A New History of the Royal Mint,* Cambridge: Cambridge University Press, 1992.

Challis, Christopher Edgar. *The Tudor Coinage,* Manchester: Manchester University Press, 1978.

Clarke, Hermann Frederick. *John Coney: Silversmith 1655-1722,* Boston, 1932. Reprint, New York: DaCapo Press, 1971.

Clarke, Hermann Frederick. *John Hull: A Builder of the Bay Colony,* Portland, Maine: Southworth-Anthoensen Press, 1940.

Clarke, Hermann Frederick, and Henry Wilder Foote. *Jeremiah Dummer: Colonial Craftsman and Merchant 1645-1718,* 1935. Reprint, New York: DaCapo Press, 1970.

Clarke, Mary Stetson. *Pioneer Iron Works,* Philadelphia: Chilton Books, 1968.

Cooper, Denis R. *The Art and Craft of Coinmaking: A History of Minting Technology,* London: Spink & Son, 1988.

Cotton, Robert. *Cottoni Posthuma: divers choice pieces of that renowned antiquary Sir Robert Cotton Knight and Baronet, preserved from the injury of time, and expos'd to public light, for the benefit of posterity*, edited by James Howell, First Edition, London: Francis Leach for Henry Seile, 1651 (Cotton's speech on the alteration of coinage appears on pp. 285-94 followed by the Answer of the Committee on pp. 295-302 and related documents on pp. 302-7).

Craig, John. *The Mint: A History of the London Mint from A.D. 287 to 1948*, Cambridge: Cambrdge University Press, 1953.

Crosby, Sylvester Sage. *The Early Coins of America; and the Laws Governing their Issue,* 1875. Reprint, Lawrence, MA: Quarterman, 1974.

Cushing, John D., editor. *The Laws and Liberties of Massachusetts 1641-1691: A Facsimile Edition, Containing Also Council Orders and Executive Proclamations*, three volumes, Wilmington, DE: Scholarly Resources Inc., 1976.

Dafforne, Richard. *The Merchants Mirrour, or, Directions for the Perfect Ordering and Keeping of his Accounts. Framed by Way of Debitor and Creditor*, Third Edition, Corrected and Revised, London: Printed by R.H. and J.G. for Nicholas Bourn, 1660.

Dasí, Tomás. *Estudio de los reales de a ocho, también llamados pesos, dólares, piastras, patacones o duros españoles*, five volumes, Valencia: [Dasí], 1950-1951.

Davis, Andrew McFarland. *Currency and Banking in the Province of Massachusetts Bay,* two volumes, first published in two parts as issues of the *Publications of The American Economic Association,* Third series, Published for The American Economic Association by the Macmillan Company, "Part I - Currency" was from vol. 1, no. 4 (December, 1900) and "Part II - Banking" was from vol. 2, no. 2 (May, 1901). Reprint, two volumes, New York: August M. Kelley Publishers, 1970.

Doty, Richard. "Making Money in Early Massachusetts," *Money of Pre-Federal America,* edited by John Kleeberg, Coinage of the Americas Conference 7, New York: The American Numismatic Society, 1992, pp. 1-14.

Dow, George Francis, editor. *Records and Files of the Quarterly Courts of Essex County Massachusetts 1636-1683,* eight volumes, Salem, MA: The Essex Institute, 1911-1921.

Earle, Alice Morse. *The Sabbath in Puritan New England,* 1891. Reprint, Williamstown, MA: Corner House Publishing, 1974.

Edwards, Graham. *The Last Days of Charles I,* Stroud, Gloucestershire: Sutton Publishing, 1999.

Ercker, Lazarus. *Treatise on Ores and Assaying,* Translated by Annelise Sisco and Cyril Smyth. [This is an English translation of the 1680, second German edition of Lazarus Ercker, *Beschreibung aller fürnemsten mineralischen Erstr- und Bergwercks Arten.* The work was first published in 1574 but the second edition of 1680 was the definitive text and was reissued several times.] Chicago: University of Chicago Press, 1951.

Ercker, Lazarus. *Fleta Minor: The Laws of Art and Nature, in Knowing, Judging, Assaying, Fining, Refining and Inlarging the Bodies of consin'd Metals. In two Parts. The First contains Assays [i.e. Essays] of Lazarus Erckern Chief prover (or Assay-Master General of the Empire of Germany) in V Books: originally written by him in the Teutonic Language and now translated into English. The Second contains Essays on Metallick Words, as a Dictionary to many pleasing Discourses. By Sir John Pettus, of Suffolk, Knight of the Society for the Mines Royal*, London: Printed for the Author, by Thomas Dawks, 1683 (second issue). [This is an English translation by John Pettus of the work of Lazarus Ercker, *Beschreibung aller fürnemsten mineralischen Erstr- und Bergwercks Arten.* The text is followed by a dictionary of terms related to metalwork by Pettus. The book was printed for Pettus, who was a deputy governor of the royal mines. A second edition of this book was issued in 1685 and another in 1686.]

Feavearyear, Albert. Edgar. *The Pound Sterling: A History of English Money,* Second Edition, revised by Edward Victor Morgan, Oxford: Clarendon Press, 1963.

Firth, Charles Harding and Robert Sangster Rait, editors. *Acts and Ordinances of the Interregnum 1642-1660,* three volumes, London: His Majesty's Stationery Office, 1911.

Fortescue, John William. editor. *Calendar of State Papers, Colonial Series, America and West Indies, 1681-1685, Preserved in Her Majesty's Public Record Office*, London: Eyre and Spottiswoode for Her Majesty's Stationery Office, 1898.

Fortescue, John William. editor. *Calendar of State Papers, Colonial Series, America and West Indies, 1685-1688, Preserved in the Public Record Office*, Norwich: The Norfolk Chronicles Company for Her Majesty's Stationery Office, 1899.

Fortescue, John William. editor. *Calendar of State Papers, Colonial Series, America and West Indies, 1689-1692, Preserved in the Public Record Office*, London: Mackie and Company for Her Majesty's Stationery Office, 1901.

Freeman Craig, Jr., "Coinage of the Viceroyalty of El Perú - An Overview," in *The Coinage of El Perú* edited by William Bischoff, Coinage of the Americas Conference 5, New York: The American Numismatic Society, 1989, pp. 1-20.

Gil Farrés, Octavio. *Historia de la moneda española,* Madrid: [1959].

Glasser, Lynn. *Counterfeiting in America: The History of an American Way to Wealth.* [no location]: Clarkson N. Potter, 1968.

Goodrick, Alfred Thomas Scrope, editor. *Edward Randolph: Including his Letters and Official Papers from the New England, Middle, and Southern Colonies in America, and the West Indies. 1678-1700,* two volumes, Publications of the Prince Society, volumes 30-31, Boston: John Wilson for The Prince Society, 1909 [this work represents volumes 6-7 of Edward Randolph of which volumes 1-5 were edited by Robert Toppan as Prince Society volumes 24-28].

Hall, Michael Garibaldi. *Edward Randolph and the American Colonies: 1676-1703* (University of North Carolina Press, 1960). Reprint, New York: Norton, 1969.

Hart, Albert Bushnell, ed. *Commonwealth History of Massachusetts,* Volume 1, Colony of Massachusetts Bay (1605-1689); Volume 2, Province of Massachusetts (1689-1775), New York: States History Company, 1927 and 1928.

Hartley, Edward Neal. *Ironworks on the Saugus: the Lynn and Braintree Ventures of the Company of Undertakers of the Ironworks in New England,* Norman: University of Oklahoma Press, 1957

Heiss, Aloïss. *Descripción general de las monedas hispano-cristianas desde la invasión de los árabes,* three volumes, R.N. Milagro: Madrid, 1865. Reprint, edited by Luis Marquina, Zaragoza: Octavio y Féliz, 1962.

Hoadly, Charles Jeremy. *The Public Records of the Colony of Conneticut,* fifteen volumes, Hartford: Case, Lockwood and Brainard, 1850-1890.

Hodder, Michael. "Cecil Calvert's Coinage for Maryland: A Study in History and Law," *The Colonial Newsletter,* vol. 33, February, 1993, serial no. 93, pp. 1360-62.

[Hodder, Michael]. *The Hain Family Collection of Massachusetts Silver Coins,* Stack's Americana Public Auction Sale January 15, 2002, New York: Stack's, 2002.

Hodder, Michael. A letter to the editor in, "Letters from Members." *The C4 Newsletter, A Quarterly Publication of The Colonial Coin Collectors Club,* volume 4, no. 2 (Fall, 1996) 19-21 [the cover says Fall, 1996 but the running headline throughout the issue states: Winter, 1996].

[Hodder, Michael]. "Massachusetts Silver Coins," pages 329-56, in *The Norweb Collection: Part I*, Public Auction October 12-13, 1987, Wolfeboro, NH: Bowers and Merena, 1987.

Hodder, Michael. "Massachusetts Silver Coins Yields Some of Their Secrets," *Coin World*, (April 10, 1995), pp. 10, 12 and 16, it is also in *The C4 Newsletter*, volume 3, no. 1 (March, 1995) pp. 24-32, but lacking an author attribution!

Hodder, Michael. "A Plea for Reason," *The Colonial Newsletter*, vol. 34, serial no. 98 (November 1994), p. 1476.

Howe, Estes. "Communication from Dr. Estes Howe, of Cambridge, in Regard to the Abode of John Hull and Samuel Sewall," *Proceedings of the Massachusetts Historical Society*, Second Series, vol. 1 (1884-1885), from the meeting of November 1884, pp. 312-26.

Hull, John. "The Diaries of John Hull, Mint-master and Treasurer of the Colony of Massachusetts Bay" [the edition and annotations to the text as well as the introductory memoir of Hull by Samuel Jennison; transcription of the shorthand passages and the compilation of the various appendices by Edward Everett Hale as stated on pp. 112-14], *Archaeologia Americana: Transactions and Collections of The American Antiquarian Society,* vol. 3 (1857), pp. 108-306 (also issued in Boston by John Wilson and Son, 1857).

Hull, John. [*John Hull's Colony Journal*], four manuscript volumes in the New England Historic Genealogical Society, Boston, Massachusetts. The work has been designated as MS Cb 110. Volume 1 is Hull's personal ledger from the 1670's while volumes 2-4 are the Massachusetts Bay accounts regarding all payments related to King Philip's War. Hull was a member of the war committee and treasurer so he maintained a record of all debts and payments incurred by the Commonwealth.

Hutchinson, Thomas. *The History of the Colony and Province of Massachusetts-Bay,* edited by Lawrence Shaw Mayo, volume 1, Cambridge, MA: Harvard University Press, 1936. [This work was first published in 1764. Hutchinson had been a Boston Selectman in 1737 and later that year was elected to the General Court. In 1749 he lost his seat in the House of Representatives but was appointed as a member of the Council, he then held a position as a judge and as a customs commissioner. In March 1771 Hutchinson became the last American-born royal governor of the colony.]

Hutchinson, Thomas. *Hutchinson Papers,* Publications of the Prince Society, volumes 1-2, New York: Joel Munsell for The Prince Society, 1865. Reprint, New York: Burt Franklin, 1967 [two volumes of documents on colonial Massachusetts covering the period to 1689 edited by Hutchinson and first published in 1769].

Jordan, Louis. *The Coins of Colonial and Early America.* James Spilman, image coordinator. A website of texts and images based on the coins in the Department of Special Collections, University of Notre Dame Libraries, with additional images from The Colonial Newsletter Foundation photofiles, at www.coins.nd.edu, 1996 with updates.

Jordan, Louis. "The Massachusetts Mint, British Politics and a Postscript on the Hull Ledger," *The Colonial Newsletter,* vol. 42, April, 2002, serial no. 119, pp. 2305-29.

Kane, Patricia E. and Francis Hill Bigelow, John Marshall Phillips, Jeannine J. Falino, Deborah A. Federhn, Barbara McLean Ward, Gerald W. R. Ward. *Colonial Massachusetts Silversmiths and Jewelers: A Biographical Dictionary Based on the Notes of Francis Hill Bigelow & John Marshall Phillips,* New Haven: Yale University Art Gallery, 1998.

Kenney, Richard. *Early American Medalists and Die-Sinkers Prior to the Civil War,* New York: Wayte Raymond, 1954. Reprint, New York: Sanford Durst, 1982.

Kleeberg, John M. "Appendix 1: A Catalogue of an Exhibition of Massachusetts Silver at The American Numismatic Society," *Money of Pre-Federal America,* edited by John Kleeberg, Coinage of the Americas Conference 7, New York: The American Numismatic Society, 1992, pp. 181-214.

Lasser, Joseph. "The Silver Cobs of Colombia, 1622-1742," in *The Coinage of El Perú,* edited by William Bischoff, Coinage of the Americas Conference 5, New York: The American Numismatic Society, 1989, pp. 121-40.

Li, Ming-Hsun. *The Great Recoinage of 1696 to 1699,* London: Weidenfeld and Nicholson, 1963.

Liset, Abraham. *Amphithalami, or, the Accomptants Closet, Being an Abbridgment of Merchants Accounts kept by Debitors and Creditors*, London: Printed by James Flesher for Nicholas Bourne, 1660.

Malynes, Gerard. *Consvetvdo, vel Lex Mercatoria, or, the Ancient Law-Merchant*, London: Printed by Adam Islip, 1622.

The Manuscripts of His Grace The Duke of Portland, Preserved at Welbeck Abbey, volume 2 [introduction signed by Richard Ward, who may have been the editor], Historical Manuscripts Commission, Thirteenth Report, Appendix, Part Two, London: Eyre and Spottiswoode for Her Majesty's Stationery Office, 1893.

Martin, Robert and Angel Pietri. "The Story of the HMS Feversham, and Massachusetts Cut Silver use in the Colonies," *The C4 Newsletter, A Quarterly Publication of The Colonial Coin Collectors Club,* volume 9, no. 3 (Fall, 2001), pp. 11-31.

Massachusetts Royal Commissions: 1681-1774, Publications of The Colonial Society of Massachusetts, volume 2, Boston: The Colonial Society, 1913.

McCusker, John J. *Money and Exchange in Europe and America, 1600-1775: A Handbook,* published for The Institute of Early American History and Culture, Williamsburg, Virginia, Chapel Hill: University of North Carolina Press, 1978.

Moody, Robert Earle, and Richard Clive Simmons, editors. *The Glorious Revolution in Massachusetts: Selected Documents, 1689-1692*, Publications of The Colonial Society of Massachusetts, volume 64, Boston, MA: The Colonial Society of Massachusetts, distributed by The University Press of Virginia, 1988.

Morison, Samuel Eliot. *Builders of the Bay Colony,* Boston and New York: Houghton Mifflin, 1930.

Mossman, Philip L. *Money of the American Colonies and Confederation: A Numismatic, Economic and Historical Correlation*, Numismatic Studies, no. 20, New York: The American Numismatic Society, 1993.

Mulholland, James A. *A History of Metals in Colonial America,* University, Alabama: University of Alabama Press, 1981.

Newman, Eric. *The Secret of the Good Samaritan Shilling,* Numismatic Notes and Monographs, no. 142, New York: The American Numismatic Society, 1959.

Newman, Eric. *The Early Paper Money of America,* Fourth Edition, Iola, WI: Krause, 1997.

News from the Goldsmiths or a Tryal of Gold and Silver, by W. T[ovey]., London: the author, 1678.

Noe, Sydney Philip. *The Castine Deposit: An American Hoard*, Numismatic Notes and Monographs, no. 100, New York: The American Numismatic Society, 1942.

Noe, Sydney Philip. *The New England and Willow Tree Coinages of Massachusetts*, Numismatic Notes and Monographs, no. 102, New York: The American Numismatic Society, 1943.

Noe, Sydney Philip. *The Oak Tree Coinage of Massachusetts,* Numismatic Notes and Monographs, no. 110, New York: The American Numismatic Society, 1947.

Noe, Sydney Philip. *The Pine Tree Coinage of Massachusetts,* Numismatic Notes and Monographs, no. 125, New York: The American Numismatic Society, 1952.

Noe, Sydney Philip. *The Silver Coinage of Massachusetts*, edited by Alfred Hoch, Lawrence, MA: Quarterman, 1973. Reprint of Noe's three ANS publications *The New England and Willow Tree Coinages of Massachusetts ; The Oak Tree Coinage of Massachusetts* and *The Pine Tree Coinage of Massachusetts*, along with his, "The Coinage of Massachusetts Bay Colony" from the *Proceedings of The American Antiquarian Society,* April, 1950, pp. 11-20; with brief prefatory material by Eric Newman and Ruth Noe Pistilese, also postscript material including extracts from Eric Newman's *The Secret of the Good Samaritan Shilling*, and a price guide by Walter Breen.

Palfrey, John Gorham. *A Compendious History of New England,* two volumes, Boston: Houghton, Mifflin and Company, 1873 and 1883.

Picker, Richard. "Variations of the Die Varieties of Massachusetts Oak and Pine Tree Coinage," *Studies on Money in Early America*, edited by Eric Newman and Richard Doty, New York: The American Numismatic Society, 1976, pp. 75-90.

Pollock, Andrew W., III. "Numismatic Register: The 17th-Century Coinage of Massachsuetts, Maryland, and the Sommer Islands," a listing of auction appearance of New England silver, in Ron Guth's, *The Internet Encyclopedia and Price Guide of United States Coins* at http://www.coinfacts.com/Administrative/numismatic_register_colonials.htm, 2000.

Prall, Stuart E. *The Puritan Revolution: A Documentary History,* Anchor Books, 1968. Reprint, Gloucester, MA: Peter Smith, 1973.

Prince, Thomas, editor. *The Mather Papers,* Collections of the Massachusetts Historical Society, Fourth Series, volume 8, Boston: Wiggin and Lunt, 1868. [This is a collection of documents and letters on colonial New England including many items relating to the Mather Family. One section concerns "Letters and Papers relating to the Regicides" containing letters and documents by and about Goffe and Wahley in America.]

Records of the Suffolk County Court: 1671-1680, in two parts, Publications of The Colonial Society of Massachusetts, volumes 29-30, Boston: The Colonial Society, 1933.

Redington, Joseph, editor. *Calendar of Treasury Papers, 1556/7-1696, Preserved in Her Majesty's Public Record Office,* London: Longmans, Green, Reader and Dyer, 1868.

A Remedie Against The losse of the Subject by Farthing-Tokens: Discovering The great abuses of them heretofor: and the Prevention of the like hereafter: By making them of such a weight as may countervaile their worth in current Coyne: And Proposing a satisfactorie way for the Exchange of those that are already dispersed abroad. With some usefull Cautions touching the receipt of certaine forraigne Coyne. Published for the good of the Commonwealth in generall, but more especially of the poorer sort. [an anonymous six page pamphlet] London: Thomas Bates, 1644.

A Report of the Record Commissioner of the City of Boston, Containing Charlestown Land Records, 1638-1802, volume 3 of the Commissioners's report, Second edition, Boston: Rockwell and Churchill, City printers, 1883.

A Report of the Record Commissioners of the City of Boston, Containing Boston Records from 1660-1701, volume 7 of the Commissioners's report, Boston: Rockwell and Churchill, City printers, 1881.

A Report of the Record Commissioners of the City of Boston, Containing Miscellaneous Papers, volume 10 of the Commissioners's report, Boston: Rockwell and Churchill, City printers, 1886.

Ruding, Rogers. *Annals of the Coinage of Great Britain and its Dependencies: from the Earliest Period of Authentic History to the Reign of Victoria,* Third Edition, three volumes, London: J. Hearne, 1840.

Sainsbury, William Noel, editor. *Calendar of State Papers, Colonial Series, America and West Indies, 1661-1668, Preserved in Her Majesty's Public Record Office*, London: Eyre and Spottiswoode for Her Majesty's Stationery Office, 1880. Reprint, Kraus, 1964.

Sainsbury, William Noel, editor. *Calendar of State Papers, Colonial Series, America and West Indies, 1669-1674, Preserved in Her Majesty's Public Record Office*, London: Eyre and Spottiswoode for Her Majesty's Stationery Office, 1889. Reprint, Kraus, 1964.

Sainsbury, William Noel, editor. *Calendar of State Papers, Colonial Series, America and West Indies, 1675-1676, also Addenda 1574-1674 Preserved in the Public Record Office*, London: Eyre and Spottiswoode for Her Majesty's Stationery Office, 1893. Reprint, Kraus, 1964.

Sainsbury, William Noel and J. W. Fortescue editors. *Calendar of State Papers, Colonial Series, America and West Indies, 1677-1680, Preserved in the Public Record Office*, London: Eyre and Spottiswoode for Her Majesty's Stationery Office, 1896.

Sewall, Samuel. *Diary of Samuel Sewall,* three volumes, Collections of the Massachusetts Historical Society, Fifth Series, volumes 5-7, Boston: John Wilson for the Society, 1878-1882.

Shaw, William Arthur. *Select Tracts and Documents Illustrative of English Monetary History*, London: C. Wilson, 1896. Reprint, New York: A. M. Kelley, 1967.

Scott, Kenneth. *Counterfeiting in Colonial America,* New York: Oxford University Press, 1957.

Scott, Kenneth. *Counterfeiting in Colonial New York,* Numismatic Notes and Monographs, no. 127, New York: The American Numismatic Society, 1953.

Scott, Kenneth. *Counterfeiting in Colonial Pennsylvania,* Numismatic Notes and Monographs, no. 132, New York: The American Numismatic Society, 1955.

Scribner, J.M. and Daniel Marsh. *Scribner's Lumber and Log Book: for Ship and Boat Builders, Lumber Merchants, Saw-Mill Men, Farmers and Mechanics*, Rochester, NY: George W. Fisher, revision of the 1882 edition, 1890.

Sewall, Samuel. *Letter-Book of Samuel Sewall,* Collections of the Massachusetts Historical Society, Sixth Series, volumes 1 and 2, Boston: Massachusetts Historical Society, 1886-88.

Shurtleff, Nathaniel, B., editor. *Records of the Governor and Company of the Massachusetts Bay in New England,* five volumes in six, Boston: William White, 1853-1854.

Suffolk Deeds, 1640-1688, twelve volumes, Boston: Rockwell and Churchill, 1880-1906.

Sumner, William G. "The Coin Shilling of Massachusetts Bay," *The Yale Review,* Old Series, volume 7 (May 1898 - February 1899), pp. 247-64 in the November 1898 issue and pp. 405-20 in the February 1899 issue. Reprint, New York: Augustus M. Kelley, 1969.

Sumner, William G. "The Spanish Dollar and the Colonial Shilling," *The American Historical Review,* vol. 3, no. 4 (July 1898), pp. 607-19.

Toppan, Robert Nixon, editor. *Edward Randolph: Including his Letters and Official Papers from the New England, Middle, and Southern Colonies in America, with Other Documents relating Chiefly to the Vacating of the Royal Charter of the Colony of Massachusetts Bay. 1767-1703. With Historical Illustrations and a Memoir,* five volumes, Publications of the Prince Society, volumes 24-28, Boston: John Wilson for The Prince Society, 1899 [two additional volumes were edited by Alfred Goodrick in 1902 as Prince Society volumes 30-31].

Toppan, Robert Nixon. "The Right to Coin under the Colonial Charters," *Publications of The Colonial Society of Massachusetts: Transactions,* vol. 1 (1892-1894), from the meeting of February 1894, pp. 216-27.

A Touch-stone for Silver and Gold Wares. Or, A Manual for Goldsmiths, by W[illiam]. B[adcock]., London: Printed for John Bellinger in Cliffords-Inn Lane, and Thomas Bassett at the George near Cliffords-Inne in Fleet-street, 1677.

Trask, William B. "Abstracts from the Earliest Wills on Record in the County of Suffolk, Mass.," *The New England Historical and Genealogical Register,* vol. 15 (1861), pp. 321-26 and vol. 16 (1862), p. 162.

Tylecote, Ronald Frank. *A History of Metallurgy,* second edition, London: Institute of Materials, 1992.

Whitmore, William Henry, editor. *Second Report of the Record Commissioners of the City of Boston; Containing the Boston Records, 1634-1660, and the Book of Possessions,* volume 2 of the Commissioners's report, Second Edition, Boston: Rockwell and Churchill, City printers, 1881 (one volume in two parts: part 1 contains the *Records* paginated viii, 1-171 and part 2 contains the *Book of Possessions* paginated xi, 1-137).

Whitmore, William Henry and Walter K. Watkins, editors. *A Volume Relating to the Early History of Boston Containing the Aspinwall Notarial Records from 1644 to 1651,* Boston: Municipal Printing Office, 1903.

Winsor, Justin, editor. *The Memorial History of Boston, Including Suffolk County, Massachusetts: 1630-1880,* four volumes, Boston: James R. Osgood and Company, 1881.

Index

❀❀❀❀❀❀❀❀❀❀❀